Multilingualism in the Chinese Diaspora Worldwide

In this volume, Li Wei brings together contributions from well-known and emerging scholars in socio- and anthropological linguistics working on different linguistic and communicative aspects of the Chinese diaspora. The project examines the Chinese diasporic experience from a global, comparative perspective, with a particular focus on transnational links, and local social and multilingual realities. Contributors address the emergence of new forms of Chinese in multilingual contexts, family language policy and practice, language socialization and identity development, multilingual creativity, linguistic attitudes and ideologies, and heritage language maintenance, loss, learning, and re-learning.

The studies are based on empirical observations and investigations in Chinese communities across the globe, including well-researched (from a sociolinguistic perspective) areas such as North America, Western Europe, and Australia, as well as underexplored and underrepresented areas such as Africa, Latin America, Central Asia, and the Middle East; the volume also includes detailed ethnographic accounts representing regions with a high concentration of Chinese migration such as Southeast Asia. This volume not only will allow sociolinguists to investigate the link between linguistic phenomena in specific communities and wider sociocultural processes, but also invites an open dialogue with researchers from other disciplines who are working on migration, diaspora, and identity, and those studying other language-based diasporic communities such as the Russian diaspora, the Spanish diaspora, the Portuguese diaspora, and the Arabic diaspora.

Li Wei is Chair of Applied Linguistics and Director of the UCL Centre for Applied Linguistics at the UCL Institute of Education, University College London, UK.

Routledge Critical Studies in Multilingualism

Edited by Marilyn Martin-Jones, MOSAIC Centre for Research on Multilingualism, University of Birmingham, UK and Joan Pujolar Cos, Universitat Oberta de Catalunya, Spain

Multilingualism in the Chinese Diaspora Worldwide

Transnational Connections and Local Social Realities

Edited by Li Wei

NEW YORK AND LONDON

First published 2016
by Routledge
711 Third Avenue, New York, NY 10017

and by Routledge
2 Park Square, Milton Park, Abingdon, Oxon OX14 4RN

First issued in paperback 2017

*Routledge is an imprint of the Taylor & Francis Group,
an informa business*

Library of Congress Cataloging-in-Publication Data
Multilingualism in the Chinese diaspora worldwide : transnational
    connections and local social realities / edited by Li Wei.
        pages cm
    Includes bibliographical references and index.
    1. Multilingualism—China.   2. Chinese—Foreign countries—History.
3. Discourse analysis—Social aspects—China.   I. Li, Wei, 1961
August 11– editor.
    P115.5.C6M85 2015
    306.44'6089951—dc23
    2015021759

ISBN 13: 978-1-138-49906-5 (pbk)
ISBN 13: 978-1-138-79424-5 (hbk)

Typeset in Sabon
by Apex CoVantage, LLC

Contents

PART III
Transnational Communities, Cultural Mediators

PART IV
Transnational Families, Transcultural Living

Figures

Tables

1 Transnational Connections and Multilingual Realities

The Chinese Diasporic Experience in a Global Context

Li Wei

To say that the Chinese are everywhere is no more a simplistic understatement than a flippant stereotypical claim. Indeed, China has been the single largest provider of migrants across the globe for many centuries. And as the studies in this volume show, Chinese migrants are found in every continent of the world. Yet the historical contexts, causes, and motivations for migration are vastly different, and the new environments they found themselves in, the ways they dealt with the challenges in their relocated lives, and their outlooks for the future are extremely diverse. There have been a number of attempts to document and analyse the complex history of Chinese migration in various parts of the world by scholars from different disciplinary backgrounds (Lim and Gosling, 1983; Gosling and Lim, 1983; Wang and Wang, 1989; Benton and Pieke, 1998; Pan, 1999, Zhou, 1999–2002; Wang, 2000; Liu, 2006; Peterson, 2012). More recently, there are renewed efforts to investigate the sociocultural changes and the emergence of new identities in the Chinese diaspora (Khoo and Louie, 2005; Kuah-Pearce-Davison, 2008; Kuhn, 2008; Tan, 2013). Nevertheless, there has been very little systematic research into the linguistic practices of the Chinese in the diasporic communities, despite the fact that language is an integral part of Chinese migration and the building of the Chinese diaspora and diasporic identities. Even less existent is the attempt to link linguistic practices with the developmental trajectory of a specific community. This volume therefore brings together for the first time contributions from well-known and emerging scholars in socio- and anthropological linguistics who are working on different linguistic and communicative aspects of the Chinese diaspora in different parts of the world and in different historical phases. Together they examine the Chinese diasporic experience from a global perspective, with a particular focus on the multilingual realities of this vast and diverse population. In this introduction, I outline some of the basic facts about the Chinese in diaspora worldwide, discuss the various terms and concepts used to describe them and analyse their experiences, highlight the role of multilingualism not simply as a product of migration but as a critical part of the process of constructing the diaspora discourses and identities, and summarise the themes across the chapters.

CHINESE MIGRATION

Migration has long been a feature of the Chinese race. The Chinese people have rarely stopped moving around within the Chinese borders to flee natural disasters, military conflicts, poverty, and oppression, to receive education and training, and to seek a better life for themselves elsewhere than their birthplaces. Overseas migration beyond the Chinese borders initially involved mainly merchants and Buddhist monks, most famously through the Silk Road and depicted in such stories as the 16th century *Journey to the West*. Li and Li (2013) reviewed the various historical accounts of the Chinese overseas migration, which became sizable in the 12th century. Significant overseas migration waves were seen during the Ming Dynasty (1368–1644) and at the beginning of the 19th century, when not only Chinese merchants travelled and settled outside China, but also workers and labourers who were drawn to the opportunities in the colonies of European powers sought work in Southeast Asia. Truly global migration, however, only began from the mid-19th century. Large-scale migration took place to the Americas, Australia, and Africa, sometimes under conditions of indentured servitude, to fill the shortages created by the decline of the slavery system. The present-day era of Chinese overseas migration began at the end of the 1940s and is continuing to this day, with a ten-year stoppage during Mao's 'Cultural Revolution', although secondary migration, i.e., migration from Southeast Asia to other parts of the world, continued right through the period.

One important and extremely complex link between Chinese migration and language—the theme of this volume—is the fact that, despite the popular claim that China has had a unified language since the First Emperor Qingshihuang (260–210 BC), who really only managed to put a stop to the diversification of the Chinese writing system in the warring regions of China at the time and imposed a unified written script through imperial proclamations, Chinese people from different parts of China speak mutually unintelligible languages. An immediate requirement for a migrant then is to learn to understand and speak a different language as soon as they move to another place. A national spoken variety of the Chinese language was only officially promoted during the Republican period (1912–1949). Known as *Guoyu*, literally National Language, it was based on the northern variety of Chinese, Mandarin, which had become a lingua franca in much of Northern and Southwestern China and was adopted by the Qing Dynasty (1644–1912) as the official language for international communication. The republicans who overthrew the last emperor of the Qing Dynasty were dominated by speakers of southern varieties of Chinese, especially Cantonese and Hokkien. But they decided to adopt Mandarin as the national variety and promoted it through the introduction of a phonetic alphabet, Guoyin Zimu (Alphabet for the National Language), later known as *Bopomofo* or *Zhuyinfuhao*. The vast majority of the Chinese overseas migration until the present-day period involved speakers of varieties other than Mandarin, as they came from the coastal areas of China. Nevertheless, bilingualism and even multilingualism in two or more regional varieties of Chinese was not uncommon amongst the migrants who went overseas. We will return to this issue later.

Given the long and complex history of Chinese overseas migration, it is very difficult, if not impossible, to come to any reliable numbers representing the total of Chinese in diaspora across the globe today. Li and Li (2013) examined some of the figures available from various sources, which helped Tan to revise the estimate from between 30 and 40 million (Tan, 2004) to between 40 and 45 million (Tan, 2013). These estimates do not include those of partial Chinese descent, i.e., children of mixed parentage. And, as some of the chapters in this volume show, intermarriage between Chinese immigrants and local people of non-ethnic Chinese origins is by no means uncommon in some places. What is fairly clear is the fact that Chinese can be found in most countries in the world. Some are descendants of much earlier migrants, whereas others are new arrivals. Many congregate in large numbers in specific geographical areas, but some choose to live apart from other ethnic Chinese. They differ significantly in socioeconomic status, education level, and occupation. They speak different languages.

TERMS AND LABELS

There are a number of terms and labels used to refer to Chinese in diaspora. Most of them are loosely defined and under-theorised, causing confusion and arguments amongst researchers. In Chinese, there are two key terms, *Haiwai Huaqiao* (海外华侨) and *Haiwai Huaren* (海外华人). *Haiwai* means 'overseas', and *Hua* means 'China/Chinese'. So the crucial difference is between *qiao* and *ren*. *Qiao* means 'sojourner'. *Huaqiao*, therefore, means Chinese sojourners, and the term is formally used to refer to Chinese citizens living outside Greater China, i.e., mainland China, Taiwan, Hong Kong and Macau, or in Chinese *liang'an sidi* (两岸四地), two sides of the Taiwan Strait and four regions. This is the term that the governments in China and Taiwan use in official documents. *Ren*, on the other hand, simply means 'person'. So *Huaren* means an ethnic Chinese person, with no reference to citizenship. *Haiwai Huaren*, though, refers to Chinese originally from Greater China who have adopted the citizenship of the countries of their residence. Moreover, the term *Huayi* (华裔) is occasionally found in official documents and research literature to refer to persons of Chinese descent. It is usually used as a modifier, for example, in *Huayi xuezhe* (华裔学者), or scholars of ethnic Chinese origin, *Huayi qingnian* (华裔青年), youth of ethnic Chinese origin. The difference between *Haiwai Huaren* and *Huayi* is that the former is typically used for the first generation of migrants who come from Greater China and have taken up residency and citizenship in another country, whereas the latter is typically used to refer to the descendants of *Haiwai Huaren*, i.e., ethnic Chinese born and brought up in places outside Greater China. Amongst the Cantonese, Hokkien, and Hakka speakers, the term 唐人, pronounced *tángrén* in Mandarin/Putong-hua, *tòhng yàn* in Cantonese, *tn̂g-lâng* in Hokkien, and *tong nyin* in Hakka is sometimes used, which literally means Tang people, a reference to the Tang Dynasty of China (618–907 AD), widely regarded as a golden era in Chinese history. Chinatown, for example, is usually known as *tángrénjiē* (唐人街), or street of the Tang people, amongst the Chinese.

When it comes to English terms, however, nothing is very precise. For a start, the word 'Chinese' could mean persons from China or Chinese nationals, in Chinese *Zhongguoren* (中国人), or ethnic Chinese, or occasionally the dominant Han ethnic group in China. But Chinese people tend not to use generic terms like this when referring to themselves. They are more likely to say that they are *Guandongren* (广东人, person from Guangdong or Canton), *Shanghairen* (上海人, person from Shanghai), *Fujianren* (福建人, person from Fujian or Hokkien), *Beijingren* (北京人, person from Beijing), or more generically, *Daluren* (大陆人, person from mainland China), *Xianggangren* (香港人, person from Hong Kong), or *Taiwanren* (台湾人, person from Taiwan). Language plays a key role in their self-identification. When one tells you that they are *Guangdongren*, they are also telling you that they are Cantonese speakers, and when they say they are *Shanghairen*, you can be fairly sure that they speak Shanghainese. The commonly occurring English term 'overseas Chinese' is equally ambiguous. It could be used, and indeed is often used, to refer to different groups of people, including Chinese migrants who have not taken up citizenships of their resident countries, those who have taken up citizenships of their resident countries, younger generations of ethnic Chinese origin living outside Greater China, and even persons of partial Chinese descent. Some, most notably Wang Gungwu (1991, 2000), attempted to differentiate 'Chinese overseas'—ethnic Chinese who have citizenships of countries other than China or Taiwan—from 'overseas Chinese'—Chinese citizens living outside Greater China. But such differentiation has not been widely adopted.

Whereas in this volume overseas Chinese is used as a blanket term to refer to a variety of people of Chinese ethnic origin living outside Greater China regardless of their citizenship, the existence of the different terms and labels, especially in Chinese, shows the different perspectives on the identity of the Chinese people in diaspora, on the issue of citizenship when talking about persons not living in their countries of origin, and on the complex relationships between the ethnic group one belongs to and the nation-state they live in. We will discuss some of these issues in the next section.

THE CHINESE DIASPORA

The discussion of the terms and labels that are used to refer to overseas Chinese raises the question: to what extent do the Chinese living outside

Greater China constitute a diaspora? The notion of diaspora is of course not new. Its original meaning was intended to describe the scattering of people between, through, and across different geographic locations. Its main reference was, for many centuries, the historical mass dispersions of the Jews, African slaves, and the Chinese coolies. The emphasis on the involuntary nature of the displacement and dispersal in the historical references was easy to see. Studies of transnational human migration in the 20th century tended to use terms such as immigrants, guest workers, asylum seekers, ethnic minorities, displaced populations, etc., to refer to the different groups of migrants in contemporary society. As the world settled into the 21st century, there has been a renewed interest in the notion of 'diaspora' as a theoretical and analytical concept. Researchers increasingly find terms such as 'immigrants' and 'minorities' unsatisfactory. Instead, as Clifford (1997) suggests, 'diasporic language seems to be replacing, or at least supplementing, minority discourse. Transnational connections break the binary relation of "minority" communities within "majority" societies' (p. 255).

An in-depth discussion of the theoretical conceptualisations of diaspora and the diasporic discourse is beyond the scope of the present chapter. As Li Wei and Zhu Hua (2013) have discussed, there are two broad approaches: one focuses on historical development of different kinds of diaspora aiming to develop a typology (e.g., Cohen, 1997), and another takes diaspora as a mentality or consciousness and critically examines the sociocultural practices and narratives of transnational individuals and groups (Clifford, 1997). Whereas both approaches involve 'an understanding of the shifting relations between homelands and host nations from the perspective both of those who have moved, whether voluntarily or not, and of the recipient societies in which they find themselves' (Quayson and Daswani, 2013: 3), the latter sees a close link between the contemporary diasporic conditions and globalisation (Cohen and Vertovec, 1999).

Safran (1991: 83–4) proposed a list of criteria for diaspora groups, in which he emphasised the following features:

- Dispersal from 'original "centre" to two or more foreign regions'
- Retention of a 'collective memory' of the homeland
- Partial or full exclusion or marginalisation from hostland society
- Desire to return to homeland
- Maintenance of homeland
- Collective consciousness/solidarity

The histories of Chinese migration to different parts of the world and the composition of the overseas Chinese population mean that not all overseas Chinese groups fulfill the criteria of diaspora in a narrow sense. Indeed, as it has already been said, overseas Chinese are a 'superdiverse' (Vertovec, 2007) population, with individuals of vastly different migration motivations and experiences, different educational and socioeconomic backgrounds and statuses, different occupations, and different languages. Yet they often find sufficient common ground to identify themselves with each other as part of a diaspora, creating an 'imagined' community (Anderson, 1991). This diasporic imagination often involves suppressing or neutralising past and present differences and establishing commonality and connectivity through which new identities can be negotiated.

Like most immigrant communities, the overseas Chinese collectively experience over time the processes of being resisted or marginalised, mainstreamed or assimilated, and memorialised. Whereas individuals may be welcomed into the hostland communities, immigrant groups as a whole tend to be received negatively at the beginning. This may be largely due to ignorance and perceived threat to the cohesion of the local community. From the immigrants' point of view, if their number is small, they may feel isolated; and if the number is large, they might encounter segregation. Either way, they may experience marginalisation. The collective coping strategies for the immigrants often involve building the so-called 'three pillars of the diaspora', namely, a community or townsmen association, a school, and a communication network and media which usually begins with information newsletters and pamphlets, moving gradually to proper newspapers and magazines, and eventually to radio, television, and, increasingly, digital and online media. Some of the chapters in the present volume document the Chinese immigrants' efforts in building the three pillars of the Chinese diaspora.

Paradoxically perhaps, the more successful an immigrant group is in building a community for themselves through establishing the three pillars of diaspora, the more pressure they may come under for mainstreaming and assimilation. Societies do not generally favour the idea of having too many different communities minding their own business. Under the discourse of community cohesion, immigrant communities, however successful and self-sufficient they may be, are pushed to assimilate with the so-called mainstream society. Of course, there are individuals and groups who do prefer to assimilate. And their efforts to do so often involve intermarriage, changing their names, and adopting a new language, as many overseas Chinese have done. Yet not everybody has the opportunity to assimilate even if they wanted to. The vast majority of immigrant groups are ignored and become invisible over time, leaving the most and the least socioeconomically successful ones to stand out. In Britain, for example, different immigrant groups are perceived and treated very differently by the general public and the media. The majority of them rarely get any notice or mention. A small number of immigrant groups are seen as problematic communities, such as the Bangladeshis in terms of their children's education achievement and the Romanians in terms of their economic and labour market status. Other groups, on the other hand, such as the Indians and the Chinese, are often held as examples of success, especially in educational and economic terms.

Many diasporic communities get memorialised over time, by both their own descendants and the mainstream society. Tsuda (2013), for example, talks about what he calls 'double nostalgias', the deflation of the romantic notions of both the homeland and the place of sojourn. Older immigrants are often invited to relive their own and their families' experiences during the earlier phases of migration and settlement and construct stories of prolonged struggle and eventual success. Younger generations are taught to learn lessons from such experiences which are constructed to be relevant to the challenges of contemporary society. All over the world, we see the setting up of museums of history of overseas Chinese migration and settlement.

As the chapters in this volume demonstrate, the Chinese form well established diaspora in many parts of the world today. But in the meantime, there are new migrant groups still going through the processes as outlined above. In both cases, however, major sociopolitical changes in China and the new world order in which China, the source nation for the overseas diaspora, is fast becoming a new world power mean that a new position needs to be negotiated in the identification with the mother nation and present place of residence. This new position, or new thinking of the Chinese diaspora, focuses on what Tsagarousianou (2004) calls 'potentialities' of diaspora, i.e., 'the various creative possibilities opened by the activities of diasporas in both local and transnational contexts' (p. 58). In Brah's terms, 'diasporas are . . . the sites of hope and new beginnings' (1996: 193); rather than looking back in a nostalgic effort of recovering or maintaining their identity, they discover or construct notions of who they are and what home is by essentially looking forward. The new thinking of the Chinese diaspora coincides with the shift of analytic interest and emphasis in the migration and diaspora research literature from mobility to connectivity and from the victimisation, uprooting, and displacement of the individuals and groups concerned to their capacity of constructing new transnational spaces of experience that are complexly interfacing with the experiential frameworks that both places of settlement and purported places of origin represent (Morley, 2000).

In keeping with the tradition of Chinese migration within the Chinese borders, a significant number of overseas Chinese undertake further and secondary migration, i.e., they move to other places once they have accumulated sufficient resources from their initial place of settlement to seek further development. It is hard to say whether this is a particularly Chinese phenomenon, as comparative data with other migrant populations are non-existent. But it is not at all uncommon to find Chinese families in North America or Western Europe who have previously lived in Southeast Asia, Australia and New Zealand, Central and Eastern Europe, or South America. In Southeast and Central Asia, the Middle East and Latin America, it is also common that the Chinese move between nearby nation-states. In the meantime, many overseas Chinese families have relatives in different parts of the world. Modern technologies and the new media have enabled many to maintain a highly transnational network with frequent and instant contacts. Such transnational networks are a concrete example of the 'potentiality' diaspora affords the migrants to enhance their sense of connectedness and diasporic imagination.

LANGUAGE AND MULTILINGUALISM IN THE CHINESE DIASPORA

As noted above, there is an intrinsic connection between language and the Chinese diaspora. Historically, it has been predominantly speakers of regional varieties of Chinese other than Mandarin who migrated beyond the Chinese borders. As a result, languages such as Cantonese, Hokkien, and Hakka, which are regarded as 'dialects' in China, dominate the overseas Chinese communities. Of course Mandarin is used. But it is used as another variety of Chinese, rather than as a national language. It is also the regional varieties of Chinese, such as Cantonese and Hokkien, that have been traditionally used as community lingua franca amongst the Chinese in diaspora, mainly because of the size of the population speaking these varieties. These language varieties have been a key binding force for the community, with townsmen associations, schools, and the media—the three pillars of diaspora—set up around them. More recently with the rise of China politically and economically in the world, Putonghua, literally 'common speech', the standardised variety of Chinese based on Mandarin that is promoted as the official language of China, has gained some prominence, and Chinese heritage schools overseas have begun to teach it.

The overseas Chinese have never attempted to spread their language beyond their own community. Where conditions afford, they have tried their best to learn the local languages and tended to privilege the learning of local languages by their children as the priority over the maintenance of their own ethnic languages. This, plus other factors, such as dispersed settlement patterns and involvement in service trades, means that a rapid language shift from varieties of Chinese to the local language, be it English, French, Japanese, or Spanish, often takes place within two generations. Whereas multilingualism is a common feature amongst the Chinese in diaspora, it means different things to different groups in different locations and to different generations within the same family. Some are multilingual in the Chinese language varieties but not in the local languages, whereas others are multilingual in various non-Chinese languages with only rudimentary knowledge of Chinese. The chapters in the present volume investigate the experiences of different groups, generations, and individuals in the Chinese diaspora in dealing with bilingualism and multilingualism and the interplay between their language experiences and the local socioeconomic conditions as well as their diasporic imaginations.

In terms of the status of the various languages, a complex pattern of polyglossia has emerged (see Table 1.1 for an illustration), with the local language as the socioeconomically High variety, the regional variety of Chinese the community High variety, Putonghua the politically High variety within certain contexts, and the other Chinese regional languages that do not belong to the immediate community and some regional forms of the local language Low varieties. The chapters in the present volume cover

Table 1.1   Polyglossia of the Chinese in Diaspora

	Within the Chinese community	Beyond the Chinese community
High	Regional variety, e.g. Cantonese, Hokkien (for everyday communication)	Local language, e.g. English, French, Japanese, Spanish (for socioeconomic/educational purposes)
	Putonghua (for political, symbolic purposes)	Putonghua (for transnational purposes)
Low	Other regional varieties of Chinese	Other regional varieties of local language

the following Chinese languages: Cantonese, Hakka, Hokkien, Mandarin, Shanghainese, Teochow, Wenzhou, as well as Putonghua, and non-Chinese languages including Arabic, English, French, Indonesian and various Borneo languages, isiXhosa, Kazakh, Malay, Russian, and Spanish.

In talking about multilingualism, literacy remains an underexplored topic. The overseas Chinese communities have set up numerous heritage language schools across the globe, and the principal objective of these schools is to teach the younger generations to read and write the Chinese characters. Literacy in Chinese is clearly an issue of concern in the Chinese diaspora. Surveys of language attitudes and ideologies amongst the Chinese have confirmed that the ability to read and write Chinese is regarded as a crucial element of 'being Chinese' (Li Wei and Zhu Hua, 2010). It often gives people a sense of maintaining their cultural heritage (Francis, Archer and Mau, 2009). In the meantime, the literacy level of the first generation adult immigrants in the non-Chinese languages of the resident place can be low. And a significant amount of language brokering is taking place through the locally born children who act as go-betweens between the family and other institutions.

As well as the effort to maintain a functional level of literacy in Chinese amongst the locally born generations, there has been an increased awareness in the Chinese diaspora of the issue of how to construct and express their identities and values through non-Chinese languages. There is little evidence of distinctive Chinese varieties of local languages used exclusively by the Chinese in diaspora, nor is there evidence of overseas varieties of the Chinese language, apart from some common learner features and dialectal influences. Improved and enhanced communication channels, often mediated by the internet, satellite technologies, and the new media, mean that new words and expressions used in China, Taiwan, Hong Kong, and Macau can be heard and replicated immediately in the Chinese diaspora. The overseas Chinese have never consciously claimed ownership of the local languages by creating distinctive language varieties of their own. Their response to the challenge of the linguistic construction and expression of identities and values seems to be translanguaging (Garcia and Li Wei, 2014) and engagement with a range of flexible multilingual practices, as the chapters in the present volume show.

THIS VOLUME

This volume aims to fill a gap in the growing body of research literature on the global Chinese diaspora by focusing on the issue of language, especially multilingualism. Specifically, the volume documents diverse multilingual practices as well as conflicting language ideologies in connection with the language users' migration trajectories and local conditions, including the sociopolitical, economic, and cultural contexts. It investigates the ways in which Chinese migrants and their descendants negotiate and renegotiate identities through their continued interactions with their heritage culture, in the current location, in similar diaspora elsewhere, and with the various 'new' cultures in both China and their current communities, including changing language values and linguistic legitimacy in new markets in migration destinations, and the enregistrement (Agha, 2003) of Chinese and other languages to index ethnolinguistic identities. It also examines the role of migration in transforming linguistic practices, ideologies, and identities, and evaluates the sociolinguistic categories conventionally evoked as a means of understanding and evaluating linguistic practices in diaspora.

The issues addressed in this volume include changing linguistic landscape and language practices and the emergence of new forms of Chinese or new forms of multilingualism, family language policy and practice, language socialisation and identity development, multilingual creativity, heritage language maintenance, loss, learning, and re-learning, and linguistic attitudes and ideologies. Sixteen chapters are grouped into four sections under the themes of 'emerging diaspora, emerging identities' (Deumert and Mabandla, Li and Jeffermans, Wang), 'changing times, changing languages' (Smagulova, Tjon, Stenberg, Setijadi), 'transnational communities, cultural mediators' (Maher, Wang, Chern, Shoniah and Riget, Lee, Lim) and 'transnational families, transcultural living' (Chen, Curdt-Christiansen, Tsung, He).

A particular strength of the volume is the geographical coverage. The studies are based on empirical observations and investigations in Chinese communities across the globe, including well-researched, from a sociolinguistic perspective, areas such as North America (Chapter 17 by He), Western Europe (Chapter 3 by Li and Juffermans) and Australia (Chapter 16 by Tsung), as well as under-explored and under-represented areas such as Africa (Chapter 2 by Deumert and Mabandla), Latin America (Chapter 6 by Clements and Chapter 7 by Tjon), Central Asia (Chapter 5 by Smagulova), and the Middle East (Chapter 4 by Wang). Studies of areas with a high concentration of Chinese migration such as Southeast Asia are represented with detailed ethnographic accounts in seven chapters (Chapters 8 by Stenberg, 9 by Setijadi, 11 by Wang et al., 12 by Lee, 13 by Lim, 14 by Chen, and 15 by

Curdt-Christiansen), and the Chinese in Japan are discussed in Chapter 10 by Maher. By bringing together studies of multilingualism in the Chinese diaspora in different parts of the world, the volume aims to shed light on the variability and fluidity of identity configurations, linguistic practices, and ideologies in different social and political contexts, and to enable us to explore the processes shaping migrants' different linguistic and migration trajectories.

The volume comes at a time when China is emerging as a new world economic, political, and sociocultural superpower and at a time of renewed and enhanced superdiversity worldwide, where the patterns and itineraries of external and internal migration are on the increase and accessible channels of communication have transformed the way in which migrants maintain and develop interpersonal bonds with their ancestral homeland and across diaspora. It is hoped that the volume will not only open a window on the new avenues for sociolinguists to investigate the link between linguistic phenomena in specific communities and wider sociocultural processes, but also seek to open a dialogue with researchers from other disciplines who are working on migration, diaspora, and identity, and those studying other language-based diasporic communities, such as the Russian diaspora, the Spanish diaspora, the Portuguese diaspora, and the Arabic diaspora.

REFERENCES

Agha, A. 2003. The social life of cultural value. *Language and Communication, 23*, 231–273.

Anderson, B. 1991. *Imagined Communities: Reflections on the Origin and Spread of Nationalism*. Rev. and extended ed. London: Verso.

Benton, G., & Pieke, F. N. 1998. *The Chinese in Europe*. Houndmills, Basingtoke: Palgrave Macmillan.

Brah, A. 1996. *Cartographies of Diaspora: Contesting Identities*. London: Routledge.

Clifford, J. 1997. *Routes: Travel and Translation in the Late Twentieth Century*. Cambridge, MA: Harvard University Press.

Cohen, R. 1997. *Global diasporas: An introduction*. London: UCL Press.

Cohen, R., & Vertovec, S. (eds.). 1999. *Migration, Diasporas and Transnationalism*. Cheltenham: Edward Elgar.

Francis, B., Archer, L., & Mau, A. 2009. Language as capital, or language as identity? Chinese complementary school pupils' perspectives on the purposes and benefits of complementary schools. *British Educational Research Journal, 35*(4), 519–538.

Garcia, O., & Li, W. 2014. *Translanguaging: Language, Bilingualism and Education*. Houndmills, Basingtoke: Palgrave Macmillan.

Gosling, L. A. P., & Lim, L. Y. C. (eds.). 1983. *The Chinese in Southeast Asia*, Vol. 2. Singapore: Maruzen Asia.

Khoo, T., & Louie, K. (2005). *Culture, Identity, Commodity: Diasporic Chinese Literatures in English*, Vol. 1. Hong Kong: Hong Kong University Press.

Kuah-Pearce, K. E., & Davidson, A. P. 2008. *At Home in the Chinese Diaspora: Memories, Identities and Belongings* (pp. xi–259). Houndmills, Basingtoke: Palgrave Macmillan.

Kuhn, P. A. (2008). *Chinese Among Others: Emigration in Modern Times*. Lanham, MD: Rowman & Littlefield.

Li, P. S., & Li, E. X. 2013. The Chinese overseas population. In C. B. Tan (ed.), *Routledge Handbook of the Chinese Diaspora* (pp. 15–28). London: Routledge.

Li, W., & Zhu, H. 2010. Voices from the diaspora: Changing hierarchies and dynamics of Chinese multilingualism. *International Journal of the Sociology of Language*, 205, 155–171.

Li, W., & Zhu, H. 2013. Diaspora: Multilingual and intercultural communication across time and space. *AILA Review*, 26(1), 42–56.

Lim, L. Y. C., & Gosling, L. A. P. (eds.). 1983. *The Chinese in Southeast Asia*, Vol. 1. Singapore: Maruzen Asia.

Liu, H. (ed.). 2006. *The Chinese Overseas*, 4 volumes. London: Routledge.

Morley, D. 2000. *Home Territories: Media, Mobility, Identity*. London: Routledge.

Pan, L. (ed.). 1999. *Encyclopaedia of the Chinese Overseas*. Cambridge, MA: Harvard University Press.

Peterson, G. 2012. *Overseas Chinese in the People's Republic of China*. London: Routledge.

Quayson, A., & Daswani, G. (eds.). 2013. *A Companion to Diaspora and Transnationalism*. Oxford: Wiley-Blackwell.

Safran, W. 1991. Diasporas in modern societies: Myths of homeland and return. *Diaspora: A Journal of Transnational Studies*, 1(1), 83–99.

Tan, C.-B. 2004. *Chinese Overseas: Comparative Cultural Issues*. Hong Kong: Hong Kong University Press.

Tan, C.-B. (ed.). 2013. *Routledge Handbook of the Chinese Diaspora*. London: Routledge.

Tsagarousianou, R. 2004. Rethinking the concept of diaspora: Mobility, connectivity and communication in a globalized world. *Westminster Papers in Communication and Culture*, 1(1): 52–65.

Tsuda, T. 2013. When the diaspora returns home: Ambivalent encounters with the ethnic homeland. In A. Quayson & G. Daswani (eds.), *A Companion to Diaspora and Transnationalism* (pp. 172–198). Oxford: Wiley-Blackwell.

Vertovec, S. 2007. Super-diversity and its implications. *Ethnic and Racial Studies*, 29(6), 1024–1054.

Wang, G. 1991. *China and the Chinese Overseas*. Singapore: Times Academic Press.

Wang, G. 2000. *The Chinese Overseas*. Cambridge, MA: Harvard University Press.

Wang, L.-C., & Wang, G. (eds.). 1989. *The Chinese Diaspora: Selected Essays*, 2 volumes. Singapore: Times Academic Press.

Zhou, N. (ed.). 1999–2002. 华侨华人百科全书 (*Encyclopaedia of Overseas Chinese*), 12 volumes. Beijing: 中国华侨出版社.

Part I
Emerging Diaspora, Emerging Identities

2 Globalization Off the Beaten Track—Chinese Migration to South Africa's Rural Towns

Ana Deumert and Nkululeko Mabandla

1 INTRODUCTION: BEYOND THE METROPOLE

In a recent paper, Xuan Wang and her colleagues (2014: 26) have argued that much existing work on globalization shows an urban bias: social scientists, including sociolinguists, have, by and large, focused their attention on 'the huge contemporary metropolis with its explosive and conspicuous diversity in people and language, its hyper-mobility and constant flux'. Peri-urban and rural areas, on the other hand, have remained understudied. There is often an implicit assumption that the effects of globalization might be less pervasive and dramatic—and thus less interesting—in non-metropolitan contexts. In order to address this imbalance in current scholarship, it is necessary to look more closely at non-metropolitan contexts. This allows us to arrive at a more 'complete' understanding of globalization by 'adding insights from places not usually or immediately identified as "globalized"' (Wang et al. 2014: 38; similar concerns have been raised by human geographers, see Woods 2007, McCarthy 2008, and Hedberg and Haandrikman 2014).

Our ongoing collaborative work responds to the call for research in non-metropolitan contexts by studying globalization in two rural towns in South Africa's Eastern Cape Province. These towns participate in what Xuan Wang and her colleagues have called 'infrastructures of globalization'. Thus, communication technologies are available in the form of mobile phones and internet cafés. In addition, new forms of transnational economic activity have transformed retail trading and created new patterns of consumption and social relation. The globalized economic activities in these towns do not involve call centers and heritage tourism, which are frequently listed as prototypical examples of globalized economic activity, closely linking North and South, but rather small-scale entrepreneurs whose import trade networks embed South Africa's rural towns in complex South-South relations, both within the country (e.g., Durban, Johannesburg, East London, Newcastle) and within the world (e.g., China, Hong Kong and Thailand).

Our focus in this chapter is on the Chinese traders who have settled in South Africa's rural towns in the last decade. They form part of a diverse international trading class, which also includes migrants from India, Pakistan, Bangladesh, Ghana, Senegal, Gambia, Eritrea, Ethiopia and Somalia. The discussion unfolds as follows: in the first part (Section 2) we outline the theoretical perspective which informs and frames our work on globalization, that is, the idea of entanglement which was formulated by the Martinican philosopher, poet and novelist Éduard Glissant. Following this we provide an overview of the history of Chinese migration to South Africa (Section 3). Section 4 describes the fieldsites and discusses the reasons behind the relocation of Chinese migrants to these parts. Section 5 takes a closer look at everyday entanglements by focusing on linguistic and semiotic practices under conditions of globalization. We understand globalization broadly as a dynamic process of social transformation that involves the global interconnectedness and mobility of goods, people, ideas and representations.

2   GLOBALIZATION AS ENTANGLEMENT

While sociolinguistic studies of globalization have long privileged ethnographic perspectives and paid detailed attention to micro-level effects, much sociological and economic work has emphasized macro-level interactions, especially those between states and transnational corporations. Sino-African relations, especially, have typically been discussed with a focus on trade agreements, large infrastructural projects, loans and foreign investments. These studies have been useful in unpacking the changing nature of global trade networks and the role of political intervention in globalization. However, they do not allow us to understand how globalization is experienced by people as they try to make lives for themselves within an increasingly global and mobile world (Harrison et al. 2012; Matthews et al. 2012; Monson and Rupp 2013). If our aim is to analyze the complexities of the everyday interrelations between China and Africa within specific localities, we need to ask questions such as the following: How do 'ordinary' people, especially those with limited amounts of capital, respond to the opportunities afforded to them by the broad structures of macro-level globalization (such as, for example, trade and visa agreements, the existence of communication technologies and a well-developed transport system for the movement of people and goods)? How do they experience globalization in the here-and-now? How do they 'make a life' and create a sense of place within new local contexts?

Central to the way we think about globalization and the everyday is Glissant's (1997) notion of entanglement (*intrication*); that is, the ways in which people, objects and ideas are linked and put in relation to one another (*mise-en-Relation*).[1] For Glissant, entanglement is what globalization—starting with colonial conquest, the experience of slavery and continuing into the present—is all about. The notion of entanglement allows us to consider diasporic, transnational connections as well as the complex, sometimes intimate, sometimes distant, interactions and relations that are formed in the new places to which people have moved. That entanglements with others are fundamental to the texture of social life has also been argued by the South African critical scholar Sarah Nuttall (2009: 1), who describes and theorizes the complexities of everyday life in post-apartheid, post-colonial South Africa as follows:

> Entanglement is a condition of being twisted together or entwined, involved with; it speaks of an intimacy gained, even if it was resisted, or ignored or uninvited. It is a term which may gesture towards a relationship or a set of social relationships that is complicated, ensnaring in a tangle, but which also implies a human foldedness. It works with difference and sameness but also with their limits, their predicaments, their moments of complication.

In other words, entanglement is not a temporary state into which we can move and which we can leave at will. Rather, it is the fundamental condition of humanity—locally and globally—which we can try to ignore, but which we cannot excise. However, this does not mean that we don't try, at times, to disengage from entanglements. National identities, especially, are typically imagined as bordered and bounded, and their historical and global entanglements have historically been silenced in discourses of nation-building. A striking example is the 2014 referendum in Switzerland that requested strict quotas for European migration, thus trying to dis-entangle the country even from its closest neighbors. A desire for dis-entanglement also exists with regard to everyday relations. In an insightful paper, Don Mitchell (2005) talks about what he calls the 'S.U.V. model of citizenship'. He uses the metaphor of an S.U.V.—a car which affords its driver maximum isolation from the surrounds—as an emerging discourse in the United States which articulates 'a right to be left alone', and which finds expression in so-called 'bubble-laws'. These prohibit others from coming too close, thus dis-entangling social relations of the everyday.

Glissant's idea of entanglement resonates well with current sociolinguistic theory in its emphasis on mobility, hybridity, mixing, creativity and the unexpected, as well as its recognition of the unbounded, interconnected and indeed rhizome-like nature of the social world and our identities within it. Entanglement as a theory of relations also echoes Mary Louise Pratt's (1991, 2008) argument for a 'linguistics of contact', which moves away from notions of community and shifts attention to the social spaces where 'cultures meet, clash, and grapple with each other' (1991: 34; on the importance of developing relational theories in the social sciences more generally, see Go 2013). Everyday interaction and improvisation are central aspects of the 'contact zone': 'subjects get constituted in and by their relations to each other', they are not separate, but co-present and, in this way, create interlocking understandings and practices (Pratt 2008: 8). The 'contact zone' is at times a 'space of imperial encounters', characterized by coercion, inequality and domination, processes which shape contemporary, neoliberal and often neocolonial globalization as well. Glissant (1997: 104–105), however, notes in his *Poetics of Relation* that domination is but one side of entanglement: it also involves relations of multiplicity, mutuality, contagion and tangency, of fascination, subservience, mockery and subversion.

Our work on Sino-African relations uses two distinct methodological lenses to trace such entanglements empirically: consumption and language. Contemporary globalization is closely tied to neoliberal market economies and consumption is a central fixture in these contexts. The presence of Chinese traders in rural South African towns has changed local market dynamics and consumption patterns: cheap consumer goods are now available to those who couldn't afford them in the past in numerous so-called China Shops. As they go about their business, the Chinese traders are brought into prolonged and intense contact with speakers of different languages. This leads to the formation of new practices of economic transaction (such as the use of language brokers, see below) and convivialities. For reasons of space—and because this chapter appears in a sociolinguistic publication—we focus here on questions of language and the everyday multilingualisms that globalization has brought about. Before turning to the fieldsites and the data, the next section provides a brief historical overview of Chinese migration to South Africa.

3   CHINA IN SOUTH AFRICA: PAST AND PRESENT

The unprecedented scope and pace of China's development has caught the imagination of policy makers, journalists and academics around the globe. An abiding concern among Western commentators especially has been the perceived threat China poses to Western influence and hegemony in the global South: Is China benevolently assisting in Africa's development? Or is it hungrily exploiting the resources of the continent and creating new markets for its consumer goods? (See Brautigam 2009.) Currently, China is one of Africa's biggest trade partners and investors, and top-level Chinese involvement has not only facilitated large infrastructural projects and investments, but also the migration of Chinese nationals (Park and Chen 2009).

Although Chinese political and economic involvement with Africa goes back to the fifteenth century, Chinese settlement has been limited in the past. This has changed dramatically over the last decade, and the number of Chinese migrants is estimated to have risen from around 100,000 in the late 1990s to more than one million in 2011 (Rice 2011; Lin 2014). Chinese migrants have settled across the continent, from Ghana to Uganda, from South Sudan to Namibia. The largest group of Chinese is currently found in South Africa, with estimates between 200,000 and 500,000 (Mohan and Tan-Mullins 2009; Li 2014).

South Africa has a complex history of Chinese migration, attracting different groups—in terms of language, educational background and economic resources—at different times. The South-Africa-born Chinese journalist and novelist Darryl Accone (2007) speaks about 'three distinct Chinas' and senses of 'Chineseness' in South Africa, each originating in a specific, historical migration stream. The three groups commonly distinguished are:

(1) *The South-African-born Chinese*, estimated at around ten thousand (Huynh et al. 2010). These are descendants of about two thousand independent Chinese migrants, mostly artisans and traders, who were attracted by the gold rush of the 1870s. The early migrants originated primarily from Guandong province in south China and were Hakka- and Cantonese-speaking. Between 1904 and 1910, over sixty thousand Chinese indentured laborers were brought to South Africa to work in the mines. However, the majority of these were repatriated in 1910, and it is unclear whether any of the indentured Chinese remained in South Africa (Yap and Man 1996). Under the segregationist policies of apartheid (1948 to 1994), South-African-born Chinese were classified as non-White and forced to reside in racially segregated townships. Here they came into contact with other groups classified as non-White by apartheid legislation, and developed complex cultural styles which were characterized by extensive mixing and hybridity (Yen 2005). In the democratic South Africa, they are the only Chinese group which is considered Black for purposes of affirmative action policies.[2]

(2) *The Taiwanese Chinese*, estimated at around six thousand (Huynh et al. 2010). The Taiwanese Chinese arrived in South Africa when the apartheid government encouraged business migration from Taiwan through various political and economic incentives (Park and Chen 2009: 26; also Hart 2002). Unlike those belonging to the 'first China' (nineteenth century migrants and their descendants), migrants from Taiwan were classified as 'honorary Whites' under apartheid, and thus granted the same privileges and rights as White South Africans. The population grew to around thirty thousand in the 1980s, but numbers have since fallen as a result of migration to North America and return migration to Taiwan. During the 1980s, there was also limited migration from Hong Kong.

(3) *New Chinese Migrants* come from the *People's Republic of China* (henceforth PRC) in numbers that are difficult to estimate due to many cases of undocumented migration. The 'new' migration started post-1994 (although there was some movement already in the 1980s), when the South African government began to orient itself toward the PRC and, eventually, cut diplomatic ties with Taiwan in 1998.

The so-called *New Chinese Migrants*, who are the topic of this chapter, are far from homogenous. Tu Huynh and her colleagues (2010) suggest that it is useful to distinguish two main groups: those arriving pre-2000, and those arriving post-2000. The first group, described in the literature as cosmopolitan and educated, includes middle managers and other professionals, originating primarily from China's East coast and its mega-cities (such as Beijing or Shanghai). Many came to work for Chinese state-owned enterprises (SOEs), and later established themselves in wholesale, import-export business as well as the manufacturing sector. The second group is quite different in their background and skills, and far larger in terms of numbers. Chinese migrants arriving after 2000 included independent small-scale traders as well as so-called 'peasants', that is, individuals without capital who found employment in the shops of relatives and associates from the home country.

Geographically, the Fujian province, which has a long history of overseas migration, features prominently as a place of origin. Philip Harrison and his colleagues (2012) estimate that about two-thirds of 'new' Chinese migrants in South Africa originate from Fujian. The growing presence of traders and 'peasant' migrants from Fujian has led to tensions and divisions among the Chinese in South Africa:

> [F]issures . . . seem to exist between those Chinese who are more settled and adapted to life in South Africa and the most recent migrants from Fujian province. These new rifts . . . have a clear class basis. . . . The more established Chinese (including now Taiwanese and some of the mainland Chinese as well as the Chinese South Africans) look down on the lower classed 'peasants' from Fujian, who are also alleged to be involved in criminal activities. (Huynh 2010: 301)

South Africa's different 'Chinas' are not only socially and historically diverse, but also linguistically diverse: South-African-born Chinese have generally shifted to English, whereas various Chinese languages are spoken by the Taiwanese and the 'new' Chinese migrants. Those migrants who settle in the bigger cities tend to conduct their business in English, and rarely learn African languages (Monson and Rupp 2013: 32). However, those who have moved to rural towns might find themselves in quite a different linguistic context: although English is used, indigenous African languages dominate in these regions.

4   TWO RURAL TOWNS: MIGRATION AND THE RESTRUCTURING OF LOCAL ECONOMIES

We have been conducting ethnographic fieldwork in two rural towns, Tsitsa and Forestville, since 2012 (ongoing).[3] The towns are located in the Eastern Cape, one of South Africa's nine provinces. The Eastern Cape incorporates large former Bantustan or homeland areas (Ciskei and Transkei), that is, areas which were designated for African settlement under colonial rule and apartheid (while the rest of the country was reserved for Whites). These areas were characterized by overpopulation and poverty, and constituted a reliable source of cheap migrant labor for the mining industry and White commercial farms. Today, the Eastern Cape remains one of South Africa's poorest provinces, and out-migration levels are high. The majority of residents in the province are Black African and speak isiXhosa, a southern Bantu language closely related to isiZulu and SiSwati. Nationally, the Eastern Cape has the lowest percentage of international migrants, i.e., residents who were born outside of South Africa (Table 2.1), and, as such, seems an unlikely candidate for a study of international migration.

Statistics, however, tell us nothing about local conditions. Gauteng, for example, has the highest proportion of international migrants. Yet, it also shows the familiar urban geography of ethnic enclaves where migrants settle among other migrants and work in the ethnic economy, running restaurants and shops which supply goods not usually available in the host country. The situation is quite different in rural towns where South Africans and international migrants live quite literally cheek-by-jowl in a heterogeneous economic landscape. Talking to Madhu, a migrant from Bangladesh about the shops located opposite Check Well, the new Chinese supermarket in Tsitsa, he provides us with a truly international list of shop owners: Pakistani, Indian, Somalian, Chinese, Ethiopian as well as Senegalese and Gambian (interview 2014). The Chinese migrants to rural towns thus find themselves not only entangled in interactions with the local African population, but also with other international migrants.

Tsitsa and Forestville, our main fieldsites, are about sixty kilometers apart. There are similarities between the two towns as well as important

Table 2.1 Percentage of International Migrants, i.e., Residents Born Outside of South Africa (Census 2011, Statistics South Africa 2012).

	Western Cape	Eastern Cape	Northern Cape	Free State	KwaZulu Natal
Population born outside of South Africa	4.8%	1.2%	1.7%	2.5%	1.7%
	North-West	Gauteng	Mpumalanga	Limpopo	
Population born outside of South Africa	4.3%	9.4%	3.8%	3.1%	

Available at: http://www.statssa.gov.za/publications/P03014/P030142011.pdf.

differences. Both towns are of a comparable size, and international traders are highly visible in the retail sector. However, while Tsitsa was part of the Transkei Bantustan until 1994, Forestville was a so-called White town. This historical difference translates into present differences. The urban landscape, for example, is carefully planned and orderly in Forestville, creating the prototypical image of a peaceful country town, whereas it appears unplanned and chaotic, loud and unruly, indeed rhizomatic, in Tsitsa. Whereas property in Forestville is mostly in the hands of the White farming class, members of the Black middle class are the main property holders in Tsitsa (Mabandla 2013). Agricultural activities are also different: whereas farming in Forestville is primarily commercial, it is mainly subsistence in Tsitsa. The municipality where Forestville is located also provides better access to services, and shows a higher degree of urbanization (Table 2.2). Although unemployment is high in both areas, the provision of social grants since 1994 has increased possibilities for consumption, even among the unemployed and 'the poor'.

When large numbers of Chinese migrants arrived in South Africa after 2000, the retail market in the urban centers of Johannesburg, Cape Town and Durban was saturated, providing only limited business opportunities, especially for those with low amounts of capital. Thus, although Johannesburg, which boasts two Chinatowns, offers a sense of community, an ethnically Chinese space away from home, many Chinese migrants have moved on in search of opportunities (Li 2014).[4] They have left the big metropolitan

Table 2.2   Selected Statistics for the Municipalities where Tsitsa and Forestville are Located (Statistics South Africa, Census 2011).

	Local municipality where Tsitsa is located	Local municipality where Forestville is located	South Africa
Population (total)	188, 226	138,141	51,800,000
Population density	67 persons per km²	27 persons km²	42 persons per km²
Black African percentage of population	99.1%	98.1%	79.2%
Access to flush toilets	4.3%	8%	57%
Access to piped water inside dwelling	4.0%	10.4%	73.4%
No internet access	83.2%	86.1%	64.8%
Urban residence	5.7%	26.7%	62.0%
Unemployment rate	48.9%	44.4%	25.2%

Available at: http://beta2.statssa.gov.za/?page_id=964.

cities that were their points of arrival and settled in smaller towns where they opened, or worked in, China Shops, selling a wide array of consumer goods produced in China. Typical goods on display are mobile phones and TV sets, kitchenwares, fashion, blankets, children's toys and stationary. Dongmei, who arrived from China in 2008, comments on the situation in Johannesburg and her subsequent move to Tsitsa, where she has been looking after her cousin's shop since 2011, as follows:

> Ja, too much Chinese coming here, because we like it . . . too much Chinese, ja, [in Johannesburg], no have work for me. This is from my cousin shop, so I come here [to Tsitsa]. (interview 2012; see also Park and Cheng 2009)

Similarly, John left Cape Town to settle in Tsitsa. In his own words, he 'followed the money', and was thus able to fulfill his dream of being his own boss (interview 2012; also Lin 2014). The fact that there is money to be made in the rural towns is also supported by the growing presence of global and national chains in these towns: SUPERSPAR (supermarket), Boxer (clothing and food), Built-It (hardware and building materials) and KFC (fast food). Thus, old general dealerships, village stores and trading stations, previously in the hands of White traders and the Black middle class, have been replaced—under the impact of globalization and neoliberal economics—with national/international chain stores and a diversity of migrant-run shops, which have brought to the area not only new types of traders, but also enabled new patterns of consumption.

Among the diversity of shops, Chinese shops are easily visible to customers. Although they do not display Chinese characters on their shop signs, the names are unmistakably 'Chinese' (Figure 2.1). During our earlier fieldtrips (2012 and 2013), Chinese traders specialized primarily in cheap

Figure 2.1   Chinese shop signs Forestville (2012) and Tsitsa (2014).

Figure 2.1 Continued

consumer goods. This had changed in 2014: Chinese migrants were found to be branching out and moving into the food business, something which previously was strongly associated with traders from South Asia (Deumert and Mabandla 2013).

5 ENTANGLEMENTS: MOORINGS AND UNMOORINGS

Although media reports have at times noted negative attitudes toward Chinese migrants in Africa, recent research (Park 2013) suggests that, at least in South Africa, attitudes are by and large positive. While there are some complaints about the low quality of goods, locally referred to as *fong kong*, there is also an appreciation of the fact that Chinese traders have made consumer goods available to the 'common people'. As one young man explained to us: 'the Chinese know, they come from communism, they make sure everyone can afford' (interview 2012). Moreover, many South Africans grew up with the presence of Chinese (the first and second China, see above), Bruce Lee movies and martial arts were popular and *fah-fee* is still played in the townships (Krige 2011). All this contributes to a sense of familiarity, which translates into predominately positive attitudes toward the 'new' Chinese migrants, who are less likely to be victims of xenophobic discourses and attacks than, especially, migrants from other parts of Africa (Park and Chen 2009). Moreover, the Chinese are not usually perceived as business competitors, as they are 'not replacing any South Africans but rather [fill] gaps that have been vacated by others. These shops have been operated by earlier immigrant groups, including those from Greece, Cyprus, and Portugal' (Park 2013: 136), as well as by White and Black traders.

Feelings of familiarity and broadly positive attitudes facilitate the integration of Chinese migrants into the daily life of rural towns and their entanglement with local ways of living. This integration is visible in a range of economic as well as linguistic practices. An important feature of Chinese shops is that they sell not only global consumer goods and fashion items, but also goods with a distinctly local flavor (albeit produced in China or in local factories run by Chinese industrialists): colorful pinafores for the newly-wed *makoti* ('bride'); African-inspired modern fashion designs; chequered blankets, an important part of traditional attire and used in ceremonial contexts; and simple enamel tableware which has long been common in these parts. Chinese businesses are thus embedded in local consumption needs. Another example of this is the popular eatery *Protea Café*, which is located on Forestville's main thoroughfare (Figure 2.2). The large restaurant, with tables and a take-away counter, offers none of the familiar dishes known from Chinese restaurants across the world. Instead, it sells distinctly local foods: cooked chicken feet, large fried curried chicken pieces, pap, a local porridge made from maize meal, as well as *vetkoek*, deep-fried doughnut-like pastry. The name too draws on local imagery: Protea is South Africa's national flower, the name of the national cricket team and a large South African hotel chain. Yet, the shop is also clearly marked as Chinese, as 'new' and different: 'New China Village Investment'. These examples illustrate the mooring of Chinese trade within local systems of knowledge and consumption. At the same time, they point to the transnational nature of the shops, and thus contribute to their unmooring from the purely local (on mooring and unmooring, see Phipps 2013).

Everyday interactions between Chinese traders and locals have led to highly localized and mixed linguistic practices among the traders. This is similar to the 'grassroots multilingualism' described by Huamei Han (2013)

Figure 2.2   Protea Cafe (Forestville, 2014).

for the reverse migration context, i.e., Africans in China. A locally acquired form of English is the main language of trade used by Chinese migrants. Thus, English is not 'brought along', but learnt in everyday interactions with local customers and other traders. Among the salient local features is, for example, the frequent use of the expressions *this side* (for 'here'), and *that side* (for 'there'). These calques are based on *kweli'cala* ('this side') and *kwelaa cala* ('that side'), and are typical in the English of many isiXhosa-speakers. The speech of the Chinese traders is often peppered with isiXhosa words. These include *batala* ('pay', a borrowing from Afrikaans *betaal*), *jonga* ('to see'), *ncinci* ('little'), *ayikho* ('it's not available', used as a stock response whenever there is a communicative breakdown in the shop), the ubiquitous South African discourse markers *ja* and *neh*, as well as kinship expressions (such as *sbali*, 'brother in law') and forms of address (*sisi, bhuti, mama*, all respectful forms of address). Mixing is not only a feature of the spoken language, but also visible in signage: a Chinese shop in Tsitsa which specializes in blankets advertises its business with the hybrid sign *BLANKET sell apha* ('Blankets sold here'), combining a second language form of English (unmarked past tense and plural) and isiXhosa. Such linguistic practices attest to an intimacy of interaction similar to that described by Nuttall (2009, cited above). It is an instantiation of Glissant's *écho-monde*: the ways in which practices resonate with one another, feed off one another, mix and entangle and create new realities in the process.

The main 'zone of contact' (Pratt 1991, 2008) between Chinese migrants and local residents is the shop (on rural shops as a space of sociability more generally, see Bauman 1972; on conviviality, see also Lampert and Mohan 2014). It is the space where learning and interaction happens. Such interactions are not limited to local customers, but also involve relations with other traders. This is visible in one of the interviews we conducted with Dongmei (see above), where she comments on the problems shopkeepers have with small-time criminals (locally referred to as *tsotsis*):

> Everyone shop got a Tsotsi taking, you see, and, I think, this year or last year is bigger problem, you see, last time is taking gun, and last week, Saturday, the Tsotsi open this, hm, next door, ja, next door, the hardware, the Tsotsi find the man, but the mister is hardware, ja, everything is bigger, the Tsotsi can't take it, so just go away, left, the Tsotsi find the man [inaudible] money, just let go [*Question: Was the owner of the shop a Chinese man?*], oh I don't know, it's Pakistan or India, I think is Pakistan. (interview 2014)

Thus, news about crime travels quickly among traders: although Dongmei might not be certain of the nationality of the next-door East Asian shop owner, who might be from India, Pakistan or Bangladesh, there is interaction, talking among one another, and a sense of shared predicament and solidarity.

That the local communicative context is experienced as deeply heterogeneous, including the 'brought along' complexity of the Chinese languages (*Pŭtōnghuà* as well as local languages), is illustrated by another extract from the interview with Dongmei:

> *How many languages are there [in Tsitsa]?*
> The Chinese, two languages, English, Xhosa and Indian language, so is five languages, Chinese, ja, too many, so many languages. (interview 2014)

Customers who come to Dongmei's shop often address her in isiXhosa, and she tries to respond as best as she can, sometimes using a few words of isiXhosa, sometimes responding in English. Only when all else fails does Dongmei rely on her bilingual (English-isiXhosa) shop assistants as language brokers. To employ local shop assistants is a common feature of all Chinese businesses in the area: the use of assistants-cum-language brokers ensures that there is always someone who can talk to customers in isiXhosa. Moreover, the local assistants also function as informal teachers, and shop owners ask them for help with learning at least rudimentary isiXhosa. Limited competence in English and isiXhosa on both sides also means that communication between Chinese employers and local assistants is not always easy. Dongmei admits that there are sometimes problems, but insists they get along if they focus on 'easy-talking', simple words and sentences to get the message across, combined with the mutual acceptance that communication requires patience (interview 2014).

Since we first met Dongmei in 2012, her life has changed a lot: from sleeping inside the shop to having her own flat, albeit small, which she shares with her husband (whom she met in China before migrating) and their newborn son. Her son, born in South Africa, was given the name Bruce. She was insistent that he needed an English name in South Africa. And since she didn't know much about English names, she solicited help from the wife of the Somali trader next door to decide on a name for her son. It is not surprising that her neighbor came up with 'Bruce', after all Bruce Lee is *the* global icon which brought Chinese culture to the continent (and the world) in the form of popular martial arts movies. Dongmei was equally insistent that Bruce will get a Chinese name in China, and that he will go to school in China. This draws attention to yet another feature of the entanglements brought about by globalization: they are not always permanent. In other words, mobility and flux are just as prevalent in South African rural towns as they are in the European metropolis. There is considerable mobility among traders: shops open and close, people move elsewhere and start afresh. In 2014, when the low exchange rate for the South African Rand put considerable pressures on those importing goods, many traders talked about business being bad and thought about moving on. Although Dongmei likes life in South Africa, she is not committed to staying: her family and her first born son are in China, and since she cannot bring them to South Africa because of visa issues, she 'must', eventually, go back:

> I must go back to China, I must go, because, my son in China, my family in China. (interview 2014)

Entanglement is a complex process: characterized not only by intimacy and relations with others, but also by resistance to it and, at times, a desire for dis-entanglement (as discussed above). Although embedded in local trade relations in her shop and everyday working life, Dongmei's family stays in Tsitsa among other Chinese from Fujian. They spend their evenings watching Chinese DVDs, and Dongmei goes to great lengths to make sure that her family has access to Chinese food. She imports Chinese rice and other ingredients from Durban and Johannesburg, but has learnt to make do with the hardy, local cabbage which she cooks for hours. Ultimately she sees her home in China, not South Africa.

Others, however, have made South Africa their home, and it is, as always, difficult to generalize. John (see above) has been in South Africa for not much longer than Dongmei. Yet, he came alone and has since married a local isiXhosa-speaking woman, with whom he has a child. He too runs a China Shop, but has also, unlike most Chinese traders, recently branched out into a type of business which is deeply local: he has opened a tavern around the corner from his shop. The tavern, like others in the area, offers entertainment to what he calls 'the common people': cheap alcohol, a pool table, jukebox and a flat screen TV which is constantly on the soccer channel. It is frequented almost exclusively by young and old isiXhosa-speaking men. And although worried about the declining exchange rate and the resulting decline in a business that relies heavily on import, he appears to be there to stay (interview 2014).

6 CONCLUSION: A GLOBAL COUNTRYSIDE

Rural international migration, although not yet well documented in scholarship, is an important aspect of contemporary globalization, and has far-reaching implications for the production of social life. The expression 'global countryside' is a 'deliberate allusion to the concept of the "global city"' (Woods 2007: 491). Yet, this does not mean that features of global cities can be mapped onto the rural or that the processes involved are similar.

Perhaps most importantly, rural migration makes it more difficult for ethnic niche economies to emerge and supports an intensity of entanglement: Chinese traders in Tsitsa and Forestville do not sell their goods in a local Chinatown, but form part of a diverse international trading class. They share social and economic spaces with traders from South Asia and Africa, mixing, talking and interacting as they negotiate the challenges of business and the realities of migrant life. Their interactions with the local population are regular and can be intimate: intermarriage, although not the norm among Chinese traders, is not an anomaly. In some ways their experiences match those of the 'first China': being embedded in local exchange networks—whether apartheid-style urban townships or rural towns—supports mixing and hybridity, the emergence of new practices which reflect the relations of 'the contact zone'. At the same time, there are moments of enclave formation (e.g., sharing living quarters with others of the same ethnicity or religion) and dreams of going home.

Glissant's notion of entanglement provides a useful conceptual framework for describing and analyzing the interactions, intimacies and moments of withdrawal that shape the everyday as international migrants and local residents go about their lives in shared spaces of activity.

Understanding globalization as entanglement has consequences for how we think about what is perhaps the most pervasive spatial image when writing about globalization: the center-margin dichotomy. In other words, if it is true that our lives with one another are deeply entangled—beyond relations of propinquity and across time/space—then there is no 'elsewhere' and what constitutes 'the center' or 'the margin' is always in the eye of the beholder, a temporarily positioned gaze from within the network, a relational 'project' rather than a reality (Drabinski 2011, 2013). Consequently, what is needed is a research agenda which is, in the words of Glissant, *tout monde*; a sociolinguistics of globalization which considers the world in its entirety and complexity: rich and poor, North and South, urban and rural, and everything in-between.

NOTES

1. For reasons of space we will not discuss another central notion of Glissant's oeuvre: opacity. That is, according to Glissant, within relations of entanglement, respect for the Other requires respect for the opacity of difference. Only by respecting the Other's opacity are we able to resist the urge toward assimilation or objectification (Britton 1999).
2. Pre-independence Chinese migration also occurred in Mauritius (where Chinese laborers arrived in the 1700s and 1800s) and Madagascar (migration since the 1800s). Both countries have sizable communities of 'indigenous' Chinese.
3. All names used in this chapter are pseudonyms. This also applies to the names of the two rural towns.
4. Chen Fanglan (2011) estimates that about two-thirds of Chinese in South Africa reside in Johannesburg.

REFERENCES

Accone, D. 2007. Chinese Communities in South Africa. *China Monitor* 21, 7–8.
Bauman, R. 1972. The La Have Island General Store: Sociability and Verbal Art in a Nova Scotia Community. *Journal of American Folklore* 85, 330–343.

Brautigam, D. 2009. *The Dragon's Gift. The Real Story of China in Africa*. Oxford: Oxford University Press.

Britton, C.M. 1999. *Eduard Glissant and Postcolonial Theory. Strategies of Language and Resistance*. Charlottesville: University Press of Virginia.

Chen, F. 2011. Chinatown in Johannesburg—A Social Survey. *China Monitor* 61, 8–11.

Deumert, A. and Mabandla, N. 2013. 'Everyday a New Shop Pops Up'—South Africa's 'New' Chinese Diaspora and the Multilingual Formation of Rural Towns. *English Today* 29, 44–52.

Drabinski, J. 2011. *Levinas and the Postcolonial. Race, Nation, Other*. Edinburgh: Edinburgh University Press.

Drabinski, J. 2013. Poetics of the Mangrove. In: *Deleuze and Race*, ed. by A. Saldhana and J.M.Adams, pp. 288–299. Edinburgh: Edinburgh University Press.

Glissant, É. 1997. *The Poetics of Relation*. Translated by B. Wing. Ann Arbor: University of Michigan Press.

Go, J. 2013. For a Postcolonial Sociology. *Theory and Society* 42, 25–55.

Han, H. 2013. Individual Grassroots Multilingualism in Africa Town in Guangzhou: The Role of States in Globalization. *International Multilingual Research Journal* 7, 83–97.

Harrison, P., Moyo, K. and Yang, Y. 2012. Strategy and Tactics: Chinese Immigrants and Diasporic Spaces in Johannesburg, South Africa. *Journal of Southern African Studies* 38, 899–925.

Hart, G. 2002. *Disabling Globalization. Places of Power in Post-Apartheid South Africa*. Berkeley/Los Angeles: University of California Press.

Hedberg, C. and Haandrikman, K. 2014. Repopulation of the Swedish Countryside: Globalization by International Migration. *Journal of Rural Studies* 34, 128–138.

Huynh, T. T., Park, J. Y. and Chen, A. Y. 2010. Faces of China: New Chinese Migrants in South Africa, 1980s to Present. *African and Asian Studies* 9, 286–306.

Krige, D. 2011. 'We Are Running for a Living': Work, Leisure and Speculative Accumulation in an Underground Numbers Lottery in Johannesburg. *African Studies* 70, 3–24.

Lampert, B. and Mohan, G. 2014. Sino-African Encounters in Ghana and Nigeria: From Conflict to Conviviality and Mutual Benefit. *Journal of Current Chinese Affairs* 43, 9–39.

Lin, E. 2014. "Big Fish in a Small Pond": Chinese Migrant Shopkeepers in South Africa. *International Migration Review* 48, 181–215.

Mabandla, N. 2013. *Lahla Ngubo: The Continuities and Discontinuities of a South African Black Middle Class*. Leiden: African Studies Centre.

Matthews, G., Ribeiro, G. L. and Vega, C. A. (eds) 2012. *Globalization from Below: The World's Other Economy*. London: Routledge.

McCarthy, J. 2008. Rural Geography: Globalizing the Countryside. *Progress in Human Geography* 23, 129–137.

Mitchell, D. 2005. The S.U.V. Model of Citizenship: Floating Bubbles, Buffer Zones, and the Rise of the 'Purely Atomic' Individual. *Political Geography* 24, 77–100.

Mohan, G. and Tan-Mullins, M. 2009. Chinese Migrants in Africa as New Agents of Development? An Analytical Framework. *European Journal of Development Research* 21, 588–605.

Monson, J. and Rupp, S. 2013. Introduction: Africa and China: New Engagements, New Research. *African Studies Review* 56, 21–44.

Nuttall, S. 2009. *Entanglements. Literary and Cultural Reflections on Post-Apartheid South Africa*. Johannesburg: Wits University Press.

Park, J. Y. 2013. Perceptions of Chinese in Southern Africa: Constructions of the "Other" and the Role of Memory. *African Studies Review* 56, 131–153.

Park, J. Y. and Chen, A. Y. 2009. Recent Chinese Migrants in Small Towns of Post-apartheid South Africa. *Revue Européenne des Migrations Internationales* 25, 25–44.

Phipps, A. 2013. Unmoored: Language Pain, Porosity and Poisonwood. *Critical Multilingualism Studies* 1, 96–118.

Pratt, M. L. 1991. Arts of the Contact Zone. *Profession* 91, 33–40.

Pratt, M. L. 2008. *Imperial Eyes. Travel Writing and Transculturation*. Second Edition. Routledge: London.

Rice, X. 2011. China's Economic Invasion of Africa. *The Guardian*, 6/2/2011; available at: http://www.theguardian.com/world/ 2011/feb/06/chinas-economic-invasion-of-africa.

Statistics South Africa, Census 2011. Available at http://www.statssa.gov.za/.

Wang, X., Spotti, M., Juffermans, K., Cornips, L., Kroon, S. and Blommaert, J. 2014. Globalization in the Margins: Toward a Re-Evaluation of Language and Mobility. *Applied Linguistics Review* 5, 23–44.

Woods, M. 2007. Engaging the Global Countryside: Globalization, Hybridity and the Reconstitution of Rural Place. *Progress in Human Geography* 31, 485–507.

Yap, M. & Man, D. L. 1996. Colour, Confessions and Concessions. *The History of the Chinese in South Africa*. Hong Kong: Hong Kong University Press.

Yen, J. 2005. Review of All under Heaven. *PINS* 31, 106–109.

3 Polycentric Repertoires
Constructing Dutch-Chinese Youth Identities in the Classroom and Online

Jinling Li and Kasper Juffermans

1 INTRODUCTION

Since the 1990s, the Netherlands are transforming from a multicultural society with a limited number of ethnic groups ("cultures") to a superdiverse society where cultural, religious and linguistic diversities are rapidly gaining complexity and losing much of their prior stability and predictability (Vertovec, 2010; Blommaert and Rampton, 2011; Arnaut, 2012). In Harris and Rampton's (2009) words, ethnicity today is without guarantees, i.e., increasingly fluid and difficult to determine in terms of groups of people (cf. Brubaker, 2002). With respect to language, observations of superdiversification have led scholars to abandon notions of languages as bounded entities and putative things in the physical world, in favour of an understanding of language as a political construction or historical invention and towards adopting an alternative sociolinguistic vocabulary with notions such as translanguaging and repertoires to describe the communicative practices and experiences in our current age of globalisation (Jørgensen, 2008; Blommaert, 2010; Creese and Blackledge, 2010).

The starting point for this paper is a recently completed ethnographic project in and around a complementary Chinese language school in the city of Eindhoven. Our study was part of a larger HERA-funded research project that investigated discourses of inheritance and identities in and beyond non-mainstream educational institutions in four northwest European urban multilingual contexts—Britain, Sweden, Denmark and the Netherlands (see e.g., Blackledge, Creese and Takhi, 2013; Jonsson and Muhonen, 2014). This chapter focuses on the linguistic practice and the contemporary identity-making of Dutch-Chinese youth. It argues for seeing language and identity as "polycentrically" organised and for considering identity construction in traditional contexts alongside new digital contexts.

In what follows, we shall first introduce the key theoretical concept of this chapter. We then sketch the historic context of the Chinese community in the Netherlands and provide some notes on our methodology. We then turn to our empirical data, collected from a complementary school classroom and a digital discussion forum, before concluding the chapter.

2 POLYCENTRIC REPERTOIRES

Polycentricity, the key notion in this chapter, is used in various disciplines of the humanities and social sciences, including geography, political sciences and sociolinguistics (e.g., Aligica and Tarko, 2012; Blommaert, 2013). It generally refers to the multiplicity of centring forces in social or spatial configurations. Whereas monocentric configurations are regulated according to a single reference point in time-space, polycentric configurations are regulated by multiple, competing centres with unequal power. Polycentric environments offer several orders of indexicality, but they are rarely equivalent: the social and cultural "order" is stratified and operates at different scale-levels—different ranges of cultural and social recognisability, recognition and scope of use. Aligica and Tarko (2012) argue that the polycentricity conceptual framework is a strong analytical structure for the study of complex social phenomena.

Social arenas for identity work are by definition polycentric, in the sense that at any moment, actors in communicative events are facing more than one "centre" from which norms can be derived. Such centres can be institutions of a formal as well as of an informal kind. Formal ones could include, for instance, the school, church, the state; informal ones can include peer groups, role models, popular culture icons and so forth. In any act of communication, participants can orient towards any of those centres for templates of "good" versus "bad" forms of communication. Thus, in a classroom, both the teacher and the classmates can be seen as "centres", and what counts as a "good" answer in relation to the teacher can be simultaneously understood as a "bad" one by the classmates. The scale of formal institutions such as the school would typically be higher than that of an informal peer group, even if some subcultural groups—think of groups oriented towards hip-hop, or communities of online gamers—operate at extremely high, global scale-levels.

The range of verbal and communicative practices that constitute an individual's language and identity we call repertoires. Drawing on Gumperz (1964: 138), repertoires are the arsenal of weapons of everyday communication that make up our linguistic and cultural selves (Busch, 2012: 504). A repertoire perspective posits that "people do not 'have' *one* identity, but *perform a repertoire* of identities by means of resources they have acquired and have at their disposal for such purposes" (Varis, Wang and Du, 2011: 267).

3 SOME BACKGROUND ON THE CHINESE COMMUNITY

The Chinese community in the Netherlands celebrated its centennial in 2011. They are one of the oldest established immigrant communities in the Netherlands, and are often seen as model immigrants for their economic, cultural and linguistic integration into mainstream society. Their number currently amounts to between 77,000 and 150,000 (CBS, 2010; Wolf, 2011). The first Chinese in the Netherlands arrived as seamen around the turn of the century and gradually settled in the Amsterdam and Rotterdam harbour districts, where they developed Chinatowns. The majority came from Wenzhou and Qingtian districts in Zhejiang province on the east coast and from Bo On in Guangdong on the south coast. A second wave of Chinese migrating to the Netherlands after the Second World War (1950–1970) settled in these Chinatowns as well as in other cities, towns and villages throughout the country, typically finding employment in the Chinese catering business. They often had complex (family) migration trajectories via Hong Kong, Vietnam, Java, Sumatra, Suriname and other regions, which is also reflected in their linguistic repertoires. Cantonese and Wenzhounese were the dominant languages of the Dutch Chinese diaspora through this period.

After 1978 and most noticeably in the 1990s and 2000s, the composition of the Chinese community in the Netherlands changed due to the political and economic changes in mainland China. More and more PRC citizens (mainly students and knowledge migrants) found their way into the Netherlands. In 2011, the Chinese were, after Germans, the second largest group of foreign students in the Netherlands. Although most of them are only temporarily residing in the Netherlands, their numbers count and have an important economic, cultural as well as sociolinguistic impact on the whole Chinese presence in the Netherlands. They now come from all over China (literally from any province). As a result, from the 2000s onwards it is no longer Cantonese that is the language of the Chinese diaspora, but increasingly Mandarin (Putonghua). As part of this development, Chinese schools in the Netherlands today have almost entirely shifted to teaching Mandarin (Putonghua) and simplified characters, where this was Cantonese and traditional characters when most schools were founded in the 1970s. Similar to reports for the UK (Li and Zhu, 2010), the hierarchy of Chinese multilingualism in the Netherlands is changing in the direction of Putonghua. Ironically, the demographic diversification of the Chinese immigrant population after 1990 leads to a linguistic homogenisation and standardisation in the sense of a Putonghuaisation of Chinese (cf. Li and Juffermans, 2014).

Eindhoven, where we centre our research, is one of the cities with both an old, predominantly Cantonese and Wenzhounese-speaking population of entrepreneurs (in the catering business mainly), and a newer, predominantly Mandarin-speaking population of so-called knowledge migrants. The Eindhoven Chinese community is younger than the Chinese communities in Rotterdam, Amsterdam and The Hague in the sense that many Eindhoven Chinese are students and technical professionals attracted to Eindhoven in recent decades by the High Tech Campus, the

Eindhoven University of Technology and the various multinational high tech companies.

4   METHODOLOGY

The empirical data used for this paper draws from a series of offline and online ethnographic observations and consists of key moments of interaction that offered insights into the dynamics of heritage and multilingual identity. We adopted a community-based approach (Li, 2014) and a sociolinguistic ethnographic path (e.g., Blackledge and Creese, 2010), working from empirical evidence towards theory with discourse analysis as our primary resource.

The central node of data collection in our project was a complementary Chinese language school in Eindhoven we observed on a weekly basis in 2010 and 2011, primarily focusing on a combined grade 11 and 12 classroom. We see schools as deeply situated in a wider context and as non-autonomous sociolinguistic spaces. Complementary schools are a particular case, as they are largely invisible and unknown in the mainstream society but highly visible and significant within the migrant community they are part of. Our fieldwork moved from observing what happens inside the classroom to what happens outside the classrooms and outside of the school, involving, for example, observations in a Chinese community tea-room annex training centre, Chinese restaurants and other organised community celebrations and activities such as tai qi and ping pong as well as in social network platforms online.

We see the Internet as part of everyday life, rather than as separate and solely virtual (cf. Varis, Wang and Du, 2011), and we approached the digital media in much the same way as historians make use of archives. We observed interactions of a metalinguistic character on three platforms, the Chinese-medium expat platform GogoDutch, the Dutch-medium teenage Asian and Proud community on the social network site Hyves, and the adolescent platform we focus on in this paper, *jonc.nl*. This view from digital media brought two methodological advantages over more classic classroom ethnographic observations. First, the voices online gave us insights into discourses of Chineseness outside of the context of complementary schooling and of people not currently in complementary education, including those who dropped out or never enrolled. Secondly, it also offered answers to the very issues we were interested in without having to ask the questions, thus devoid of some of the traditional sociolinguistic observer's paradox effects (Juffermans, Blommaert, Kroon and Li, 2014). The blurring of the offline/online dimension of data collection generates different and unexpected voices and insights, facilitating the collection of richer data (Baker, 2013). Our online data collection similarly focused on key moments of data that offer insights into multilingual identity repertoires.

5 CONSTRUCTING DUTCH-CHINESE YOUTH IDENTITIES IN THE CLASSROOM

The first example we shall discuss is drawn from our classroom observations. The school, like other Chinese schools in the Netherlands, is a community-run and self-financed institution operating outside of the mainstream education system, convening on Saturday mornings. Although the majority of the school's students are Cantonese speakers, the school does not provide Cantonese lessons (anymore) and the teaching materials are now in Putonghua (Mandarin) and provided by the PRC. Most teachers are also more recent migrants from the PRC, rather than from Hong Kong or Taiwan, and Mandarin rather than Cantonese speakers. A glimpse of the textbook series shows that many folk stories and national fairy tales appear in the curriculum, pointing to the intended creation of a collaborative memory of Chinese history and culture coordinated in Beijing.

On the Saturday in November 2010 when we observed the discussion we turn to below, there were eight students present, aged 17 to 20. Four students are enrolled in university; the other four attended secondary schools of the type giving direct access to university studies. Xin, Mei and Qiang (not their real names) are of third generation Hong Kong Cantonese background and their home language is mainly Dutch. Hong, Yuan and Ming are of respectively Wenzhou and Fuzhou backgrounds and have Wenzhounese and Fuzhounese as their main home language. Tao, who is the central character in this classroom discussion, is a 1.5th-generation migrant from Beijing and of Mandarin language background: his parents came to the Netherlands in the 1990s to pursue postgraduate university education and settled in Eindhoven after they completed their studies.

The class teacher, Ms. Sun, had been engaged in teaching at the Chinese school in Eindhoven for over a decade. Born in Fujian province in the late 1950s, she experienced the political turbulence and the aftermath of the Great Leap Forward (1958–1961) and the Cultural Revolution (1966–1976) as well as the Economic Reforms of 1978. Ms. Sun completed a university degree in Beijing in the mid-1980s and moved to the Netherlands with her husband as he pursued his PhD in Eindhoven in the early 1990s.

On the first day of the school year, Ms. Sun asked the students to speak only Chinese in class: questions could only be asked and answered in Chinese, i.e., in Mandarin or Putonghua. Our classroom observations suggest that the students "translanguaged" (Creese and Blackledge, 2010) a lot between varieties of Chinese and Dutch and were all very interested and committed to learning Chinese. They made efforts to address the teacher in Chinese on most occasions, wrote their notes in a combination of Chinese and Dutch and talked with their peers before and during classes more exclusively in Dutch. The teacher encouraged the students to speak Chinese most of the time, but did not enforce this in a very repressive manner, thereby keeping a pleasant and interactive atmosphere in the classroom.

Despite—or because of—the friendly atmosphere, students often engaged in ideological debate with their teacher, contesting the contents of the textbook and her teaching and juxtaposing this with Dutch norms and values they simultaneously or concurrently identified with. The teacher-student discussion we turn to below is not rare; similar discussions repeatedly occurred during our observations. The discussion was triggered by a discussion of the text, "The Song of the Little Brook". This text is a well-known Chinese folk story written in 1959 during China's Great Leap Forward campaign, which meant to transform China into a modern communist society through rapid industrialisation and collectivisation. Creese, Wu and Blackledge (2009: 363) explain that folk stories are productively used as heritage texts in complementary education throughout the world, and are applied to "endorse traditions, values and beliefs, and to invoke features of the collective memory of community". As such, folk story literacies often have a clear ideological and political message.

This text tells the story of a personified little brook that never runs dry but sings and runs through the landscape day and night without stopping, and playfully and cheerfully finds its way over pebbles and rocks, grasses and branches without ever taking a rest. The brook resists various challenges from a dead branch and dry grass, a crow and a rusty iron boat to take a rest or stop running, but tirelessly continues running day and night without ever stopping. It becomes bigger and stronger as other brooks join it, turns into a little stream and ultimately a big river that flows into the boundless, happy blue sea. Throughout its infinite existence, the brook is happy and smiles and melodiously sings. The story culminates in the coda "never stop to take a rest, never stop running!" The growth of the little brook is meant as a metaphor for the socialist revolution and construction of China, praising hard work and achievement.

It is this story that is printed in the textbook as educational material for Chinese children in the diaspora half a century later. This, perhaps unsurprisingly, causes some contestation in the classroom, as evident in the translated fragment below of the original classroom discussion in Mandarin with occasional code-switching to Dutch (marked by italics). For reasons of space, all fragments are given in their English translation only.

FRAGMENT 1: "NO FEELING?"

Ms. Sun	Such a text, what do you think of it? Tao, how do you feel about this text?
Tao	I don't have any feeling.
Ms. Sun	No feeling? No *feeling*? Such a text, what does it tell us?
Xin	Nothing.
Ms. Sun	Nothing? It personifies things, personification, right? It personifies the brook, the brook works very hard, never takes a rest, running straight to the sea. In fact, it is just like the life of people. From the moment you were born until you die, the experience of our life is just like the brook, understand?
Tao	Not necessarily.

This is how the classroom discussion begins: Ms. Sun asks her class how they feel about the text. However, the students show little interest in the assignment ("I don't have any feeling", "Nothing"). They do not cooperate with the teacher and claim to have no feelings at all about the text, and assert that it doesn't tell them anything. The teacher does not give up. In the next turn, the teacher explains the context and the moral implication of the story—more or less in the spirit of the Great Leap Forward—stressing the value of hard work as a good way of life. Tao contests the teacher's point of view. In the following fragments, the students begin actively interpreting the story with their own understanding.

FRAGMENT 2: "YOU JUST WANT TO BE LIKE THE DUTCH"

Ms. Sun	Not necessarily? He tells us that people should always work hard until the day you die. Do not stop, understand?
Tao	I don't-
Ms. Sun	-don't *agree?* Hehe . . . don't agree with me, *okay*, then tell us about your opinions. Yea, what kind of life do you want? You just want to be like the Dutch, have a comfortable life?
Tao	You do what you want to do.
Ms. Sun	((Smiling)) The brook also does what he wants to do; he wants to go to the sea. Doesn't he mean the same?
Tao	Not the same.
Qian	But that brook, he doesn't have a single friend. He flows without stopping. He can't stop to play [. . .]

In this section, Tao keeps rejecting the teacher's interpretation of the story and the dispute is lifted to an intercultural conflict, with the teacher impersonating traditional Chinese values and Tao constructing a Dutch attitude, which is characterised by the teacher as not sufficiently ambitious, only aimed at having "a comfortable life". The story illustrates how one should lead one's life: "Work hard, pursue and explore". This is questioned by Qiang, who remarks that in such a life there is no time for friendship or enjoyment.

FRAGMENT 3: "MY WAY OF THINKING IS DUTCH"

Ms. Sun	He only talks about his opinion, eh.
Tao	Yea, yea, yea, but the fishes and shrimps couldn't catch up, and then they will be forgotten.
Ms. Sun	Right, they are dropped off by society, by environment. Things are often like that, right? So if you don't work hard, you'll be eliminated.

Tao	So I think if you don't make great efforts you'll be eliminated, I think this is not very well written. Because every individual should decide what he wants, not everyone wants to, wants to rush to the top, to win, because most of the people will fail, only a few can come to the top, then the people who fail will be very unhappy, isn't it? So if you fail, let it be.
Tao	If you didn't climb to the top, then you've lost. If all eight people in our class, including you, all want to be number one in the exam, but of course there is only one. In this case, the other seven will lose.
Ms. Sun	*No, no, no*, your thinking is very narrow. In our class, one can, of course, be number one in his field. And you can also be number one. He can be number one in economics, and you can be number one in your French. Each has its own directions of development, its own definition. It's different.
. . .	. . .
Tao	For some people, even if they try hard, they will also lose!
Hong	*You don't need to always win.*
Tao	This text draws attention to the fact that if you do not reach the top, then you are lost. If you, on your way, step out, then that is considered a negative thing, so to say . . .
Ms. Sun	He just implies that you should make great efforts, work hard, and then you'll make progress.
Tao	Chinese ought to work hard. That's too much.
Ms. Sun	I think that the Netherlands absolutely makes people lazy, make people making no efforts.
Tao	Dutch people are more *efficient* than Chinese. Chinese have no choice.
Ms. Sun	Chinese all over the world work hard.
. . .	. . .
Tao	My way of thinking is Dutch.
Ms. Sun	((Students chat with each other in Dutch.)) Speak Chinese! ((Bell rings.))

In this fragment, the dispute becomes more serious. Tao begins to build an argument that there is more in life than just hard work and that such a life can be a lonely life. He brings in the fish and the shrimps that are unscrupulously left behind as the brook becomes a river and a sea. Ms. Sun responds that life is like that, "if you don't work hard, you'll be eliminated". Tao continues his case: in a class of eight, only one can be the best, leaving seven losers if life is only about winning and being the best. For Ms. Sun, everybody can be a winner in something, if only you work hard. The discussion also explicitly turns to national categories again as they argue about Chinese and Dutch values: for Ms. Sun, "the Netherlands makes people lazy", whereas for Tao, "Dutch people are more efficient than Chinese". Ms. Sun and Tao take up opposite ideological positions on their shared "bicultural identity" (De Korne, Byram and Fleming, 2007).

The whole discussion culminates in Tao's claim that his "way of thinking is Dutch". Contestations and negotiations over the interpretation of the story ran through the entire discussion and point to the different cultural frameworks the teacher and students respectively applied in making sense of this old Chinese folk story. The different perspectives held by the teacher and the students, whether intended or not, create a fruitful platform for language learning.

Whereas the teacher seemed to believe that teaching "language" and "culture" through folk stories was a means of reproducing "Chinese" identity, in the young people's minds, the imposition of such Chineseness was explicitly challenged and renegotiated in the classroom. The students assertively considered themselves as Dutch citizens fully participating and entrenched in Dutch culture and society, and rejected the deeper metaphorical meaning and moral lesson embedded in the story. Being Dutch-Chinese is not a wholesale package of identity that one subscribes to all inclusively. It is rather a repertoire of identity options of which some parts are compulsory and barely negotiable and yet others are chosen and replaceable. There are degrees and types of Chineseness, Dutchness and other-nesses with which one can identify or disidentify.

6   CONSTRUCTING DUTCH-CHINESE YOUTH IDENTITIES ONLINE

Having discussed the classroom episode above, we now introduce data drawn from a Netherlands-based digital platform where issues of Chinese identity are discussed. We focus on the public discussion forum of *www.jonc.nl*, a social network site of JONC (*Jongeren Organisatie Nederlandse Chinezen*), a national organisation *of* and *for* Chinese youth in the Netherlands. JONC describes itself as an organisation for Dutch-Chinese youth or young adults in the age range of 18 to 35, and its website as a virtual meeting place for young persons of Chinese heritage living in the Netherlands. By referring to themselves as Dutch-Chinese rather than Chinese-Dutch, they focus on the part of their identity that requires, in their view, elaboration and discussion. The emphasis is on "cherishing" their Chinese descent by bringing Dutch-Chinese youth together "in a relaxed atmosphere of Western openness" (www.jonc.nl, "Over ons").

The thread we discuss below was initiated in August 2007 by a contributor with the screen name Faraway. The topic asks a double question, "How often have you been to China and do you speak the language well?" Because the thread is fairly long, we provide only a part of the discussion and in translation only (the original being in Dutch, with occasional code-switching to English as marked by italics).

FRAGMENT 4: "EVEN THE ENGLISH OF JACKIE CHAN IS BETTER THAN MY CHINESE"

Topic	*How often have you been to China and do you speak the language well?*
Faraway 06-Aug 07:53	My Mandarin and WenZhounese are not super great but I do understand everything + that I have enough time before I will live on my own . . .
Pooky *06-Aug 10:50*	And with my Cantonese I can manage just fine so far in daily (vacation) life. My Mandarin is uh . . . uh . . . uhh . . . 😊 I can only just hear the difference between Mandarin and whichever other Asian language, but that's it . . . 😊😊
(One post omitted)	
Dennis 06-Aug 14:52	Have been 5 x to China and Hong Kong but my Cantonese *sucks big time* and hakka (from origin) is also *shit*. My Mandarin is non-existent but it's still fun to go there.
BORNINHK1971 *06-Aug 21:48*	I have never been to China if I don't count HK and Macau. My knowledge of Mandarin is not so good although I took Mandarin classes.
Jason *07-Aug 01:01*	Cantonese is good, because I speak far too decent too civilised so that they hear immediately that you're from abroad. Mandarin is *okay*. Can understand everything and make myself understood fairly well and read Chinese, which is no unnecessary luxury if you regularly travel to China.
Eek *07-Aug 13:31*	And language: Cantonese is fine for me, speak and understand fluently . . . Reading is also ok good. Mandarin I can understand (if not super fast) speaking is a bit brackish for me (too insecure about tone heights). And all other dialects I don't know . . . With Wenzhounese can pick up a thing or two I think (1 % 😊) and the oh so bad 'Wai Thou' I can also pick up 75 %.
Pooky *07-Aug 15:57*	LOL 😊 . . . I appear to be speaking Cantonese with an indefinable accent, which makes most *sales people* initially think I'm from 'Tai Lok'. If I make clear that I cannot understand Mandarin, they try their 2nd (or 3rd) option out on me; Vietnamese or Japanese . . . 😊😊 Reading Chinese I can't either, never learned. Still, I have no problems with customs, visa and more of those annoyances, thanks to my travel documents. 😊

Boer *07-Aug 23:02*	My Cantonese is rotten, even the English of Jackie Chan is better than my Chinese. I can on the other hand understand it well. In HK I often talk English with the sales people, even if that's mostly to irritate them. Mostly, they say 'Nee Koon Mat Lang Yeh?' in return, what that means I leave up to you. 😊
(One post omitted)	
KiWi *08-Aug 08:37*	Principally I speak Cantonese (followed Saturday school in Amsterdam) and a little Mandarin (but with my level, I really can't survive). I still want to travel sometime from Shanghai to Beijing (or the other way around), but then I need to brush up my Mandarin first.

The linguistically focused part of the initial question builds on (at least) three assumptions. First, all the members of *jonc.nl* should have skills in a specific language ("the language"), which we could label Chinese for simplicity. Second, a high degree of linguistic skills is expected and, in this sense, preferred. This is evident from the formulation of the question: it is asked if you speak the language *well*. The third assumption concerns Chinese being one language. Together this means that everybody who accepts the position as addressees in this interaction is inserted into the position as (competent) speakers of "the language".

The contributors only partly accept these assumptions. When talking about their linguistic skills, they all break up the category of the (Chinese) language in named (sub)registers such as Mandarin, Cantonese, Wenzhounese and Hakka. Clearly they are aware that Chinese does not exist as a bounded category. One exception concerns the written language, where all registers spoken in China share a common norm; this is the basis for Jason's claim that he reads Chinese rather than Mandarin or Cantonese. The assumption regarding their relation to China and the implied obligation to be skilled speakers of Chinese is accepted. Everybody indicates that their proficiency in at least one of the Chinese registers is imperfect, and many offer apologetic evaluations for their self-perceived lack of proficiency. For instance, Pooky characterises her Mandarin as "eh . . . eh . . . ehh . . . ", that is, not very good. Her statement is followed by a blushing emoticon, which indicates her lack of comfort with this. Dennis says that his Cantonese "sucks big time", using this exact expression, that his proficiency in Hakka—described as his family's language—is "shit" and that his Mandarin is "non-existent". Boer says that his Cantonese is "rotten" (*belabberd*). He claims that Jackie Chan's English is better than his Chinese—which is meant as a funny comparison and a negative self-assessment. KiWi's level of Mandarin is allegedly insufficient for surviving, which evidently is a bad thing, and she indicates that in order to fulfil her dream of travelling from Shanghai to Beijing she needs to improve her Mandarin—i.e., invest in her Chinese repertoire—first.

The contributors characterise the way they speak Chinese as insufficient. Pooky says that she appears to speak Cantonese with an indefinable accent and Hong Kong sales people think she is from Tai Lok, Vietnam, or Japan. Jason says his Cantonese is too civilised and this "gives off" his foreigner identity. Eek says he speaks Mandarin in a brackish way because he is not confident with the tonal distinctions. This confirms the characterisation of the young people as different from genuine and competent native speakers of Chinese. But it also positions them as something else but genuine Chinese. They are foreign, they have an accent, and their linguistic deficiencies are typical of foreigners rather than of native speakers of Chinese; the tonal distinctions are a notoriously difficult dimension to master for learners who speak non-tonal languages. Boer recognises this implicitly, as he writes that he often speaks English with sales persons in Hong Kong, mainly to irritate them. This is probably irritating because he is identified as Chinese and therefore required to speak Chinese, according to a monolingual norm. He cites a typical reaction to his inappropriate use of English in Hong Kong as *Nee Koon Mat Lang Yeh* ("What are you saying?"). In short, Boer identifies as non-Chinese when in China, and he uses Dutch spelling conventions rather than traditional Chinese characters, Jyutping or Cantonese pinyin to render this Cantonese phrase in his post (compare: *nei⁵ gong² mat¹yeh⁵ wa²?*). This of course is an excellent example of translanguaging, in which Boer demonstrates his complex belonging to the group of Chinese speakers. He speaks, and does not speak, Cantonese. He shows his orientation to a Dutch centre of normativity rather than a Chinese one (notice also that his screen name is Dutch).

This leads to our last point, concerning written language. As mentioned, the young speakers predominantly deploy Dutch, and a Dutch that gives an impression of being non-accented, native, fully adequate writing. In this way, it contrasts strikingly with the picture they draw of their Chinese. Also, an alternative (Dutch) normative centre is present during the entire interaction, simultaneously with the orientation to an (imagined) Chinese centre. This does not mean that their written language is completely in accordance with the institutionally accepted Dutch Standard. We find non-standard features, such as the English spelling of Malaysia instead of standard Dutch *Maleisië* (Faraway) and the constructions "voor me zelf [op mezelf] woon" (Faraway), "onze [ons] team" (Dennis), "na [naar] China" (Eek), "omdat we . . . ben [zijn] gegaan" (Jason). Yet, again this language use (and normative transgression) is normal in the informal genres of online discussion boards and it is demonstrated by language users recognised as natives. There is no reason to link it with foreignness. A different type of non-standard writing is found in word-internal capitalisation and spacing: "WenZhounees" (Faraway), "Gui Lin" (Jason), "Wai Thou" (Eek). Similar forms were observed elsewhere: the Asian and Proud thread features an occurrence of *ShangHai's* (for Shanghainese). We find it reasonable to analyse this as a way to mark aesthetically the character-segmentation in Chinese. This thereby also illustrates how the young people orient to different normative centres simultaneously. It is, in other words, a sign of the polycentric character of the interaction.

To sum up, to Dutch-Chinese youth, Chinese appears to be a complex matter, and in order to discuss it they draw on different normative centres. First, Chinese is composed of several named registers. Second, nobody simply speaks it or doesn't speak it. Everybody speaks some registers of Chinese, and nearly always not as well as they would like to. Their skills in Chinese are evaluated predominantly negatively and as insufficient in comparison with an unspecified norm. Third, even though as Dutch-Chinese they are positioned as native speakers, several of the contributors report to be speaking with accents, thereby indexing their non-nativeness. Fourth, all of this goes on in fluent Dutch, which in itself demonstrates the common orientation to a normative centre located within a Dutch rather than a Chinese context. They are, and are not, speakers of Chinese and they are, and are not, Chinese.

7 CONCLUSION

Both data samples discussed above illustrate the complexity and multilayeredness of Dutch-Chinese identities, as well as the internal diversity of what constitutes Chinese. The examples also illustrate how little identity is simply given and how much young people of Chinese heritage in the Netherlands actively seek and construct, as well deny and negotiate, the identities they inhabit. In the classroom, participants found an identity in opposing the teacher's and the textbook's claims of a Chinese identity that reproduces old communist values. They found an identity in Tao's alignment with individualist, Western/Dutch values and in his somewhat rebellious articulation of these in the classroom ("my way of thinking is Dutch"). On the discussion forum, we saw young people virtually connecting in search of a common identity as Dutch-Chinese. They seemed to find identity in sharing experiences of travelling to China and talking about their abilities and limitations as speakers of Chinese.

The overall picture of multilingual identity that emerges is one of intense polycentricity: Dutch-Chinese youth in the Netherlands organise their identity work in relation to a number of simultaneously occurring but context-specific centres of language and identity—Dutch, PRC/Hong Kong, Asian/Western, Cantonese/Mandarin, home town, age, gender, etc.—that provoke differing, sometimes conflicting orientations towards complexes of legitimacy and authenticity with respect to Dutch-Chinese identity. Rather than assuming that young people's identities would necessarily be "dual" or "hyphenated", we consider that people articulate a whole repertoire of inhabited and ascribed identities and that they do so by means of a complex display and deployment of cultural resources. The learning of Chinese language and literacy in the complementary classroom generates a particular set of resources, allowing the organisation of different micro-identities. Tao, Faraway and friends are not merely displaced Chinese subjects, but also Dutch young people receiving their mainstream education in and through Dutch. As a result, they embrace some Chinese cultural and linguistic resources, while rejecting others and while all along recognising the incomplete and unfinished character of their Chinese repertoires.

ACKNOWLEDGEMENTS

Both authors gratefully acknowledge support from HERA, which funded the data collection and partly our jobs as part of the CRP "Investigating Discourses of Inheritance and Identities in Four Multilingual European Settings". We thank project coordinator Adrian Blackledge and the members of the IDII4MES team in Birmingham, Stockholm, Copenhagen, Tilburg and now beyond, for the many discussions we had between 2010 and 2012. We also thank Li Wei for including our paper in the invited colloquium "Multilingualism in the Chinese Diasporas" he organised at the 2013 International Symposium on Bilingualism in Singapore. We alone, of course, are responsible for any shortcomings that remain.

REFERENCES

Aligica, P.D. & Tarko, V. 2012. Polycentricity: From Polanyi to Ostrom, and beyond. *Governance: An International Journal of Policy, Administration, and Institutions* 23 (2), 237–362.

Arnaut, K. 2012. Super-diversity: elements of an emerging perspective. *Diversities* 14 (2), 1–16.

Baker, S. 2013. Conceptualising the use of Facebook in ethnographic research: as tool, as data and as context. *Ethnography and Education* 8, 131–45.

Blackledge, A. & Creese, A. 2010. *Multilingualism: A Critical Perspective*. London: Continuum.

Blackledge, A., Creese, A. & Takhi, J.K. 2013. Language, superdiversity and education. In *Multilingualism and Multimodality: Current Challenges for Educational Studies*, I. De Saint-Georges and J.-J. Weber (eds.), 59–80. Rotterdam: Sense.

Blommaert, J. 2010. *The Sociolinguistics of Globalization*. Cambridge: Cambridge University Press.

Blommaert, J. 2013. *Linguistic Landscapes, Ethnography and Superdiversity: Chronicles of Complexity*. Bristol: Multilingual Matters.

Blommaert, J. & Rampton, B. 2011. Language and superdiversity. *Diversities* 13 (2), 1–22.

Brubaker, R. 2002. Ethnicity without groups. *Archives Européennes de Sociologie* 43 (2), 163–89.

Busch, B. 2012. The linguistic repertoire revisited. *Applied Linguistics* 33 (5), 503–23.

CBS. 2010. Herkomst van Chinezen in Nederland. In *Bevolkingstrends: Statistisch Kwartaalblad over de demografie van Nederland. Jaargang 58, 1e kwartaal, 6–6.* Den Haag: Centraal Bureau voor Statistiek.

Creese, A. & Blackledge, A. 2010. Translanguaging in the bilingual classroom: A pedagogy for learning and teaching? *The Modern Language Journal* 94 (1), 103–15.

Creese, A., Wu, C.-J. & Blackledge, A. 2009. Folk stories and social identification in multilingual classrooms. *Linguistics and Education* 20, 350–65.

De Korne, H., Byram, M. & Fleming, M. 2007. Familiarising the stranger: Immigrant perceptions of cross-cultural interaction and bicultural identity. *Journal of Multilingual and Multicultural Development* 28 (4), 290–307.

Gumperz, J. J. 1964. Linguistic and social interaction in two communities. *American Anthropologist* 66 (6, 2), 137–53.

Harris, R. & Rampton, B. 2009. Ethnicity without guarantees: An empirical approach. In *Identity in the 21st Century: New Trends in Changing Times*, M. Wetherell (ed.), 95–199. London: Palgrave Macmillan.

Jonsson, C. & Muhonen, A. 2014. Multilingual repertoires and the relocalisation of manga in digital media. *Discourse, Context and Media* 3 (2–3), 48–61.

Jørgensen, J. N. 2008. Polylingual languaging around and among children and adolescents. *International Journal of Multilingualism* 5 (3), 161–76.

Juffermans, K., Blommaert, J., Kroon, S. & Li, J. 2014. Dutch–Chinese repertoires and language ausbau in superdiversity: A view from digital media. *Discourse, Context and Media* 3 (2–3), 78–100.

Li, J. & Juffermans, K. 2014. Learning and teaching Chinese in the Netherlands: The metapragmatics of a polycentric language. In *Learning Chinese in Diasporic Communities: Many pathways to being Chinese*, X. L. Curdt-Christiansen and A. Hancock (eds.), 97–115. Amsterdam: John Benjamins.

Li, W. 2014. Researching multilingualism and superdiversity: Grassroots actions and responsibilities. *Multilingua* 33 (5–6), 475–84.

Li, W. & Zhu, H. 2010. Voices from the diaspora: changing hierarchies and dynamics of Chinese multilingualism. *International Journal of the Sociology of Language* 205, 155–71.

Varis, P., Wang, X. & Du, C. 2011. Identity repertoires on the Internet: Opportunities and constraints. *Applied Linguistics Review* 2, 265–84.

Vertovec, S. 2010. Towards post-multiculturalism? Changing communities, conditions and contexts of diversity. *International Social Science Journal* 61 (199), 83–95.

Wolf, S. 2011. *Chinezen in Nederland.* Utrecht: Forum: Instituut voor Multiculturele Vraagstukken.

4 Sojourner Tongues
Language Practices Among the Chinese of Cairo

Jie Wang

INTRODUCTION

Although many Chinese visitors, especially Muslims, passed through North Africa on their way to Europe for centuries, there seems little specific evidence of a Chinese presence in Cairo before the early twentieth century. In the 1930s, there were only somewhere around sixty Chinese persons in Cairo, and the number remained very small until the late twentieth century (Zhou, 2002). Thanks to a small group hailing from Northeast China arriving at the beginning of the 1990s to seek business opportunities,[1] the number of Chinese in Cairo had risen to around 300 individuals by 1999 (Zhou, 2002). Like elsewhere in North Africa (except Tunisia), the Chinese population in Cairo has risen dramatically in the early twenty-first century as migration networks expanded and bureaucratic and financial barriers began to weaken. By 2006, around 5,000 Chinese people were working, living, or studying in Cairo ("Overseas Chinese," 2006). One estimate for the population today is 10,000 (Anonymous, 2013). Consequently, the demographic expansion of Chinese migrants in Cairo has attracted some attention from the Western mainstream media, particularly the prospect of a booming Chinatown (Nasser, 2012; Sheils, 2014).[2] However, in my interviews with Chinese respondents resident in Egypt for at least fifteen years or longer, everyone agreed that their presence in Egypt is neither connected to Chinatowns in other African countries, nor could any population concentration in Cairo justify the identification of a Chinatown there. In their comments, many respondents returned to the basic fact that Egypt is not a country which welcomes or integrates immigrants in general,[3] and thus, their staying in Egypt is temporary. It is based on this view among the Chinese in Egypt that this chapter adopts the term *transmigrant* or transnational migrant to refer to the Chinese in Cairo, accentuating their transient nature.

Studies of language use in Chinese diaspora tend to skew toward the more permanent, self-reflective, and adaptive communities. Yet, transient communities are an important category of the transnational experience of Chinese ethnic groups, and their approach to and experience with multilingualism—limited and practical as it is for many—deserve attention alongside the more frequently privileged narratives of linguistic adaptation and integration.

I noticed the disjunction between Western narratives and Chinese realities the first time that I visited Cairo in 2006, and it is primarily this disparity in terms of perception toward the Chinese diaspora in Cairo that prompted my interest in the topic. My personal experience of multilingual practice as a transnational subject who has lived in the Arab world and later studied in Europe leads me to inquire: how do the Chinese people in Cairo recruit and deploy multiple languages? And what are the connections between their use of languages and their transnational mobility?

First-hand data collection occurred in Cairo from 28 December 2013 to 20 January 2014, and again from 16 August to 10 October 2014, starting from networks of Chinese migrants whom I had known from my previous visits to Cairo in 2006 and 2009, and my residence elsewhere in the Arab world. Drawing on participant observations, I conducted a series of semi-structured and ethnographic interviews with Chinese people living, working, and studying in Cairo, while also consulting the limited secondary literature.

This chapter aims to show that the Chinese diaspora in Cairo as a whole is transient in that they have moved bodily across national borders while harboring a goal of returning back to China or of going on to Western countries after adequate accumulation, either financially or academically. Thus, unlike linguist Christian Dustmann (1999), who concluded that "language fluency is negatively and significantly affected by the migrant's return propensity" (p. 312), and that "language proficiency is positively related to the total intended duration of the migrant in the host country" (p. 306), I argue that there is little connection between Chinese transmigrants' linguistic capital and their intended stay in Cairo.

Nancy H. Hornberger (2007) has called for transnationalism to be distinguished from immigration by focusing on the difference in terms of an individual's link to the host country and the home country (see also Trueba, 2004). To be transnational, the occupations or activities of the individuals concerned should "require regular and sustained social contacts over time across national borders for their implementation" (Portes et al., 1999, p. 219), rather than consisting simply of occasional contacts, visits, and activities across the borders of members (Yi, 2009). Language, both oral and written, can be used to form and represent people's identities (Guzzetti & Gamboa, 2004). However, literature on economic development and globalization suffers a "lack of (or at best myopic) attention to linguistic issues" (Jacquemet, 2005, p. 259). Marco Jacquemet (2005) pointed out that "the majority of scholars have been, until recently, quite unwilling to find [linguistic] zones of engagement with globalization theory. When they do, the dominant discourse has privileged the dystopic pole, thus depicting the worst possible scenario: linguistic imperialism, endangered languages, language loss, and language death" (p. 260). Thus, addressing the Cairo case in an empirical way from a linguistic perspective holds promise for attending to the macro-level of the reality of the transnational field as well as to its internal heterogeneity from a micro-level of daily dialogical encounters, in addition to complementing sociological theories of migration and transnationalism and advancing the notion of transnationalism.

This chapter is structured as follows. Firstly, taking the religion of Islam as a departure point, I examine how Arabic language functions among Chinese Muslims in Cairo, who account for a large portion (probably more than half, albeit the absence of any statistics, this is a crude estimate) of the local Chinese population. The second section focuses on how those coming to Cairo under the capitalist flow, including vendors, peddlers, individual businessmen, and Chinese private and state-owned company staffs use Arabic and English. Then, Chinese publications and civic associations of Chinese concerns in Egypt are discussed, with an exploration of how the transmigrant Chinese employ their mother language, in Egyptian society, and for what purposes. Finally, the multilingual experience of the small, young Egypt-raised generation of Chinese, the majority of whom are of kindergarten or primary school age, living in Cairo with their parents, is discussed.

FROM PILGRIM TO BUSINESSMAN: CHINESE MUSLIMS IN EGYPT IN HISTORICAL PERSPECTIVE

A historical story known as the *Huihui Yuanlai* (Origins of the Hui), which was first printed in 1712 AD, indicates a "crucial link between Chinese Muslims and the Islamic heartlands by stating that Muslims came to China following the order of none other than the Prophet himself" (Benite, 2004, p. 85). While employing Persian as the lingua franca for communication with non-Chinese Muslims in the Tang and Song periods (618 AD–1279 AD) (Liu, 2010), Chinese Muslims started prioritizing Arabic in light of "the revival of Arabic studies in China from the late eighteenth and, more sustainably, from the late nineteenth century" (Green, 2013, p. 5). At the beginning of the 1900s and before the establishment of the People's Republic of China in 1949, educated Hui had access to journals of the Arab world, such as the Egyptian periodicals *al-Manar*, *al-Majallah al-Azhar*, *Nur al-Islam*, *al-Fath* and *al-Irshad* (Green, 2013). In China's Republican era (1912–1949), Chinese Muslims founded their own journals, such as the *Yuehua* (月华) journal (1929–48) in 1929 by reformist Hui scholars at the Chengda Normal School in Beijing's Tongsi Mosque, a post secondary school for Muslims. In the period from 1911 until 1937, thirty other new Muslim journals were founded in Beijing alone (Gladney, 1996).

During the Republican period, Chinese Muslims began also to seek to integrate themselves more substantially into networks of global Islam. One of the aspects of this growing self-awareness was a renewed influence on religious education, including the study of Arabic. Pang Shiqian, a Hui intellectual of this period, wrote that 20% of Egyptian Muslims were literate, 40% of Syrian Muslims were literate, and that 10% to 12% of the whole Chinese population was literate, whereas only 5% or 6% of Hui Muslims were literate (in Chinese) (Pang, 1951). Contacts with the Arab world were initiated as part of a general effort to improve Hui education. Systematic Chinese study visits to Egypt were initiated in 1930, when the Association of Muslims in Yunnan Province sent an official request to Al-Azhar, Egypt's oldest university, about dispatching Chinese Muslims to conduct Arabic and Islamic studies there; the first batch of students, including Pang, arrived in 1931 (Pang, 1951).

Between the 1930s and 1949, a total number of six groups of Chinese Muslims were dispatched by Kunming Mingde High School,[4] Shanghai Islamic Normal School, Chengda Normal School,[5] and other institutes (Wei, 2013). These contacts stopped after the founding of the People's Republic (1949) and were not renewed until 1982, when the Islamic Association of China sent ten students to Al-Azhar (Wei, 2013), followed by another gap until 1993, when a bilateral cultural exchange agreement was signed between Egypt and China, including an item stipulating that each year twenty-five Chinese Muslim students could enroll at Al-Azhar to pursue Arabic or Islamic studies on full scholarships provided by the university (Wei, 2013). These scholarship students have been joined by many more studying at their own costs. Due to a vacuum of officially published data, it is hard to pinpoint the exact scale of Chinese Muslim students in Egypt nowadays. However, one respondent studying in Al-Azhar explained that because tuition at Egyptian universities is free for Muslims, including international Muslim students, and because of the low living cost in Egypt,[6] many Chinese Muslims are able to afford their Arabic or Islamic studies at Al-Azhar or other Egyptian universities. Thus the number of students coming to Egypt by themselves largely surpasses that dispatched by the Chinese government.[7]

The life and linguistic practices of Chinese Muslims in Egypt can be further elucidated by a few individual cases. Zhang Jin, a Hui Muslim from Shandong province, has been living in Cairo for thirteen years. After his graduation from Al-Azhar, he decided to give up a decent governmental job in Shandong, remaining in Cairo and starting his own business. Nowadays, he is one of the most successful Chinese businessmen in Cairo, running his own factory of extracting granite and exporting it to China. He also operates the only private bilingual (Chinese and Arabic) newspaper of foreign capital *China Weekly* in Egypt, and is the executive deputy president of the Egyptian-Chinese Cultural Exchange Association, while having other roles such as the Egyptian representative of a world tour of Chinese paintings and calligraphy. He previously worked as an interpreter in the first few years after his studies at Al-Azhar. The frequent contacts with local people in his part-time job not only improved his language skills, but also allowed him to see the huge business potentials in the Egyptian market. He speaks fluent Egyptian Arabic, and employs only one interpreter, an Egyptian girl recently graduated from Cairo University with a Bachelor's degree in Chinese studies, working for the Egyptian-Chinese Cultural Exchange Association. He explained that he does not need interpreters working for his factory, because his Chinese workers only need to deal with technical issues, and he handles all dealings with Egyptians personally.[8] Ma Sheng is another Hui businessman whose career has followed a similar trajectory to that of Zhang Jin. Beginning his studies in Al-Azhar, Ma worked as an interpreter, and now runs his own factory of recycling plastics and then producing fiber and selling it to Egyptian state-owned factories or exporting it to other Gulf countries, such as Kuwait. He has been living in Egypt for twenty years, recruiting no interpreter because he is able to manage all issues requiring Arabic personally. His brother, who also speaks fluent Egyptian Arabic, helps him operate the factory.

For many Chinese Muslim[9] students, the successful career path of Zhang Jin's and Ma Sheng's is their ideal model—moving from university studies into being an interpreter for Chinese companies, and from there into an independent entrepreneur. Indeed, many Chinese Muslim students have started doing business in different fields in Cairo, from operating Chinese restaurants to internet cafés. Ahmad Saeed Street is reported by the media as the center of the Chinese community in Cairo (Nasser, 2012), and Li's Beijing Internet Café is located on this street, adjacent to several Chinese restaurants offering Western Chinese Muslim fare. Although this Internet Café has been there for more than ten years, Li, a Muslim student from Yunnan Province, informed me that he had only purchased it from the previous owners—a couple from Northeast China, one year before when the couple decided to leave Egypt. Li's wife, who was about to register for Arabic Studies at Al-Azhar, and another Chinese student from the same province of Yunnan, were helping him run the café.[10] The customers are Chinese students, almost all of them young men playing Chinese computer games with other Chinese students at the same café for hours at a stretch. I stayed for a while to observe them in the café, and noticed that their communication was frequently interlarded with words from colloquial Egyptian Arabic such as حبيبي (*Habibi*, dear), ماشي (*Mashi*, ok), كويس (*Kuwis*, nice), يلي (*Yalla*, come on), etc. However, the future of these students seems far from being promising, considering how much time they spend at the café and the difficulty of acquiring colloquial Arabic, which is largely different from the Modern Standard Arabic taught at Al-Azhar. Recalling his school days, Zhang Jin remembered that he could not communicate with Egyptians in even one complete Arabic sentence after learning Modern Standard Arabic for one or two years.[11] Enrollment in Arabic Studies, while providing a foundation, does not supply on its own the linguistic knowhow for Chinese students to find a place in the local economy.

Jiang Peng is a twenty-year-old Muslim from Northeast China. Having failed the national university entrance examination in China, he enrolled in computer science at a local adult education college. As the first person in his hometown to go abroad, he chose Egypt, because one of his brother's friends was already living there. He heard that being an interpreter for Chinese companies could be lucrative. While awaiting the chance to register at Al-Azhar,[12] he is learning Modern Standard Arabic from scratch at a local language school. This school offers thirteen levels of Arabic, and each level will take one month to accomplish, with five hours of intensive daily study for six days a week. According to Jiang Peng's description, after finishing all thirteen levels, he could be qualified of working as an interpreter. However, when being asked how many levels he has finished, he said he had only finished three levels in a year's time, because he has failed several exams. He has begun to consider returning to China.[13] He describes his Arabic level as basic, remaining unable to communicate with local people. Thus, although the Muslim Chinese students in Cairo form the only group with substantial bilingual proficiency, their experiences can be very different, from incomplete or failed language acquisition to successes, as in the cases of Ma Sheng or Zhang Jin.

INDEPENDENT CHINESE BUSINESS IN CAIRO: A STUDY OF LIMITED LANGUAGE ACQUISITION

As the majority ethnic group in China, Han Chinese comprises at least half of the Chinese migrant population in Egypt. They can be broadly identified into contract migrants who are in Egypt under the auspices of Chinese (both state-owned and private) enterprises, and individual entrepreneurs at varying scales of economic importance. For the contract migrants whose return time is not self-determined, their linguistic practice is similar to the experience elsewhere, in countries such as Libya. By the time such workers leave Egypt, they will have learned no Arabic, made no Egyptian acquaintances, eaten little or no Egyptian food, undertaken no domestic or regional tourism, observed no local holidays, and seen no more than drive-through glimpses of Egyptian life, returning to China once the contract, which usually lasts for two to three years, expires (Wang & Stenberg, 2014). They, and the majority of Chinese non-Muslim managers, never expect to learn Arabic or English, because the gap caused by language between them and local people will be filled by both Egyptian and Chinese interpreters.

Of greater relevance is the experience of various Han Chinese individuals, including peddlers and venders selling mobile phones in the massive local open markets, such as Ramsis or Khan el Khalili Bazaar, or doing door-to-door selling in several poor local communities, such as Ain Shams—an occupation it seems only Chinese would take, whose long-term existence in Egypt has produced a particular kind of multilingual practice, and whose presence first attracted the Western media's attention to the Chinese of Cairo (Badawi, 2014). These peddlers and vendors, without any Arabic knowledge before coming to Egypt or the funds to employ interpreters, seem to be able to communicate with the local customers without any great obstacles, making use of limited but useful Egyptian simple phrases and with the help of calculators.

Liu Jing, a Han ethnic, married, middle-aged women from Qingtian of China's Zhejiang Province, has been selling mobile phones in Ramsis market for two years. I spent one hour with her on a Wednesday afternoon, during which at least twenty Egyptian people stopped in front of her small desk, on which more than ten phones of different brands and models were displayed. Their pleasing appearance attracted some Egyptians to ask about the price. Speaking with an impeccable Egyptian accent and by using several independent words and phrases rather than complete sentences, Liu told them the price, and reminded them that these mobile phones are made in China and carry no guarantee. When the customers wished to bargain, she would first further exhibit the phone, letting them see how many modern functions it is equipped with, and then use a calculator to confirm the final price. Within an hour, she sold two phones by using her limited Arabic and the calculator. This brief process, which took less than ten minutes, reflects the relationship between her linguistic-communicative experience and her current linguistic-communicative competence (Blommaert & Backus, 2011). Before coming to Egypt, she had been to Indonesia and Dubai, selling mobile phones there. She clearly knows what the customers are most concerned with and what the potential troubles might be with the local people. Therefore, once arriving in Egypt, she quickly learned the most pragmatic but basic trade Arabic of Egyptian accent from earlier Qingtian arrivals, and later supplemented this to a small degree by interaction with Chinese Muslim students. However, she complained that language remains a problem for her, and she cannot learn more Arabic from the community which she is living in—one residential building in Cairo accommodating around one hundred people from the same place, Qingtian (Zhejiang Province). They were all doing the same trade, and their Arabic seemed to be at more or less the same level. Outside work, their lives are conducted in Qingtian dialect and occasionally Mandarin. Liu's isolation from the Egyptian society leads to her incapacity of recognizing the local people's real intention. In the hour I spent with her, I was surprised by Liu's patience with the potential customers for the phones. From their questions, it was easy for me[14] to recognize who was seriously considering buying, and who only wanted to have a look. In addition, Liu's response to the questions demonstrated her lack of local cultural knowledge, which always accompanies linguistic practices (Blommaert & Backus, 2011). For instance, some Egyptians were curious about my presence, and asked her who I was. Her answer was, "my friend". But to avoid unnecessary troubles in Arab countries, it would be wise for a foreign female to say "my sister".

In Egypt, the fields of extracting granite and exporting marble to China seem to be monopolized by groups of certain origins in China.[15] However, unlike Qingtian mobile phone venders and door-to-door sellers from Northeast China who lack a financial and social foundation and live on the margin of Egyptian society, the private factory bosses and individual businessmen in the granite and marble trade and in other businesses usually recruit local Egyptians as their interpreters. While interviewing one Syrian factory executive who has business cooperation with one Chinese factory in plastics recycling, he said that he found no obstacle at all in dealing with the Chinese of the Chinese factory, because the Egyptian interpreters employed by the Chinese factory are adequate for their conversations. However, Zhao Xing, the Chinese staff who is in charge of financial issues for this Chinese factory, faces problems in communicating with Egyptians when the interpreters are not in the factory. Having stayed in Egypt for several months, he has learned some basic Egyptian expressions, such as امشي (*Imshi*, go away), شوية شوية (*Shuwia Shuwia*, slowly slowly), etc. Although these phrases sound impolite, they enable the Egyptians to understand his intention. Both Syrian and Egyptian respondents who had frequent interactions with the Chinese reported that some expressions spoken by Chinese people are not polite at all and sound quite harsh. Over time, however, they have grown used to the idea that these expressions are a result of the fragmentary knowledge of Arabic of the Chinese there. Language does not seem to be an issue for many Chinese who run businesses in Cairo. In each business, such as Chinese restaurant, spa, etc., there are usually one or two persons who are relatively strong in language, either in Arabic or in English, and who are naturally delegated to dealing with Egyptians or foreigners from other countries. The rest of the staff either totally rely on him or her, or use body language and limited Egyptian words to express their intentions.

China Pearl Aromatherapy Club had only been open for a few months in the affluent Zamalek neighborhood of Cairo when I visited it in January 2014. No staff member speaks Arabic, but the owner, a middle-aged Chinese woman, could speak English due to her several years of experience of selling clothes in Jordan[16] before coming to Cairo. Although all the services are in traditional Chinese medicine, and most of the customers are Chinese in Cairo, some Arabs from Gulf countries, in addition to local people, also frequent the Club. Li Xiao, the brother of the owner, as well as the receptionist, explained to me how he interacted with Arabs: first, he shows the service item with price written in English. If the Arab customer says something he does not understand, he will use his body language to point all over his body from head to toe, with questioning: Kulu Kulu? (كل كل, all of it), which means do you want to do the massage for the whole body? Then he will point at the item of whole body massage, most of the time, the customers will nod. He does not find it necessary to employ staff who can speak Arabic, because the Arab customers can explain their needed service through body language. It was only in the very beginning of their business that they employed one Egyptian who can speak Chinese to help them with marketing. After a few months, their club became known in the town, so they recommended this Egyptian interpreter to work for a four-star hotel run by a Chinese state-owned company registered in Cairo.

COMMUNITY ORGANIZATIONS AND
THE EGYPT-BORN CHINESE

As the population has grown, Chinese language newspapers and magazines have emerged. In 2008, the bimonthly *Sino-Egyptian Friendship: Chinese in Egypt Journal* was founded by the chair of the Egypt Cairo Chinese Women's Association, a businesswoman from Hong Kong, Li Xinxin, who has been living in Egypt for twenty-six years (Guo & Yu, 2008). In the following year, another bimonthly Chinese language journal was founded by the China Council for the Promotion of Peaceful National Reunification in Egypt and the Egypt Chinese Solidarity Council. On the cover of the former journal *not for sale* is printed, and on the latter it says *circulated only within Chinese in Egypt*, indicating that these Chinese language journals are aimed at the Chinese community in Egypt. These publications can be picked up for free at Chinese restaurants. They are also circulated by publishers to those working with the Chinese companies in Egypt. Both journals contain advertisements posted by Chinese restaurants, Chinese hair salons, Chinese vegetable delivery centers, Chinese traditional medical centers, etc., in addition to passages introducing Arab society, Arab culture, and Arab politics. Some Chinese in Egypt also contribute stories about living in Egypt, alongside brief news of official activities held in Egypt. The contents of these contributed writings are fairly simple—one Chinese student in the Netherlands, happening to look through my research materials, remarked that it seemed pitched lower than materials for middle school students in China. Clearly, the publications are intended for utilitarian purposes, be it for interaction with Arabs, provision of services, or softening the feeling of estrangement by sharing the experience with a community in print. The intended readership shares an experience of being a Chinese person in Egypt, and suggests at least a rudimentary community.

Unlike the Chinese language journals solely circulated among the Chinese community in Cairo, a third publication, *The China Weekly* newspaper, is strategically directed at both the Arab countries as a whole and the Chinese community in Egypt. As a newly established newspaper in 2012, *The China Weekly*, registered in the UK, may well be the first Arabic language newspaper owned by non-Arab foreigners to be sold legally in the Middle East and North Africa. Zhang Jin, the president of *The China Weekly*, likened the experience of running this newspaper to a process of nurturing a child, and said that the message the newspaper delivers to the Arab countries was much more significant than the financial profit gained from it.

Twice a month, Chinese and Arabic versions of this newspaper are printed. Only the Arabic language edition is for sale, at a cheap price of one Egyptian pound. The print run is 20,000 copies, whereas the Chinese edition, circulated within the Chinese community for free, has a print run of only 500 copies. Zhang also sends Arabic copies to Sudan and Jordan by mail, of 200 copies each time, where Zhang Jin's personal Chinese friends help him circulate it free of charge among Arabs there. When I asked some Egyptians and Syrians living in Cairo about their impression of this newspaper, some of them pointed out its strong pro-PRC (People's Republic of China) political views, whereas others remarked on the beauty of the writers' use of the Arabic language. Indeed, the president of *The China Weekly*, Zhang Jin, told me a story that the Egyptian editor described Mao Zedong as the great architect, and before printing out the Arabic version of the newspaper, Zhang Jin came across this expression and angrily asked him to change the word "architect", because this designation was typically used for Deng Xiaoping in China's political and economic discourses. The contents of the two different language versions differ noticeably. Approximately half of the Arabic version content is usually on Sino-foreign relations, particularly in support of Chinese stances on particular international issues, and other pages are about introducing Chinese culture and bilateral cultural and economic agreements. The Chinese language version is quite similar to the Chinese language journals. One interesting phenomenon is that all the competition announcements and activities posted in the journals and newspapers are sponsored or supported by either the Chinese embassy in Cairo or other Chinese associations, such as the China Council for the Promotion of Peaceful National Reunification in Egypt or the Egyptian-Chinese Cultural Exchange Association.

It is self-evident that *The China Weekly*, although not a government publication, is at least informally concerned with fostering a favorable public opinion in Egypt about the People's Republic of China. Zhang, as a successful bilingual Chinese businessman in Egypt, is deeply invested in good bilateral relations. If he is an example of a mature migrant subject trying to act through print media to improve Chinese and Egyptian mutual perceptions, Chinese children in Egypt can suggest whether a Sino-Egyptian subject is likely to emerge.

Almost none of the Chinese presently in Egypt reported considering settling down there, with an exception of a few women married to Egyptian men.[17] Some Chinese families, however, have brought their children to Cairo, and in some cases even the children's grandparents. One example is Li Xia, dispatched by Peking University to the Confucius Institute in Cairo University as a Chinese language teacher. She brought her parents to help her take care of her six-year-old son, and enrolled him in an international kindergarten in Cairo. Linguistically, she is concerned that her son is suffering from the vacuum of Chinese learning, although she is heartened by his rapid adoption of English. Nevertheless, because of the weakness of mathematics education in Egypt in general, she has decided to send her son back to China once he reaches the age for entering primary school. None of the four family members are learning Arabic.

Most of the Chinese living in Egypt send their children to international schools, and to Deren Chinese School on Friday and Saturday afternoons, the latter of which is operated by the Chinese community via the assistance of the Egypt Chinese Solidarity Council. Several Chinese women are paid teachers, teaching children basic Chinese. There are around twenty students in this private school, all of whom are around kindergarten age.

The most prominent Chinese in Cairo are the exceptional Muslim Chinese families of Ma, Yan, and Tan, who were high officials and local power lords in the Northwestern Army of Kuomintang (KMT, or Chinese Nationalist Party), and who played a central role in the history of Northwest China in the first half of the twentieth century. Fleeing to Egypt from Qinghai Province in 1950 after their defeat by the communists in China, they were granted residency in Egypt by King Farouk over the opposition of all the other members of the royal family. Nowadays, the third generation of the Ma family is living in Cairo, still holding Chinese passports and never losing Chinese mainland citizenship.

Ge Zi, the descendant of Ma Liankui, married one of the grandsons of Ma Bufang in the early 1990s, both of whom were aligned against the Chinese Communist Party. It was an arranged marriage between their two families, and she had no knowledge at all of Arabic nor English. She served in the army in Northwest China before coming to Cairo. Her husband, Ma Wei, was born in comfortable circumstances in Cairo and holds a Chinese mainland passport. Ge Zi embarked on Arabic studies at Al-Azhar, but dropped out in 1995 when she found a job as an Arabic-Chinese interpreter when she was visiting the commodities fair in Cairo. According to her recollection, at that time almost none of the Chinese in Cairo could speak Arabic. Her Arabic developed rapidly, largely because her husband, whose family originated in Qinghai Province, could only speak Arabic and the Northwest Chinese dialect. Her twin daughters are now Egyptian university students pursuing Arabic studies. Ge Zi hopes that they will find places as senior Chinese-Arabic interpreters for the Chinese government. Their English is also good, because they entered a language institute in their middle school and attended international high school. Ge Zi emphasized that Ma Bufang, the patriarch of the family, paid attention to language education. Once they arrived in Cairo in the 1950s, they hired private tutors for English and Arabic learning. Ge Zi regarded her daughters' oral Chinese level as acceptable, but their knowledge of Chinese culture and history as insufficient. Her daughters speak Egyptian Arabic with their father, Northwest dialect with their grandparents, and standard Mandarin with their mother. The other descendants of the Ma family are living in different countries of Jordan, Saudi Arabia, and Canada, and most of them married Arabs. However, Ge Zi stated that she personally would be displeased if her daughters were to marry Egyptians.

Another rare example of a new Sino-Egyptian is Hani Yan, perhaps the first Egyptian-born Chinese national. His father, originally from Shandong Province, arrived in Cairo in the 1930s and married an Egyptian woman. Although having very little knowledge of Chinese language, he holds a Chinese passport, and has to fly to China twice a year in order to renew his Egyptian visa, carrying with him a document that has been issued by the Chinese embassy in Cairo, stating that he is a genuine citizen of the PRC. During my stay in Cairo, I attempted to make contact with him. The Chinese people who tried to assist me in approaching him inform me that Yan seldom has contact with the Chinese community in Cairo, and follows entirely an Egyptian way of living.

Several Egyptian universities, such as Cairo University and Ain Shams University, have offered Bachelor's, Master's, and even Ph.D. degrees in Chinese language and literature since the 1990s. A variety of bilateral cultural exchange activities, visits, civic Chinese learning courses, and Chinese cultural workshops have operated under the aegis of Chinese Cultural Center in Cairo, which belongs to the Cultural Department of the PRC embassy in Cairo. These initiatives ensure a relatively stable flow of Egyptians who are sufficiently competent in Mandarin to communicate with Chinese.

CONCLUSIONS

Underpinning the transnational movements of the Chinese to Egypt is of course the economic growth of China as well as the market potential of Egypt. The Chinese community in Cairo, with its limited multilingualism, should thus be seen as a byproduct of the competitive price of certain Chinese commodities as well as labor. Arabic, in particular Egyptian Arabic, brings convenience in doing business in Egypt, but is not the necessary premise. The religious ties between the Hui and the Egyptians end up serving the purposes of the market, rather than spiritual enhancement. The Muslim connection does serve, however, to produce individuals such as Zhang Jin, who are heavily committed to friendly Chinese-Egyptian relations. Recently, Zhang has started drafting an Egyptian dialect dictionary, hoping to help more Chinese in Cairo overcome linguistic obstacles.

Local context "plays a critical role in mediating the scope and depth of migrants' transnational practices" (Yi, 2009, p. 115). Although there are individuals with fascinating life stories who demonstrate features of the integration or assimilation familiar from the received narratives of immigrants elsewhere, the Chinese in Egypt are largely composed of Han individuals who learn only rudimentary business Arabic, and Muslims, the majority of whom are Hui ethnic group,[18] whose education allows them to find work as Egyptian Arabic-Chinese interpreters. On the periphery of these Chinese communities are also the numerous Egyptian graduates of Chinese-language programs who find employment as interpreters for Chinese firms.

Concepts such as multilingualism are liable to privilege narratives. It is important, however, to remember how many individuals and societies live in marginal states of multilingualism with only enough access to another language in order to make ends meet.

ACKNOWLEDGMENTS

The completion of this research article was not a solo work. The author would like to thank Executive Deputy President of the Egyptian-Chinese

Cultural Exchange Association Mr. Ma Qiang, Mrs. Ma Ge, and Mr. Basel Turkmani and his family members for their assistance of all kinds during her fieldwork in Cairo. She would also like to thank Chinese, Egyptian, and Syrian respondents for sharing their experiences in formal and informal interviews. The author also owes debts to Josh Stenberg. He provided constructive and critical comments on the draft paper.

NOTES

1. There is no source on the Internet or in the literature about the first group of people coming to Egypt in the beginning of the 1990s. However, when I asked several Chinese who have been living in Cairo for at least fifteen years about which group came to Cairo first, they all said "the Northeasterners", who initially joined the commodities fairs held in different countries and settled down in Egypt. Usually one person who first settled in Cairo would bring many of his relatives there later on.
2. Chinese migrants discussed in this article include those hailing from the mainland, but exclude Uyghur Muslims, due to my inadequate access to Chinese Uyghur Muslims in Cairo.
3. The respondents also spoke of other reasons that make the existence of Chinatown in Cairo seem impossible. However, surprisingly, they all first mentioned the Egyptian policy of not welcoming foreigners living permanently in Egypt.
4. Ming De High School was a private school established in 1929 by Hui Muslims.
5. It was established in 1925 by several Muslims. It is located inside a mosque in Shan Dong Province in China.
6. The respondents told me that ten thousand Renminbi, around 1,250 Euro, would be sufficient for a modest living in Cairo.
7. The interview took place on 2 February 2014 in Cairo.
8. The interview took place on 10 February 2014 in Cairo.
9. Here I refer to not only Hui Muslims, although they account for the majority of the Chinese Muslim population.
10. The interview took place on 5 February 2014 in Cairo.
11. The interview took place on 5 February 2014 in Cairo.
12. The Chinese Muslim students studying at Al Azhar told me that in 2013, Al Azhar didn't accept any foreign student due to the unstable political situation inside Egypt.
13. The Interview took place on 7 February 2014 in Cairo.
14. I have spoken Arabic for more than ten years, and have lived in Arab countries for six years.
15. People from Shandong Province are running factories extracting granite, while those from Chengtou of Fujian and Yunfu of Guangdong are exporting marble to China.
16. I didn't ask her if she understands or speaks Jordanian Arabic. However, based on my knowledge of Arabic, Jordanian Arabic is quite different from Egyptian Arabic.
17. All Chinese suggest to me not to marry an Egyptian man.
18. There are ten historically Islamic minorities in China, including Hui, Uyghur, Kazak, Dongxiang, Kyrgyz, Salar, Tajik, Uzbek, Bonan, and Tatar.

REFERENCES

Badawi, K. (2014). *The migratory silk road: Chinese in Egypt* [Video File]. Retrieved from http://vimeo.com/97196920

Benite, Z. B. D. (2004). From 'Literati' to 'Ulama': The origins of Chinese Muslim nationalist historiography. *Nationalism and Ethnic Politics, 9*(4), 83–109.

Blommaert, J., & Backus, A. (2011). Repertoires revisited: 'Knowing language' in superdiversity. *King's College London Working papers in Urban Language & Literacies, 67*, 1–26.

Dustmann, C. (1999). Temporary migration, human capital, and language fluency of migrants. *The Scandinavian Journal of Economics, 101*(2), 297–314.

Gladney, D. C. (1996). *Muslim Chinese: Ethnic nationalism in the People's Republic* (No. 149). Cambridge, MA: Harvard University Asia Center.

Green, N. (2013). From the silk road to the railroad (and back): The means and meanings of the Iranian encounter with China. *Iranian Studies*, (ahead-of-print), 1–28.

Guo, C. J., & Yu, Z. W. (2008). *<Lv ai Hua ren Tong xun> Chuang kan Fa xing.* Retrieved from http://news.xinhuanet.com/newscenter/2008–01/31/content_75 33772.htm

Guzzetti, B. J., & Gamboa, M. (2004). Zines for social justice: Adolescent girls writing on their own. *Reading Research Quarterly, 39*(4), 408–436.

Hornberger, N. H. (2007). *Biliteracy, transnationalism, multimodality, and identity: Trajectories across time and space.* GSE Publications, 149.

Jacquemet, M. (2005). Transidiomatic practices: Language and power in the age of globalization. *Language & Communication, 25*(3), 257–277.

Liu, Y. (2010). *A Lingua Franca along the Silk Road: Persian Language in China between the 14th and the 16th Centuries.* na.

Nasser, M. (2012). *The area that could become Cairo's own Chinatown.* Retrieved from http://www.bbc.co.uk/news/world-middle-east-20454495

Overseas Chinese Affairs Office of the State Council. (2006). *Ai ji Hua qiao Hua ren Jing ji Fa zhan Xian zhuang ji Qian jing.* Retrieved from http://www.gqb.gov.cn/news/2006/0613/1/2585.shtml

Pang, S. Q. (1951). *Ai ji jiu nian.* Beijing: Yue hua wen hua fu wu she.

Portes, A., Guarnizo, L. E., & Landolt, P. (1999). The study of transnationalism: pitfalls and promise of an emergent research field. *Ethnic and racial studies, 22*(2), 217–237.

Sheils, C. (2014). *Exploring Cairo's Chinatown.* Retrieved from http://www.cairoscene.com/ViewArticle.aspx?AId=13481-Exploring-Cairo's-Chinatown

Trueba, E. T. (2004). *The new Americans: Immigrants and transnationals at work.* Lanham MD: Rowman & Littlefield.

Wang, J., & Stenberg, J. (2014). Localizing Chinese migrants in Africa: A study of the Chinese in Libya before the Civil War. *China Information, 28*(1), 69–91.

Wei, S. J. (2013). *Ai ji Liu xue Sui yue.* Retrieved from http://www.china774.com/Vip/index.asp?mod=club&do=ts&Qid=456&Tid=29611

Yi, Y. (2009). Adolescent literacy and identity construction among 1.5 generation students: From a transnational perspective. *Journal of Asian Pacific Communication, 19*(1), 100–129.

Zhou, N. (2002). *Hua qiao Hua ren Bai ke Quan shu.* Zhong guo Hua qiao Chu ban she.

Part II

Changing Times, Changing Languages

5 The Dungans of Kazakhstan
Old Minority in a New Nation-State

Juldyz Smagulova

INTRODUCTION

This chapter focuses on the historical development of the Dungan community in Kazakhstan and the changes in their linguistic practices over time. The social, political and economic transformations following the collapse of the Soviet Union have led to shifts in the state's and local communities' ideologies regarding language, identity and nationhood. Kazakhstan's enforcement of a Kazakh nation-state has challenged the value of Russian, a language most Soviet minorities have shifted to. At the same time, the opening of Kazakhstan's market, migration, new communication technologies and globalization have created new opportunities for the diaspora to maintain their ethnic language and identity. Dungans have been able to reestablish ties with the 'historical home' communities in China. They travel to China for business, tourism and educational purposes and many have access to Chinese mass media via internet, satellite TV, etc.

In light of these sociopolitical transformations, this chapter examines the language attitudes and linguistic practices of the Dungan community in Kazakhstan. Using data collected through ethnographic interviews and a critical reading of publications by Kazakhstan Dungan community members, it also explores tensions between nationalism and minorization by addressing issues related to multilingualism and identity from the point of view of members of the Dungan community. Special attention is given to "the various practices in which a minority is constituted and perpetuated, as well as the various practices by means of which such constituted minorities react and resist these processes" (Blommaert 2010: 14).

BACKGROUND

The Dungan[1] diaspora (also called the Hui people or Chinese Muslims[2]) is one of the oldest in Kazakhstan. The first Dungans arrived to the region at the end of the 19th century in two main waves. The first immigrants were refugees from the Gansu and Shaanxi provinces of China fleeing from massacre after the unsuccessful Dungan-Uyghur revolt (also called Muslim revolt) of 1863–1877 against Manchu rule. They arrived to the Zhetysu area (see Figure 5.1 below), then the part of the Russian Tsarist Empire, in fall-winter of 1877–78. According to Rimsky-Korsakoff (1992), 5,444 Dungans arrived and established three compact settlements in Yrdyk, near Osh (current Kyrgyzstan) and Karakonuz (now named Masanchi, Kazakhstan). The second wave came between 1881 and 1884 from the Ili River valley after the Treaty of St. Petersburg (1881) between the Russian and Chinese Empires. The territory of Ili (or Kuldja) sultanate was occupied by Russia in 1871 during the Dungan revolt, when the power of Imperial China in the Ili basin region virtually collapsed. In 1864, Dungans and Uyghurs got full control of eastern Turkestan and established a new state—the Ili sultanate (1864–1881) with its capital in Kuldja. The new sultanate proclaimed war with the Russian Empire, which manifested in numerous attacks of the rebels on Russian troops and settlements in the border areas. Thus the official reason for occupation was protection of the Russian borders and citizens and prevention of the spilling out of the upheaval to the Russian side of the border. In 1881, after the Chinese Empire reestablished their rule in the region, the Russian troops withdrew from the Kuldja region and most of the former sultanate territory was returned to China. The residents of the area were given the opportunity to stay or to move to the Russian Empire. The area west of the new Russia-China border running along the Ili Valley was retained by Russia for the settlement of those residents who chose to become subjects of the Russian Empire.[3] 1,147 Dungan households (or 4,682 people) from the Kuldja region opted for Russian citizenship and settled in Vernyi (now Almaty, Kazakhstan), Zharkent (a small town established in 1881 after the St. Petersburg treaty on the new Russian-Chinese border, now Kazakhstan), Pishkek (now Bishkek, Kyrgyzstan) and along the thousand kilometer route from Kuldja to Bishkek. The map below shows the areas of greatest concentration of the Dungan people in modern Kazakhstan and Kyrgyzstan.

Among modern day Dungans, the first settlers who came in the 19th century are referred to as "old Dungan" in contrast to those who came to Kazakhstan in the 1940s–60s. During the turmoil of the October revolution, civil war, hunger and repression, some of these first settlers returned to China. Also, since the border between the two countries was open, many travelled back and forth for various reasons: trade, education, family visits, etc. Because these Dungans were Soviet citizens (holders of Soviet passports), many returned during the repatriation of Soviet citizens in the 1940s–50s. The Soviet repatriation program, which aimed to bring in labor for rebuilding agriculture and industry, was very successful. According to official data, during the 1950s, 230,000 people left China, but it is likely that the actual number of repatriates was higher (Ablazhey 2003).

Starting from the 1960s, migration from China became much more chaotic. During the so-called "Black Years" (1959–61) when hunger struck China, about 200,000 people, mainly Kazakhs and Uighurs from Xinjiang,

Figure 5.1   Map
Map source: http://www.joshuaproject.net/people-profile.php?peo3=12145

applied for repatriation. But because of the Chinese government's protest, the Soviet administration decided to end the repatriation program. It caused mass unsanctioned crossings of the border during 1962–63. After that the border was sealed and any cross-border activities stopped until the early 1990s. There is no data on how many Dungans arrived during the last migration wave, but interviews with community members and the review of self-publications (such as autobiographies) clearly show that the number was high. Four out of thirteen informants I interviewed arrived in the USSR in the 1950s–60s. These newcomers settled within or in close proximity to the existing Dungan villages. Many of them were well educated, multilingual and had extensive administrative experience; they formed the core of the Kazakhstan Dungan intelligentsia.

The Dungan community in Kazakhstan was 36,945 people in 1999 and 51,944 people in 2009 (1999 and 2009 National Surveys); they represented 0.2% of the total Kazakhstan population. Demographic growth was largely due to the high birth rate among Dungans. They are geographically concentrated in two southeastern areas of Kazakhstan. By large the community remains agricultural, only 17% of Dungans live in cities. In comparison to other ethnic groups living in Kazakhstan, Dungans have a considerably lower level of education. Table 5.1 compares educational attainment among selected ethnic groups. As we can see, less than 10% of Dungans went to university and less than 9% received secondary technical or vocational training.

Table 5.1   Educational Level of Adult Population by Ethnicity (%)

	University	University incomplete	Secondary technical	Vocational	Secondary comprehensive (high school)	Secondary basic (middle school)	Primary
Kazakhs	30.2	2.1	25.9	2.3	32.1	6.8	0.7
Russians	24.4	1.9	39.3	3.1	22.5	7.9	1.0
Uzbeks	15.4	0.9	18.0	3.3	53.2	8.4	0.7
Ukrainians	19.7	1.5	39.3	3.6	23.8	10.5	1.5
Uyghur's	17.1	1.6	22.4	1.7	47.9	8.4	0.9
Tatars	27.2	2.2	37.0	3.0	22.1	7.6	0.9
Germans	15.1	1.7	33.8	3.9	29.6	14.0	1.9
Koreans	47.1	2.9	28.1	1.3	16.5	3.8	0.3
Dungans	8.9	0.7	8.1	0.4	68.0	12.5	1.3
Kurds	8.3	0.8	10.9	1.0	46.1	28.1	4.6
Total	27.2	2.0	29.7	2.6	30.2	7.6	0.8

Source: 2009 National survey

During the early Soviet era of active promotion of minorities, Dungans were recognized as a nationality. Although they were not assigned their own territory, the state maintained old and formed new compact settlements in rural areas and carved for them an economic niche in the agricultural sector. Within the framework of the Soviet policy on nationalities and minority languages, described by Yuri Slezkine (2000: 313) as "the most extravagant celebration of ethnic diversity that any state had ever witnessed", Dungans as an officially recognized minority were given the opportunity to develop a standardized national language, received the right to publish[4] and to educate in Dungan (even though the Dungan language was just taught as a subject in lower grades in certain secondary schools in the areas of compact settlement). Like many other Soviet minority languages, Dungan got a new phonetic alphabet; first it was a Latin-based script (1928) and then a Cyrillic-based script (1952). To develop the new standard, in the 1930s there was established a Dungan section in the Union of Writers and State Department of Publishing (in Kyrgyzstan), whose responsibility was to produce literature in Dungan. To prepare pedagogical cadre, two teacher colleges were opened: the Dungan pedagogical college in Almaty and the Dungan department in the Kyrgyz pedagogical college. A research institution, Center of Dungan Studies, was founded in Frunze (now Bishkek, Kyrgyzstan) and a smaller center was opened in Almaty. Scholars working in these centers developed textbooks of the Dungan language, compiled dictionaries and conducted research in the area of Dungan studies.

However, with a shift in the Soviet language policy in the 1960s to Russification, support of minority languages had weakened and many minority-language schools were closed. Russian often became the only language of education available. Not surprisingly, this led to language shift among many minorities, including Dungans. According to the 2009 Census, 96.3% of Dungans claimed Dungan as their native language, yet the data on reported language proficiency hinted at language shift from Dungan to Russian. In 1999, only 48.9% of Dungans reported speaking fluency in Dungan, at the same time 35.9% and 95.1% of them reported speaking proficiency in Kazakh and Russian respectively (Suleimenova et al. 2007).

METHODOLOGY: ETHNOGRAPHIC INTERVIEWS

The present study draws upon the data from a series of ethnographic interviews conducted in December 2012–May 2013 in Almaty, Kazakhstan. The data was collected through snowball sampling. Because I am not a Dungan, I had to use my personal connections to gain access to the community. I was referred to my first informant by a colleague. This informant then introduced me to people who came from the Kurdai area (see Figure 5.1) and those who work at a local bazaar. I was referred to my second informant, who is a key figure in the Almaty Dungan cultural center, by an acquaintance at the Committee of Languages under the Ministry of Information and Culture of the Republic of Kazakhstan. This and other ethnic cultural centers are part of the Assembly of the People of Kazakhstan[5]—a political organization whose aim is to represent the political interests of ethnic minorities. Through latter connections, I was able to gain access to activists of the Dungan cultural center.

Altogether I interviewed 13 people aged from 17 to 90. They include four females and nine males. All the interviewees are Kazakhstan citizens. Four respondents were born in Kuldja, China, and came to Kazakhstan in the early 1960s. The interviewees have different levels of education (four have a university degree, two have special technical training and seven have finished high school). At the time of the interview all (except one respondent) lived either permanently or temporarily in the Dungan neighborhood—a former Soviet farm called "Zarya Vostoka" (translated to English as "Dawn of the East"), now part of the Zhetysu district of the Almaty city. The table below summarizes information about the interviewees.

Semi-structured ethnographic interviews focused on five broad sets of topics: (1) Migration and settlement; (2) Family and community; (3) Daily routines and language practices; (4) Transnational contacts; (5) Attitudes and ideologies.[6] The interviews were conducted in Russian, excepting the interview with the oldest respondent, who chose to speak in Kazakh (only because I do not know Dungan or Uyghur). The interviews typically lasted between 20 and 30 minutes each, although some lasted more than an hour. All the interviews were tape-recorded and transcribed. Sections of the interviews were translated for the purpose of this paper. What follows is

Table 5.2 Interviewees: Summary

Age	Gender	Place of birth	Education	Occupation	Language of education
1. 90	male	Kuldja, China	Gymnasium, courses for government workers (both in Xinjiang)	Government worker (pre-cultural revolution Xinjiang, China); retired, agriculture (Soviet times); a head of community's elders; author of memoir "Dungans—Past and Present" (2008)	Uyghur
2. 65	male	Kuldja, China	High school (in Xinjiang)	Retired, bus driver (Soviet times); translating and mediating services (since the 1990s)	Chinese
3. 58	male	Tokmak, Kyrgyzstan	High school and two year courses for teachers of Dungan	School teacher of Dungan (until 1972); imam (religious leader)	Russian
4. 56	male	Almaty, Kazakhstan	University	Retired, police officer; one of the activists of the Almaty Dungan association	Russian
5. 52	female	Kuldja, China	University, graduate school	University instructor	Russian
6. 54	female	Kuldja, China	High school	Agriculture; housewife	Russian
7. 18	male	Kurdai, Kazakhstan	High school	Self-employed, trade (at "Barakholka" bazaar)	Russian

Age	Gender	Place of birth	Education	Occupation	Language of education
8. 18	male	Kurdai, Kazakhstan	High school	Self-employed, trade (at "Barakholka" bazaar)	Russian
9. 29	female	Tokmak, Kyrgyzstan	University	Self-employed, trade (at "Barakholka" bazaar)	Russian
10. 23	female	Almaty, Kazakhstan	Technical school (paralegal)	Assistant at the Dungan Cultural Center, Almaty	Russian
11. 23	male	Kurdai, Kazakhstan	Polytechnic university (engineer)	Self-employed, trade (at "Barakholka" bazaar), agriculture	Russian
12. 18	male	Kurdai, Kazakhstan	High school	Self-employed, trade (at "Barakholka" bazaar)	Russian
13. 17	male	Kurdai, Kazakhstan	High school	Self-employed, trade (at "Barakholka" bazaar)	Russian

a discussion of what the interviewees said regarding the five topics stated above. This data is supplemented by a critical reading of publications and internet materials produced or reprinted by the Dungan association and the members of the community.

MIGRATION AND ESTABLISHMENT OF THE DIASPORA

"Catastrophic origin" is an archetypal narrative among many old (e.g., Jewish) and new (e.g., Palestinian) diasporas; such narratives, as research indicates, often serve as a way of legitimizing community (Cohen 1996: 507). Among Dungans, the story of traumatic scattering from an original homeland is also predominant in imagining their diaspora. History texts published in the Soviet and post-Soviet times typically describe a heroic march of the Dungan refugees through the mountains from China to Central

Asia. The same information is duplicated on the official site of the diaspora (http://dungane.kz). The story is reiterated in academic papers, for example, in a well-known paper by Rimsky-Korsakoff (1992). The symbolic value of one specific "date of birth" of the community is also evidenced by the celebration of 135 years since the arrival of Dungans to the Zhetysu area (part of Kazakhstan and Kyrgyzstan) in the fall of 2013. There were a number of various events (the biggest of which was an expedition through the mountains on bikes that repeated the journey of the first migrants) to commemorate what is believed to be a new beginning for people who were about become extinct if not for the warm welcome from the Russian Tsarist administration and the kindness of the locals.

When asked about the origin of their diaspora, most interviewees retell the same story with minor variation. The first extract comes from an interview with an urban, college-educated male who is 55 years old and is retired from the police force.

Russian	English translation
1. китайцы вырезали 800 тысяч дунган	Chinese knifed 800 thousand Dungans
2. даже если младенец в коляске мальчик	even if baby in a carriage was a boy
3. то его подкидывали и так	he was thrown up and this way
4. дедушка рассказывал	(my) grandfather told
5. что когда бежали	that when fleeing
6. мальчиков переодевали в девочек	boys were dressed as girls
7. в Казахстан дошло всего десять процентов	to Kazakhstan came only ten percent
8. очень много погибло	very many died

The next extract is from an interview with a young 26-year-old male who came to Almaty from the Kurdai area (a place on the border between Kazakhstan and Kyrgyzstan densely populated by Dungans living in several Dungan villages) to work at a bazaar. This version is a more poetic interpretation of the events—a mixture of mythical (use of mythological themes of a dream in line 1 and a flood in lines 17–22) and real (reference to Dungans' livelihood in line 9 and religion in line 14).

Russian	English translation
1. императору китайскому и сон приснился	and the Chinese emperor had a dream
2. дунган ну вычистить	well to exterminate Dungans
3. и так как я слышал	and from what I heard

Russian	English translation
4. 15 лет война шла	the war lasted 15 years
5. 15 лет война шла и немеренно людей там	the war continued and countless people there
6. дунган полтора миллиона	million and a half Dungans
7. китайцев вообще немеренно	even more countless Chinese
8. четыре с половиной миллиона	four and a half million
9. и представляете война так	and imagine war like this
10. пятнадцать лет как воюют	fifteen years of fighting
11. и надо успеть еще огород садить	and (one) has to have time to plant
12. и зимой и летом 15 лет война шла	and winter and summer for 15 years the war had continued
13. и в один прекрасный день вот	and one day this
14. они говорят вот	they say this
15. что война не кончается	that the war is not ending
16. и вот аллах видит же все	and Allah he sees everything
17. и десять дней короче дождь шел	and in short it had rained for ten days
18. и дождь шел	it had rained
19. но никто не утонул	but no one drowned
20. но вода по горло выше	but the water was up to the neck and higher
21. наводнение	flood
22. и так 10 дней	and ten days like this
23. и вот этот император так осознал	and then the emperor realized
24. что дунган, мусульман нельзя обижать	that he can't persecute Dungans, Muslims
25. и он приказал, чтобы перестали вообще преследование	and he ordered to stop the chase
26. и вот дунгане через тянь-шаньские горы дед говорил перешли	and Dungans crossed the Tian-Shian mountains my grandfather said
27. ну дунгане это непростой народ	well Dungans are not usual people
28. так дед сказал	that (is what) my grandfather said

All in all, local construction of the community relies on typical narratives of forced migration and preservation of "homeland" culture. However, because throughout modern history (the 19th–21st centuries) Central Asia has witnessed the emergence and disappearance of states and ethnic groups, the drawing and re-drawing of borders and movements of people in different directions, it is no wonder that the interviews reveal much more complex multidirectional flows of people and cultures than are depicted by the dominant 'catastrophic origin' discourse. The third extract, below, tells us about migration following the 1881 Treaty of St. Petersburg. The oldest interviewee (90 years old, male) shares a story (told in a rather prosaic, matter-of-fact manner) about his grandfather, who was the first in his family to move to the Zhetysu area. He tells that his grandfather initially came from Gansu to Xinjiang, and then along with others passed to the Russian side of the new border. The interviewee's grandfather and other Dungans settled in the Sheleck (former Chilik) area (180 km east of Almaty) and started to grow rice.

Kazakh	English translation
1. Жібек жолы кезінде	in times of the Silk Road[7]
2. Күлжаға Гансу күеден келген екен	he came from the Gansu province to Kuldja
3. Жібек жолы кезінде	in times of the Silk Road
4. сауда караванға лесіп	he, following a trade caravan,
5. Күлжаға келген	arrived to Kuldja
6. Синзянға	to Xinjiang
7. содан 1882 өзгерістер болған кезде	after changes of 1882
8. осы жакка өткен	he crossed to this side

The interviews also revealed that the local Dungan community, especially the Almaty one, was not as isolated as it is presented to be by the dominant diaspora discourse. Before 1963, when the China-Soviet border was sealed, people had traveled back and forth for various reasons. Many "old" Dungans went to Xinjiang in the 1920s–1930s during the turmoil caused by the October Revolution, civil war, collectivization and repression. The father of the oldest interviewee ran away with his family to Kuldja in the late 1920s during the civil war and hunger. One of the interviewees told that her mother went to study at a medical training school in Kuldja in 1952 where her grandfather had relatives and lived there until 1958. She also said that her paternal grandfather did barter trade and thus routinely crossed the border to bring small goods from China to exchange them for food.

During the 1950s–60s, when the political situation in Xinjiang changed after the Ili rebellion of 1944, absorption of the independent "Three districts" into the PRC and the Chinese communists taking power in the region in 1949, the Cultural Revolution and hunger (the latter referred as the "Black years" in a couple of interviews), many returned to the USSR. Because these people (Russians, Uyghurs, Kazakhs, Dungans and others) were holders of Soviet passports, they or their children were eligible for repatriation to the Soviet Union. One of the interviewees (female, 43 years old) even goes so far as to say that her grandparents and father, who arrived in Kazakhstan in 1958, came back to their motherland:

Russian	English translation
1. так как мои дедушка, бабушка и отец	because my grandfather, grandmother and father
2. родились в Жаркенте (.) [. . .]	were born in Zharkent
3. они решили вернуться на историческую родину	they decided to return to the historical homeland

The last extract in this section is from the interview with a 65-year-old male who was born in Kuldja and came to Kazakhstan at age 16. The excerpt captures how people were forced to change their place of residence several times and adapt to new languages and cultures in order to survive. I would like to point to lines 2 and 9 where, similarly to the previous interviewee, relocation to the USSR is constructed as homecoming.

Russian	English translation
1. отец покойный был гражданинном Советского Союза	my late father was a citizen of the Soviet Union
2. он изъявил желание вернуться	he expressed desire to return
3. хотя и работал в видном месте	even though he worked in a good place
4. он был начальником областной милиции Кульджинской	he was a head of the regional Kuldja militia
5. после окончания высшей школы[8] в Пекине	after graduating from university in Beijing
6. работал начальником безопасности	he worked as a head of security
7. потом перешел в гражданское	then he transferred to civil (service)
8. и работал секретарем горкома партии	and he was a secretary of the town committee of the Communist party
9. в этой должности он изъявил желание вернуться	in this post he expressed desire to return
10. видимо политика	must be policy
11. если бы не приехали	if he didn't leave
12. при культурной революции его бы убрали	during the Cultural revolution he would be removed
13. они старые люди знали	they, the old people, knew
14. отсюда уехали в 20-ые годы	from here they left in the 20s
15. он учился в Москве	he studied in Moscow
16. грамотный молодой человек	(he) was a well-educated young man
17. он родился в Алма-Ате[9] на улице Дунганская	he was born in Alma-Ata[9] on the Dungan street[10]

(*continued*)

Russian	English translation
18. и мать тоже родилась в Алма-Ате	and mother too was born in Alma-Ata
19. уехали	they left
20. там поженились	got married there
21. здесь учился на русском языке	here he studied in Russian
22. там на уйгурском	there in Uyghur
23. знал китайский	he knew Chinese
24. папа между прочим все доклады свои писал на русском	by the way dad wrote all his speeches in Russian

Although interviews highlight the fact that local diaspora is a result of multiple cross-border movements, the narrative of refugees and survivors who found a new home in Zhetysu in the 19th century is dominant. Why does the community imagine (Anderson 1983) itself as a linguistically and culturally homogeneous diaspora within a nation-state rather than a diverse cross-border minority? Undeniably, the "catastrophic origin" narrative, defining the point of origin and point of destination (Cohen 1996), fits very well with both past Soviet and modern Kazakh nationalist ideology based on territorializing ethnic identity. On the other hand, reiteration of the old narrative under the new postmodern conditions, especially in the materials published and reprinted by the Dungan association, suggests that this traditional imaginary of Dungans as victims and outside settlers is being used instrumentally. Laruelle and Peyrouse (2009) argue that:

> Being a "politically correct" minority, which, besides, is well integrated in Central Asia and often viewed favorably, they benefit from an environment that is ripe for developing their economic niche. Even if this niche remains modest by comparison to overall Sino-Central Asian trade, it constitutes an important element in the social strategies being put into place by the community. (p. 111)

This is not to say that local Dungans do not self-problematize their identity. As Barabantseva (2011: 97) observes:

> The ongoing negotiations of a Kazakhstan national identity around Kazakh ethnic identity rather than the purported idea of multiculturalism . . . , and Russia's active engagement with ethnic Russians in Kazakhstan and other post-Soviet states . . . creates favorable conditions for Dungans in Kazakhstan, and other Central Asian states, to revisit their Chinese roots and rethink their relationship with China.

According to interviews, community members identify themselves as Dungans. When asked what differentiates their group from others, interviewees unanimously state that the main distinctive feature is Muslim religion; it is followed by culture and food. All informants illustrate the distinctiveness of their culture by referring to weddings, especially pointing out the traditional bride's clothing and food served at the wedding party. Although language is viewed as a traditional core value, it seems to have less importance in comparison to other cultural values. In fact, no respondent mentioned language when they were probed about their identity and even when I asked more explicitly, "What role does a language play in ethnic identification?" An interview with a 56-year-old imam, a religious leader, only highlights the lesser role of language in comparison with religion. When asked in what language service is conducted in the local Dungan mosque—by all respondents identified as a key cultural institution—he revealed that services are offered in Kazakh, the state language, or Russian, because younger attendees are not able to follow a sermon in Dungan.

At the same time, most informants pointed out that their diaspora is a small part of a demographically strong ethnic group. "Нас миллионы" [There are millions of us], stated one of the informants during the interview, referring to the 10 million Hui people in China. This is frequently followed by description of the uniqueness of the language and culture that local Dungans preserved, typical for diaspora narratives. Informants would say, "They are different" or "They are more Chinese than Dungan". Many recognize different histories of language contact by stating that "Our language is different" or "We use Russian words, they use Chinese".

The next section analyzes identity construction through the lenses of language practices. Its aim is to draw attention to shifting language affiliations and practices as a result of the changing affective, economic and practical roles of the Dungan diaspora.

MULTILINGUALISM

The interviews show that all respondents value multilingualism very highly and that all are at least bilingual in Dungan and Russian. Many are proficient to some degree in several languages.

Dungan: In interviews, it emerges that Dungan speakers use their mother tongue for communication with community members in domestic and traditional work-related domains. The proficiency level in Dungan is highest for older speakers and those who live in only Dungan villages of the Kurdai area. In Almaty, it is typical to use Dungan with elders but Russian with and among younger generations.

Code-switching and code-mixing are common:

Russian	English translation
1. (язык) ну у нас смешанный	well, our language is mixed
2. я если честно сказать	tell the truth
3. все на дунганском языке затрудняюсь	to say all in Dungan is difficult
4. без русского языка не могу	without Russian I can't

Whereas elder interviewees lament about it, younger people seem to have a much more relaxed attitude to code-mixing and accept it as something unavoidable. As we see in the extract below, a young woman justifies code-mixing by saying that speakers of other languages do it as well:

Russian	English translation
1. ну я вижу что и казахи смешивают языки с русским	well I see that Kazakhs too mix their language with Russian
2. и уйгуры	and Uyghurs
3. получается это дунгане тоже	thus and Dungans too
4. это уже неизбежно	it is unavoidable
5. всякие слова которые вышли сшас	all words that just appeared
6. они как бы не переводятся	they are kind of untranslatable
7. получается что все на русский переводится	thus everything is translated to Russian

There is no formal education available in Dungan in Almaty. Most children attend Russian-medium schools, although the interviews show that there is a growing trend of enrolling children in Kazakh-medium schools. For a short period of time (circa 2003–2005), Dungan was taught as a subject by a teacher invited from Kyrgyzstan, but because of a lack of financial resources, currently there is no formal teaching of Dungan available in Almaty.

Literacy in Dungan is low. Even those who learned Dungan as a subject in secondary school seem to have limited, if any, literacy skills in Dungan. Many interviewees do not necessarily see literacy in their mother tongue as important or necessary as there are no books in the language. A former Dungan language teacher, now imam, summarizes the situation as very dire: schools no longer have state support in maintaining Dungan and thus have no teachers, no books. Even in the Dungan villages of Sartobe and Masanchi, teachers do not have textbooks: "Один учебник на весь школа может быть" [Sometimes they have only one text per whole school]. In fact, I had a very difficult time trying to obtain a textbook in Dungan. The only copy I saw was a primer published in 1987 in then Frunze (now Bishkek), Kyrgyzstan. Another reason for the lack of literacy could be dialect differences between local Almaty code and the standard Dungan developed on the basis of the Gansu dialect of Kyrgyz Dungans.

Russian: It is a lingua franca and a second official language in Kazakhstan. Before Kazakhstan's independence, compulsory secondary education for Dungan communities was available in Russian only. All interviewees report fluent oral proficiency and literacy in Russian. In many urban families, Russian is also a second home language. It is a preferred language for media (TV, films, radio, newspapers, internet, etc.). Most books people have and read are in Russian, and thus at home children are primarily exposed to literacy in Russian.

However, the derussification language policy and a dominance shift from Russian to Kazakh in post-Soviet Kazakhstan appear to have triggered changes in attitudes toward Russian, which are manifested in shifts in parental choices of the language of education. It appears that Russian is no longer perceived as the sole language of social inclusion. As interviews indicate, whereas many parents still opt for educating their children in Russian, some now prefer a Kazakh-medium school.

Uyghur: Many Almaty Dungans report proficiency in Uyghur, three out of thirteen interviewees reported oral fluency in Uyghur and two more said they can also read and write in Uyghur. There are two reasons for that: Firstly, all Dungans in Kazakhstan came from (second and third wave of migrants) or through (first wave of migrants) Xinjiang, where Uyghur was the main language of communication and education. Thus many Dungans who came with the third wave received their education in Uyghur. They read and write in Arabic-based Uyghur script.

Secondly, for centuries Dungans lived side by side with Uyghurs, first in Xinjiang, and then they also settled together after they crossed to the Russian side of the border. Uyghurs are one of the largest ethnic minorities in Kazakhstan; villages where Uyghurs live compactly have always had Uyghur-medium schools. The interviews showed that Dungans who lived in these predominantly Uyghur villages in the 1940s–60s attended Uyghur-medium schools. For instance, one interviewee reported that her mother, who graduated from a secondary school in 1952, studied in an Uyghur school; she was Dungan-Uyghur bilingual but did not know any Russian. She learned Russian much later, after their family moved to Almaty in 1960. The same interviewee said that her older brother (born in 1950 in Kuldja) also studied in an Uyghur-medium school after their family came from China in 1958. It seems to be the case today as well. Some Dungan children attend the Uyghur-medium school that is located in their neighborhood. A younger interviewee (female, 25 years old) from "Zaria Vostoka" says that she and many others learned Uyghur through everyday interaction with peers, the majority of whom were Uyghurs.

Uyghur is also a lingua franca between local Dungans and Chinese Hui. One of the interviewees, for example, said that because her Chinese was not good enough, when she visited her relatives in Kuldja or when she phoned them (which occurred regularly), she spoke Uyghur.

Kazakh: Kazakh is the state and official language in Kazakhstan. Current language policy aims for a gradual increase in use of Kazakh in all official and public domains. All interviewees report some level of proficiency in Kazakh. Since education in Kazakh became available, there is a growing trend of enrolling children in a Kazakh-medium schools instead of Russian-medium schools. Three interviewees said that young children in their families are enrolled in Kazakh-language schools, whereas their older siblings study in Russian. Those who study in Russian study Kazakh as a required school subject.

Because many Dungans speak Uyghur, learning related Turkic Kazakh and Kyrgyz languages appears to be relatively easy for them. Even the earliest reports about the Dungans' first settlements, for instance, mention that "a few Dungan know how to read, write, and speak Russian; but we should note here that Dungans in general do not find this language easy to learn. On the other hand, many Dungans speak Kirghiz tolerably well" (Tsibuzdin and Shmakov 1897, translated by Rimsky-Korsakoff 1992: 258). Proficiency in Uyghur facilitates acquisition of Kazakh today as well. The extract below is from an interview with a 65-year-old male.

Russian and Kazakh (in italic)	English translation
1. а казахский язык	and the Kazakh language
2. это уже после провозглашения независимости	it's after the proclaiming independence
3. на основании уйгурского язык	on the basis of Uyghur
4. мы просто чуть-чуть поменяли акценты	we just changed accents a bit
5. и все	and that's all
6. и стали уже	and we already
7. *қазақша сөлейп тұрамыз*	*are speaking Kazakh*

Whereas only two females reported learning Kazakh in an educational setting as a second language in college, others have acquired it through everyday interaction. This is especially true for Dungans from Kurdai, where residents of neighboring villages are ethnic Kazakhs who often have limited or no proficiency in Russian.

Four interviewees said that they themselves or their family members watch news and films in Kazakh and listen to Kazakh music. Kazakh is also a language of the religious services and interaction in mosques; it is required by the state.

Kyrgyz: Many Dungans in Almaty are recent migrants from Kyrgyzstan. Two interviewees reported proficiency in Kyrgyz. Political instability, economic hardship and ethnic conflicts, for instance, a violent clash in Iskra in 2006 and attacks on Dungans and Uyghurs in Tokmak in 2010, forced many Dungans to relocate to Kazakhstan.

Chinese: Kazakhstan Dungans are predominantly speakers of the Shaanxi dialect of Chinese. But no interviewee said that he or she speaks Chinese; all perceive their native code as a distinct language. Due to extended language contact, the local Dungan is influenced by Russian and Turkic languages (Uyghur, Kazakh and Kyrgyz), an influence which is most pronounced in extensive borrowing from these languages. Despite dialectal differences and different language contact situations, interviewees claim intelligibility with Chinese (although I cannot tell which dialect of Chinese they refer to) when interacting with Chinese speakers in China or in Almaty. Only one interviewee, who was born and received his schooling in China, said that he watches Chinese television, even though it is easily available via satellite TV. He was also the only one who is able to write or read in Chinese. The extract below is from an interview with a 25-year-old female who works in the Almaty Dungan cultural center. In 2011, she visited China for the first and only time; there she met her Chinese relatives with whom she had no difficulties interacting:

Russian	English translation
1. ездила в Китай	I went to China
2. общалась на дунганском языке	(I) conversed in the Dungan language
3. без проблем	with no problems
4. единственное в ресторане меню не могли прочитать	we only could not read menu in restaurants
5. они нам переводили	they translated for us

Spoken, even if only dialectal, proficiency in Chinese allowed members of the Dungan community to engage in and benefit from mediating activities, such as as cross-border trade and work for Chinese companies. As one male respondent (65-year-old) put it: "У меня был язык. Этот язык меня и кормил" [I knew the language. This language fed me].

Four out of thirteen interviewees visited China after the border was opened and others plan to or dream about visiting their ancestor's land. In recent years the Chinese government, via the Association of Dungans, has sponsored tours to China and provided scholarships to Dungan students to study in Chinese universities. The number of Dungan students studying in China has increased from three students in 2002 to fifty students in 2009. Interestingly, in the official discourse, learning Chinese seems to have a clearly instrumental value as a mediating tool. In this light, the words of the Chair of the Kazakhstan Association of Dungans, Kh. Daurov, are particularly revealing: "Наши дети дунган, которые изучают китайский язык, в будущем станут важным звеном в развитии китайско-казахстанских отношений" [In the future our Dungan children who are learning the Chinese language will become an important link in development of Chinese-Kazakhstan relations] (interview in "People's Daily" 人民日报, 31 December 2010, online Russian edition).

The illustration below is an announcement by the Center of Chinese language in Kazakhstan, working under the auspices of the Kazakhstan Dungan association. The ad is Russian; it invites candidates to apply to study in leading Chinese universities, such as Beijing, Shanghai, etc.

Arabic: Devoted Muslims, to be able to read the Quran, have to learn to read in Arabic. According to the interviews, in some families children are taught basic literacy either at home by adults or at local mosques. However, it appears that in most cases the knowledge of Arabic is limited to recognition of words without much comprehension of the text. The exception

Figure 5.2 Study in China Advertisement.

was the oldest, 90-year-old, interviewee who studied in an Uyghur-medium school in Kainuk and then in Ili pedagogical gymnasium (both in Xinjiang) in the 1940s. He writes in Uyghur using Arabic script.

English: In Kazakhstan English is a state-promoted foreign language; it is a required school subject in the secondary school and university. It means that all Kazakhstan children are exposed to English in an educational context. Three female interviewees claimed high proficiency in English; two of them were trained as teachers of English and the youngest was studying it at one of the many language courses.

As Canagarajah and Silberstein (2012: 83) have noted, "multilingualism and multiculturalism shouldn't be treated as a third state between home and host communities, without commitment to either . . . [h]ybridity should be treated as a strategy and not a stable state or end product." Multilingualism, as we see, allows Dungan community members to tactically align themselves with different groups and adapt to changing sociopolitical contexts while sustaining their ethnic identity.

LANGUAGE SHIFT

Whether multilingualism is prized or taken for granted, still some community members raise concerns about it. As we see from the following extract, a young mother of two wonders about the value of multilingualism if one does not speak her native language.

Russian	English translation
1. учим другие языки	we learn other languages
2. наш язык забывается	our own language is forgotten
3. наши дети забудут язык	our children will forget the language
4. потом вырастут	then they will grow up
5. получается кто?	who do they become?
6. он не китаец, он не дунган, он не уйгур, он не казах	he is not Chinese, he is not Dungan, he is not Uyghur, he is not Kazakh
7. он никакие языки конкретно не будет знать	he won't know any language properly

The interviews provide evidence of distinct language shift toward Russian among the younger generation, or as one of the youngest respondents said, "anyone born after 1980".

Whereas all interviewees expressed some level of commitment to intergenerational transmission of Dungan, there were differences in the level of commitment across the group. Some said they speak only Dungan with children at home, whereas others showed less commitment, admitting that it is acceptable for kids to have some receptive competence and very basic conversational skills. For example, a young 29-year-old mother of two primary school aged children, who reported speaking Dungan with her own parents and husband, admitted that her aim is to slow down the attrition of Dungan.

Russian	English translation
1. у нас нету книг ничо такого	we have no books or anything
2. просто я щас с ними стараюсь	now I just try with them
3. чтобы дунганский не забыли	so that they won't forget Dungan

Urban interviewees aged 25–55 disclosed that their proficiency in Dungan is somewhat limited, and all urban interviewees said that younger members of their families have limited or very limited proficiency in Dungan. For example, in the extract below, a 65-year-old male who arrived to Kazakhstan at age 16 and is a fluent speaker of Dungan and standard Chinese laments about his grandson's lack of knowledge of their native language.

Russian	English translation
1. утрата язык чувствуется	loss of language is felt
2. вот у меня внук например	my grandson for example
3. он на русском разговаривает	he speaks Russian
4. в школу ходит на русском языке	he attends Russian language school
5. с детьми со своим сверстниками	with kids with his peers
6. он же на русском разговаривает	he speaks in Russian
7. а дома чуть-чуть так мы по дунгански	at home we (speak) little Dungan
8. слушает понимает	(he) understands listens
9. а говорить он уже не может	but he already cannot speak

Even in the Kurdai area, where Dungans live in close-knit isolated communities, the success of language transmission seems to rely on the presence of monolingual or dominant Dungan-speaking elders. As a 43-year-old female from Kurdai states:

Russian	English translation
1. утраты языка не ощущаю	I don't feel language loss
2. по крайней мере в нашей семье	at least in our family
3. родители с нами жили	parents lived with us
4. и поэтому дети говорят на дунганском	and that's why kids speak Dungan

The data shows that recent socioeconomic changes in Kazakhstan have made it progressively difficult to maintain the Dungan language, particularly in Almaty, for a number of reasons: dissolution of large Soviet farms, urbanization, demographic changes and lack of state support. It is well known that minority groups have better chances of maintaining their language when they live concentrated in a certain area. This was the case for the Dungan community until the late 1980s–early 1990s. However, after the collapse of the Soviet Union, large soviet farms (совхоз) were dissolved and the land was privatized. It resulted in freeing masses of people, and thus a rapid rise in unemployment among rural communities. Whereas all the rural residents received a plot of land, very few were able to start private farms because of a lack of investment capital and structural support. Some turned to subsistence agriculture for survival; many left farming and moved to urban areas in search of job opportunities and a better life. Interviews and observation at a local bazaar suggest that for many, relocating to Almaty is the only way "to escape from the agricultural crisis" (Laruelle and Peyrouse 2009: 106). In fact, all three young males I interviewed have recently moved to the city to work at the local bazaar; two of them brought their families to the city as well (one is too young to be married). These young men still participate in agricultural activities; they go back to their villages during the work-intensive periods to help during the seeding and harvest seasons. However, the money the extended family earns by selling produce is not enough to support them, and thus young men are forced to seek additional income opportunities.

On one hand, because these young men typically work for small businesses owned by their relatives or people from the same village, they report maintaining their close family ties and speaking Dungan. On the other hand, these informants complain that their urban peers are not very proficient in Dungan and often mix Dungan and Russian. However, they are most concerned about their children's limited opportunities to acquire their mother tongue, especially after children start school. Lack of institutional support, especially absence of schooling in Dungan or learning Dungan as a mother tongue in a school, aggravates the situation.

In addition to the lack of institutional support, collapse of the traditional trade and way of living, there were other changes that propelled a language shift in the Almaty Dungan community. The interviews indicate that the boundary maintenance and compartmentalization of languages necessary for language maintenance (Fishman 1991) are lacking in the case of Almaty Dungans. The former Soviet farm *sovkhoz* "Zaria Vostoka" was in close proximity to the city; Dungan farmers supplied the metropolitan area with produce while enjoying relative isolation. The families lived compactly on two or three adjacent streets, whereas the majority of the village residents were Uyghurs. As the city expanded because of rapid population increase, largely due to uncontrolled rural-urban migration, "Zaria Vostoka" became part of Almaty's new "Zhetysu" district. What is more, next to the neighborhood there has emerged the region's biggest bazaar,

"Barakholka"—a site of more than 20 adjoining markets with more than 15,000 sales outlets. It is one the major places of employment and sources of income in the Almaty region. According to estimates by Kaminskii and Mitra (2012), about 250,000 people are directly or indirectly employed at Barakholka, and the bazaar's annual sales are 1.742 million dollars. Having an international bazaar next door opened various job and business opportunities. Capitalizing on their language proficiency and contacts in Xinjiang, a significant number of Dungans are engaged in cross-border trade, tourism or joint-venture projects with China (Laruelle and Peyrouse 2009). At the same time, because of "Barakholka," the formerly isolated community became a desirable place to work and to live for city migrants. According to interviews, "Zaria Vostoka" has become considerably more multiethnic, but particularly the interviewees note the rise in the number of oralmans—ethnic Kazakhs repatriated to Kazakhstan from other countries (mainly from Uzbekistan and China). In the context of growing ethnic and linguistic diversity after the disappearance of the community's borders, modernization and urbanization, it has become more difficult for local Dungans to maintain their cultural traditions and language.

The Dungan community that has exhibited stable bilingualism for more than a century is now experiencing rapid language shift. The case of Dungan also makes it clear that whereas close family, community and work networks are of crucial importance, the conditions in the greater society and wider social changes may easily override them. The data shows that although Dungans in the urban milieu still heavily depend on their family and community networks, the destruction of traditional farms and thus almost forced modernization of the community have propelled language shift. This case also highlights that governmental support in providing resources is necessary for minority language maintenance. After the collapse of the Soviet system, Kazakhstani Dungans, as have many other minority groups, have been neglected. The community has no schools, no teachers and no literacy resources that could ensure the longevity of the Dungan language.

CONCLUSION

In line with arguments that diaspora is an adaptive form of social organization (Cohen 1996) and that diasporic communities constantly "negotiate diverse social and institutional relations with other, especially dominant, communities" (Canagarajah and Silberstein 2012: 82), this chapter is an attempt to challenge the local traditional orientation to diaspora as an archetypically dispersed population who have managed to preserve their unique culture and identity. The interview data demonstrate that the Dungan community is more decentered and more mobile than a traditional victim narrative allows. The interviews also reveal that the diaspora is linguistically diverse and linguistic resources are used strategically to negotiate identities and group membership. The case of the Dungan diaspora serves as a good reminder that "once we stop treating diaspora as bounded, territorialized, static, and homogeneous, we begin to appreciate the role language and discourse play in its construction" (Canagarajah and Silberstein 2012: 82).

This chapter is an initial attempt to outline the role of language in imagining and negotiating Dungan diaspora identities. It is clear that further, more interactional, studies are needed to understand how identities and relationships are constructed and performed, to describe tensions and difficulties diaspora members face in the host community and ultimately to advance studies of language identity.

NOTES

1. The origin of the name "Dungan" is discussed in Allies (2010), Rimsky-Korsakoff (1992).
2. Dungans are Sunni Muslims.
3. When discussing border disputes between Russia and China, one has to remember that these lands were the traditional migration area of several Kazakh nomad tribes.
4. The first newspaper in Dungan appeared in 1932.
5. More information is available at http://www.assembly.kz.
6. The questionnaire was designed by Li Wei.
7. Silk Road refers to a number of trade routes that used to connect China and Europe.
8. Высшая школа is a term used for courses for Communist party higher rank members.
9. Alma-Ata is an older Soviet name for Almaty.
10. When Dungans arrived in Vernyi (Almaty) in 1881–84, a special district named Dungan sloboda (there were also Uyghur and Tatar districts) where Dungans settled was established. Dunganskaya was one of the main streets in that district. Now it is Masanchi Street, after a famous ethnic Dungan revolutionary, Magazy Masanchi. Although the name of the street refers to the old history, it is no longer a place of Dungans' settlement.

REFERENCES

Ablazhey, N. [Аблажиев, Н.] (2003). *Level and consequences of re-immigration from China to the USSR* [Масштабы и последствия возвратной миграции из Китая в СССР]. Institute of history, Northern Branch of the Russian Academy of Sciences [Институт истории СО РАН]. Retrieved from http://sibistorik.narod.ru/project/modern/018.html

Alles, E. (2010, September 22). The Chinese-speaking Muslims (Dungans) of Central Asia: A case of multiple identities in a changing context, Asian Ethnicity. *Asian Ethnicity* 6(2), 121–134. Retrieved November 4, 2013, from http://dx.doi.org/10.1080/14631360500135716

Anderson, B. (1983). *Imagined communities: Reflections on the origin and spread of nationalism*. London: Verso.

Barabantseva, E. (2011, November 16). Modern China: Who are "overseas Chinese ethnic minorities"? China's search for transnational ethnic unity. *Modern China 38*(1), 78–109. Retrieved from http://mcx.sagepub.com

Brophy, D. (2005). Taranchis, Kashgaris, and the "Uyghur Question" in Soviet Central Asia. *Inner Asia 7*, 163–184.

Bloomaert, J. (2010). *Policy, policing & the ecology of social norms: Ethnographic monitoring revisited.* Working Papers in Urban Language & Literacies, Paper 63. Retrieved from http://www.kcl.ac.uk/innovation/groups/ldc/publications/work ingpapers/63.pdf

Canagarajah, S., & Silberstein, S. (2012). Diaspora identities and language. *Journal of Language, Identity & Education 11*(2), 81–84. Retrieved November 7, 2013, from http://dx.doi.org./10.1080/15348458.2012.667296

Cohen, R. (1993). Diasporas and the Nation-State: From victims to challengers. *International Affairs, 72*(3), 507–520. Retrieved November 7, 2013, from http://www.jstor.org/stable/2625554

Collins, J., & Slembrouck, S. (2005). *Multilingualism and diasporic populations: Spatializing practices, institutional processes, and social hierarchies.* University of Albany, University Ghent 25, 189–195. Retrieved from www.elsevier.com/locate/langcom

Dzhanshanlo, Р. Е. [Джаншанло Р. Е.]. (2011). *Essays on the history of the Dungan* [Очерки истории дунган]. Almaty: LEM Press.

Fishman, J. (1991). *Reversing language shift: Theoretical and empirical foundation of assistance to threatened languages.* Clevedon: Multilingual Matters.

Gladney, D. C. (1991). *Muslim Chinese: Ethnic nationalism in the People's Republic.* London: Council of East Asian Studies, Harvard University.

Hong, D. (2005). A comparative study on the cultures of the Dungan and the Hui peoples, Asian Ethnicity. *Asian Ethnicity 6*(2), 135–140. Retrieved November 7, 2013, from http://dx.doi.org/10.1080/14631360500135765

Kaminski, B., & Mitra, S. (2012). *Skeins of silk: Borderless bazaars and border trade in Central Asia.* World Bank. Retrieved from http://www.caps.am/materi als/sectors/trade/Silk_road_bazars.pdf

Laruelle, M., & Payrouse, S. (2009). Cross-border minorities as cultural and economic mediators between China and Central Asia. *China and Eurasian Forum Quarterly 7*(1), 93–119.

Pavlenko, A. (2006). Russian as a lingua franca. *Annual Review of Applied Linguistics, 26*, 78–99.

Rimsky-Korsakoff Dyer, S., Tsibuzgin, V., & Shmakov, A. (1992). Karakunuz: An early settlement of the Chinese Muslims in Russia. *Asian Folklore Studies 51*(2), 243–278. Retrieved November 11, 2013, from http://ww.jstor.org./page/info/about/policies/terms.jsp

Slezkine, Y. (1994). The USSR as a communal apartment, or how a socialist state promoted ethnic particularism. *Slavic Review 53*(2), 414–452. Retrieved January 6, 2014, from http://www.jstor.org/stable/2501300

Smailov, A. (ed.) (2011). *The results of the 2009 national census of population.* Astana: Statistical Agency of the Republic of Kazakhstan.

Suleimenova, E., Shaimerdenova, N., & Akanova, D. (2007). *The languages of people of Kazakhstan* [Языки народов Казахстана]. Almaty, Arman-TB Press.

Yavakhunov, I. [Явахунов И.] (2008). *Dungan—past and present* [Дунгане—прошлое и настоящее]. Almaty: Art Print Press.

6 Chinese-Spanish Contact in Cuba in the 19th Century

J. Clancy Clements

1 INTRODUCTION

Perhaps the most extensive study carried out on immigrant speech is that by Wolfgang Klein and Clive Perdue, reported on in a number of studies and in the 1992 book *Utterance Structure: Developing Grammars Again.* One main question these researchers sought to answer was: Is a second language variety learned naturalistically based on recognizable organizational principles? After studying 40 adult learners over a period of two and a half years from as near as possible to the beginning of the learning process, they identified three general constraints on utterance production: the focus of an utterance appears at the end (pragmatic), the controller of an utterance appears at the beginning (semantic), and three basic syntactic structures are apparent:

- noun phrase 1 + verb + (noun phrase 2)
  {noun phrase 2}
- noun phrase 1 + copula + {adjective}
  {prepositional phrase}
- verb + noun phrase
  (found in presentational constructions, e.g., *there is* + NP)

That is, an utterance has the verbal element after the first noun phrase and before the second phrasal constituent (if there is one) unless it is a presentational construction, in which case the first noun phrase follows the verb.[1] With regard to utterance development, Klein and Perdue found that, at first, utterances were organized around noun phrases (nominal utterance organization [NUO]), which then expanded to include a verbal element unmarked for tense, aspect, or mood (infinite utterance organization [IUO]), which sometimes developed such that an utterance included nominal elements and a verbal element marked for tense, aspect, or mood (finite utterance organization [FUO]). They reported that whereas not all speakers in the study developed the FUO, all speakers displayed the IUO stage. Klein and Perdue call this variety based on the IUO the 'basic variety', which they characterize as relatively homogeneous and whose organization was guided largely by the above-mentioned pragmatic, semantic, and syntactic constraints. Linguistic features attributable to the specific properties of the first languages were reported to be more characteristic of later developmental stages.

The second-language (L2) Spanish variety examined in this study was spoken in Cuba in the latter half of the 19th century by first-language (L1) Chinese speakers who most likely spoke Cantonese. It is well known that, from a typological perspective, Spanish and Chinese are highly distinct from one another: Chinese is an aspect-marking, isolating tone language with no morphology whereas Spanish is a tense-and-aspect-marking, fusional language with a rich nominal and verbal morphology. In a situation of indentured labor in 19th century Cuba, one would hypothesize that Cantonese speakers in a Spanish-speaking environment would acquire whatever elements they needed in order to understand and make themselves understood. The expectation would be, then, that such speakers would have developed an infinitival utterance organization for the most part. But as we will see, the data suggest that the Cantonese speakers whose Spanish is portrayed have also transferred some traits of their L1 in their restructuring of Spanish.

In the next section, a brief account of the sociohistorical situation of Chinese indentured labor in 19th century Cuba will be briefly presented, and then I will address the manner in which Spanish is restructured by Cantonese speakers, as portrayed by Jiménez Pastrana (1963).

2 SOME SOCIOHISTORICAL BACKGROUND ON THE CHINESE IN 19TH AND 20TH CENTURY CUBA

When one thinks of slavery in Cuba, perhaps the first link one typically makes is to Africa, specifically to West Africa, from where the ancestors of the vast majority of the Afro-Cubans were brought to the island two or more centuries ago. In his treatise on the Atlantic slave trade, Curtin (1969: 88–89) gives a speculative geographical distribution of slave imports during the whole period of the slave trade, estimating that around 5,093,000 slaves were imported to the Caribbean Islands and South America (excluding Brazil). Of these, roughly 26% (1,331,000 slaves) were sent to Spanish-speaking countries. According to Curtin's figures, 53% (702,000) of these were imported to Cuba alone.

During the first half of the 19th century, the African slave trade in Cuba became illegal and the laws prohibiting it were increasingly enforced. Alarmed by the slave revolts of the early 1800s in Haiti, movements began in Cuba with the purpose of settling whites on farms and in villages in Cuba, not only to infuse the labor force with new power, but also in part to counterbalance the large black population and thereby diminish the possibility of revolt. The black population in Cuba began to outnumber the whites around 1791, and according to Kiple (1976), this situation lasted up until 1846. Corbitt (1971: 2) notes that in 1841 in Cuba there were 589,333 blacks (58%) (436,495 slaves and 152,838 free coloreds) and 418,211 whites (42%).[2] This situation made Cuban plantation owners uncomfortable, and as a consequence incentives were offered to planters to hire workers from Spain, but with little success. The Spanish government then agreed to a plan drawn up by the Junta de Fomento to introduce Chinese coolies into Cuba, following an idea the British had used in their colonies. From June 3, 1847 onward, the arrival date of the first Chinese coolies from China, nearly 500,000 came to the island (Corbitt 1971: 6). In this study, I discuss some details of the ecology of the Chinese in Cuba between 1847 and the late 20th century, focusing on the relations between the Chinese, the Africans, the Afro-Cubans, and the development of the Chinese variety of Spanish. I then examine the traits found in some of the sources of Chinese Spanish.

2.1 The Period of Chinese Indentured Labor (1847–1877)

Until 1762, when the English occupied Havana for ten months, the Spanish crown had a vice grip on trade with her colonies, including the slave trade in Cuba. In the 1760s, trade barriers began to break down, and this allowed an influx of slave labor, followed by a rapid development in Cuban agriculture, which in turn led to the need for additional slave labor. But just as slave labor between the 1760s and 1791 became more accessible to Cuban landowners, the slave revolts began in Haiti (then Saint Domingue). Caught between the need for labor and the fear of revolts of their African slaves, Cuban plantation owners turned to the idea of trying to attract white labor. Corbitt (1971: 1–4) reports on the less than successful attempts by the *Junta de Población Blanca* ('Committee of White Population') to lure white labor to Cuba while slave labor continued to be exploited.

In 1821, the African slave trade was curtailed by the treaty signed by Spain and Britain to outlaw the slave trade. However, enforcement of the treaty was weak to non-existent and Cuban plantation owners were still able to import illegal slave labor. In 1835, Britain obtained another treaty to enforce the first one, which obliged the Cuban plantation owners to look elsewhere for their labor needs.

In 1842, some high profile Cuban businessmen and planters founded the *Junta de Fomento* ('Promotion Committee'), which took over some of the duties and budget of the *Junta de Población Blanca*. This committee hatched the idea of offering prizes to the planters who attracted the highest number of white settlers from among the Catalans, Canary Islanders, and Galicians in Spain (Corbitt 1971: 3), but the experiment attracted only around 1,000 settlers in two years, far fewer than they had hoped for. As the members of the *Junta de Fomento* were becoming increasingly desperate to find labor, the English firm Zulueta and Company, which had been trafficking in Chinese indentured labor for Great Britain, presented them with the idea of importing laborers from China.

The *Junta de Fomento* saw several apparent advantages to this proposal. First, the Chinese would be considered white, so the stipulation that white labor be sought would be fulfilled. Second, from the experience of the Spaniards in The Philippines, the Chinese were viewed as docile and hard-working, and would thus be ideal laborers.[3] Third, it was thought that the supply of Chinese laborers, referred to as *culíes* or coolies would be plentiful.[4] The reaction of the Spanish government to the plan, recorded in a Royal Order of July 3, 1847, was favorable. Interestingly, according to Corbitt (1971: 5–6), it was roughly one month earlier (June 3 and 12, 1847) that two ships carrying the first Chinese immigrants (515 able-bodied laborers) arrived in Havana. Thus began the exploitation of Chinese coolie labor in Cuba, which would last until 1877.

After the first two shipments of coolies to Cuba, problems arose between China and Great Britain regarding the trafficking of coolies to the Caribbean, and so their importation to Cuba was temporarily suspended (Jiménez Pastrana 1963: 37–38). On August 5, 1851, the *Junta de Fomento* agreed to a plan to import more Chinese (Corbitt 1971: 14–15), and permission was granted to two firms to import 3,000 coolies over two years time. Around 1855, the practice of using Chinese laborers on the plantations was evaluated by the planters. Although the experiment received mixed reviews, overall it was considered a success, the importation of coolies continued, and by the end of 1860, around 49,077 Chinese indentured laborers had been taken to Cuba (Corbitt 1971: 18).

During this time, problems of abuse of the coolies and other problems with the importation of Chinese indentured labor to Cuba led to riots and protests in Hong Kong and in Chinese cities, such as Amoy (Xiamen, in Fujian province), one of the major ports used to ship the laborers to Cuba. As a consequence, Britain closed its port in Hong Kong to the coolie trade and the Chinese imperial authorities adopted the policy of beheading the recruiting agents. As a result, by 1859 only the Portuguese colony of Macau was used to ship Chinese laborers to Cuba (Corbitt 1971: 19). Virtually all the people taken to Cuba were men from Canton Province who spoke Cantonese.

In 1859–1860, some regulations were established to safeguard the Chinese laborers being shipped to Spanish colonies, and the Spanish government, which had called a temporary halt to the shipments of Chinese laborers to the New World, bestowed its blessing on the resumption of the trade, after which coolie importations rose sharply (e.g., 6,223 coolies were taken to Cuba between January 1 and July 21, 1861).

As mentioned, the importation of coolies to Cuba continued until 1877. Although the Cuban planters favored the further importation of coolies, the Spanish government entered into a treaty with Peking that shut down the coolie trade and closed a painful chapter in Chinese-Spanish relations (Corbitt 1971: 23).

The year-by-year arrival of coolies in Cuba between 1847 and 1859 is shown in Table 6.1. Corbitt (1971: 52) notes that these figures, while not complete or necessarily entirely accurate, are the most reliable ones available. After 1859, he adds, there is no complete information about the number of coolies taken to Cuba. He further states that the tabulation of the arrivals reported in the daily shipping column of the newspaper *Diario de la Marina* from 1847 to 1874 gives a total of 114, 232 (1971: 24). Thus, between 1859 and 1877, roughly 71,731 coolies were transported to Cuba.

After coolie trade was halted in 1877, Chinese immigrants continued to arrive in Cuba but under substantially different circumstances (Corbitt 1971: 92). Of those who were in Cuba as coolies, if the available estimates are reliable, less that 40% of them lived to complete their eight-year term of 'service' (Corbitt 1971: 88). Corbitt (1971: 90) also notes that for every Chinese man who achieved success in Cuba, there were dozens who eked out a bare existence against innumerable odds, or who were able to gather together sufficient means to buy a return passage to China (1971: 90).

In 1899, when the Spanish were finally defeated and the Cuban flag was raised over the island, Corbitt (1971: 92) estimates that around 15,000 Chinese remained. According to the census of 1899, the Chinese men were mainly day laborers (54%), servants (19%), merchants (13%), and peddlers (3%), with other professions making up the remaining 11%. In the same census, only 20 Chinese women were listed as having professions.

Chinese immigration to Cuba during the republic is hard to ascertain because of what Corbitt (1971: 95) calls the 'hopelessly conflicting statistics on the subject.' The figures maintained by the Chinese consulate in Havana reveal that, between 1903 and 1916, 6,258 Chinese arrived in Cuba, and that between 1917 and 1924 some 16,005 came to the island. Around 1930, the reports on the number of Chinese in Cuba continue to display a wide range of estimates, from 30,000 (Chinese consulate) to 150,000, a number

Table 6.1 Number of Coolies Arriving in Cuba from 1847 to 1859

Year	No. of Ships	Coolies Embarked	Coolies Landed	Deaths	Death Rate
1847	2	612	571	41	6.7
1853	15	5,150	4,307	843	6.37
1854	4	1,750	1,711	39	2.23
1855	6	3,130	2,985	145	4.635
1856	15	6,152	4,968	1,184	19.245
1857	28	10,116	8,547	1,589	15.51
1858	33	16,414	13,385	3,129	18.45
1859	13	6,799	6,027	778	11.355
TOTAL	116	50,123	42,501	7,722	15.2

reported by the Cuban newspaper *El Mundo*. Corbitt (1971: 105) maintains that even the estimate of 150,000 was probably too low.

At the beginning of the Second World War, estimates of Chinese in Cuba range from 18,000 (those registered at the Chinese consulate) to 30,000. During this time, the Chinese kept to themselves with respect to Cuban politics, although they were deeply interested in the politics of the homeland and maintained in Cuba off-shoots of the different Chinese political parties (cf. Ramos Hernández et al. 2000). Corbitt (1971: 113–15) reports that whereas some Chinese nationalized to meet legal stipulations in Cuba, overall they adjusted to citizenship requirements for Cuban work permits by other means and maintained their strong relationship with the homeland. Given that most Chinese men had wives in their homeland, there continued to be few Chinese women in Cuba. For example, of the 18,484 Chinese registered at the Chinese consulate in 1942, only 56 were women. The large majority of Chinese continued to be from the Canton area.

Well after the cessation of Chinese indentured labor, Chinese continued to come to Cuba throughout the 20th century. Today there are still roughly 400 'pure Chinese' that maintain Cantonese; and as of 2008 Mandarin is even offered by an organization called *Grupo Promotor Chino* ('Chinese Promotion Group'), which is in charge of developing activities on Chinese culture in Cuba. La Habana still has a Chinatown, which was built towards the end of the 1990s. Thus, the ties between the Chinese Cubans and China still remain relatively strong.

2.2   Chinese and the Spanish Language

With regard to the acquisition of Spanish on the part of the Chinese coolies, Corbitt (1971: 11, after Erenchun 1856: 778–779) quotes the well known scholar Antonio Bachiller y Morales, who wrote in 1856 that:

> [h]omicides, rebellions and uprisings were repeated on some plantations, while more tactful masters obtained better results. A large part of the problems arose from lack of competent interpreters. At present, although there are still some that doubt the advantage of this type of immigrant, the early difficulties occur less frequently, a fact that is due in great part to the coolies' being directed by men who speak their language.

Nine years after the first Chinese had arrived in Cuba, there was no indication that they had learned Spanish, nor would it be expected of them, because these laborers lived and worked together with fellow Cantonese speakers and likely used their native language almost exclusively.

In 1874, a recruiting agent named Francisco Abella, who had transported more than 100,000 Chinese to various countries, including Cuba, wrote about the recruiting process that, '[b]efore loading the transports the

Portuguese authorities would address a group of coolies through an inter-preter, who often knew only one of the eleven dialects spoken in China, ask-ing them if they were willing to embark' (in Corbitt 1971: 41). This system changed, according to Abella, in that five or six interpreters came to be used by the recruiters, each speaking a different dialect of Chinese. Although these statements suggest that a great majority of those Chinese going to Cuba were speakers of one or more varieties of Chinese, they were largely varieties of Cantonese.

The varieties of Spanish found in Jiménez Pastrana (1963), taken from documents that attempted to capture the manner in which the Chinese spoke Spanish, exhibit characteristics consistent with naturalistic second language acquisition, and the infinite utterance organization discussed in section 1, with evidence of L1 transfer.[5]

In general, then, it seems that the Chinese learned enough Spanish to fulfill their needs in the jobs they had. For example, one story tells of a cook who learns how to speak Spanish, arguably because of his position (Corbitt 1971: 77). However, it is also clear from the documents and statistics in Corbitt (1971) that the Chinese, although some fought alongside whites and Afro-Cubans in two wars in the 19th century, generally were not linguisti-cally integrated in Cuban society at that time.

3   STRUCTURE OF CHINESE SPANISH OF 19TH CENTURY CUBA

In this section, I discuss who were the probable speakers of 19th century Chinese Spanish, and discuss some salient characteristics of their speech. We draw on data found in Jiménez Pastrana (1963).

3.1   The speakers of Chinese Spanish in 19th Century Cuba

In section 2.1 above, I mentioned that from 1847 to 1859 the Chinese who arrived in Cuba embarked from various ports; two of the most prominent were Amoy (Xiamen) in Fujian province where Min dialects were and are spoken, and Macau, where Cantonese dialects were and still are found. After 1859, ships carrying Chinese to Cuba embarked only from Macau. Records from that time indicate that Chinese from various dialects, tantamount to different languages in some cases, were recruited for Cuba. Initially, then, I assume that the Chinese arriving in Cuba were speakers representing vari-ous Min and Cantonese dialects, but over time increasingly more Cantonese dialect speakers were recruited to work in Cuba. This assumption is sup-ported by the fact that the Chinese population today in Cuba largely is of Cantonese origin.

Almost all of the Chinese arriving in Cuba in the 19th century were lit-erate and shared the same writing system (Corbitt 1971: 63). Moreover, they all shared the same culture, especially as compared to the culture predominant in Cuba in the mid-19th century. I assume that speakers of each of the Min or Cantonese varieties could and would cluster into same-dialect groups, such that they could maintain their variety of Chinese in Cuba. Thus, thrown into a quasi-slave situation in Cuba, the bonds between the different dialect speakers among themselves, and even speakers across dialects, were beneficial for survival. I assume, as well, that such bonds were cultivated and maintained to the extent that they improved the chances of survival.

To our knowledge, there are generally two main sources of evidence for 19th century Chinese Spanish speech. I commented already on the sources found in Jiménez Pastrana's (1963) history of the Chinese between 1847 and 1930. The other general source is literary texts in which Chinese speech is portrayed. I prefer to draw primarily from Jiménez Pastrana (1963) (a historian), given that the portrayal of Chinese speech in the sources he uses seems to us to constitute a serious attempt to approximate as close as possible the Chinese Spanish of that time.

Although Lipski (1999) calls the variety of Spanish spoken by the 19th century Chinese a pidgin, this depends on the definition of the term pidgin. Lipski's definition seems to be closer to that advanced by Hall (1966), according to which even a highly unstable incipient pidgin constitutes a pidgin proper. If we define pidgin according to Bakker (1994), as a linguistic system with its own set conventions and rules which can be spoken to different degrees of proficiency, there is little sociohistorical evidence to support the existence of a Chinese pidgin Spanish in this sense, especially given that the Chinese at that time had no apparent motivation to speak anything other than Chinese among themselves. The variety found in Jiménez Pastrana (1963), I argue, is closer to a naturalistically learned L2 variety, i.e., Chinese 19th century immigrant Spanish. This view is also suggested by quotes of dialogue found in Jimenez Pastrana (1963) between Cuban superiors and Chinese soldiers in which the Cubans speak colloquial Spanish and the Chinese in their variety of Spanish. An illustrative exchange is shown in the following extract (1), a dialogue between a Spanish-speaking captain and a soldier originally from Canton, in which the captain speaks standard Spanish and the soldier speaks in what I consider to be a second-language variety of Spanish (Jimenez Pastrana 1963: 100). In this conversation between the Captain and Achón, I have marked Achón's speech in bold and added the standard colloquial Spanish version of his speech so the reader can appreciate the difference between the two varieties.

(1)

> Captain: Mira, Achón; a los oficiales les está prohibido usar armas largas. ('Look, Achon; the officials are prohibited from using long rifles.')
> Achón: **¿Qui cosa usa Ficiá?** (Standard Sp: ¿Qué usan los oficiales?) ('What do officers use?')

Captain: Machete y revólver. Es una orden superior. . . . ('Machete and revolver. It's an order from above.')

Achón: **Londi ta Ginilá Maceo, que yo va pleguntá si son vel esi cosa?**(Standard Spanish: ¿Dónde está General Maceo?, que (yo) voy a preguntar si {es verdad esa cosa/si son verdad esas cosas}) ('Where is General Maceo? I'm going to ask him if that thing is true.')

Of note in this exchange is that there is no attempt on the part of the captain to accommodate his interlocutor linguistically.[6] Achon uses one verb form (except for *son* 'they are') and no plural marking the nouns, both of which are also traits found in Chinese Immigrant Spanish.[7] The choice of 3PL *son* is interesting because it is also found in the speech of one Chinese Immigrant Spanish speaker as the default equative copula. Moreover, its Portuguese counterpart *sang* (< Ptg. *são* 'they are') is the default copula form in Macau Creole Portuguese (Pinharanda Nunes 2010: 163).

Having discussed the background of the Chinese laborers in Cuba and considered some of the salient traits of their variety of Spanish, we now turn to a more systematic examination of its features.

3.2   Some Key Traits of 19th Century Chinese Spanish (19CCS)

Not surprisingly, the phonological traits in 19CCS found in the texts in Jiménez Pastrana (1963) are largely those found in Chinese Immigrant Spanish. Here I use the adapted list of traits for Chinese Pidgin English found in Shi (1991). Table 6.2 contains the traits in the lefthand column and the source of respective traits in the righthand column.

However, there are some differences between 19CCS and CIS. Although the confusion of liquids is attested in Jiménez Pastrana (1963), it is only as the replacement of [r] by [l] as in (2), but not as [l] by [r], as we encounter in CIS.

Table 6.2   Phonological Traits of Chinese Coolie Spanish

Trait	Source
a. r → l, l → r	Chinese
b. b, d, g devoicing (g → k)	Chinese
c. š → s and s → š	Chinese
d. voicing of stops	Chinese
e. three types of syllable simplification strategies	
i. vowel epenthesis	Chinese
ii. cluster simplification	Chinese
iii. deletion of syllable coda	Chinese
f. preference of CV structure	Chinese, other
g. retention of closed syllables in—s	Spanish

(2)

> nosotlo (< Sp. nosotros 'we, us'; JP, 75)
> dinelo (< Sp. dinero 'money'; JP, 80)
> quiele (< Sp. quiere 's/he wants'; JP, 99)
> tiloteo (< Sp. tiroteo 'shootout'; JP, 100)
> lifle (< Sp. rifle 'rifle'; JP, 100)

No cases of voiced stop devoicing are found in Jiménez Pastrana or in the literary sources consulted (Bueno 1959, Feijóo 1960, 1965). There is one possible case of voicing of a voiceless stop in the form *pasa*, shown in (3). In one CIS speaker, we found she had conflated the form *pasa* 'pass by, move on' and the phrase *vas a* 'you go to', with the interpretation 'go.' It is possible, then, that *pasa* in (3) could represent a voiceless *vas a* with the meaning 'go, went.'

(3)

> Nosotlo principia peleá Lemelio, Cienfuego,
> at the beginning fight Remedios, Cienfuego
> nosotlo *pasa* la Trocha, nosotlo vinimo Camagüey. . . (JP, 76)
> we went/moved on the Trocha we came-1PL Camagüey
> 'At the beginning, we fought in Remedios and Cienfuego; we went to
>   Trocha, we then went to Camagüey.'

Syllable simplification is found in 19CCS, examples of which contain cluster simplification or coda consonant deletion, but not epenthetic vowel insertion. Examples of the first two phenomena are given in (4) and (5) respectively.

(4)

> gobieno (< Sp. gobierno 'government'; JP, 76)
> life (< Sp. rifles 'rifles'; JP, 75, 76)
> libe (< Sp. libre 'free'; JP, 76)

(5)

> españó (< Sp. español 'Spanish'; JP, 73)
> pañól (< Sp. español 'Spanish'; JP, 99)
> señó (< Sp. señor 'sir'; JP, 91)
> ficiá (< Sp. oficial 'official'; JP, 100)
> tilá (< Sp. tirar 'shoot'; JP, 100)

Note that in (5) there are examples of apheresis, the elision of the word-initial syllable, attested to in Jiménez Pastrana but not in CIS. The effects of cluster simplification in the speech reported on by Jiménez Pastrana suggest a notable preference for CV syllable structure, also apparent in CIS. Interestingly, in the literary sources, as well as in Jiménez Pastrana, there is only one instance of a plural noun (*no tenel amigos* (< Sp. *no tener amigos* 'not have friends'), although in Jiménez Pastrana (1963), nouns such as *life* and *cásula* 'shells' are used in a plural context but not pluralized. This suggests that the latter source is closer to CIS.

As far as morphosyntactic phenomena are concerned, we find that 19CCS and CIS are highly comparable. The traits to be considered are listed in Table 6.3. The predominant order found in 19CCS is SVO order (Table 6.3a), examples of which are given in (6). There are no examples of transitive clauses with overt objects in which the object is not postverbal.

(6a)

¿Tú **quiele pollo**? Mata **capitán pañol**.
2SG.FAM want-3SG chicken kill captain Spanish
'If you want to eat chicken, kill a Spanish captain.'

(6b)

Tú no da pa nosotlo *cásula*.
2sg NEG give for us shell
'You don't give us any ammunition.'

Relative to the verb, adjuncts (Table 6.3b) usually appear after it, as in the examples in (7).

(7a)

Luego nosotlo *viene Oliente*.
then we comes Oriente
'Then we came to Oriente.'

(7b)

Tó la gente camina pa la Camagüey.
all the people walks for the Camagüey
'All the people walked to Camagüey.'

However, there is an interesting example, shown in (8), in which an instrument adjunct phrase appears preverbally, as in Cantonese, the native language of the vast majority of the Chinese in Cuba at that time.

Table 6.3 Morphosyntactic Traits

Trait	Likely Source
a. SVO word order	IUO, Spanish, Chinese
b. S Adjunct V word order	Chinese
c. No passive voice	Other
d. Classifier equivalent to English *piece*	Not present
e. N + N (with genitive or modifier relation)	Chinese
f. No prepositions as such	There are prepositions
g. Adv + Adj	Spanish, Chinese
h. V + IO + DO order with no marking for IO or DO	Chinese
i. Adv + V + NP	Chinese
j. V + N + Adv	Spanish, Chinese
k. *ya* completive	Other, Chinese
l. Evidence of other TMA markers	Other
m. Copula with Ns, absent with Adjs.	Chinese
n. In-situ and fronted *wh*-words	Spanish, Chinese[a]
o. Bimorphemic *wh*-words	Other
p. No equivalents of *yes* and *no* to questions	Spanish[b]
q. Negation: *no* before the predicate	Spanish, Chinese
r. Double negation: *antes nunca no pensado* 'I had never thought [about it] before.'	Not present
s. Headless relative clauses	Chinese

[a] fronted
[b] there are

(8)

Yo mimito *con lifle* tilá pañole tlentacinco tilo

1sg EMPH with rifle shoot Spanish thirty-five shots
'I myself shot 35 rounds at the Spaniards.'

Cantonese has a similar construction, with a comitative or instrumental phrase with an equivalent of 'with', as in (9).

(9)

Jeui hóu tùhng ngàhnhòhng je chin.
most good with bank borrow money
'It's best to borrow money {with/from} the bank.'

(Matthews and Yip 1994: 143)

In the 19CCS corpus, there is no evidence of a passive voice, a classifier element, or the N + N construction in the corpus (Table 6.3c-e). There is, however, a clear example of a N *de* N construction, shown in (10), a feature also found in CIS.

(10)

> Generá de nosotlo muere aquí.
> general of we/us dies here
> 'Some of our generals died here.'

Regarding prepositions (Table 6.3f), verbs of motion in 19CCS carry either no directional marker (11), or appear with the element *pa* (< Spanish *para* 'for') as a marker of direction (12). The lack of prepositions is the norm in one CIS speaker's speech (cf. [13]), although not in another's (cf. examples in [14]).

(11a)

> Baja Ø la plasa españó, y pelea.
> go.down the square Spanish and fight
> 'Go down to Spanish Square and fight.'

(11b)

> nosotlo vinimo Ø Camagüey . . . luego nosotlo viene Ø Oliente.
> 1PL came-1PL Camagüey then we comes Oriente
> 'We came to Camagüey . . . then we went to Oriente.'

(11c)

> Nosotlo pasa Ø la Trocha.
> we goes the Trocha
> 'We went to Trocha.'

(12a)

> Tó la gente camina *pa* la Camagüey.
> all the people walks for the Camagüey.
> 'All the people walked to Camagüey.'

(12b)

> Tú dise nosotlo va *pa* la Camagüey
> 2sg.FAM says we goes for the Camagüey
> 'You tell us to go to Camagüey.'

(13a)

> yo **llegá Ø Madrid**, . . . **vive Ø Madrid** casi cuanto año?
> I arrive Madrid live Madrid almost how-many year
> 'I arrived in Madrid, I lived in Madrid almost how many years?'

(13b)

> **Pero Ø España,** español nada nada, no sabe.
> but Spain Spanish nothing nothing NEG know-3SG.PRES
> 'But in Spain, I knew nothing, nothing of Spanish.'

(14a)

> Momento no pensaw poro vuelva **poro** mi país
> momento NEG thought-PPART poro return poro my country
> 'For the moment, I don't plan on returning to my country.'

(14b)

> Me viene **por** aquí.
> me comes poro here
> 'I came here.' (from Clements 2009: 147)

With locative adjuncts, we find a lack of marking, as illustrated by the examples in (15).

(15a)

> Nosotlo principia peleá Ø Lemelio.
> we at.the.beginning fight Remedios
> 'At the beginning, we fought in Remedios.'

(15b)

> Nosotlo peleá Ø Camagüey.
> we fight Camagüey
> 'We fought in Camagüey.'

(15c)

> Nosotlo tá Ø Oliente.
> we is Oriente
> 'We were in Oriente.'

(15d)

> Nosotlo peleá Ø Oriente.
> we fight Oriente
> 'We fought in Oriente.'

There are no data in the 19CCS sample related to adverb-adjective order (Table 6.3g). However, there are important data in the sample relating to object marking (Table 6.3h). We find one example of an IO marked by its immediately postverbal position, shown in (16).

(16)

> Tú dise nosotlo va pa la Camagüey.
> 2sg-FAM says we/us goes for the Camagüey
> 'You tell us to go to Camagüey.'

Although we have one example of V-IO-DO order, there is no established pattern in 19CCS of V-IO-DO order with no marking on the IO or DO. However, we do find a fairly consistent pattern of V-IO-DO order, in which the IO is marked with the element *pa* (< Spanish *para* 'for'). The examples are given in (17). Whereas in Spanish the default order is V-DO-IO, in these examples the order is V-IO-DO, following the Chinese (and Cantonese) order. Nevertheless, in (17c), we have an example attributed to a Chinese doctor, who uses the default order found in Spanish.

(17a)

> *Tú no **da pa nosotlo** life.*
> 2sg-FAM NEG gives for we/us rifle
> 'You don't give us rifles.'

(17b)

> *Tú no **da pa nosotlo cásula**.*
> 2sg-FAM NEG gives for we/us shell
> 'You don't give us shells.'

(17c)

> *Yo le **da medicina pa la gente poble**.*
> 1sg CL.3SG.IO gives medicine for the people poor
> 'I give medicine to the poor people.'

In one CIS speaker's speech, we find ample use of *pa* (< Spanish *para* 'for') as an IO marker (cf. examples in [17]), whereas in another CIS speaker's speech we find the Chinese pattern.

In our corpus, there are no clear examples of Adv-V-NP order (Table 6.3i), but we do find one example of V-NP-Adv (Table 6.3j), shown in (18).

(18)

> Suleto tiene arma por la mañana.
> insurgent has arm at the morning
> 'The insurgents (who) had guns in the morning.'

Although the 19CCS sample contains no instances of *ya* 'already' used as a tense-aspect marker (Table 6.3k), we do encounter a particle reminiscent of the progressive aspect marker, the use of *ta*, mentioned in footnote 5 above and shown again in (19), that is reminiscent of a present or an imperfective marker.

(19)

> No señó, pa mí no sabe, *ta* trabaja, quema carbón.
> NEG sir, for me NEG knows AUX works, burns coal
> 'I didn't see armed insurgent people in the morning. No sir, I
> don't know, I was working, burning carbon.'

Regarding the use of the copulas *ser* and *estar* (Table 6.3m), there are various examples of *ta* (< Spanish *estar* 'be [resultative or locative]'), shown in (20), and of *soy* 'I am' and *son* 'they are' in (21).

(20a)

> Tó la gente *ta* qui jabla bonito na má.
> all the people is here talk pretty nothing more
> toda la gente que está aquí habla bonito nada más
> 'All the people who are here talk pretty, nothing else.'

(20b)

> 'Nosotlo *tá* Oliente, nosotlo peleá Oliente
> we is Oriente we fight.INF east
> nosotros estuvimos en Oriente, nostros peleamos en Oriente
> 'We were in Oriente, we fought in Oriente.'

(20c)

> Londi *ta* Ginil Maceo?
> dónde está General Maceo
> 'Where is General Maceo?'

(21a)

> Cuidado, yo *soy* cabo José.
> careful 1sg am private José
> 'Watch out, I'm private José.'

(21b)

> que yo va pleguntá si *son* vel esi cosa?
> COMP 1SG goes ask if are true that thing
> que yo voy a preguntar si son verdad esas cosas
> 'I'm going to ask him whether these things are true.'

The presence of *soy* is likely due to a fixed phrase. In the text, the context clarifies that the soldier in question would routinely utter (21a) when others addressed him. It is interesting to note that in the small corpus, there are no instances of zero copula.

With regard to fronted and in-situ wh-words (Table 6.3n), there are two instances of a fronted wh-word: one shown above in (20c), and the other below in (22). The latter is of note because it is bimorphemic: *qui cosa* 'what thing' (with mid-vowel *e* raised to *i* instead of the standard *qué* 'what'). Such bimorphemic wh-words are considered to be more transparent and consequently not uncommon in certain restructured language varieties (cf. Muysken and Smith 1990, and Clements and Mahboob 1999). These were also found in Chinese Pidgin English (cf. Shi 1991).

(22)

> *Qui cosa* usa Ficiá?
> ¿Qué usan los oficiales?
> what thing uses official
> 'What do the officials use?'

Regarding the use of *si* 'yes' or *no* 'no' to yes-no questions (Table 6.3p), we have one example of a negation of a question, given in (23).

(23)

> ¡No es un chino manila, *no*!
> NEG is a Chinese Manila NEG
> 'I'm not a Chinaman!'

The use of the sentence-final negator *no* in this sentence suggests African influence, as argued by Schwegler (1998: 235), Ortiz (1998: 113–115).

Finally, in our small corpus we find one example of a headless relative clause (Table 6.3s), shown in (24). As is evident from the comparison between the 19CCS sentence and its Spanish equivalent below it, the relative pronoun *que* (whose place is marked with the symbol Ø) is absent.

(24)

> Tó la gente Ø ta qui jabla bonito na má.
> all the people is here talk pretty nothing more
> toda la gente [que] está aquí habla bonito nada más.
> 'All the people who are here talk pretty and nothing else.'

With regard to discourse properties of 19CCS, we note one object deletion, which occurs when the information is recoverable from the discourse context. There are several examples of this phenomenon, shown in (25).

(25a)

> Si tiene dinelo paga pala mí. Si no tiene, no paga Ø
> if has money pay-3SG.PRES for me. if NEG has NEG pay-3SG.PRES
> 'If you have money, you pay me. If you don't, you don't pay.'[8]

(25b)

> Si tú pue cogé Ø Ø coge; y si no, Ø leja.
> if you can catch-INF catch-IMP and if NEG leave-IMP
> Si tú puedes cogerme, cógeme, y si no, me dejas [en paz].
> 'If you can catch me, catch me; otherwise leave me alone.'

Of these two examples, it is possible to find null objects in Spanish as well for (25a), but in standard Spanish it is impossible to delete the animate direct objects, as in (25b).

4 CONCLUSION

In this study, we have seen that both the sociohistorical and the linguistic evidence suggests that the variety of Spanish spoken by the Chinese laborers in the 19th century was in all likelihood not a pidgin, with its own conventionalized vocabulary and grammar, but rather individual instances of naturalistic second language acquisition. As indentured laborers, the Chinese would have spoken Chinese among themselves, even though several dialects of Cantonese were surely represented. Although there is anecdotal evidence, found in a short story (cf. Bueno 1959: 66), that foreigner talk was used in addressing the Chinese, there is no historical evidence that any restructured variety of Spanish emerged in the communication between Cubans and Chinese. The practice of shipping laborers to Cuba from China lasted around

30 years (1847–1877). Thus, the period of time was not conducive to the creation of a Chinese pidgin Spanish variety either.

The linguistic evidence, based on a comparison between 19CCS and Chinese Immigrant Spanish (cf. Clements 2003, 2005, 2009: 124–157) suggests that the two varieties are highly similar and that they both are good examples of Klein and Perdue's (1992) 'basic variety' of naturalistically learned L2 Spanish, discussed in the introduction above. And although the sociohistorical evidence suggests that the Chinese and Africans did not interact, there is some evidence that at least some of the Chinese had enough contact with Afro-Cubans to be influenced by their speech, apparent in the African language trait of the sentence-final negation particle (i.e., *¡No es un chino manila, **no**!*).

The external ecology of the Chinese in Cuba and the linguistic data coincide to give a picture of a people who learned enough Spanish to fulfill their needs and desires, but whose children (the second generation, most of which had Cuban mothers) spoke Cuban Spanish, with few or no features of their first-generation ancestors.

NOTES

1. A number of target and source languages were studied: Punjabi and Italian speakers learning English, Italian; Turkish speakers learning German, Turkish; Arabic speakers learning Dutch, Arabic; Spanish learning French; and Spanish and Finnish speakers learning Swedish.
2. One of Corbitt's statistics differs minimally from Kiple's: the former cites the number of Whites at 418,211, whereas the latter uses an adjusted figure of 418,291. We take Kiple's figure to be the more accurate one.
3. The expression *manila chino* was used by the Spanish colonizers to refer to Chinese indentured laborers, also in Cuba. See example (28) for an example of the expression in the mouth of a Chinese soldier fighting for Cuba against the Spanish.
4. According to the OED, the term 'coolie' probably derived from Gujarati *kulī*, initially the name of a tribe in Gujarat that migrated to South India. There, the term apparently mixed with Tamil *kūli* 'hire' and eventually came to denote hired laborers or burden carriers.
5. There are some notable exceptions. One is the use of a sentence-final negator, as in (i). Assuming the data is an accurate reflection of the Spanish of Chinese Cuban soldiers, this feature is most likely due to the influence of Afro-Cuban Spanish (cf. Ortiz López 1998, Schwegler 1998).

(i) ¡No es un chino manila, **no**!
neg is a Chinese Manila neg
'I'm not a Chinaman!'

A second and third feature involves case and tense-aspect marking, respectively. In example (ii), the logical subject of a stative predicate *sabe* 'know-3sg. pres' is marked as the grammatical object, assuming that here *pa* (< Spanish *para* 'for') is a case marker. This is not a feature of Cantonese, where pronominals are not marked for case in analogous constructions (see the example in [iii]). The third feature is the particle *ta* (< Spanish *está* 'is-AUX') underlined in (ii). This could be a case of simple reduction, which is common and widespread in Spanish, but *ta* would need to appear with the gerund form *trabajando* 'working.' The form *trabaja* could also be an instance of reduction. It is not clear from the transcription where the stress lies (*trabája* or *trabajá*). There are too many unknowns to be able to say anything more concrete about *ta* here.

(ii)　No señó, pa mí no sabe,　　　*ta* trabaja,　　quema carbón.
no sir　for me neg know-3sg.pres　is work-3s.prs　burn-2sg.prs　charcol
'No, sir. I don't know. I'm just working, making charcoal.'

(iii)　Ngo m-zi　　　aa.
1　sg neg-know　　prt
'I don't know.'

(iv)　ngo zou-gan je,　　　siu-gan　mui.
1　sg do-imp thing, burn-imp　coal
'I'm doing things (working), burning coal.'

6. In one short story collection (Bueno 1959: 66), we found evidence of foreigner talk, that is, evidence of accommodation on the part of a native speaker communicating with a non-native Spanish speaker: "¿Capitán, tú estar triste, tú pensar en Cantón . . . " le decía Acacio, poniendo los verbos en infinitivo para que lo entendiera mejor ' "Captain, you be sad, you think about Canton . . ." Acacio was saying to him, putting the verbs in the infinitive so that he would understand better.' In this story, however, the Spanish of the Chinese captain is stereotypically portrayed in that all verbs are in the infinitive, all instances of *r* are rendered as *l*, all copulas are deleted, etc.
7. Here, Chinese Immigrant Spanish refers to the speech of two native Chinese speakers who are immigrants in Spain. The traits of their speech are discussed in Clements (2003, 2005, 2009: 124–157).
8. Spanish can delete an object in discourse if it is a mass term (noncount noun or bare plural). In this example, *dinero* 'money' is a mass term and can be unexpressed in Spanish.

REFERENCES

Bakker, Peter.1994. *Pidgins, in Pidgins and creoles*, edited by Jacques Arends, Pieter Muysken, and Norval Smith. Amsterdam: Benjamins.

Bueno, Salvador. 1959. *Los mejores cuento cubanos*, tomo I. La Habana: Segundo Festival del Libro Cubano.

Clements, J. Clancy. 2009. *The linguistic legacy of Spanish and Portuguese: colonial expansion and language change*. Cambridge: Cambridge University Press.

Clements, J. Clancy. 2005. Immigrant speech, creoles, and the 'basic variety': a usage-based account of some traits in the Portuguese-based creoles. *Journal of Portuguese Linguistics* 4.149–165.

Clements, J. Clancy. 2003. The tense-aspect system in pidgins and naturalistically learned L2. *Studies in Second Language Acquisition* 25.245–281.

Clements, J. Clancy and Ahmar Mahboob. 1999. Wh-words and question formation in pidgins/creole languages, *Language change and language contact in pidgins and creoles*, edited by John McWhorter. Amsterdam: John Benjamins, 459–497.

Corbitt, Duvon Clough. 1971. *A study of the Chinese in Cuba, 1847–1947*. Wilmore, KY: Ashbury College.

Curtin, Phillip. 1969. *The Atlantic slave trade: a census*. Madison: University of Wisconsin Press.

Erenchun, Felix. 1856–59. *Anales de la Isla de Cuba*. Havana: Imprenta La Habanera.

Feijóo, Samuel (ed.). 1965. *Cuentos populares cubanos*. Selección. La Habana: Bolsilibros Union.

Feijóo, Samuel (ed.). 1960. *Cuentos populares cubanos*. Tomo I. La Habana: Universidad Central de Las Villas.

Hall, Robert, 1966. *Pidgin and creole languages*. Ithaca NY: Cornell University Press.

Jiménez Pastrana, Juan. 1963. *Los chinos en la liberación cubana*. Havana: Instituto de Historia.

Kiple, Kenneth F. 1976. *Black in colonial Cuba, 1774–1889*. Gainesville: University Presses of Florida.

Klein, Wolfgang and Clive Perdue. 1992. *Utterance structure: Developing grammars again*. Amsterdam: Benjamins.

Lipski, John. 1999. Chinese-Cuban pidgin Spanish: implications for the Afro-Creole debate, in *Creole genesis, attitudes, and discourse*, edited by John R. Rickford and Suzanne Romaine. Amsterdam: Benjamins, 215–233.

Matthews, Stephen and Virginia Yip. 1994. *Cantonese: A comprehensive grammar*. London: Routledge.

Muysken, Pieter, and Norval Smith. 1990. Question words in pidgin and creole languages. *Linguistics* 28. 883–903.

Ortiz López, Luis A. 1998. *Huellas etno-sociolingüísticas bozales y afrocubanas*. Frankfurt an Main: Vervuert.

Pinharanda Nunes, Mário Rui Lima de Oliveira. 2010. *estudo da expressão morfo-sintácticva das categorias de tempo, modo, e aspecto em Maquista*. Unpublished Doctoral Dissertation. University of Macau.

Ramos Hernández, Reinaldo, Arturo A. Pedroso Alés and Flor Inés Cassola Triamma. 2000. Barrio chino de La Habana. *Cataruo* 2(2). 57–75.

Schwegler, Armin. 1998. El palenquero, in *América negra: Panorámica actual del los estudios lingüísticos sobre variedades hispanas, portuguesas, y criollas*, edited by Matthias Perl and Armin Schwegler. Madrid, Spain: Iberoamericana, 219–291.

Shi, D. 1991. Chinese Pidgin English: Its origin and linguistic features. *Journal of Chinese Linguistics* 19.1–40.

7 Shifting Identities, Shifting Practices
The Chinese-Speaking Communities in Suriname

Paul Brendan Tjon Sie Fat

1 LANGUAGE AND IDENTITY IN SURINAME

Suriname is located on the North-Eastern coast of South America, between 2°–6° Northern latitude and 54°–58° Western longitude, borders in the East with French Guiana, in the South with Brazil, in the West with Guyana and in the North with the Atlantic Ocean. The total land area of Suriname is ca. 164,000 km². According to the results of the eighth census, as per 13 August 2012, Suriname has 541,638 inhabitants, approximately 44.2% of whom live in the capital of Paramaribo.[1]

The ethnic variety of Suriname's population stems from labour policies under a Caribbean plantation economy: chattel slavery from Africa, indentured labour from China, India and Indonesia. According to the 2012 census, Suriname's strong population is comprised of 27.4% East Indians (persons originating from the Indian sub-continent), 15.7% Creoles (of African or mixed descent), 13.7% Indonesians, 21.7% Maroons,[2] and 13.4% 'mixed'.[3] The smaller census categories include 3.8% Indigenous (the Amerindian peoples of Suriname), 1.5% Chinese and 0.3% Caucasian.

As a former colony of the Netherlands, Dutch is the official language. The lingua franca, Sranantongo, is widely spoken. The other languages include the Maroon Creoles, Amerindian languages and Asian languages (Carlin & Arends 2002).[4]

1.1 Surinamese Multiculturalism, Ethnic Identity and Language

Suriname is frequently presented as a 'multiculturalist hotspot', based on superficial observations of racial and linguistic variety. Ethnicity, rather than class, gender or body, is the dominant social distinction invoked by the term multiculturalism. However, ethnic identification is usually about access to resources, if one considers that the major ethnic contrasts are generated in Surinamese ethnopolitics and economic relations (such as ethnic ownership economies). Surinamese ethnopolitics are the most complex of the region, and not only invoke a particular spectrum of ethnic groups with their particular histories, folkloric cultures and languages, but also reproduce them in the form of political constituencies (Tjon Sie Fat 2009).

This 'groupism'—the idea that ethnic groups are etic rather than emic categories (Brubaker 2004)—is bolstered by the common use of 'culture' as a euphemism for ethnic difference, a pars pro toto for ethnic identity. Surinamese multiculturalist discourse is 'groupist', i.e., ethnic groups are seen as real entities that are internally homogenous and externally bounded. But lived reality is different; it is and has always been about hybrid identities rather than a single monolithic reference.

Language, an important marker of ethnic borders in Surinamese multiculturalist discourse, is assumed to be as monolithic, unchanging and primordial as the group it is associated with. In fact, multilingualism is widespread, with the majority of the population (which is urban) having a repertoire that includes Dutch, Sranantongo and more often than not at least one 'ethnic' language (Leglise & Stoll 2014). Language practices are complex, and linguistic hierarchies reflect hierarchies of class and gender that underlie representations of ethnicity in Suriname (Carlin et al. 2014).

What amounts to ideologies of language and ethnic identity feed into each other and reinforce the notion of ethnicity as groups, and groups as communities. A colonial-era anthropological notion of 'tribes' continues to be used to describe the Maroon and Amerindian peoples of the Surinamese interior; tribe stands for ethnicity, for a bounded community, and a speech community, which in turn defines a tribe and the ethnic group. The term 'Chinese community' is persistently used in Suriname, and here too groupism is both the result and the cause of language being used as an ethnic marker and racial attribute.

2   CHINESE IN SURINAME

The category of 'Chinese' is highly variable and extremely porous in Suriname. The label covers both an indigenous ethnicity within Surinamese multiculturalist discourse and immigrants from the People's Republic of China (PRC). It does not distinguish between various regional or linguistic backgrounds, nor between the assimilated and newcomers, or take into account levels of cultural hybridity. None of the various regional and linguistic subgroups that now typify the ethnic Chinese segment in Suriname are as homogenous or bounded as insiders or outsiders claim. The oldest subgroup, Sanyi Hakka, display the most variation with regard to self-identification, linguistic repertoires and multiple ethnic identities.

Even so, Chinese are considered a fundamentally homogenous ethnic group in Suriname. As I said elsewhere, the Dutch term *Chinees* ('Chinese') covers and conflates a diverse range of meanings, and obscures cultural and linguistic variety that is changing under migration (Tjon Sie Fat 2014). By its very nature Chinese social organisation in Suriname reinforces the impression of the Surinamese public and state that 'the Chinese community' is a real, bounded entity. Ethnic Chinese elites position themselves as gatekeepers by manipulating (real or imagined) linguistic and cultural barriers, and use ethnic sociocultural institutions (*shetuan* 社團) as platforms for 'Chinatown politics' to gain status among the in-group and to convince the State that they are representatives of a constituency (Tjon Sie Fat 2012).

2.1 Origins

The history of ethnic Chinese in Suriname is very much a history of Overseas Chinese, linking 'sojourners' (華僑 *huáqiáo*) to a homeland (僑鄉 *qiáoxiāng*) typically via chain migration and money transfers, that developed out of indentured labour. In the case of Suriname, the majority of Chinese indentured labourers came via Hong Kong from the Sanyi[5] region in the nineteenth century. By the early twentieth century a fairly typical Overseas Chinese community had developed, with sociocultural organisations, Suriname-born generations, retail trade as an economic niche and constant chain migration.

Ongoing immigration and inescapable assimilation resulted in the apparent paradox of ethnic Chinese as unassimilated outsiders as well as increasingly hybridised; *Tongap*, migrants who spoke Kejia[6] as a community language, Sranantongo as a service language in their shops and generally no Dutch, versus *Laiap*, the local-born, culturally or genetically hybridised generation, that spoke Dutch, Sranantongo but less and less Kejia (Tjon Sie Fat 2009). Local, hybridised Hakka populations are not unique to Suriname, but have a parallel, for instance, in the *tusan* of Peru (Lausent-Herrera 2010).

After the founding of the PRC in 1949, direct chain migration from the *qiáoxiāng* was no longer possible. Sanyi Hakka joined the sudden influx of refugees to Hong Kong, and eventually remigrated to Suriname around the 1970s; adapted to urban Hong Kong culture and the Cantonese language, these migrant cohorts came to be known in Suriname as 'Hong Kong Chinese' (Tjon Sie Fat 2009). The balance between immigration and assimilation appears to have swung in favour of assimilation after Surinamese independence in 1975, with migration to the Netherlands increasing and immigration from China stalling.

By the 1990s, following economic reforms and concurrent relaxation of restrictions on emigration in the PRC, immigration from the PRC dramatically increased (Tjon Sie Fat 2009).

The main difference between New Chinese, as these migrant cohorts were soon called, and the older Chinese cohorts in Suriname was the nature of the link between mobility and economic strategies. The newest cohorts were intertwined with cheap commodities; they were obviously facilitating the globalisation of Chinese goods, but were they following the spread of cheap commodities around the globe, or were those cheap commodities following in the wake of their outmigration?

New Chinese have many different regional and linguistic backgrounds, as we will see. However, most people in Suriname are not aware of any differences; it is the split between 'Old Chinese' / Hakka / 'Surinamese Chinese' and New Chinese that is the most salient distinction to Surinamese observers. Immigration continues, and the range of regional backgrounds and Chinese languages spoken in Suriname continues to fluctuate.

2.2 Chinese Languages

The older, Sanyi Hakka migrant cohorts brought with them Kejia varieties, initially from what is now central Dongguan Municipality, and later more southern varieties, down to those of the New Territories in Hong Kong. Later Sanyi Hakka migrants cohorts also brought other Chinese languages, such as the 'Hong Kong Chinese' of the 1960s who brought the prestige variety of Hongkongese Cantonese, or the Sanyi Hakka among the New Chinese who brought Putonghua (PTH), the prestige variety and standard language of the People's Republic of China, as well as the most recent versions of the hometown dialect. New Chinese migrant cohorts came from virtually every part of coastal China, but most speak: Wu (Oujiang Wu: Wenzhou, Wencheng, Ruian), Northeastern Mandarin (Dongbei, Qingdao), Yue (Guangzhou, Taishan, Dongguan), Min (Qiongwen Min: Hainanese); Minzhong (Xianyou); Minbei (Fuzhou), Kejia (non-Sanyi varieties, in particular Taishan Kejia).

After just twenty years, New Chinese have not assimilated into Surinamese society as much as the 160-year-old Sanyi Hakka cohort. Topolects have not developed, and given the more pronounced transnational nature of the New Chinese, it is by no means certain that localised varieties will emerge. Twenty years ago New Chinese migrants, as a group, were very much like the first Sanyi Hakka cohorts; they spoke their hometown dialects, quickly learned basic lingua franca Sranantongo, had no Dutch. A local-born generation is emerging, and children raised in Suriname speak a similar range of languages to the children of the Sanyi Hakka: intra-ethnic languages (that is, the hometown dialect and Putonghua), inter-ethnic languages (Sranantongo and increasingly Dutch), and English.[7]

The hometown dialects of the New Chinese migrant cohorts are strong markers of regional identity, and are essential to socioeconomic networks in the way Sanyi Kejia used to be in the past. The 'unlearnable' Oujiang Wu varieties signal in-group status, and are vital within Zhejiangese sociocultural and entrepreneurial networks in Suriname. Fujianese dialects only do so to a limited extent, and Fujianese *huiguan* organisation in Suriname requires Putonghua over the mutually incomprehensible Minnan, Minzhong and Minbei varieties. The Hainanese are linguistically far more homogenous than the Zhejiangese and Fujianese, rather like the Sanyi Hakka migrants, although speakers of Hainanese in Suriname are not as worried about the status consequences of speaking their hometown language as are speakers of Sanyi Kejia.

2.3   Positioning Chinese Languages in Suriname

In Suriname, Chinese languages are firmly associated with migrants as an ethnic border marker. Two factors determine the way Chinese languages are positioned in Suriname: language ideology of Chinese immigrants on the one hand, Surinamese attitudes towards Chinese on the other.

2.3.1   *Chinese Migrants' Attitude to Language*

The first Sanyi Hakka migrants had left Guangdong Province not very long after the nineteenth century Punti-Hakka wars. In this period, Hakka identity was ethnicised in the struggle between the established (punti, 本地: 'autochthons') and the outsiders (Hakka, 客家: 'allochthons'), and language in particular became a vital marker of Hakka belonging (Cohen 1995). The earliest Sanyi Hakka migrant cohorts appear to have been practically monolingual when they arrived, with just a minority able to speak *p'akwa* (白話, 'vernacular': Cantonese) or *tsinngi* (真語/ 正語, 'real/proper language': Mandarin). The contrast between *punti* language (本地話) and Kejia quickly lost any meaning in Suriname, where Punti identity did not exist.[8] Kejia was a *tuwa* (土話, 'local patois') of very low status, below Cantonese, and far lower than Mandarin.

Up to the arrival of the Hong Kong Chinese in the 1970s, the low status of Kejia was constructed in relation to the Surinamese context, in particular Dutch; Kejia was the only form of Chinese that mattered, and only contrasts between 'proper' Kejia and localised 'Laiap Kejia' indicated some in-group status hierarchy. As we will see below, high-status Cantonese, introduced by the Hong Kong Chinese, eventually replaced Kejia as the public medium, and now Mandarin in the form of Putonghua (PTH) is overtaking Cantonese in public discourse and replacing Kejia as the default intra-ethnic lingua franca.

New Chinese migrants are infused with the idea that the unity of the Chinese State is represented in cultural and linguistic unity (Tjon Sie Fat 2014). The Embassy of the People's Republic of China in Suriname consciously and unconsciously reinforces this discourse by way of PTH and written Chinese in its communication with ethnic Chinese in Suriname, either migrants or Overseas Chinese.

2.3.2   *Local Attitudes to Chinese*

Surinamese attitudes towards Chinese have always been ambiguous to say the least. These are shaped by general, originally nineteenth-century racist notions of Chinese as the eternal Other (cf. Keevak 2011), local multiculturalist discourse that informs Surinamese ethnopolitics as well as more recent anxieties with regard to the increasing 'Chinese' presence in Suriname in the form of the more visible influence of the People's Republic of China and the growing influx of New Chinese migrants (cf. Tjon Sie Fat 2009). Chinese migrants are highly visible in Suriname, phenotypically, linguistically as well as culturally, and their basic strategy was traditionally to lie as low as possible to avoid any possible repercussions.

The first obvious examples of public anti-Chinese sentiments, and the only clear instance of anti-Chinese government policy, started in the late 1920s (Tjon Sie Fat 2009), a period when Chinese were demonised in other Latin American and Caribbean countries (Hu-DeHart 2010). In a survey of Creole attitudes towards other ethnic groups during the early 1960s, Van Renselaar noted that about a third of his respondents held a negative view of Chinese, mainly because Chinese shopkeepers were considered exploiters (Van Renselaar 1963: 103, 105).[9] A slightly earlier survey on multicultural attitudes of East Indians showed that less than half of the respondents held a positive view of Chinese (Speckmann 1963: 88).[10] With the arrival of New Chinese in the 1990s, anti-Chinese sentiments gained new momentum (Tjon Sie Fat 2009), and persist to the present day.[11]

Such negative Surinamese attitudes towards Chinese are based on stereotypes of Chinese that include the widespread image of Chinese language as monolithic, ugly and unlearnable (Tjon Sie Fat 2009). Negative outsiders' attitudes dovetailed with Hakka notions of Kejia as a low-status language to be avoided in decent company, and multilingual speakers would self-deprecate spoken Chinese language towards non-Chinese. Although Cantonese was the high-status variety among Old Chinese, its use too was avoided in non-Chinese company, and was not presented as an important identity marker.

3   LANGUAGE CHANGE, SHIFTS, ATTRITION: THE CASE OF KEJIA

Three dimensions of language acquisition and shift affect all Chinese migrants in Suriname. First, all migrants in Suriname who cannot isolate themselves as expats eventually recognise the need to learn Sranantongo, and Chinese migrants quickly acquire it, to the extent that all ethnic Chinese are assumed to be able to speak it. Secondly, speakers of hometown dialects generally have to deal with changeable intra-ethnic lingua francas, Cantonese in the case of Sanyi Hakka cohorts thirty or forty years ago, currently PTH for all Chinese migrants. Finally, there is the generation gap inherent in the migrant experience. The children of migrants generally speak a different set of languages than their elders; they usually are fully competent in spoken and written Dutch, whereas migrant adults tend to be fully literate in Chinese.

It is surprisingly difficult to collect quantitative data to support any statement about the survival or demise of Kejia in Suriname, mainly because speakers of any Kejia variety, both Old and New Chinese, are all multilingual and can choose to remain hidden behind any other Chinese variety. Without applying some type of language proficiency test, it is also difficult to gauge actual language use and competency, as speakers tend to under-report their own fluency or over-report the use of Kejia in various contexts. The inherent difficulty of distinguishing different sub-populations within the ethnic Chinese group from the outside, as well as a general inability from the inside to distinguish between variation within Kejia, also compound methodological difficulties.

But in general it is possible to claim that Kejia is not consistently maintained in Suriname, and that the majority of the speakers of the different varieties do not worry about its possible demise. Kejia is a language to bridge generation gaps, but not something one uses with one's peers; it signals lack of sophistication, of being out of touch with the modernity of places like Hong Kong. To non-Hakka migrants, it betrays one's Overseas Chinese identity in Suriname, and marks one as not quite loyal to pan-Chinese sentiments and very likely out of touch with developments in the People's Republic of China. It is increasingly a language of familiarity, of old social networks and of Sanyi migrant heritage, instead of what it used to be: the dominant everyday language of ethnic Chinese.

Kejia smoothes participation in *huiguan* rotating savings and credit association (ROSCA), but the increasingly skewed proportion of newcomers versus the established means less trust, so Kejia no longer guarantees the kind of Sanyi Hakka in-group identity necessary to find a ROSCA sponsor. Kejia is also less essential because Chinese entrepreneurial networks are no longer Hakka networks, which means that one needs PTH. Participation in sociocultural events which are aimed at the broader ethnic Chinese segment requires PTH. Kejia is still not used in public Sanyi Hakka settings, and even Cantonese now increasingly shares the stage with PTH.

In short, there are three main factors that determine the fortunes of Kejia in Suriname: assimilation, language ideology imported from Hong Kong and the growing influence of the discourse of global Chinese identity. We will discuss each below.

2.1 Assimilation

Assimilation has two meanings in Suriname with regard to the language situation of the Sanyi Hakka. The first is the loss of Kejia among younger generations; the second is the local divergence of the ancestral dialect.

2.1.1 *The Problem of Language Maintenance*

Very typical for the Sanyi Hakka experience in Suriname was the reluctance of early migrant men to communicate a sense of heritage to their Suriname-born children, resulting in a very fundamental break between the Tongap and Laiap generations; Laiap seem to be people 'without a history' (Tjon Sie Fat 2009). Later Hakka families in Suriname were more likely to have an immigrant mother, and Kejia was also more likely to be maintained in the family context. Kejia is maintained with some difficulty as a family language in many other places with Hakka populations (Shao 2001; Lim & Hsiao 2007, 2009). Kejia is thus only a limited heritage language in Suriname, in the sense that it does not universally communicate a broad Hakka cultural heritage or community feeling.

Local-born children of Sanyi Hakka migrants integrate into the Surinamese educational system, and their experience is not unlike that of children of Chinese migrants in the USA: they quickly learn that the national language, which is the language of education, is essential for social acceptance and social mobility in the host society, and a language gap opens between them and their immigrant parents (cf. Wong 1978). No data exist on school attendance of ethnic Chinese children in Suriname, but anecdotal evidence suggests that it is consistently high, and in any case the stereotype of the overachieving ethnic Chinese student is common in Suriname. There are also no data on Dutch language competence among young ethnic Chinese in Suriname, but it is very hard to find any who do not speak Dutch, even considering the increased migrant influx since the 1990s.

All young Sanyi Hakka descent I interviewed in 2002 and in 2012 considered spoken Chinese to be essential for the Chinese identity of their descendants. But remarkably, none seemed to realise that their own experience might be typical of their future children; they hardly ever exclusively spoke any variety of Chinese, especially Kejia, to people their own age. Kejia, either 'real' Sanyi Kejia or the Laiap topolect, was not valued as a heritage language. To these young people, spoken Chinese meant a variety with higher status, an international range and access to modernity—everything Kejia would not provide. Despite the sincere intentions of the interviewees, there was no reason to believe that any Chinese variety would survive into the next generations, if young speakers remained in Suriname.

In fact, the fortunes of Kejia are waning everywhere in the world. The only place where Kejia would seem to be safe is Taiwan; in reaction to Taiwanese nationalism, an image of a 'multicultural Taiwan' has arisen, in which different Chinese dialect communities have equal rights, just like the aboriginal Taiwanese communities (Wei 2006; Wang 2007).

2.1.2   *Localised Kejia: 'Laiap Kejia'*

In Suriname, Kejia is strongly associated with the Sanyi Hakka, although they themselves tend to distinguish different levels of competence, such as 'Laiap speech', 'Hong Kong speech', and almost mythical 'proper Kejia'. Other Hakka migrant communities elsewhere have also developed localised varieties, some more distinctive than others (Shao 2001, Ungsitipoonporn 2008). Laiap Kejia (*lai²ap⁵ hak³ga¹wa³*) is the localised variety of the Sanyi hometown dialect. It is associated with Laiap generations because of its lexical, phonological and syntactic peculiarities (Tjon Sie Fat 2002). Its vocabulary contains archaic items, neologisms that developed in isolation from China, local toponyms and Sranantongo loans. Some vowels reflect the dialect of the Qingqi area in Dongguan Municipality, while tones may be reduced. Syntactically, it diverges from the hometown variety mainly in the way the perfective aspect is interpreted, parallel to Sranantongo. 'Laiap' also indicates the low status of this particular variety of Kejia.

It must be noted that there is no baseline of 'proper' Kejia. The language of the early migrants, from which Laiap Kejia developed, has not been recorded, and informants tend to refer to the speech of modern Sanyi Hakka immigrants, either Tongap or New Chinese, as 'proper Kejia'. It is implied that the language of the *qiáoxiāng* is pure and proper by virtue of not being 'polluted' by the Surinamese context. The available material on Kejia in the Sanyi area suggests that some tones and consonants are not exactly the same as those of Laiap Kejia (Bǎoān Dìfāng Zhì 1997; Dōngguǎn Dìfāng Zhì 1998; Zhang 1999, Xie & Huang 2007). Either the descriptions of the Surinamese and Chinese material are inaccurate or the dialects have started to diverge with regard to phonology.

2.2   The Influence of Hong Kong

As stated above, transmission of Kejia was typically gendered. In the 1960s and 1970s, Kejia-speaking men married in Suriname what they considered to be Hakka women from Hong Kong, who spoke Hong Kong Cantonese to their Suriname-born children. Virtually all non-Communist Chinese cultural influences were from Hong Kong, implicitly teaching Hongkongese language ideology, in particular the higher status of Cantonese versus Kejia. Trips to China were more often than not visits to relatives on the mother's side, and in the cultural context of Hong Kong, speaking Kejia was not an option. The Hong Kong migrants brought with them the language ideology of the former British crown colony. Kejia now was a *tuwa* as it was in the Pearl River Delta, and eventually Cantonese replaced Kejia as the language of public events.

Up to 1950, Kejia was the dominant Chinese variety in Hong Kong, but that changed with the influx of refugees from all over the PRC, which favoured the emergence of Cantonese as a lingua franca, a British educational policy that promoted Cantonese as the vehicle for teaching Chinese literacy, urbanisation and the swift economic rise of Hong Kong (Zhou & Liu 1998; Lau 2005). The shift from Kejia to Cantonese is speeding up, and Kejia may already be considered endangered in Hong Kong (Zhou & Liu 1998; Lau 2005; Lee 2008). The influence of Hong Kong is felt everywhere Kejia is spoken; it is being replaced by Cantonese as a community language (Lim & Hsiao 2007, 2009; Ungsitipoonporn 2008).

More recent migrant cohorts and their Suriname-born descendants use a variety that is closer to Hong Kong Kejia ('New Kejia' according to Lau 2005), heavily larded with Cantonese vocabulary and influenced by Hong Kong Cantonese, with its more varied phonology as a result of English loans (Bauer 1984, 1985). Since the return of Hong Kong to the PRC in 1997, the status of Cantonese in Hong Kong is no longer uncontested. Even before the handover of the former crown colony, it was clear that Cantonese would be threatened by PTH in the realms of education, administration and economy (Bruche-Schulz 1997).

2.3 Global Chineseness

The variety of Chinese that has the most impact in Suriname is PTH. It dominates all other Chinese varieties in Suriname as the intra-ethnic lingua franca with the widest reach and is ubiquitous as the basis of modern written Chinese, and the increasing pluriformity among the Overseas Chinese of Suriname, as well as the increasing presence of the People's Republic of China in Suriname, conspire to make Putonghua practically indispensible for anyone within the Chinese segment. Putonghua is also the only form of Chinese that has a good chance of—limited—spread beyond the boundaries of Chinese ethnicity, as an international and commercial language.

PTH is an essential element in the discourse of unified, global Chineseness that is part of PRC nationalist ideology. Despite the fact that the language is developing, it is touted as the medium of Chinese identity (Li 2004). PTH and all other incarnations of standard Mandarin before it were considered superior to the dialects, and the idea was that Chinese modernity would cause the extinction of dialect variation; even so, the PRC recognises the use of the southern dialects (Cantonese, Min, Kejia) as a means of reaching out to the Chinese world outside the PRC (Erbaugh 1995). The notion of a unified, homogenous and standardised Chinese cultural identity mediated through PTH is promoted through modern transnational media, in particular TV and the Internet.

2.3.1 Written Chinese

Written Chinese merits separate treatment because it is basically written PTH, and as such strongly supports the spread of that language. The first variety of written Chinese in Suriname was the style based on Mandarin *guānhuà* that still somewhat resembled Classical Chinese (*wényán* 文言) and which was read aloud in literary Kejia pronunciation. That particular written form was replaced before the Second World War by the more modern standard of the Republic of China, which was more thoroughly based on Mandarin. Eventually the subtly different Putonghua standard became the norm in Surinamese Chinese newspapers. The successive forms of written Chinese were all taught in the Chinese schools, from the *jiàoyùtuán* (教育團) organised by the *huìguǎn* sociocultural organisations, to the current Chinese (primary) school.

Character literacy has always been the most important prerequisite for being 'fully Chinese' in Suriname among all migrant cohorts as well as the local-born descendants of Chinese migrants. Character literacy has always been the most important prerequisite for being 'fully Chinese' in Suriname among all migrant cohorts as well as the local-born descendants of Chinese migrants. For Old Chinese, to not know characters was to be doomed to the depths of Laiap ignorance—people who look Chinese, but 'don't know anything'. Literacy for the Suriname-born generation was hardly ever more than familiarisation with Chinese characters, and so the literacy gap coincided with the immigrant generation gap and the gap between migrants and local-born.

New Chinese migrants can be safely assumed to be fully literate, most to middle school level. The problem starts with the local-born generations, or very young migrant children. Children of the Old Chinese migrant cohorts are fully integrated into the Surinamese educational system, at all levels. There are no data on how many children of New Chinese attend Surinamese schools. Although the current Chinese school now can function rather more as an expat school than its predecessors, it does not substitute for the Surinamese educational system, and not all Chinese migrant children are enrolled there.[12] The point is that Chinese literacy is very difficult for migrant children to acquire, and maintain, in Suriname. Despite the best intentions of parents, assimilation pressure in Suriname is high, and children are unlikely to become fully competent users of Chinese characters unless they are sent to a fuller Chinese-language environment somewhere else.

The basic pattern of literacy loss among Chinese migrants still holds, but there are important differences with the past, the most important being technological innovations. Chinese-language media in Suriname developed parallel to regular Surinamese media. From newspapers,[13] via radio, television,[14] mobile phones and Internet,[15] interactivity has steadily increased. There are now far more possibilities and opportunities to read and, more importantly, write Chinese.[16] And because the modern written Chinese standard is very much equivalent to the spoken standard of PTH, it is overshadowing all other Chinese varieties as the 'only Chinese'.

4   CONCLUSION

The most noticeable changes in the Chinese linguistic situation in Suriname are the result of renewed immigration. On the face of it, the situation is more varied than ever, with larger numbers of speakers of many more Chinese varieties, more Chinese-language media and the rise of Putonghua, which is replacing Kejia as the main intra-ethnic language. Less noticeable to outsiders is the steady fading of Kejia under the influence of integration and language ideologies initially from Hong Kong and now from the PRC.

Over the course of a century and a half, the Sanyi migrant cohorts have steadily assimilated into the Surinamese population. Sanyi migrants dominated the retail sector in Suriname, and as a result they came to be associated with Sranantongo, the Surinamese lingua franca. Kejia was not consistently transmitted to the Laiap generations, mixed or simply local-born. School attendance has always been high among ethnic Chinese children in Suriname, and Dutch-language education enabled social mobility, which in turn enhanced Dutch-language contact. Among the Laiap generations, Kejia became limited to the family context, and among many families with a Chinese background, Kejia has been forgotten.

The link between Kejia and Hakka identity weakened in Suriname. 'Hakka-ness' meant little in the absence of other contrasting Chinese cultural identities in Suriname, and as the only Chinese variety spoken there, Kejia was simply 'Chinese'. The low status associated with Kejia and identification as Hakka in China were masked, but not replaced, by the ambiguous meanings of Chineseness in Suriname. After the founding of the PRC, migration to Suriname passed through Hong Kong, and by the 1960s and 1970s, Sanyi migrants were urban Hongkongese. These 'Hong Kong Chinese' were increasingly Cantonese-speaking, with the shift to Cantonese in Hong Kong as an indirect result of the birth of the PRC. Transnational Chinese media of the time were Hongkongese and in the prestigious Cantonese language, which reinforced a steady shift away from Kejia in Suriname.

Renewed migration from the 1990s onwards increased the population of ethnic Chinese and broadened the Chinese cultural and linguistic variety in Suriname. But rather than providing a renewed impetus for Hakka identity, the newly contrastive presence is discouraged in the cultural and nationalistic ideology promoted by the PRC embassy in Paramaribo. Putonghua is promoted by the PRC via its embassy over all other Chinese languages as a marker of pan-Chinese identity linked to a strong Chinese State. This globalised Chineseness dovetails with the groupist notion of monolithic Chinese identity in Surinamese multiculturalism to recreate an image of Chinese in Suriname as uniformly 'Chinese-speaking' and loyal to an alien power.

The consequence of all this is the likely disappearance of Kejia in Suriname. First to go will be Laiap Kejia, doomed by the age of its speakers and its low status, lower than the already low status of 'proper' Kejia. The variety spoken by young Sanyi Hakka, so focused as they are on the modernity of Hong Kong, will also eventually disappear, elbowed out by Hongkongese Cantonese and Putonghua. Assimilation into Surinamese society will continue, whereas in a Chinese cultural context in Suriname, Putonghua will become increasingly relevant. In principle, the languages of the New Chinese migrants could follow suit; processes of assimilation are already underway, new arrivals are changing from outsiders into established, contact with Dutch is increasing and all groups are under pressure to conform to the image of global Chineseness. Glocalisation, or being caught between the pull of globalisation and the push of local reality, will determine how quickly and completely language change will play out.

REFERENCES

Băoān dìfāng zhì 寶安地方誌 (Baoan local gazetteer). 1997. Shaoguan: Guangdong People's Publishing House.

Bauer, Robert S. 1984. The Hong Kong Cantonese speech community. *Cahiers de linguistique—Asie orientale* 13 (1). 57–90.

Bauer, Robert S. 1985. The expanding syllabary of Hong Kong Cantonese. *Cahiers de linguistique—Asie orientale* 14 (1). 99–111.

Brubaker, Rogers. 2004. *Ethnicity without Groups*. Cambridge MA / London: Harvard University Press.

Bruche-Schulz, Gisela. 1997. 'Fuzzy' Chinese: the status of Cantonese in Hong Kong. *Journal of Pragmatics* 27. 295–314.

Carlin, Eithne, & Jacques Arends (eds). 2002. *Atlas of the Languages of Suriname*. Leiden: KITLV Press.

Carlin, Eithne, Isabelle Leglise, Bettina Stoll, Paul Tjon Sie Fat (eds). 2014. *In and Out of Suriname: Language, Mobility and Identity*. Brill: Leiden / Boston.

Cohen, Myron L. 1995. The Hakka or 'Guest People': Dialect as a Sociocultural Variable in South-Eastern China. In: Nicole Constable (ed.), *Guest People; Hakka Identity in China and Abroad*. Seattle: University of Washington Press. 36–79.

Dōngguǎn dìfāng zhì 東莞地方誌 (Dongguan local gazetteer). 1998. Shaoguan: Guangdong Renmin Chubanshe.

Erbaugh, Mary S. 1995. Southern Chinese dialects as a medium for reconciliation within Greater China. *Language in Society* 24. 79–94.

Hu-DeHart, Evelyn. 2010. Indispensable enemy or convenient scapegoat? A critical examination of sinophobia in Latin America and the Caribbean, 1870s to 1930s. In: Walton Look Lai & Tan Chee-Beng (eds.), *The Chinese in Latin America and the Caribbean*. Leiden / Boston: Brill. 65–102.

Keevak, Michael. 2011. *Becoming Yellow: A Short History of Racial Thinking*. Princeton & Oxford: Princeton University Press.

Lau, Chun Fat. 2005. A dialect murders another dialect: the case of Hakka in Hong Kong. *International Journal of Society and Language* 173. 23–35.

Lausent-Herrera, Isabella. 2010. Tusans (*tusheng*) and the changing Chinese community in Peru. In: Walton Look Lai & Tan Chee-Beng (eds.), *The Chinese in Latin America and the Caribbean*. Leiden / Boston: Brill. 143–183.

Lee, Sherman. 2008. *A Study of Language Choice and Language Shift among the Hakka-speaking Population in Hong Kong, with a Primary Focus on Sha Tau Kok* / 香港客家人的語言選擇和語言轉移研究以沙頭角爲主要焦點. [Ph.D Thesis], City University of Hong Kong.

Leglise, Isabelle, & Bettina Stoll. 2014. Language practices and linguistic ideologies in suriname: results from a school survey. In: Eithne Carlin, Isabelle Leglise, Bettina Migge & Paul Tjon Sie Fat (eds), *In and Out of Suriname: Language, Mobility and Identity*. Brill: Leiden / Boston. 13–57.

Li, Chris Wen-Chao. 2004. Conflicting notions of language purity: the interplay of archaising, ethnographic, reformist, elitist and xenophobic purism in the perception of standard Chinese. *Language & Communication* 24. 97–133.

Lim, Khay-Thiong & Hsin-Huang Michael Hsiao. 2007. The formation and limitation of Hakka identity in Southeast Asia. *Taiwan Journal of Southeast Asian Studies* 4 (1). 3–28.

Lim, Khay-Thiong & Hsin-Huang Michael Hsiao. 2009. Is there a transnational Hakka identity?: examining Hakka youth ethnic consciousness in Malaysia. *Taiwan Journal of Southeast Asian Studies* 6 (1). 49–80.

Scholte, Jan Aart. 2005 (2000). *Globalization: A Critical Introduction*. Second revised and updated edition. Houndmills / New York: Palgrave MacMillan.

Shao, Huijun. 2001. 毛裏求斯華人社會語言概況 (The sociolinguistic situation of the Sino-Mauritians). 方言 / *Dialect* 3. 238–243.

Speckmann, J.D. 1963. De houding van de Hindostaanse bevolkingsgroep in Suriname ten opzichte van de Creolen. *Bijdragen tot de taal-, land- en volkenkunde* 119. 76–92.

Tjon Sie Fat, Paul Brendan. 2002. Kejia. A Chinese language in Suriname. In: Eithne B. Carlin, Jacques Arends (eds), *Atlas of the Languages of Suriname*, Leiden: KITLV Press. 233–248.

Tjon Sie Fat, Paul Brendan. 2009. *Chinese New Migrants in Suriname; the Inevitability of Ethnic Performing*. [Ph.D Thesis], University of Amsterdam.

Tjon Sie Fat, Paul Brendan. 2010. Old migrants, new immigration and anti-Chinese discourse in Suriname. In: Walton Look Lai & Tan Chee-Beng (eds.), *The Chinese in Latin America and the Caribbean*. Leiden / Boston: Brill. 185–209.

Tjon Sie Fat, Paul Brendan. 2012. Old and new Chinese organizations in Suriname. In: Zhang Jijiao & Howard Duncan (eds.), *Migration in China and Asia: Experience and Policy* International Perspectives on Migration, Vol. 10. Springer: Dordrecht / Heidelberg / New York / London: Springer. 189–206.

Tjon Sie Fat, Paul Brendan. 2014. They might as well be speaking Chinese. In: Eithne Carlin, Isabelle Leglise, Bettina Migge & Paul Tjon Sie Fat (eds), *In and out of Suriname: Language, Mobility and Identity*. Brill: Leiden / Boston. 196–228.

Ungsitipoonporn, Siripen. 2008. The Bangkok Hakka phonology. *Mon-Khmer Studies* 38. 158–208.

van Renselaar, H.C. 1963. De houding van de Creoolse bevolkingsgroep in Suriname ten opzichte van andere bevolkingsgroepen (in het bijzonder ten opzichte van de Hindostanen). *Bijdragen tot de taal-, land- en volkenkunde* 119. 93–105.

Wang, Lijung. 2007. Diaspora, identity and cultural citizenship: the Hakkas in 'Multicultural Taiwan'. *Ethnic and Racial Studies* 30 (5). 875–895.

Wei, Jennifer M. 2006. Language choice and ideology in Multicultural Taiwan. *Language and Linguistics* 7 (1). 87–107.

Wong, Bernard. 1978. A comparative study of the assimilation of the Chinese in New York City and Lima, Peru. *Comparative Studies in Society and History* 20 (3). 335–358.

Xie, Liuwen & Huang Xuezhen. 2007. 客家方言的分區(稿) (Classification of Kejia [draft]). 方言 / *Dialect* 3. 238–249.

Zhang, Donghui. 2010. Language maintenance and language shift among Chinese immigrant parents and their second-generation children in the U.S. *Bilingual Research Journal* 33. 42–60.

Zhang, Zhenjiang. 1999. 語言資料三篇 (three articles on linguistic material). In: 廣東族群與區域文化研究調查報告集 (Collected research in Guangdong regional and ethnic studies), Guangzhou: Guangdong Higher Education Press. 498–546.

Zhou, Bosheng & Liu Zhenfa. 1998. 香港客家話向粵語轉移的因素和趨勢 (Factors and trends in the shift from Kejia to Cantonese in Hong Kong). 方言 / *Dialect* 3. 225–232.

NOTES

1. *Resultaten 8ᵉ Volks- en Woningtelling in Suriname, Volume 1: Demografische en Sociale Karakterstieken en Migratie (Results of the 8th Population and Household Census in Suriname, Volume 1: Demographic and Social Characteristics and Migration)*, SIC 284/2013–05. Paramaribo: General Bureau of Statistics.

2. Maroons are descendants of Africans who fled the plantations and settled in the interior of Suriname, primarily in the eighteenth and nineteenth centuries, and settled themselves in tribal community structures along the larger rivers. There are currently six Maroon groups: Saamaka, Ndyuka, Pamaka, Matawai, Kwinti, Aluku.

3. Census categories are based on self-identification of interviewees. The general consensus in Suriname is that 'mixed' includes people who under other circumstances might self-identify as 'Creole'.

4. Maroon languages and their dialects: Ndyuka/Aluku/Boni/Pamaka, Kwinti (not fully classified, related to Ndyuka); Saamaka/Matawai. Amerindian languages: Arawakan: Lokono, Mawayana; Cariban: Kari'na, Wayana, Trio,

Akuriyo, Tunayana, Sikïiyana, Waiwai. Asian languages: Sinitic: varieties of Kejia, Yue, Wu, Min, Northern Chinese. Numbers of speakers are unknown. Some languages, such as Mawayana, are reduced to a handful of speakers, whereas others, such as Surinamese Dutch, are spoken to some degree by the majority of the population.

5. *Sanyi* 三邑, 'the three districts', is one term for what Surinamese Hakka refer to as the *fuidung'on* area in the eastern part of the Pearl River Delta in Guangdong Province: Dongguan, Bao'an, Huiyang.

6. Hakka identity and language are too easily assumed to be interchangeable. In order to distinguish between language labels and ethnonyms, we will use *Hakka* (based on the Cantonese reading of the characters of the label) for the ethnic group, and *Kejia* (based on the Mandarin reading of the characters) to refer to the language.

7. For Sanyi Hakka children born and raised in Suriname these would be Kejia, Putonghua in later generations, Sranantongo, Dutch and English.

8. Punti is often called Cantonese, but it refers to the language of the locals. In the case of the Sanyi Hakka migrants, *punti* language meant the Yue dialect of Dongguan (東莞話): Yue > Guangfu > Dongguan.

9. 15.9% regarded Chinese positively. Unfamiliarity with Chinese, probably due to lack of contact, was reflected in the large number of Creole respondents who had no opinion (45%).

10. 16% regarded Chinese negatively, whereas 24% had no opinion. Given that 60% of interviewees had a positive view of the Dutch, one might wonder to what extent the Dutch researcher unwittingly biased the responses.

11. On the morning of 8 August 2012, I heard a radio talk show host, Wayne Telgt, end the daily current affairs talk show on Radio ABC with a rant containing the main anti-Chinese tropes: Chinese immigration is an invasion, there are too many Chinese businesses in Suriname, Chinese immigration was a conscious policy of previous governments to manipulate the balance of ethnic constituencies, 'real Surinamese' will soon have to learn 'the language of the Chinese' in school, etc.

12. In 2012 the Chinese School (中文學校) in Paramaribo had a pre-school group (70 children) and six primary school levels, following the primary school curriculum of the People's Republic of China (258 students). There were evening classes for non-Chinese speaking students ('Surinamese and mixed Chinese'), the total of which had shrunk to 15 students.

13. The Kong Ngie Tong Sang sociocultural association publishes the *Xunnan Ribao* (洵南日報, 'Suriname Daily'), and the Chung Fa Foei Kon sociocultural association publishes the *Zhonghua Ribao* (中華日報, 'China Daily'). In practice, however, both combine as a single Chinese-language daily paper, with an edition of about one thousand copies. There are no real subscriptions. The embassy of the People's Republic of China donated hardware to modernise production, but also censors content. Both newspapers now also have a website: http://www.chungfadaily.com for *Zhonghua Ribao*, and www.kntsdagblad.com for *Xunnan Ribao*.

14. *Surinaamse* [sic] *Chinese Televisie Station* / 廣義堂蘇里南電視臺 (channel 45).

15. There are no data on New Media use among Chinese speakers in Suriname, but there is no question that access is widespread.

16. For Chinese migrant children, literacy generally meant reading newspapers, letter-writing, writing simple notes, taking orders in restaurants. Their parents would also keep shop accounts in Chinese, read novels and a few individuals would also compose poetry. The basic literacy skills that the *huiguan*-run Chinese schools in Suriname historically provided would generally fade with lack of practice. Exactly how e-mail, social media and text messages influence character literacy would be interesting to know.

8 Multilingualism and the West Kalimantan Hakka

Josh Stenberg

THE MULTIPLICITY AND MULTILINGUALISM OF BEING SINO-INDONESIAN

There has been a considerable amount of work surrounding Chinese Indonesian sociolinguistics. All Chinese Indonesian communities are multilingual, and their patterns of use may involve several Indonesian languages (e.g., standard Indonesian, Javanese, Sundanese, Betawi, Balinese, etc.), several Chinese languages (e.g., Hokkien, Hakka, Mandarin, Teochow, Cantonese, etc.), and Western languages (increasingly English as a foreign language, but historically also Dutch and occasionally French). Which specific languages are in play, in what proportion, and in what context they are used varies heavily over time and from region to region, and is also affected by social class and level of education.

In academic literature, not all communities have been given equal weight, and sometimes regional situations are erroneously presented as reflecting the situation of the nationwide population. As a consequence of demographics and economic dynamics, there is a heavy and understandable focus, in sociolinguistics as elsewhere, on the Sino-Indonesian communities of Java, and to a lesser extent Sumatra.[1] The linguistic landscape of the substantial Chinese community of Kalimantan, like their history, is less widely known, and cannot easily be integrated into the national narrative. Given both the size of the Chinese population and the diversity of Indonesia, it is in fact rarely appropriate to think of Sino-Indonesians as a monolithic or even coherent entity, although in practice it is often necessary to speak in those terms.

This chapter, which is based on interviews conducted in West Kalimantan in January–February 2013, news materials, existing secondary scholarship and ongoing correspondence with informants in Singkawang and Bengkayang, seeks to provide an overview of the linguistic habits of the Chinese of the province of West Kalimantan (Kalimantan Barat), with a focus on Singkawang.

THE CHINESE OF WEST KALIMANTAN TODAY

Since the late eighteenth century, there has been a Chinese community in the area now known as West Kalimantan (Kalimantan Barat; colloquially often Kalbar), the triangular province which forms the western coast of Borneo, between Tanjung Sambar in the south, up to the border with Sarawak at Tanjung Datu and stretching deep inland where the Schwaner and Müller Mountains form the border with Central and East Kalimantan. The equator runs through the province just north of the capital Pontianak. The fourth largest of Indonesia's thirty-four provinces, West Kalimantan represents over 7% of Indonesia's area, but at 4.4 million, its population is under 2% of the national total.

It is also among the provinces with the highest proportion of ethnic Chinese Indonesians. According to the 2000 census, it was second in proportion of total (9.62%) after Bangka Belitung; and in absolute numbers second only to Jakarta (359,202 people, forming almost 15% of the national figure for ethnic Chinese).[2] Chinese populations are found throughout West Kalimantan, although they are concentrated in the two urban areas of Singkawang and Pontianak. What little political success there has been for Indonesian Chinese political parties in recent years has also largely been in West Kalimantan.[3]

The coastal city of Singkawang is the second-largest city and probably the Indonesian urban area with the highest proportion of Chinese. In Singkawang, 2007 government data for both religion and ethnicity gives a Chinese population of 79,421 (53.75%) and a Buddhist population of 78,668 (42.53%), although these numbers are problematic, not least because the ethnic table results give a total population over 37,000 smaller than the religious table.[4] One frequently cited proportion for Chinese population in the city is 42%,[5] although former mayor Hasan Karman told researcher Margaret Chan that he believed it to be 60%,[6] whereas some publications claim up to 70%.[7] In any event, it seems certain that Singkawang Chinese form the plurality, especially in urban areas. Originating as a Hakka town, its name can be approximated as meaning 'where the mountains meet the sea' (Mandarin *pinyin*: Shankouyang).

In most parts of Indonesia today, ethnic Chinese mostly do not speak a Chinese language. In the areas where whole communities still do, especially in Sumatra, the Chinese language they speak is Hokkien. Most West Kalimantan Chinese, however, speak Hakka or Teochew. Hakka are the second-largest Chinese subethnic group in Indonesia, with one scholar estimating the number of Hakka in Indonesia at 1.2 million, among 6 million Chinese,[8] with historic communities outside of Kalimantan especially descending from the tin mines of Bangka and Belitung.

Singkawang Hakka people are known to *pribumi* (i.e., "authochtonous", non-Chinese) Indonesians in Kalimantan Barat generally as *orang khek* (being the Hokkien pronunciation of the character *ke*).[9] Hakka in West

Kalimantan varies substantially from varieties spoken in Mainland China, Taiwan, and elsewhere in Southeast Asia. Within the Hakka of West Kalimantan, there are also considerable regional differences, enough so that mutual comprehension is not perfect. These distinctions were noticed already by Dutch administrators and linguists, and reflect the movement of Hakkas from various parts of eastern Guangdong to various parts of West Kalimantan.[10] Hakka from areas such as Hepo in Jieyang, or from Lufeng, Haifeng, Fengshun and Huilai were largely bilingual in Teochew and Hakka, whereas those from Meixian spoke a more "pure" or "soft" variety of Hakka. Today, the former dialect is associated with Singkawang, and the latter with the section south of the Duri River and on towards the northern sections of Pontianak, across the Kapuas River. South of the Kapuas River, in central Pontianak, Teochew is largely spoken, although many speak Hakka as well.[11]

The use of Hakka as the predominant Chinese language, and a co-dominant language overall, in Singkawang marks the area as highly unusual in Southeast Asia. Hakka use has sometimes been inhibited in Southeast Asia, vis-à-vis, for instance, Hokkien, even where Hakka populations have been large. Hakka populations were in many places poorer and more rural than Hokkien or Cantonese,[12] allowing the latter languages to develop as the intra-Chinese lingua franca. In Singkawang and environs, however, Hakka predominates even when individuals are of other Chinese origins.

One anthropologist found that "when two Chinese speak Indonesian with each other, it signifies distance and formality,"[13] and only the youngest Singkawang Hakka are at all likely to speak Indonesian with each other. Older speakers (above sixty or seventy) often have limited ability to speak Malay or Indonesian, and those in their forties and fifties sometimes retain a pronounced accent. Younger speakers have a native command of Indonesian, and are likely to use Indonesian with non-West Kalimantan Chinese. Younger respondents reported that they would do so also with Teochew-speaking Pontianak Chinese, whereas elders said they would use a mix of Hakka and Teochew to communicate. Naturally, communication with Java Chinese occurs also in Indonesian. Most Singkawang Hakka have limited means of communication with non-Hakka Chinese from outside the Malayic-speaking world, although knowledge of Mandarin is growing.

CHINESE COMMUNITIES AND HISTORIC MULTILINGUALISM IN WEST KALIMANTAN

West Borneo in the eighteenth century was deeply marked by the arrival of Hakka gold miners. The *kongsi* system of mining communities, which were substantially independent of nominal Dutch control, elected their own leaders and exerted substantial control over Malay and Dayak subjects.[14]

American missionaries, visiting from China in 1838, noted that at Mandor and its surroundings, the population "called themselves Canton men, but speak the Kheh [Hakka] dialect."[15] Having visited in 1834, the English traveller and administrator George Windsor Earl wrote of Singkawang that the male population of the town was entirely Chinese, with only one resident Malay man; many Chinese were married to Dayak women, who "as wives and mothers" were highly spoken of for "their exemplary conduct."[16] Thus, the early Hakka population can be presumed to be the descendants of the subjects of the eighteenth century *kongsi*, many of whom, especially in the early stages of their history, had married local women, largely Dayaks. Because of the density, high proportion and relative autonomy of the Chinese population, this did not result in the same degree of acculturation as observed in Java.

At this early stage, Earl also remarked upon the ability of some Dayaks to speak Chinese:

> The Dyaks, even those who reside constantly with the Chinese settlers, can never attain the pronunciation, or even a correct knowledge of the idiom of the language spoken by the latter, a circumstance which does not arise from any deficiency of intellect or application in the Dyaks, since they acquire a perfect knowledge of the Malay and Bugis tongues with the greatest facility.[17]

Although Earl is pointing out what he perceives as flaws in Dayak ability to speak Hakka (although one might question his ability to judge the question, speaking no Chinese himself), the deprecation of accent or lexical ability suggests that a high working knowledge of Hakka was common among Dayaks. One hundred and eighty years later, an (Indonesian-language) written response I elicited from a Singkawang Hakka to a question on non-Chinese competence in Hakka reads, "Malay/Dayak people who live near Hakka people are sure to speak Khek [i.e., Hakka], and even if it is less than fluent they will understand 100% the meaning of spoken Hakka."[18] Various recent studies attest to the same phenomenon.[19] It seems probable that a high level of competence of Hakka among non-Chinese inhabitants has been common for the better part of two centuries.

Earl also encounters a Chinese man travelling with two Dayaks, who translated Earl's Malay into a Dayak language.[20] In another place, Earl, describing (presumably) Hakka as "certainly more barbarous in its pronunciation than any I have ever heard spoken by the people of China," finds that "one of my interpreters, a native of the east coast of that empire, had acquired a perfect knowledge of it,"[21] probably indicating that a Hokkien had learned Hakka to communicate with the Chinese of West Borneo. W. L. Ritter, a colonial official in Sambas between 1826–34, describes a Dayak who flees from his people and gets a job because he can speak Chinese,[22] whereas the language of the Salako people, a Dayak group, has extensive loanwords from Hakka in their lexicon, pointing to a long historical interaction.[23]

Taken as a whole, Earl's evidence includes Dayaks who speak Hakka; Hakka who speak Malay and Dayak languages; and Hokkiens who have learned Hakka. By the second half of the nineteenth century, the learning of language was reciprocal: interior traders learned Dayak languages, and Dayaks learned Hakka. Malay was the lingua franca for interactions between Malays, local-born Chinese, Dayaks, and Dutch officials. Overall, the picture is of a highly polyglot Chinese community within a highly polyglot territory.[24]

There is also evidence, however, that many Chinese—especially those living in *kongsi*—spoke no non-Chinese language. Invited by the Chinese "governor" to visit, Earl had to wait for the arrival of his interpreters because no one present could understand Malay. Likewise, Pieter Adriani, who visited the "Chinese districts of the West-*afdeeling* (province) of Borneo" between 1879 and 1882, reported finding, on a visit to Montrado, that "the Chinese we encountered here as well as en route understood not a word of Malay, so that we had to use gestures to communicate. One might fancy one had been displaced into the Heavenly Kingdom; everything here was Chinese: the houses of the inhabitants, the language, the inscriptions, the signs, people's clothing, in a word, the whole environment was a faithful picture of Southern China."[25] Over the three years in the area, Adriani abandoned an attempt to learn Chinese, and used Malay with Chinese "most of whom were able to speak it" as well as in conversation with Javanese and Malays.[26] Until the mid-nineteenth century, colonial authorities struggled to place people into their appropriate ethnic groups, suggesting fluidity in terms of cultural practice, linguistic among others.[27]

The multilingualism of the area seems to have continued unabated throughout the colonial period. The Dutch census in 1930 for West Kalimantan gave the Hakka-speaking proportion of the Chinese population at 57.4%, Teochew at 32.5%, and Cantonese (4.4%), Hokkien (3.8%) and others (1.9%) as small minorities of the total population of 66,800.[28] In some areas, Hakkas continued to mix, especially with Dayaks, and raised the children as Chinese, speaking Hakka[29] as well as Dayak languages and doubtless often Malay. Although theatre scholar Matthew Isaac Cohen writes that in 1920, "more than 99% of the west coast's Chinese spoke a Chinese language rather than Malay; Hakka effectively functioned as interethnic lingua franca," there seems little doubt that even if Chinese schools and institutions remained the "defining elements in Pontianak's civic life,"[30] it would have been usual if not universal for Chinese to speak Malay as well, and *bangsawan* and Malay operas were being performed alongside forms of *xiqu*. Nor should the presence of Dutch or English in the pre-Independence patchwork of languages be overlooked: a survey of Catholic schools in Borneo in 1939 reveals seven Dutch-Chinese schools, one English-Chinese school, and nine Chinese-language primary schools. There was one station, however, in Nyarumkop, where Dayaks and Chinese were educated together in Malay. The Catholic mass was sometimes celebrated in Hakka.[31]

Whereas the ability to speak European languages increased, Chinese language diversity was probably decreasing in the late colonial period and after independence. An article in a 2008 edition of a Singkawang bilingual (Chinese-Indonesian) magazine suggested that the descendants of Singkawang Chinese came in fact from many parts of southern China, but that Hakka—having formed the early mining population—had become the dominant commercial language in the city of Singkawang. At home, people had continued to speak Teochew, Hokkien and other languages, although after 1949 few or no immigrants could arrive. The influx of Hakka to the city of Singkawang from the hinterland due to the 1967 anti-Chinese violence resulted in a concentration of Hakka-speakers in Singkawang and a consolidation of Hakka as the lone Chinese language.[32]

The suppressions of Orde Baru, which elsewhere in Indonesia created generations of Chinese Indonesians who spoke no Chinese language, do not seem to have basically impacted the ability of Singkawang Chinese to speak Hakka, although they ensured universal knowledge of Indonesian and decimated knowledge of Mandarin by cutting off Chinese-language education and causing the departure of many of the most committed educators and Chinese ethnic nationalists.

An American missionary writes that when he was in West Kalimantan in 1974, urban Singkawang was almost entirely Hakka-speaking, and that older Chinese had difficulty expressing themselves in Indonesian unless they had a store.[33] Those who were then in their thirties (i.e., born in the 1930s and 1940s) could speak Indonesian, although generally used Hakka except when in government offices, and would bring a translator with them if necessary to conduct affairs at the government offices. In 1984, French Indonesianist Denys Lombard wrote of "general use" of Indonesian among young Chinese in West Kalimantan, and relatively high levels of schooling.[34]

Today, one finds that only older, more rural and poorer populations have difficulty with Indonesian. An additional feature of multilingualism is that persons of education (of whatever ethnicity) switch registers between a local variety of Malay and the more formal standard Indonesian.[35] In conversation, Singkawang Hakka refer to the local language as "Malay" rather than "Indonesian," which may however also indicate the tendency to use ethnic labels for linguistic practice. One Hakka respondent described the local variety as closer to Malay than Indonesian, giving the example of the final /a/ in Indonesian often being pronounced instead with the *schwa* found in Malay (*berapa* pronounced as *berape*). It seems there is little research on the Malay of the region, and that its features are not well understood.[36] Further affecting the linguistic map of the region are the many Javanese, Sundanese, and Madurese migrants who, besides speaking their own languages, likely will by their presence promote the more frequent use of standard Indonesian as a means of interethnic communication.

The multilingualism and indeed the mixed heritage of the community in West Kalimantan should not be taken to mean that all Chinese consider themselves Indonesians. Heidhues writes of the colonial period that "most Chinese continued to feel they were a group apart, children of a distant homeland,"[37] and Hui found that there continue to be conflicting loyalties in the community. My own field research suggested unsurprisingly that older Singkawang Hakka were more committed to a singular Chinese identity, whereas younger persons were more likely to express pride in being from Singkawang as reflecting both an ethnic Chinese identity and a pragmatic and sometimes patriotic attitude towards Indonesia.

HAKKA MULTILINGUALS IN CONTEMPORARY SINGKAWANG

Multilingualism finds expression in Singkawang daily life in numerous ways. There is substantial mixing of languages, particularly among the young. When using Hakka, people are liable to insert Indonesian words, because the younger generation was entirely educated in that language. Those spending time in Jakarta increasingly use Indonesian and Betawi words in their Hakka usage. During the festival season, Chinese New Year *duilian* (couplets) rub shoulders on Spring Festival dioramas with slogans in Indonesian, such as "We are all brothers," and political parties, churches and community organisations set out flyers wishing all a happy Imlek (Spring Festival) and Cap Go Meh (Lantern Festival).

Because most Singkawang Hakka cannot read or write Chinese, they SMS and Facebook in a mixture of phonetic representations of Hakka (according to Indonesian phonetic rules) interspersed with Indonesian and English vocabulary. A common nickname of Singkawang, "Kota Amoy," combines the Indonesian word for city with the Hakka word for "younger sister," referring among other things to the frequency with which local Hakka become brides for Taiwanese men. This population movement, which in many cases constitutes human smuggling, is also one of the themes of the most prominent writer from Singkawang, the novelist poet and dramatist Hanna Fransisca. Resident in Jakarta, she intersperses her Indonesian prose with Hakka terms in works such as the short stories *Sulaiman Pergi ke Tanjung Cina* (Sulaiman Goes to Cape China) and the drama *Kawan Tidur* (The Friend Is Sleeping).

Multilingualism must also be navigated in terms of Singkawang popular culture, which features a small local film and music scene. The movies largely feature sentimental plots, mixed with aspects of local Hakka culture, frequently involving the supernatural. They are acted in Hakka and subtitled in Indonesian and sometimes traditional Chinese characters. They are preceded by advertisements for local businesses, which deal with the language issue in the same manner. One director I interviewed told me that his hope was to sell his work also to Hakka communities elsewhere in Indonesia. The movies, however, feature Mandarin pop songs in their soundtracks. One of the movies also features a *pribumi* character who speaks Hakka. The YouTube video comments display good examples of the written forms of Singkawang's mixed Hakka and Malay forms of expression: e.g., "Gokil n lucu, an ho siaaauuu" (Crazy and funny, very funny").[38] YouTube also hosts dubbings of sections of Stephen Chow movies in Singkawang Hakka, a few of which have racked up over 50,000 views.

Some of the most interesting contemporary expressions of multilingualism appear in Singkawang's tourism industry, such as the Lantern Festival, known in Indonesia as the Cap Go Meh festival, a term derived, like other festivals, from the Hokkien and Teochew (although not the Hakka) word for what in China is known as Yuanxiaojie. The Lantern Festival is popular and important throughout Southern China and the diaspora, but in Singkawang it has a crucial ritual position while also forming the centrepiece of the local government's attempts to make Kalimantan Barat a tourist destination primarily for Chinese, including those from Java, Singapore, Hong Kong, Malaysia, Taiwan, and the Mainland.

Between the Spring Festival (known in Indonesia as Imlek, derived from the Hokkien term for the lunisolar calendar *yinli*) and Cap Go Meh, the organising committee of the Cap Go Meh festival presents performances on the pitch of the local football stadium. Hawkers are set up on the outskirts, selling food and beer, and T-shirts and caps inscribed "Kota Amoy," "United States of Amoy" or "I ♥ SKW." In 2013, I attended several of the shows in the stadium, which attracted a varied audience of Singkawangers, Chinese and non-Chinese, as well as a substantial proportion of tourists from the region and beyond. The majority of the emceeing was in Hakka, with an increasing admixture of Indonesian as the day of Cap Go Meh approached and tourist numbers swelled. Mandarin pop singers performed, some of them local and others brought in from Malaysia. On one occasion, school girls in jilbabs, knee-length dresses and black stockings were singing and dancing *I Love You Baby*, followed by another group performing a dangdut routine in full traditional Malay dress. Frequently the banter between emcees moved easily between Hakka and Indonesian, with the apparent presumption that both were understood. In another number, girls from a local Chinese school performed a dance of ethnic harmony, dressed up in Chinese, Malay and Dayak costumes. Despite the admixture of Indonesian, English and Mandarin, the dominant language was Hakka, a remarkable fact given that the event was part of sanctioned municipal celebrations, that a substantial portion of the audience was non-Chinese and that Hakka has no official status in Singkawang, or indeed anywhere. However, it also deserves mention that some Malay leaders and nationalist elements have decried the official sanctioning of Singkawang's culture as likely to create "another Singapore." It is also true that the concept of an Indonesian city promoting itself as an expression of Chinese culture remains fraught with tension that plays out at the level of municipal politics, education, religion and intercultural social interaction.

However usual multilingualism may get, its practice is far from universal. An example of entrenched monolingualism in Singkawang is the case of the Hakka marionettes known as *wayang gantung* in Indonesian, *chiao thieu* in Hakka and *qiaotouxi* in Mandarin. Unlike the Sino-Javanese puppet form *wayang potehi*, which descends from Minnan forms and is now performed in Central and East Java by ethnic Javanese *dalangs*, *wayang gantung* is now all but extinct, not least because the genre is difficult to assimilate into the general discourse on *wayang*. The only living master, 71-year-old Chin Nen Sin, had been inactive for two years when I visited in 2013, and he regards it as unlikely that anyone will pick up the art. It is performed only in Hakka—Mr. Chin and many others of his generation do not speak Indonesian or Mandarin well—and has made no obvious adjustment or acculturation to local conditions. Although the local government does feature it on their website and did devote a publication to it, it is not surprising that there is limited official enthusiasm for a type of performance that has not adapted much to accommodate the state or non-Chinese ethnicities.

Unlike post-1998 Java or Sumatra, there were for many years few opportunities in West Kalimantan to learn Mandarin. Although there are a few people in the older generation who learned Mandarin from the pre-Orde Baru *huaxiao* (Chinese schools), even the majority of the generation that was of school age in that period did not have the financial means to attend *huaxiao*, and many had little or no schooling at all. For the same reason, very few Chinese in Singkawang are literate in Chinese. Although the Chinese identity of Singkawang is always visible, the actual knowledge of characters is generally weak, being restricted to those who both have Chinese schooling and are over the age of fifty-five or sixtyt. Singkawang Hakkas are thus generally in the position of being unable to read their mother tongue, although all but the elderly are fully literate in their language of education, Indonesian.

A MULTILINGUAL VIGNETTE

Writing in a Mainland *huaqiao* publication in 1999 to commemorate the fiftieth anniversary of the establishment of the People's Republic of China, the Singkawang Chinese author Huang Zhenling, who left in 1963, recounts a story about Singkawang in that era which turns on linguistic issues.[39] In 1949, students (including Huang) and teachers of Nan Hwa Middle School are sitting in a café, listening to the "repeated victories of China's People Liberation Army" on a radio, rare at the time. At hearing Mao's words on October 1, everyone weeps with excitement at the foundation of the PRC. In West Kalimantan, "Chinese (Hakka, Teochew) had become the tool of human communication, in Singkawang and elsewhere, people spoke Hakka—even Indonesians, local [colonial] officials and missionaries were competent [*tongxiao*] in it."

The body of the story concerns the dispute of the right of Nan Hwa to raise the new PRC flag alongside the Indonesian flag on December 27, 1949, after Indonesian authorities had acknowledged the right of foreign nationals to hoist their own flag as well as the Indonesian flag to celebrate the foundation of the nation. A Chinese policeman with KMT sympathies appears, demanding that the flag be taken down. After a prolonged dispute, the headmaster cedes, which causes unrest among the student population. The policeman strikes a student with the butt of his gun. The headmaster pushes the policeman's gun away and forbids him to strike the student with it. The policeman tells other (non-Chinese) policemen, in Indonesian, that an attempt is being made to steal the gun. They open fire, and all flee.

The headmaster is arraigned on charges of inciting the students to take the gun. Even though the independence of Indonesia has been recognised, the judge is still Dutch, and an interpreter is present to render testimony and judgment. A non-Chinese policeman testifies that the headmaster incited the students. The headmaster asks the policeman if he understands Chinese; he answers that he does not. It is thus proven that he could not have understood the headmaster's words, and because he cannot have known the purport of the headmasters' words, he is thus bearing false testimony. The case is dismissed.

Thus, for an event in 1949, four languages appear: Hakka is the language in which the Chinese are speaking among themselves, Mandarin is the patriotic national language in which the radio is broadcasting, Dutch is the residual judicial language and Indonesian is used as the lingua franca. The Chinese policeman uses the incomprehension of his colleagues to act upon an internal Chinese political issue; the Dutch judge examines the linguistic capacity of the witness to rule on the case. The anecdote, besides providing a snapshot of the extensive multilingualism of Singkawang at the moment of the establishment of both Indonesia as an independent country and of China as a People's Republic, also demonstrates how the multilingualism of a community may nevertheless be composed of many barriers. The limits of multilingualism are at the heart of both the dispute and its resolution by a judge who is himself linguistically removed from the proceedings. The history of publication of the story—written in Chinese about a community which, although Chinese-speaking, largely cannot read Chinese, and with an implicit Mainland audience—is a reminder that there is another Singkawang multilingualism: the many "returnees" to Mainland China and Hong Kong since the 1960s, who continue to speak Indonesian languages as well as Singkawang Hakka while residing in the "Homeland."

Singkawang Chinese are thus in fact a multilingual diasporic community twice or three times over: once through the historical processes which created a Hakka-speaking community in Borneo in the eighteenth century, and the second time through the emigration of Singkawangers, first to China in the 1950s and 1960s, and in the last fifty years as brides and factory workers to Taiwan, as well as small traders to Jakarta and elsewhere on

Java, Malaysia, Singapore and the Western world. Among my respondents in Singkawang were many who were returning for the Lantern Festival, and they included people who had learned Mandarin and Taiwanese for use in Taiwan (the largest group), Singapore or Malaysia. Others in Jakarta spoke Singkawang Hakka to their children, who responded in Betawi; one woman's daughter had married a Pontianak Teochew, and thus had to speak to her grandchildren in Indonesian. Another woman, having worked at a Chinese restaurant in London with Northeastern Chinese colleagues for a year, had learned Mandarin but no English.

We can add to this the unusual circumstance in Singkawang for non-Chinese persons to have competency in Chinese outside the borders of China and without formal education, although there are similar anecdotal reports also from North Sumatra and Riau. It is thus relevant to conceive of the Chinese communities of Singkawang as much of a *source* of diasporic multilingualism as an expression thereof. In their extension of knowledge of Hakka beyond self-identified ethnic borders, Singkawang can also raise the question of ethnic borders of diaspora from an uncommon perspective. Whereas "Chineseness" often comes under scrutiny wherever identified ethnic Chinese communities lose linguistic and cultural markers, it is seldom challenged through the acquisition of Chinese characteristics (such as knowledge of Hakka) from communities that are not identified and do not self-identify as Chinese.

DECLINE OF DIASPORIC NON-MANDARIN CHINESE LANGUAGES

Whereas proponents of linguistic diversity and multilingualism can regard present-day West Kalimantan, as indeed all of Indonesia, as a cause for celebration, the future of Hakka and Teochew as important local languages is in doubt. Only the relative remoteness and great density of the Chinese population in West Kalimantan communities has retained the use of Hakka and Teochew as the dominant lingua franca. In the coming years, as West Kalimantan continues to develop, the Chinese individuals will be even more closely linked into Chinese and Indonesian identity networks.

Javanese, Sundanese and Balinese Chinese underwent processes of acculturation and intermarriage which reduced knowledge of Chinese, while at the same time re-Sinicisation movements in the late nineteenth century privileged Mandarin as a way of uniting the Chinese community and relating to the "motherland." West Kalimantan Chinese, although multilingual, were a sufficiently dense and conservative population to retain overwhelming use of Hakka and Teochew until the present day. Likewise, pan-Chinese educational and institutional initiatives—which produced in Java a class and generation (by no means a majority, but substantial) of fluent Mandarin speakers (often with continuing knowledge of Hokkien or Hakka, as well as native knowledge of Indonesian and

Javanese or Sundanese)—had a much lesser effect on West Kalimantan Chinese communities. Finally, the Orde Baru pressures, which in Java so effectively suppressed learning of any Chinese language in the generations born in the 1960s, 1970s and 1980s, had more limited linguistic effect on the densely Chinese communities of West Kalimantan (as well as in Hokkien areas of Sumatra). The effects of the post-1998 Mandarin revival, currently in progress, which make Chinese accessible to some among the (generally more educated) young Javanese Chinese—have also had much lesser effects in West Kalimantan. Thus, all the changes and movements that occurred in Java have been felt in West Kalimantan, but their influence was unable to disrupt the general pattern of near-universal Hakka and Teochew transmission.

But in an era of increasing wealth in West Kalimantan, in tandem with the increasing technology for broader communication, this apartness is unlikely to last. The two tendencies—towards closer integration into the Indonesian national identity, and closer integration into the pan-Chinese diasporic imaginary—will ensure that use of Hakka and Teochew will diminish in West Kalimantan, just as the vibrant Hokkien-speaking communities of North Sumatra are likely also to move incrementally towards the standard national languages of Indonesian and Mandarin.

These patterns are part of a slow international decline of non-Mandarin varieties of Chinese and of course of small languages in general, a feature of globalisation that is unlikely to change. The Chinese diaspora community, although often multilingual in terms of ability in Chinese/non-Chinese languages, is becoming increasingly consolidated around Mandarin in terms of Chinese languages. Whereas this attrition plays out unevenly, its effects are felt everywhere, and even places where non-Mandarin dialects are very strong (such as West Kalimantan or North Sumatra) are tending increasingly to Mandarin/non-Mandarin bilingualism.

Whereas there remain regions, especially in Southeast Asia, where Hakka, Hokkien, Cantonese or Teochew dialects remain dominant, at a national and international level, this is becoming increasingly rare. At the same time, even in highly distinctive language areas in China such as Wenzhou, Quanzhou or Nantong, residents report that generations now growing up prefer Mandarin, or have tendencies to speak their dialect in forms that are phonetically and lexically Mandarinised. The tendency of non-Mandarin languages to weaken in the Mainland feeds back into the weakness in diaspora, as new migrants leaving today from Wenzhou, Guangdong or Fujian are more likely to speak Mandarin as well as their local dialect. Children born outside of China—if they speak a Chinese language—are then more likely to learn only Mandarin. New members of long-established diasporic communities will have little reason to perpetuate an ethnic or linguistic identity of increasingly minor global relevance. Kalimantan Hakkas are at an early stage in the process, which in the industrialised world is also decreasing the varieties of French, German or Japanese.

The economic and political rise of Mainland China is another major factor. In an era where Mainland China was politically and economically isolated, there was less of an incentive to foster Mandarin in diasporic communities. Now in North American communities, for example, language education in Cantonese, once usual, is growing less common. At present, the power and opportunities of Mainland China produce a strong preference in favour of Mandarin at both the community and post-secondary levels. According to local Singkawang respondents, all better local schools now offer Mandarin courses, whether state or private. There are also Mandarin courses, some of them free, on offer in Singkawang. One respondent reported that children born after 2000 were showing considerable proficiency in Mandarin.

I personally observed also that, with Hakka being spoken at home, the availability of television programming—often CCTV—in Mandarin, was aiding the younger generation in gaining comprehension of the language. One respondent called them the "luckiest generation;" whereas their parents were prevented from learning Mandarin in schools, younger people were fortunate to "learn Mandarin with government support." By 2011, there were fourteen Mandarin language schools and two trilingual (English-Mandarin-Indonesian) day schools in Singkawang, and the 2011 Singkawang Association of Mandarin Teachers reported 120 members, many of them young Singkawang Hakka speakers sent for teacher training to Mainland China, mostly Guangdong.[40] Although it seems doubtful that there is state financial support for Chinese-learning activities in Kalimantan Barat, the commitment of the local government to a tourism-based economy entails at least tacit support for increasing Mandarin proficiency.

Thus, Mandarin—drawing on the existing fluency of the community in Hakka—looks likely to gain substantial ground as Kalimantan Barat is integrated more and more in international Chinese channels of communication. As education continues to improve, English will become a more substantial foreign-language presence. And, with the continual exposure to Indonesian media, the local variety of Malay may gain more features of colloquial standard Indonesian. The generation of West Kalimantan Chinese who are now young may in fact be even more multilingual, as their Mandarin and English improves, while they retain local Malay, Indonesian and Hakka. Thereafter, however, the prospects are likely to follow general global, and Indonesian, trends of decreased linguistic diversity.

CONCLUSIONS

Communities such as those of Kalimantan Barat are reminders of what earlier Chinese communities in Maritime Southeast Asia might have been like, where there is both a great variety of Chinese languages spoken by their respective communities of origin, and a variety of archipelagic languages being spoken throughout a region. The relative isolation of Kalimantan

Barat has prevented the influence of Indonesian, Mandarin or English from being as profoundly felt as elsewhere. As Singkawang and the rest of Kalimantan Barat are increasingly integrated into larger economies and medias, linguistic change will be one way of measuring how larger imagined communities (Chinese and Indonesian) gain power over local identities. The progress of the standard languages of Indonesian and Mandarin, alongside ideas of the "modern" or the "international" associated with English will, as everywhere, chart the phasing out of local particularities.

Mary Somers Heidhues' historical work of West Kalimantan traces the province's development, producing a picture which shows the Chinese as being absolutely formative for the local culture. Singaporean anthropologist Hui Yew-Foong's work *Strangers at Home* explores the dichotomy of West Kalimantan Chinese as being *from* West Kalimantan but always estranged from it. This chapter has tried to indicate (on a far more modest scale) how the same essential problematic can be approached from the field of sociolinguistics.

Linguistically, as well as culturally, historically, religiously, politically and economically, the Chinese of West Kalimantan do not comfortably fit notions of the Indonesian Chinese. Ien Ang has written that it "is by recognizing the irreducible productivity of the syncretic practices of diaspora that 'not speaking Chinese' will stop being a problem for overseas Chinese people,"[41] but the West Kalimantan Chinese demonstrate that the reverse need not be true either: that is to say, continuing to speak Chinese does not guarantee non-syncretism, nor does it necessarily link a community closely to a central concept of cultural or political China. Indeed, it is in some way the modest pace and the lateness of change in this region which ensures great difference, linguistic and otherwise, from the incredibly rapid alterations in Mainland China.

Although continuing to speak Hakka and Teochew, locally inflected Indonesian as well as potentially Iban or Selako, and although learning Mandarin or English, West Kalimantan Chinese are a productive, syncretic community—one may also wish to consider that they are in important ways an autochtonous one. The experience of the community, especially before the present generation, also demonstrates that multilingualism and adaptation do not necessarily produce hybrid identities: even today, the older Chinese generation identifies most closely with Hakka identities, whereas orientation towards Indonesia is found mostly among younger people, and remains relatively weak compared to other Chinese Indonesian groups. The linguistic traits associated with "Chineseness," including the linguistic pattern of speaking Hakka and not speaking Mandarin, are however a local phenomenon, because one would be hard-pressed to find elsewhere a population, including the young, that largely speaks Hakka (or in Pontianak, Teochew) but no other Chinese language.

The project of recognising the diversity of Chinese experiences, and valorising them independently rather than as orbiting satellites of a monolithic political or cultural motherland, need not define itself in terms of use or non-use of Chinese languages. Indeed, in an era where dialects are in decline in Mainland China, the predominance of Hakka and Teochew in West Kalimantan accentuates the singularity of that province in a diasporic context quite as much as it does in the Indonesian national context.

Without a doubt, studies are equally warrantable for communities elsewhere in Kalimantan, as well as in Sulawesi, Papua or Nusa Tenggara; more could be done to contextualise communities in a Southeast Asian linguistic landscape, particularly because the West Kalimantan patterns of multilingualism are as much linked to Singapore and Malaysia as they are to Sumara and Java.[42] In Indonesia, therefore, Chinese multilingualism is a highly regional affair; in fact, this article attempts to lay out just one case in the panoply of Chinese Indonesian multilingualisms, in the hope that it can help to balance narratives on the Chinese Indonesian experience which tend to privilege urban elites.

NOTES

1. For a sociolinguistic study of the Chinese community in East Java, see, for instance, Oetomo, Dede. 1987, *The Chinese of Pasuruan: Their Language and Identity*. Canberra, A.C.T., Australia: Dept. of Linguistics, Research School of Pacific Studies, Australian National University.
2. Ananta, Aris, Evi Nurvidya Arifin and Bakhtiar. 2008. "Chinese Indonesians in Indonesia and the Province of Riau Archipelago: A Demographic Analysis." In *Ethnic Chinese in Contemporary Indonesia*, edited by Leo Suryadinata, 17–47. Singapore: Chinese Heritage Centre and Institute of Southeast Asian Studies. See 25–27.
   The 2000 census counting of Chinese was problematic for numerous reasons, and it is likely that North Sumatra, for instance, undercounted its Chinese residents. Also noteworthy is that the Province of Riau had not separated into the Province of the Riau Archipelago and a province which retains the old name. According to the authors, Riau Archipelago's numbers in the census, if separated, also create a slightly larger proportion of Chinese that West Kalimantan.
3. Hoon, Chang-Yau. 2008. *Chinese Identity in Post-Suharto Indonesia: Culture, Politics and Media*. Brighton: Sussex Academic Press, 85.
4. In Wulandari, Benedikta Juliatri Widi Wulandari. 2010. *Wayang Gantung*. Departeman Kebudayaan dan Parawisata, Pontianak: Balai Pelestarian Sejarah dan Nilai Tradisional Pontianak, 30, 38. Wulandari cites a now defunct Singkawang website, but since her work is a government publication, I gather that she is using official figures.
5. Hui, Yew-Foong. *Strangers at Home: History and Subjectivity Among the Chinese Communities of West Kalimantan, Indonesia*. Leiden: Brill, 2011, 22. He cites official figures from *Profil Kota Singkawang 2005*.
6. Chan, Margaret. "The Spirit-Mediums of Singkawang: Performing "Peoplehood." In *Chinese Indonesians Reassessed: History, Religion and Belonging* edited by Siew-Min Sai and Chang-Yau Hoon, 138–158. See p. 142.
7. E.g., Syafaruddin, Usman M, and Isnawita Din. "Beli" Istri Mulai 8 Jeti: Fenomena Amoy Singkawang. Yogyakarta: Media Pressindo, 2010, 48. The same text gives the absolute number as 50,000 and the percentage of Khek (i.e., Hakka) among Chinese as 90%.

8. Wang Dong. Kejia xue daolun. Taipei: Nantian, 1998, 4.

9. The term *pribumi* is used in Indonesia for those ethnic groups who are deemed to be "sons of the land," and form all but a small minority of the population. Deriving ultimately from Dutch racial policy, the pribumi/non-pribumi distinction is problematic but less cumbersome than "non-Chinese Indonesians."

10. Somers, Heidhues M. F. 2003. *Golddiggers, Farmers, and Traders in the "chinese Districts" of West Kalimantan, Indonesia.* Ithaca, N.Y: Southeast Asia Program Publications, Southeast Asia Program, Cornell University, 36–37.

11. Hui 21–22; Huang Hui-chen. "Yinni Shankouyang Kejiahua Yanjiu."National Central University, M.A. thesis ROC 97 [2008], 8 11.

12. Thiong, L. Khay and Michael Hsiao. "Dongnanya Kejia rentong de xingcheng yu juxian." *Taiwan dongnanya xuekan.* (2007): 3–28.

13. Hui 21 n72.

14. Heidhues 16–125.

15. Doty, E. and W.J. Pohlman. "Tour in Borneo from Sambas, through Montrado to Pontianak, and the adjacent settlements of Chinese and Dayaks, during the autumn of 1838." *Chinese Repository 8 (1839)* 307.

16. Earl, George W. *The Eastern Seas: Or, Voyages and Adventures in the Indian Archipelago, in 1832-33-34, Comprising a Tour of the Island of Java—Visits to Borneo, the Malay Peninsula, Siam &c.: Also an Account of the Present State of Singapore with Observations on the Commercial Resources of the Archipelago.* London: W.H. Allen, 1837. 210; 259. Accessed at the Internet Archive https://archive.org/details/easternseas00earlgoog

17. Earl 276–77.

18. Personal communication by e-mail, November 4, 2013.

19. Heidhues 36 N69, Adelaar 9, Hui 22.

20. Earl 296–297.

21. Earl 277.

22. Heidhues 36 N69.

23. Adelaar 9.

24. Heidhues 36–37.

25. Adriani, Pieter. 1898. *Herinneringen uit en aan de Chineesche Districten der Wester-Afdeeling Van Borneo, 1879–1882: Schetsen En Indrukken.* Amsterdam: Campagne, Vol. 1, 39.

26. Adriani 135; 168.

27. Heidhues 22.

28. Maekawa, Kaori. 2002. "The Pontianak incidents and the ethnic Chinese in wartime Western Borneo". In *Southeast Asian Minorities in the Wartime Japanese Empire*, edited by Paul H. Kratoska, 153–169. See 154.

29. Heidhues 149.

30. Cohen, Matthew I. 2006. *The Komedie Stamboel: Popular Theater in Colonial Indonesia, 1891–1903.* Athens, Ohio: Ohio University Press, 317.

31. Aritonang, Jan S, and Karel A. Steenbrink (eds). *A History of Christianity in Indonesia.* Leiden: Brill, 2008. 507–508.

32. Wu Liu. "Shankouyang de Kejiahua." *Buletin Permasis.* 2008. Edition 10. Reproduced on the Singkawang Yahoo Group. http://www.mail-archive.com/singkawang@yahoogroups.com/msg04409.html

33. Personal communication, 2013. The missionary prefers not to be named.

34. Lombard, Denys. "Guide Archipel IV: Pontianak et son arrière-pays." *Archipel : études interdisciplinaires zur le monde insulindien.* 28 (1): 77–97. See 88.

35. Shin, Chong. 2007. "Masyarakat Tionghoa Kalimantan Barat: Tinjauan Pemilihan Bahasa di Kota Sekadau." *Linguistik Indonesia.* 25 (1): 19–33. See 27.

36. Adelaar, K. Alexander. 2005. *Salako or Badameá: sketch grammar, text and lexicon of a Kanayatn dialect in West Borneo*. Wiesbaden: Harrassowitz.
37. Heidhues 196.
38. From the comments on the trailer for *LI BUN KU in new era*, a story of Hakka culture hero Li Wengu, re-set in contemporary Singkawang. http://www.youtube.com/watch?v=IspRPKhXhvo
39. Huang Zhenling. "Wushi nian qian women zai Yinni sheng guoqi." *Qiaoyuan* (1995): 8–9.
40. "Yinni Shankouyang Jiaoshihui" (Teacher's Association of Singkawang, Indonesia) at the *Dongnanya Guojia Huawen Jiaoyu Rencaiku* (Human Resources Database for Mandarin Education in Southeast Asian Nations) http://202.116.28.31/hjDepartment.aspx?IDX=23&CMD=List. Singkawang Mandarin-language education also features frequently in the Pontianak insert of the *Guoji ribao* (International Daily), and featured on the *DAAI* television station, which is owned by the Indonesian branch of Tzu Chi.
41. Ang, Ien. 2001. *On Not Speaking Chinese: Living Between Asia and the West*. London: Routledge, 35.
42. See also Oetomo 208.

REFERENCES

Adelaar, K. Alexander. 2005. *Salako or Badameá: sketch grammar, text and lexicon of a Kanayatn dialect in West Borneo*. Wiesbaden: Harrassowitz.

Adriani, Pieter. 1898. *Herinneringen uit en aan de Chineesche Districten der Wester-Afdeeling Van Borneo, 1879–1882: Schetsen En Indrukken*. Amsterdam: Campagne, Vol. 1.

Ananta, Aris, Evi Nurvidya Arifin and Bakhtiar. 2008. "Chinese Indonesians in Indonesia and the Province of Riau Archipelago: A Demographic Analysis." In *Ethnic Chinese in Contemporary Indonesia*, edited by Leo Suryadinata, 17–47. Singapore: Chinese Heritage Centre and Institute of Southeast Asian Studies.

Ang, Ien. 2001. *On Not Speaking Chinese: Living Between Asia and the West*. London: Routledge.

Aritonang, Jan S, and Karel A. Steenbrink, eds. 2008. *A History of Christianity in Indonesia*. Leiden: Brill.

Chan, Margaret. 2013. "The Spirit-Mediums of Singkawang: Performing "Peoplehood." In *Chinese Indonesians Reassessed: History, Religion and Belonging* edited by Siew-Min Sai and Chang-Yau Hoon, London: Routledge, 138–158.

Cohen, Matthew I. 2006. *The Komedie Stamboel: Popular Theater in Colonial Indonesia, 1891–1903*. Athens, Ohio: Ohio University Press.

Doty, E. and W.J. Pohlman. 1839. "Tour in Borneo from Sambas, through Montrado to Pontianak, and the adjacent settlements of Chinese and Dayaks, during the autumn of 1838." *Chinese Repository*, 8: 284–307.

Earl, George W. 1837. *The Eastern Seas: Or, Voyages and Adventures in the Indian Archipelago, in 1832–33–34, Comprising a Tour of the Island of Java—Visits to Borneo, the Malay Peninsula, Siam &c. : Also an Account of the Present State of Singapore with Observations on the Commercial Resources of the Archipelago*. London: W. H. Allen.

Hoon, Chang-Yau. 2008. *Chinese Identity in Post-Suharto Indonesia: Culture, Politics and Media*. Brighton: Sussex Academic Press.

Huang Hui-chen. ROC 97 [2008]. "Yinni Shankouyang Kejiahua Yanjiu." National Central University, M.A. Thesis.

Huang Zhenling. 1999. "Wushi nian qian women zai Yinni sheng guoqi." *Qiaoyuan* 5, 8–9.

Hui, Yew-Foong. 2011. *Strangers at Home: History and Subjectivity among the Chinese Communities of West Kalimantan, Indonesia*. Leiden: Brill.

Lombard, Denys. 1984. "Guide Archipel IV: Pontianak et son arrière-pays." *Archipel : études interdisciplinaires zur le monde insulindien*, 28 (1): 77–97.

Maekawa, Kaori. 2002. "The Pontianak incidents and the ethnic Chinese in wartime Western Borneo". In *Southeast Asian Minorities in the Wartime Japanese Empire*, edited by Paul H. Kratoska, London: RoutledgeCurzon, 153–169.

Oetomo, Dede. 1987. *The Chinese of Pasuruan: Their Language and Identity*. Canberra, A.C.T., Australia: Dept. of Linguistics, Research School of Pacific Studies, Australian National University.

Shin, Chong. 2007. "Masyarakat Tionghoa Kalimantan Barat: Tinjauan Pemilihan Bahasa di Kota Sekadau." *Linguistik Indonesia*, 25 (1): 19–33.

Somers, Heidhues M. F. 2003. *Golddiggers, Farmers, and Traders in the "Chinese Districts" of West Kalimantan, Indonesia*. Ithaca, NY: Southeast Asia Program Publications, Southeast Asia Program, Cornell University.

Syafaruddin, Usman M. and Isnawita Din. 2010. *"Beli" Istri Mulai 8 Jeti: Fenomena Amoy Singkawang*. Yogyakarta: Media Pressindo.

Thiong, L. Khay and Michael Hsiao. 2007. "Dongnanya Kejia rentong de xingcheng yu juxian." *Taiwan dongnanya xuekan*, 4(1): 3–28.

Wang Dong. 1998. *Kejia xue daolun*. Taipei: Nantian.

Wu Liu. 2008. "Shankouyang de Kejiahua." *Buletin Permasis*. Edition 10. http://www.mail-archive.com/singkawang@yahoogroups.com/msg04409.html

Wulandari, Benedikta Juliatri Widi. *Wayang Gantung*. 2010. Departeman Kebudayaan dan Parawisata, Pontianak: Balai Pelestarian Sejarah dan Nilai Tradisional Pontianak.

"Yinni Shankouyang Jiaoshihui". 2014. At *Dongnanya Guojia Huawen Jiaoyu Rencaiku*. http://202.116.28.31/hjDepartment.aspx?IDX=23&CMD=List. Accessed October 2, 2014.

9 Being Chinese Again
Learning Mandarin in Post-Suharto Indonesia

Charlotte Setijadi

INTRODUCTION

For thirty-two years under former President Suharto's New Order regime (from 1966–1998), the teaching of Chinese languages in schools was banned in Indonesia. During this period of total assimilation, public displays of Chinese characters, along with other forms of Chinese cultural expressions, were prohibited, allegedly for the sake of national unity. From 1966–69, hundreds of Chinese medium schools and Chinese language press were closed in Chinese settlements throughout the archipelago, and the formal teaching of Chinese languages in Indonesia effectively ceased. As a result, the majority of contemporary Chinese Indonesians no longer have the ability to speak, let alone write in, Chinese.

As has been extensively documented, the situation only changed when, after months of economic crisis, political instability and student protests demanding the resignation of President Suharto, the chaos culminated in large-scale lootings, destruction of properties and rape of ethnic Chinese women between 12 and 14 May 1998 in Jakarta, Solo and other major cities (see Hoon, 2007; Purdey, 2006). Soon after, the New Order regime collapsed and a new era of reform (*reformasi*) began, with promises of civil society, democracy, civil liberties and justice. The post-Suharto sociopolitical atmosphere could not be more different for the ethnic Chinese, whereby almost immediately, subsequent *reformasi* governments abolished almost all assimilationist policies, ushering in a 'revival' of Chinese identity (see Hoon, 2007; Setijadi, 2010). Since 1998, there has been a steady increase in the number of Chinese language courses and programs at Indonesian schools and universities, particularly in areas with large ethnic Chinese populations.

Indeed, after three decades of assimilation, many Chinese parents—the majority of whom do not speak Chinese themselves—want their children to learn Chinese in order to 'reconnect' to a 'lost' Chinese identity. At a more pragmatic level, they are also deeply aware of the potential economic advantages of knowing Mandarin for the purposes of their children's future career advancement, trade and *guanxi* with rapidly rising China. This pragmatism is reflected in the overwhelming popularity of Mandarin (particularly the standardised *Putonghua* variety used as the national language in China) as *the* language to learn, and not regional dialects such as Teochew, Hakka or Hokkien, originally spoken by the majority of Chinese migrants in the Indonesian archipelago. The youth themselves seem to embrace learning Mandarin with many increasingly engaging in code switching between English, Mandarin and Indonesian in social interactions. In addition, the ability to speak or at least understand Mandarin also enables young Chinese Indonesians to further imagine themselves as part of a modern pan-Chinese youth identity they see in transnational Mandarin and Cantonese films, TV series and pop culture.

Looking at all these trends, the ability to speak Chinese (particularly Mandarin) appears to play an important part in the construction of Chinese identities in the post-Suharto era. Thus far, however, little is known about the linguistic practices and beliefs of contemporary Chinese Indonesians. Furthermore, considering that only fifteen years ago, Chinese languages and culture were banned, questions also need to be asked regarding how the 'return' of Chinese languages in public are perceived by Chinese and non-Chinese Indonesians. Using ethnographic interviews with twenty-five young Chinese Indonesians[1] ages 18 to 35 from both genders conducted in Jakarta from 2008–2012, this chapter examines how young post-Suharto Chinese view their ethnic identity and belonging in relation to their ability (or inability) to speak Chinese. This chapter also discusses the tensions between competing ideologies on ethnicity, nationalism and culture as embodied in the daily negotiations of which language(s) to speak and when.

CHINESE INDONESIANS, CHINESENESS AND CHINESE LANGUAGES IN INDONESIA

The prohibition of Chinese languages during the New Order period was only one example of the many instances of anti-Chinese discrimination that had occurred almost consistently throughout the history of Chinese settlement in the Indonesian archipelago. Whereas the Chinese had had a long history of migration to Indonesia that began in pre-colonial times, the Dutch colonial policy of racial segregation successfully perpetuated a negative image of the Chinese as economically dominant 'essential outsiders' who did not sympathise with the plight of the native ('*pribumi*' in Indonesian) population (Chirot and Reid, 1997). Throughout the periods of Dutch colonialism, independence struggle and the early days of the Indonesian Republic, the Chinese's belonging and national identity in Indonesia remained ambiguous at best, regardless of the fact that many ethnic Chinese were nationalists who supported the independence cause. As Filomeno Aguilar, Jr. suggests, in the course of Indonesian nationalist awakening, the Chinese were attributed a definite, distant place of origin—China—and thus the descendants of Chinese migrants became 'indelibly linked to the first-generation immigrants and, in an unbroken chain, remained forever aliens' (2001: 517).

Chinese Indonesians themselves were, and always had been, a heterogeneous group consisting of people that came from various regions in China, spoke different languages (Hakka, Hokkien, Cantonese and Teochew being the four major spoken languages), held different political views and felt varying degrees of belonging towards the Indonesian nation. The traditional groupings of Chinese Indonesians as either '*totok*' ('pure' Chinese with no mixed ancestry) or '*peranakan*' (acculturated Chinese, usually with mixed Chinese-native Indonesian ancestry) illustrate the different 'types' of Chinese in Indonesia with different connections to the Chinese homeland, language and culture[2] (see Coppel, 1983). Unlike the *totok* Chinese who maintained Chinese traditions, culture and language in Indonesia, the *peranakan* Chinese mostly identified with the cultures of their local regions, spoke local languages instead of Chinese and developed their own unique hybrid culture from a mixture of Chinese and local cultural influences. Nevertheless, the discourse of '*Masalah Cina*' (the 'Chinese Problem') in Indonesia collapsed the diversity of ethnic Chinese lives into one alleged problem that needed to be 'fixed' with a convenient phraseology.

Following the alleged failed communist coup of 30 September 1965 (G-30S/PKI in the national terminology), in which many ethnic Chinese individuals and organisations were implicated, President Suharto's New Order regime 'took control' of rising anti-Chinese sentiment with a series of assimilationist legislations (see Cribb & Coppel, 2009). In 1966, Cabinet Presidium Decision 127 required all ethnic Chinese to discard their Chinese names and adopt 'Indonesian-sounding' ones. In 1967, Presidential Instruction Number 14 on Chinese Religion, Beliefs, and Traditions effectively banned any Chinese literature and public displays of cultural expression in Indonesia, including the prohibition of Chinese characters. Furthermore, as part of the 'Basic Policy for the Solution of the Chinese Problem' (Presidential Decision No. 240 of 1967) and other measures, only one heavily monitored Chinese-language newspaper was allowed to continue and all Chinese language schools were eventually phased out. Buildings and properties owned by Chinese educational organisations were seized and 'nationalised' for use by state-run schools. Sai Siew-Min (2010) estimates that, in the late 1960s, the ban on Chinese language education affected 629 schools, 6,478 teachers and 272,782 students in eleven cities across Indonesia.[3]

The prohibition of Chinese languages throughout the New Order was consistent with the prevalent national language ideology at the time that viewed the elimination of 'non-native' languages such as Chinese as necessary for national unity. Since the beginning of the Indonesian nationalist movement in the early twentieth century, the Malay language came to be seen as a strong contender as the emerging nation's *lingua franca* because it was perceived as a common language of the natives (Kahin, 1963). At the historic Second Youth Congress on 28 October 1928 when youth delegations from native ethnic groups across the archipelago pledged their oath (known from then on as the 'Youth Oath') towards a unified Indonesian nation, modernised Malay (renamed 'Indonesian') was adopted as the language of the new nation, privileged above all other native and non-native languages. The centrality of Indonesian as the language of national unity was evident in its teaching as a compulsory language in schools and as the only language of politics, trade and national culture, although the government was committed in principle to protecting local languages. As non-native languages spoken by a sociopolitically 'problematic' ethnic minority, the prohibition of Chinese languages was easily justified. In this regard, the banning of Chinese reflected the popular view of Chinese Indonesians as essentially foreigners within the framework of Indonesia's ethno-nationalist ideology.

Ariel Heryanto (2006) argues that the effect of the assimilation policies was the lasting image of Chineseness as ideologically unclean, dangerous, shameful and therefore in need of erasure. Connections with China in the late 1960s had strong communist connotations, and anyone caught speaking in Chinese was viewed with strong suspicion and anger. Chinese languages became confined to the private domains, and many parents stopped teaching their children Chinese altogether. Over the three decades of assimilation from 1966 to 1998, Chinese Indonesian language, culture and identity were in many ways 'erased' or at least hidden from public view, although their forced assimilation also had the paradoxical effect of accentuating the group's essential foreignness in the national imagination.

As mentioned before, the end of the New Order marked the beginning of a new Chinese identity politics that started with demands for the abolition of assimilationist laws and justice for the victims of the May '98 rapes and riots (see Budiman, 2005; Purdey, 2006; Turner, 2003). Indeed, post-Suharto governments were only too eager to prove their commitment to human rights issues and move away from the harmful legacies of the New Order and May 1998 by implementing new laws that recognised the rights of Chinese Indonesians. The Habibie government (1998–1999) started off these reforms through a Presidential Instruction that abolished the use of the terms *'pribumi'* and *'non-pribumi'* in official government documents. In the year 2000, the newly elected President Abdurrahman Wahid (1999–2001) revoked bans against Chinese languages, religion and cultural expressions, allowing Chinese culture to be practiced in public once more. President Megawati Sukarnoputri (2001–2004) made *Imlek* (Chinese New Year) a national holiday in 2002 as an official gesture of recognition for both Chinese Indonesians and the Confucian (*Konghucu*) religion that was added as one of the state's six official religions. The stark contrast between the New Order and the post-Suharto era led many ethnic Chinese to view the *reformasi* era as a time for the revival of Chinese culture in Indonesia.

One of the most noticeable changes that occurred in the post-Suharto era is the return of Chinese languages and script in the public domain.

Previously banned, Chinese characters could be seen on posters, banners and store decorations, particularly during annual *Imlek* celebrations. More and more, Mandarin and other Chinese languages are being spoken in public by Chinese Indonesians who feel that it is now 'safe' to speak Chinese in front of *pribumi* Indonesians. Perhaps more significantly, the fall of the New Order has seen what Leo Suryadinata calls 'a watershed for Chinese education' (2008: 4). In the last fifteen years, the demand for Mandarin, particularly among Chinese Indonesian students, has led to language courses being offered in many private and public schools, often as part of the National Plus curriculum, according to which classes are delivered in a combination of Indonesian, English and Mandarin. The number of private Mandarin language course providers has also mushroomed in the last decade, especially in urban residential areas with large concentrations of middle to upper class Chinese Indonesian families (see Kaboel & Sulanti, 2010). On their part, the PRC government is clearly encouraging the demand for Mandarin language in Indonesia with the opening of seven Confucius Institutes attached to universities in major Indonesian cities. Additionally, in the past five years, a number of alumni organisations made up of older generation Chinese Indonesians who were ex-graduates of Chinese-medium schools, such as the disbanded *Tiong Hoa Hwee Koan* (Chinese Association) schools, had re-established their pre-Suharto schools with the mission to revive Chinese education for post-Suharto youth. Such organisations include the PaHoa alumni group that established the PaHoa National Plus School in the outer suburbs of Jakarta, the PaChung group that established two schools in Jakarta and the MaChung group that established MaChung University in Malang, East Java (see Setijadi, 2010).

For many middle- and upper-class Chinese Indonesian families, it makes sense to send their children for Mandarin extracurricular lessons or to National Plus schools, especially if they plan on sending their children to China or Taiwan for language or tertiary education. Indeed, in recent years, more and more Chinese Indonesian youth from affluent families go to China not only for language study but also for tertiary education degrees. For instance, data from the Indonesian embassy in Beijing suggest that whereas in 1998, only around 1,000 Indonesian students studied at Chinese universities, in 2012 the number had risen to over 9,000 (Priyambodo, 2012). This is a growing trend away from the dominance of Western countries such as Australia, the US and the UK as the common destinations for Indonesian students pursuing overseas education. Whereas non-Chinese Indonesian students are included in this figure, a large majority are ethnic Chinese youths with hopes of creating a future employment niche for themselves not only with an overseas university degree but also knowledge of modern Chinese language and society. Many among them also hope that their Chinese ethnicity will increase the possibility of future advantageous *guanxi*[4] connections for career advancement and trade opportunities with China and other Chinese-speaking countries.

'YOU'RE NOT A REAL CHINESE IF YOU CAN'T SPEAK CHINESE': LANGUAGE IDEOLOGY AND CHINESE INDONESIAN IDENTITY

At the core of this post-Suharto 'revival' of Chinese language use and education is a belief that Chinese Indonesians must now seize the opportunity to re-learn Chinese languages and reclaim a Chinese identity that was lost to the generations that grew up under the New Order. The term 'lost generation' has been frequently used by scholars, observers and the Chinese Indonesian public more generally to refer to the post-1965 generation who never learned Chinese, possess little or no knowledge of Chinese culture and had been made to feel ashamed about being Chinese (see Hoon, 2007; Suryadinata, 2008). Many of the older, Chinese-educated *totok* Chinese in particular expressed concerns that contemporary young Chinese Indonesians do not know their identity and the long, proud history of the Chinese people. In an interview, Teddy Jusuf, a former Indonesian Army General and prominent Chinese Indonesian elder who himself was Chinese-educated in the 1940s, complained that:

> The [Chinese] youth today cannot speak Mandarin, do not know Chinese culture, and had become completely dissociated from their family's name and heritage. . . . They do not know who they are. . . . It is the job of the older generation to encourage the youth to learn about their Chinese identity again. . . . In particular they need to learn Mandarin so they can understand the culture. (author's translation from Indonesian)

In a similar vein, Koko Tanumihardja, a PaHoa alumni and founder of the new PaHoa School remarked:

> I remember going to school at the old *PaHoa* school in Patekoan, and I also remember the sadness I felt when the government forcibly closed the school. . . . Not just our school but also all Chinese schools in Indonesia. It was a tragedy for the Chinese, because without the schools, we lost all sense of who we are and the values that set us apart as a people. My children for example, can't speak Mandarin, although I did try to instil Chinese moral values as much as I could while they were growing up. . . . The younger generation now, they are lucky that they could have Chinese education again. . . . Chinese schools like *PaHoa* need to be resurrected so that the younger generation can re-learn what was lost. (author's translation from Indonesian)

Evident in what *Pak* (Mister) Teddy and *Pak* Koko said is a common idea among Chinese Indonesians that the ability to speak Chinese is intrinsically linked to Chinese culture and identity.

The belief in the cultural significance of Chinese language is prevalent among Chinese people both in China and in overseas Chinese diaspora around the world. As scholars note time and time again, most Chinese—even those who do not speak Chinese themselves—hold the position that without the ability to speak Chinese, a Chinese person could never be a 'complete' Chinese (see Li & Zhu, 2010; Tu, 1991; Wang, 1991). Here, the ability to read and write in Chinese is desirable, but a Chinese person should at least be able to speak Chinese. For ethnic Chinese living in overseas Chinese diaspora, the issue is arguably even more complicated considering that, as Chinese who live in the 'periphery,' Chinese languages and culture are often preserved with particular zeal as the means by which overseas Chinese (*huaqiao*) could maintain their connection with China as the mythical homeland. In her book *On Not Speaking Chinese: Living Between Asia and the West*, Ien Ang argues that for ethnic Chinese in diaspora, the inability to speak Chinese is 'a condition that has been hegemonically constructed as a lack, a sign of loss of authenticity' (2001: 30). According to this logic, Chinese persons who somehow 'lost' the ability to speak Chinese are constructed as inauthentic or 'fake' Chinese, both by others and by themselves.

Indeed, during interviews with young Chinese Indonesians, this ideology about the importance of Chinese language to identity is prevalent and would often come up during conversations about how the youth view their Chineseness in relation to their ability (or inability) to speak Chinese. For example, in an interview with Ben and Fenny, two 30-year-old *peranakan* Chinese, they joked about how they were 'fake' Chinese (*cina palsu*) because they did not know how to speak Chinese:

Ben:	It is actually quite funny that the *pribumi* call me Chinese because actually, a real Chinese person would never pass me as a Chinese [laughs].
Interviewer:	What do you think makes a real Chinese person?
Ben:	Well, for one, you'd have to be able to speak Chinese, which I can't.
Fenny:	That's right, I'm a fake Chinese too like Ben [laughs]. My grandparents could still speak Chinese [Hakka], but my parents were never taught properly and could only speak a little bit of Chinese. But my siblings and I, we can't speak any Chinese at all.
Ben:	So your family gets faker and faker [as Chinese] with each generation [laughs].
Fenny:	Yeah, you can say that, we got diluted over time! [laughs]
Ben:	Everyone knows that you're not a real Chinese if you can't speak Chinese.

(author's translation from Indonesian)

For young people like Ben and Fenny, the experience of realising their status as a so-called 'fake' Chinese could sometimes be a harsh one, as discovered by Alex, a 32-year-old male from a *totok* Chinese background who felt hurt when he thought that people in mainland China did not regard him as a 'real' Chinese while on a family trip to China:

> Growing up, I was always told that I should be proud of being a Chinese, and our family spoke Hokkien at home. I only knew very little Mandarin, but when our family went to China for holiday, I tried speaking in Mandarin to shopkeepers and when ordering food. . . . But the shopkeepers would talk back to me really fast, and I couldn't understand what they were saying! They just looked at me like they were angry at me for not being able to speak proper Chinese. . . . I felt so sad because I felt like I didn't belong there [in China] and that I was not a real Chinese. . . . Now I know that other Chinese people, especially those in the mainland, don't regard us Chinese Indonesians as Chinese anyway. (author's translation from Indonesian)

Although Alex's experience of being regarded as inauthentic is quite common among overseas Chinese and members of other diaspora, the Chinese Indonesian experience is unique because, feeling like they are neither accepted as Indonesian nor Chinese, many Chinese Indonesians are unsure about where they belong.

In many ways, being able to speak Chinese carries a particular symbolic significance for Chinese Indonesians in the post-Suharto era as they now struggle to reclaim what is perceived as a lost Chinese identity. If in the past, speaking in Chinese was seen as something shameful and politically dangerous, now the tables have turned and being able to speak Chinese is considered an asset that needs to be acquired quickly. Furthermore, at a time when Chinese Indonesians are seeking to redefine their ethnic and national identities following more than three decades of assimilation, more and more contemporary Chinese from *totok* and *peranakan* backgrounds are learning Mandarin as a way to forge connection to a pan-Chinese identity. Feeling like they could never be regarded as a 'true' Indonesian by the *pribumi*, many young Chinese Indonesians are reorienting themselves towards China and Chinese culture, and learning Mandarin is often viewed as the most effective way to do so.

THE RISE OF CHINA, MANDARIN AND ISSUES IN CONTEXT

One of the most interesting aspects of the post-Suharto return of Chinese languages has been the privileging of Mandarin as *the* language to learn among Chinese Indonesian youth. If in the past, the Chinese in Indonesia mainly spoke southern Min languages such as Hokkien, Hakka and Teochew, today, the emphasis is on the learning and use of Mandarin as the official language spoken in the PRC, Taiwan and Singapore. Regional Chinese languages traditional to Chinese Indonesian families were rendered useless, as they would not give the Chinese Indonesians any advantage in terms of education, trade or future career paths. For example, in a group interview with Henry, Jimmy and Maria, three university students in their early twenties who all studied at the same Mandarin language tuition centre in Jakarta, all three participants had similar views about the importance of Mandarin in comparison to the original languages spoken by their families:

Interviewer:	So what made you guys decide to learn Mandarin?
Henry:	I want to do my Master's degree maybe in China or Taiwan, so I need to learn Mandarin in order to do that.
Maria:	I was just interested in learning because even when I was a teenager, I always liked watching Chinese films and TV series, so I wanted to learn the language [laughs].
Jimmy:	My parents wanted me to learn Mandarin and I thought that it would be a good skill to have too.
Interviewer:	So do your parents or grandparents speak Mandarin too?
Jimmy:	No, my family were originally from Kuntien [Pontianak], so they spoke Teochew.
Henry:	My family was from Bangka and at home we still speak Khek [Hakka].
Maria:	I think my late grandfather knew Mandarin because he went to a Chinese school, but our family spoke Khek. I can't speak Khek though because I never learnt it.
Interviewer:	So how come you are learning Mandarin now and not your family's traditional languages?
Henry:	Because it would be useless to learn Khek [laughs].
Maria:	Yeah [laughs] we wouldn't be able to use the language much, and Khek doesn't get used much anywhere.
Henry:	And Mandarin is the language for education, business and all that so it is useful for us to know Mandarin.
Jimmy:	It [Mandarin] would help us communicate with people in China, Singapore, and in other places too. It is going to take over English as the global language in the future.

(author's translation from Indonesian)

As discussed by Li Wei and Zhu Hua (2010), whereas overseas Chinese living in diaspora have traditionally been dialect dominant, globalisation and the rise of China as a global politico-economic power mean that Mandarin is gaining particular prestige among the Chinese diasporas. In the same paper, Li and Zhu gave the example that all Cantonese schools for British Chinese children in the UK now also teach Mandarin, whereas none of the Mandarin schools teach Cantonese.[5] The situation is very similar in Indonesia, where virtually all of the schools, universities and private course providers that claim to teach Chinese only teach Mandarin and none of the other Chinese languages. Traditional languages such as Hakka, Hokkien and

Teochew are only taught and maintained at home, and mainly used to communicate among families and networks that originated from the same local regions in Indonesia (e.g., Khek is still commonly spoken among the Hakka Chinese from Bangka, Hokkien among the Chinese from Medan, etc.). It is true that Mandarin had been a dominant language even in pre-assimilation Chinese medium schools, such as the THHK or Xinhua schools. However, the post-Suharto situation is different in that most Chinese Indonesian families no longer spoke their traditional familial languages anymore. As the younger ethnic Chinese learn and communicate in Mandarin rather than Hakka, Hokkien or other Chinese languages, the concern is that these languages will eventually 'die off' in Indonesia as a result.

Another issue with the teaching of Mandarin in Indonesia is that, because the teaching in Mandarin on a large scale is a relatively new phenomenon, almost all of the materials used in classes and tuitions are imported from China, Taiwan, Singapore or Malaysia. Furthermore, the shortage of good quality Mandarin teachers in Indonesia means that Mandarin language schools and course providers resort to hiring expatriate teachers from China or Taiwan. As one Chinese Indonesian Mandarin language teacher tells me, consequently, very little of the teaching materials used in classes relate to the culture or everyday lives of Chinese Indonesians. Furthermore, this teacher also tells me that because many Mandarin teachers come from China, local teachers like him worry that PRC-sanctioned Mandarin pronunciation and manner of speaking would be the standard for Chinese Indonesians. Such concerns highlight the uncertainties that revolve around the dominance of Mandarin and the potential for mainland Chinese 'cultural imperialism' among Chinese Indonesians in the future.

Voices of apprehension have also come from *peranakan* Chinese Indonesians who feel unrepresented by the recent trend among *totok* Chinese to speak Mandarin and orientate themselves towards China. This kind of view is evident in a conversation between Christa, a 34-year-old female from a *totok* background, and David, a 33-year-old from a *peranakan* background. During the joint interview, the two disagreed about the effects of the resinification of *totok* Chinese Indonesians, which in David's opinion creates a negative stereotype of all ethnic Chinese:

David:	It makes me uncomfortable that, now, a lot of Chinese are speaking Mandarin in public.
Interviewer:	Why does it make you feel uncomfortable?
David:	Because it creates a bad impression for all Chinese. Can you imagine what the *pribumi* would think when they hear a bunch of Chinese people speaking in Chinese? I think the Chinese forget that the [May '98] riots weren't that long ago. . . . Just because now we can speak in Chinese, doesn't mean that we should be insensitive.

Christa:	I disagree with you David, I think you're being unfair. The Chinese have every right to speak in Chinese, or in whatever language they want to. I can speak Mandarin, but that doesn't mean that I'm any less Indonesian or that I'm insensitive to the *pribumi*.
David:	What I mean is this: I think it doesn't look good for the Chinese to suddenly be all 'Chinese' once we were allowed to. . . . Doesn't that just confirm all the things the *pribumi* thought about us as not being Indonesian? Besides, my family is *peranakan* and we never spoke Chinese at home. . . . I see no reason to start doing so now.

(author's translation from Indonesian)

Reflected in the conversation between Christa and David is the long-standing social, cultural and political differences that exist between *totok* and *peranakan* Chinese. Whereas the *totok* Chinese in general seem to be embracing the opportunity to speak Mandarin, many *peranakan* Chinese like David reject it altogether.

Here, although the differences between the two 'groups' are not as pronounced as what they used to be prior to assimilation, contemporary Chinese Indonesians still differentiate themselves from each other based on the *totok/peranakan* distinction, particularly when discussing the reasons for their chosen cultural orientations. At the crux of differing *totok* and *peranakan* attitudes towards China, Chinese culture and language is the reality that, even in the post-Suharto era, debates still rage about where the ethnic Chinese are (or should be) located in the greater scheme of Indonesian national belonging. In a country where national identity is still very much defined by ethno-nationalist ideology, many Chinese and *pribumi* Indonesians continue to view Chinese and Indonesian identities as essentially incompatible. For the Chinese, the choice of which language to speak and when is fraught with sociopolitical considerations related to the kind of belonging they aspire to.

CODE-SWITCHING AND THE NEGOTIATION OF CHINESE INDONESIAN IDENTITIES

Among the young ethnic Chinese who aspire to speak Mandarin, there is a recent trend of engaging in the practice of code-switching in everyday speech, particularly when they are in the company of other Chinese who also aspire to speak Mandarin. Code-switching, or the practice of alternating between two or more languages during a single speech act, is a feature of bi- and multilingualism that has been amply researched over the past three decades (see Auer, 1988; Milroy & Muysken, 1995). However, it is not until relatively recently that scholars started to investigate how bi- and multilingual speakers utilise code-switching as a linguistic strategy in the construction of ethnic identity (see Block, 2007; Blommaert, Collins & Slembrouck, 2005; De Fina, 2007). Here, scholars have found that the act of code-switching can be transformative for the speakers because it allows the speakers to creatively bring together their personal histories and social contexts in order to make sense of their multilingual identities (see Garcia, 2009; Li, 2011). The result is the creation of new language spaces where hybrid identities are negotiated. Language proficiency almost does not matter in this regard because the rules and boundaries of code-switching continuously change according to the speakers' life experiences and needs.

For Chinese Indonesian youth who aspire to speak Mandarin, code-switching between Indonesian and Mandarin (and sometimes English) is a speech strategy that allows them to speak Mandarin, even when they only know very few Mandarin sentences or phrases. Such code-switching acts usually only occur when the young people are in the presence of other friends who also know some Mandarin, or—as was the case during interviews for this research—they find themselves in a situation where they feel like they need to emphasise their Chineseness. Whereas words from other Chinese languages, such as Hokkien, often also get used in code-switching, in recent times, Mandarin as the language most young Chinese learn is the language most commonly used for code-switching. For example, the following excerpt was recorded during a group interview with Ling Ling, Melia and Andri, three friends in their early twenties who all spoke beginner level Mandarin:

Interviewer:	*Jadi kalian bisa ngomong Mandarin?*
	(So do you guys speak Mandarin?)
Andri:	[laughs] *ya, kalau yi dian dian Zhongwen bisa lah.*
	(well, if it is just a little bit of Mandarin then I can do a bit.)
Ling:	Ling: *Ahhh, gaya si Andri sok bisa, tapi kalau disuruh ngomong depan orang pasti dia bù h o yìsi!* [laughs]
	(Ahhh, Andri is just playing it up, if he has to speak it in front of other people then I bet that he'd be embarrassed!)
Interviewer:	*Kenapa kok malu kalau ngomong Mandarin di depan orang lain Andri?*
	(Why do you get embarrassed if you have to speak Mandarin in front of other people Andri?)
Andri:	*Karena gue cuma tau dikit-dikit tapi sok tau* [laughs].
	(Because I only know a bit but I pretend to know a lot.)
Melia:	*Iya terus abis itu dia panik kalau diajak ngomong yang susah, dia wo bù zh dào lah, wo bù zh dào!*
	(Yes but then he panics when someone then starts talking complicated [Mandarin] to him, he'll go I don't know, I don't know!)
	sample: (author's translation from Jakartan dialect Indonesian and Mandarin)

Neither Ling Ling, Andri or Melia came from Mandarin-speaking families and, like so many other post-Suharto Chinese youth, they only started learning and speaking Mandarin at their private schools during compulsory Mandarin language classes. Initially uninterested by the language, they became more motivated users of Mandarin during their university years when they realised its potential usefulness. Here, code-switching is not only a way for friends to practice their limited Mandarin with one another; it is also a way to reaffirm each other's Chineseness. As Andri claimed during the interview, 'it is nice to be able to speak in a language of the Chinese people' (author's translation from Indonesian).

Indeed, one of the most common situations in which the Chinese youth I observed code-switched with one another was when they wanted to say something to each other without wanting the *pribumi* to understand what they were saying. For instance, Ling Ling, who admits to frequently using Mandarin words or sentences when speaking with her ethnic Chinese friends said, 'I like being able to speak Mandarin because that means that I can speak in Mandarin with my friends without the *f ngui*[6] understanding what we're saying. . . . It is like having a secret language' (author's translation from Indonesian). Asked whether she ever gets worried about whether the *pribumi* would get offended when she speaks in Mandarin near them, Ling Ling answered:

> Well, I guess so, there was this one time that my friend and I were speaking in Mandarin, and then this [*pribumi*] man told us off and said that we should speak Indonesian because we're in Indonesia. . . . But I think that's not fair because we have the right to speak our own language now. . . . The *pribumi* themselves also have languages that we don't understand like Sundanese or Batakese, so why shouldn't we be able to speak our own language? (author's translation from Indonesian)

A number of other young Chinese interviewed shared the same opinion as Ling Ling, with Singapore or Malaysia often cited as positive examples of Southeast Asian countries where Chinese could coexist with other languages like Malay, Hindi and English in the public domain. However, as is the case with many other sociocultural aspects of Chinese Indonesian lives, the issue of language choice is complex and laden with uncertainties about how much Chinese is acceptable in public. For now, the increasing use of code-switching among young people indicates that many contemporary Chinese Indonesians are experimenting with Mandarin as a means of identification. Consequently, as new spaces for identity expression are created, the meanings and boundaries of Chineseness in Indonesia are also continuously being redefined.

CONCLUSION

In this chapter, I have presented the case of Mandarin language learning and use among young Chinese Indonesians in the post-Suharto era. At a time when Chinese Indonesians are free to 'be Chinese' again, learning and speaking Mandarin has become one of the most important ways in which Chinese identities are expressed. The demand for Mandarin is evident in the large number of schools, universities and private course providers that started offering Mandarin language teaching in recent years, and the number of Indonesian tertiary and language students in the PRC and Taiwan is presently at an all-time high. Here, motivations for learning Mandarin vary from the sentimental (e.g., wanting to reconnect to a 'lost' Chinese identity) to the pragmatic (e.g., wanting to keep up with the rise of China and tap into the potential for *guanxi*). Regardless of their motivation, however, one defining feature of Chinese Indonesians currently learning or speaking Mandarin is a sense of renewed pride in their Chinese ethnicity where, for the first time in a long time, Chineseness is seen as an asset and no longer a sociopolitical liability. Speaking Chinese in public is seen as increasingly acceptable, and more and more young Chinese Indonesians are engaging in code-switching between Indonesian and Mandarin in everyday speech with each other.

Nevertheless, there are pertinent issues associated with the return of Chinese languages in post-Suharto Indonesia. For one, the vastly popular preference for Mandarin as *the* language to learn and speak among the young people means that regional languages such as Hokkien and Hakka traditionally spoken by Chinese families are under the threat of eventually becoming extinct in Indonesia. This privileging of Mandarin above regional Chinese languages is consistent with the trend seen in other Chinese diaspora worldwide, where the promotion of Mandarin as the official language of the PRC has increased its authenticity, prestige and demand among overseas Chinese (see Gao, 2012; Li & Zhu, 2010). From a theoretical point of view, the fact that many Chinese Indonesian families are encouraging their young to learn Mandarin as a way to reconnect to a 'lost' Chinese identity even though their ancestors never spoke Mandarin highlights the constructed nature of language ideology and ethnic identity. Furthermore, the return of Chinese languages in the public domain raises questions about how this process of resinification is perceived, not just by *pribumi* Indonesians, but also by ethnic Chinese who feel uncomfortable about the trend. As discussed in this chapter, many Chinese Indonesians from *peranakan* backgrounds had always felt wholly Indonesian and thus consider the recent move to speak Mandarin and reorient towards China to be unrepresentative of the *peranakan* sociocultural heritage. Some of these Chinese Indonesians also feel anxious about the potentially harmful effects of post-Suharto resinification on the already fragile political image of the Chinese in Indonesia.

Issues surrounding the politics of language among ethnic Chinese in the post-Suharto era are intrinsically linked to the long-standing Chinese 'problem' in Indonesia. For contemporary Chinese Indonesians, choosing which language(s) to speak and when is not a simple matter, and the decision whether to speak Chinese or not is ultimately a statement of individuals' sense of ethnic and national belonging. For now, however, recent trends suggest that Mandarin will continue to gain popularity among younger Chinese Indonesians, particularly as China gains more international prominence politically, economically and culturally. As Mandarin becomes more widely spoken among Chinese Indonesians, the characteristics and boundaries of Chineseness in Indonesia will continue to be redefined. As such, more critical reflections are needed in the future in order for scholars to analyse what these changes mean, both for Chinese Indonesian identity politics and the study of language politics in Chinese diasporas.

NOTES

1. The names of research respondents have been changed in order to protect their anonymity.
2. '*Totok*' Chinese are generally regarded as less intermingled with the local communities and still very much culturally orientated towards China. The term '*peranakan*' on the other hand generally refers to the Chinese who have lived in Indonesia for centuries—in many cases even of mixed ancestry—and have intermingled with local cultures. Such distinction should only be seen as a common and convenient way to differentiate between *totok* and *peranakan* as, even within these two groups, the Chinese were far from unified and most of their political decisions were motivated by pragmatism and self-preservation. Scholars now generally regard the *totok-peranakan* distinction to be outdated, but the terms are still frequently used by Chinese Indonesians when referring to the degrees to which their families adhere to Chinese cultural traditions (see Hoon, 2007; Tsai, 2008).
3. These figures were official statistics released by the Education Ministry. For in-depth accounts and analyses of events leading to the language ban, see Coppel (1983).
4. *Guanxi* (pronounced kuan-shi) literally means 'relation' or 'relationship' as a noun, and 'relate to' as a verb, although as commonly used in contemporary Chinese society it refers more narrowly to 'particularistic ties' (Jacobs, 1980). According to Thomas Gold, Doug Guthrie and David Wank, these relations are based on ascribed or primordial traits such as kinship, native places and ethnicity, and also on acquired characteristics such as attending the same school, serving in the same military unit and doing business together (2002: 6). Because of the emphasis on primordial traits, it is generally understood among the Chinese (both in pan-Chinese countries and in the diaspora) that their shared ethnicity means that they will benefit from mutual preferential treatment when dealing with each other (see Ong, 1999).
5. The promotion of Mandarin at the expense of regional languages has been well noted in recent sociolinguistic research. For more on the topic, along with examples from other Chinese-speaking counties and communities, see Gao (2012), Tan (2006) and Wang & Ladegaard (2008).
6. '*Fāngui*' is a Mandarin term meaning 'dark foreigner' and it is a derogatory term often used by Chinese Indonesians to describe the *pribumi*.

REFERENCES

Aguilar Jr., F. V. (2001). "Citizenship, Inheritance, and the Indigenizing of 'Orang Chinese' in Indonesia." *Positions: East Asia Cultures Critique* 9(3): 501–533.

Ang, I. (2001). *On Not Speaking Chinese: Living between Asia and the West.* London, Routledge.

Auer, P. (1988). A Conversation Analytic Approach to Code-switching and Transfer. *Codeswitching: Anthropological and sociolinguistic perspectives.* M. Heller. Berlin, Walter de Gruyter: 187–213.

Block, D. (2007). "Bilingualism: Four Assumptions and Four Responses." *International Journal of Innovation in Language Learning and Teaching* 1(1): 66–82.

Blommaert, J., J. Collins and S. Slembrouck (2005). "Spaces of Multilingualism." *Language & Communication* 25(3): 197–216.

Budiman, A. (2005). Portrait of the Chinese in post-Soeharto Indonesia. *Chinese Indonesians: Remembering, distorting, forgetting.* T. Lindsey and H. Pausacker. Singapore, ISEAS Publications: 95–104.

Chirot, D. and A. Reid (1997). *Essential Outsiders: Chinese and Jews in the Modern Transformation of Southeast Asia and Central Europe.* Seattle, University of Washington Press.

Coppel, C. (1983). *Indonesian Chinese in Crisis.* Kuala Lumpur, Oxford University Press for Asian Studies Association of Australia.

Cribb, R. and C.A. Coppel (2009). "A Genocide That Never Was: Explaining the Myth of Anti-Chinese Massacres in Indonesia, 1965–66." *Journal of Genocide Research* 11(4): 447–465.

De Fina, A. (2007). "Code-switching and the Construction of Ethnic Identity in a Community of Practice." *Language in Society* 36(3): 371–392.

Gao, X. (2012). ""Cantonese Is Not a Dialect": Chinese netizens' defence of Cantonese as a regional lingua franca." *Journal of Multilingual and Multicultural Development* 33(5): 449–464.

Garcia, O. (2009). *Bilingual Education in the 21st Century: A Global Perspective.* Oxford, Wiley-Blackwell.

Gold, T., D. Guthrie and D. Wank (2002). *Social Connections in China: Institutions, Culture, and the Changing Nature of Guanxi.* Cambridge, Cambridge University Press.

Heryanto, A. (2006). *State Terrorism and Political Identity in Indonesia: Fatally Belonging.* Singapore, Taylor & Francis.

Hoon, C.Y. (2007). *Reconceptualising Ethnic Chinese Identity in Post-Suharto Indonesia.* Doctor of Philosophy, University of Western Australia.

Jacobs, J.B. (1980). *Local Politics in a Rural Chinese Cultural Setting: A Field Study of Mazu Township, Taiwan.* Canberra, Contemporary China Centre, Australian National University.

Kaboel, A. and N.M. Sulanti (2010). Bahasa Mandarin Dimana-Mana: Studi Kasus di Wilayah DKI Jakarta. *Setelah Air Mata Kering: Masyarakat tionghoa Pasca Peristiwa Mei 1998.* J.-L. Thung and I. Wibowo. Jakarta, Penerbit Buku Kompas: 208–231.

Kahin, G.M. (1963). *Nationalism and Revolution in Indonesia.* Ithaca, NY, Cornell University Press.

Li, W. (2011). "Moment Analysis and Translanguaging Space: Discursive Construction of Identities by Multilingual Chinese Youth in Britain." *Journal of Pragmatics* 43: 1222–1235.

Li, W. and Z. Hua (2010). "Voices from the Diaspora: Changing Hierarchies and Dynamics of Chinese Multilingualism." *International Journal of the Sociology of Language* 205: 155–171.

Milroy, L. and P. Muysken (1995). *One Speaker, Two Languages: Cross-disciplinary Perspectives on Code-switching.* Cambridge, Cambridge University Press.

Ong, A. (1999). *Flexible Citizenship: The Cultural Logics of Transnationality.* Durham, Duke University Press.

Priyambodo, R. H. (2012). Indonesian Students in China Set Up Association. *Antara News*.

Purdey, J. (2006). *Anti-Chinese Violence in Indonesia, 1996–99*. Honolulu, University of Hawai'i Press.

Sai, S. M. (2010). "Pugilists from the Mountains: History, Memory, and the Making of the Chinese-Educated Generation in Post-1998 Indonesia." *Indonesia* 89: 149–178.

Setijadi, C. (2010). "Cautiously Promoting Humanism: A Chinese school tries to promote 'universal' humanism." *Inside Indonesia: Special Issue on Multicultural Education*.

Suryadinata, L. (2008). Chinese Indonesians in an Era of Globalization: Some major characteristics. *Ethnic Chinese in Contemporary Indonesia*. L. Suryadinata. Singapore, Institute of Southeast Asian Studies: 1–16.

Tan, C. (2006). "Change and Continuity: Chinese Language Policy in Singapore." *Language Policy* 5: 41–62.

Tsai, Y.-l. (2008). *Strangers Who Are Not Foreign: Intimate Exclusion and Racialized Boundary in Urban Indonesia*. Doctor of Philosophy, University of California Santa Cruz.

Tu, W.-M. (1991). "Cultural China: The Periphery as the Center." *Daedalus* 120(2): 1–32.

Turner, S. (2003). "Setting the Scene Speaking Out: Chinese Indonesians after Suharto." *Asian Ethnicity* 4(3): 337–352.

Wang, G. (1991). *China and the Chinese Overseas*. Singapore, Times Academic Press.

Wang, L. and H. J. Ladegaard (2008). "Language Attitudes and Gender in China: Perceptions and Reported Use of Putonghua and Cantonese in the Southern Province of Guangdong." *Language Awareness* 17: 57–77.

Part III

Transnational Communities, Cultural Mediators

10 Multilingualism in the Chinese Community in Japan

John C. Maher

1 HISTORICAL DEVELOPMENT

1.1 Language Contact and Processions of the Exotic

The *Kultursprache* that is 'Chinese-Japanese' in Japan can be illustrated by two signal examples: the first from historical sociolinguistics, the second from cultural semiotics.

Firstly, it must be noted that Chinese-Japanese contact goes back to the 9th century—in terms of language history, Late Old (*chuko*) Japanese (Heian)— when grammars and dictionaries were being prepared (*Shinsen jikyo*, 'Newly Compiled Mirror of Chinese Characters', 898–901 and *Ruiju myogisho*, 'Classified dictionary of pronunciations and meanings, annotated', 1081). Chinese characters had been imported into Japan in the 6th century in the absence of a vernacular script (Gottlieb 1995 and Loveday 1996). High status Chinese was the variety superimposed on vernacular Japanese and employed by the literate elite (administrators, Buddhist priests, etc). Some kind of language planning took place whereby the Chinese writing system was adopted and a decision was made, in the 10th century, to replace older pronunciations (go-on) of Chinese characters with the Northern Chinese readings (kan-on).

Secondly, we draw attention to the famed *Edo Nobori* (going up to Edo) tributary processions during Japan's Edo period (1603–1868), in which officials from the Kingdom of the Ryukyus were obliged to perform following the Satsuma clan's invasion of the Ryukyu in 1609. The shape of these diplomatic expeditions copied the Ryukyuan embassy missions to the Qing court in Beijing (Beasley 1955). There were 400 to 1000 officials and considerable efforts were made to emphasise the foreignness or exoticness of this mission. Specifically, it was a Chinese parade. The Ryukyuans wore Chinese clothes, played Chinese music and used Chinese titles and names. Their language (Ryukyuan) could be easily confused in the popular imagination as Chinese. Why the Chinese charade? Quite simply, Satsuma political prestige was enhanced as a bogus 'ruler of a foreign country' by having Okinawans masquerade as Chinese. Extraordinarily, the influence survives today in the cliché believed by some Japanese that Okinawans are similar to Chinese and different ethnically from Japanese.

The phenomenon of massive linguistic borrowing from Chinese and its impact on literary practice and transcultural exchange connects with the processional charade *nobori*, encapsulating the paradox of ethnicity and appearance, minority marginalisation and linguistic presence. This occurs in a nation struggling with the claims of language ideology and modernity—as Heinrich (2012) has demonstrated in Okinawa within the context of multilingual Japan. These ancient and pre-modern phenomena underpin and inform the present, even as, in the 21st century, the actual presence of Chinese in Japan has evolved into something different (see Shao 2014): the massive force of Chinatowns, the legacy of war, the influx of migrant workers and students, the dramatic increase in the learning of Chinese, continuing transnational migration and evolving fluid identities.

1.2 Diglossia and Literacy

I doubted that I had arrived in Japan because I saw many Chinese characters, and almost all Japanese products I had known in Vietnam had the company names in western languages. . . . I was so confused that I may have arrived in China or Hong Kong when I saw many Chinese characters in the harbour of Yokohama.

(Vietnamese refugee 'boat person'. Kawakami 2012)

As a historical phenomenon of language as social practice, in the textual world Chinese and Japanese exist alongside each other in a diglossic relation. Crucially, this pertains to the spectrum of writing in the educational context, or put differently, in 'literacy practices' which involve the construction of knowledge and values, beliefs and feelings connected with the reading and writing of particular texts within particular contexts (Barton & Hamilton 2012). There is an assortment of terminology for diglossia. The 'classical' (Ferguson 1959) version is usually contrasted with 'extended' diglossia (Fishman 1967). A common language situation that exists throughout the world, generally diglossia refers to the coexistence of two varieties of the same language throughout a speech community. Often, one form is the literary or prestige dialect and the other is a common dialect spoken by most of the population. Employing Greek root prefixes for these two varieties, we might contrast 'endo-diglossia' (where two languages are related) with 'exo-diglossia' (where languages are not related or are distantly related). In the case of Japan, knowledge of Kanbun (漢文), the Chinese classics, has long been a prestige commodity (sic. 'prestige dialect'—see proviso below regarding H or Higher form).

The impact of Chinese on literacy and literature among the educated classes in Japan, until the end of the Edo period, was significant. For the educated elite, Kanbun (Chinese classics) were read not as Chinese per se (the 'higher' or H form per se) but rather as a 'higher' Japanese. This paradoxical situation I shall term 'inverted diglossia' to describe the context in which an L spoken variety (Chinese) contrasts with an unrelated prestige spoken variety (Japanese) whose written version constitutes an H variety of the other language. To summarise, Chinese as a spoken language was considered inferior, the L (Low) form to the H (High) written language and it was the latter that was regarded as the ideal form.

Whilst spoken Chinese was viewed as a degenerate form, the situation changed dramatically when it began to be studied as a foreign language starting from the Edo period and almost entirely in the Kansai region (Osaka). The motivation was overseas trade and commerce. In the Edo period, Osaka was the booming trading centre of Japan. In 1722, 124 brokers in the Doshomachi 道修町 quarter of Osaka, still now the core of the pharmaceutical trade of Japan, received official permission to act as a trade association (*kabunakama*). In 1871, the first Kangaku Gakusho 漢学学所 was set up by the Japanese Foreign Ministry whilst many private commercial Chinese schools were established.

Every child must learn the Chinese classics in primary and secondary school. It comes with the heavy cargo of cultural consciousness that food, religion, clothes, poetry, the arts and philosophy derive, in various degrees, from China. The Chinese classics have formed the ideological underpinning of Chinese-Japanese diglossia. High school textbooks focus mostly on philosophers, such as Confucius, Mencius, Lao Tzu and Chuang Tzu of the Hundred Schools of Thought during what is often called the Golden Age of Chinese philosophy. 'High school Chinese' is not the language of 'real people'.

It was the literary syncretism propelled by the volatile mix of Chinese, Japanese and European languages that set the stage for the emergence of Japan's powerful literary presence in the 20th century. The platform that helped solidify a bourgeois elite in the Chinese communities in Japan—of the Edo period and fin de siècle—was the symbolic respect with which Japanese intellectuals regarded Chinese literature. The unifying effect of literature began in school when an increasingly well-educated population—Japanese and Chinese—were obliged to study the Chinese classics.

1.3 Chinatowns

Japan has three main Chinatowns in Yokohama, Nagasaki and Kobe, originating as residential areas of Chinese merchants who settled in Japan. Urban traces of older thriving conglomerations of Chinese exist in Kanda-machi (Tokyo) and Tojin-machi (Fukuoka), whilst neo-Chinatowns flourish and impact on the linguistic landscape, as in the Nippori area of Tokyo's Ueno district.

Nagasaki was hometown to Chinese sailors, merchants and entrepreneurs during the 'exclusion' period (1639–1858) when the Tokugawa Shogunate adopted a closed-door policy for the rest of the country. Nagasaki Chinatown 長崎新地中華街, also known as Shinchi Chinatown, remains Japan's oldest Chinese community established as early as the 17th century.

Chinatowns are a symbolic presence of the Chinese diaspora and culture, a massive tourist destination and an economic engine of the region. It is my contention that the foundation of the Chinese community and Chinatowns in Japan was laid, paradoxically, during the exclusion period. The draconian foreign policy of Japan (1633–1868) dictated that no foreigner could enter nor could any Japanese leave the country on penalty of death. Strict regulations were applied to commerce and foreign relations by the central government. Trade with China was also handled at Nagasaki. After Yokohama, Kobe and Nagasaki opened at the start of the Meiji period, Chinese immigrants poured into the ports, many accompanying western diplomats and traders as compradors and employees from Chinese ports. Hundreds of interpreters (some bogus) were employed in the ports and diplomatic missions: the Edo government itself commissioned a group of reliable multilingual Chinese or Totsuji (Chinese negotiators).

A social construct, replete with tropes (sic. 'oriental orientalism', Leung 2012), the Chinatown of Japan is as fundamental a part of tourist Japan as Disneyland—except that people live there. Yokohama Chinatown is the largest Chinatown in Asia. Most of the Chinese population of Yokohama live in Chinatown, and it has been home for almost a hundred years. In 1867, a Chinese population of 660 started to assemble Yokohama Chinatown. At the close of the Taisho period (1912–1926), the figure was 6,280. In 1947, there was a wave of 'newcomers' from Taiwan and northeastern China. Restaurants at that time numbered 61. In 2011, with an overall population of approximately 22,500, there were 250 restaurants and shops. Developed from the old port, the shopping malls (shotengai) and streets of Yamashita-cho (500 square meters), under the ten gates, to the annual festivals and the Kanteibyo Temple come fifteen million visitors annually.

2 ONGOING CHANGES AND SUPERDIVERSITY

2.1 Work, Migration and Citizenship

Typologically, the Chinese community can be divided into the following categories, along with the main languages of preference in the speech community:

1. *Ro-* or *Kyu-kakyo*. The traditional communities of *Kyukakyo* (old overseas) resident over several generations: Cantonese mother tongue, some Mandarin, Japanese as a second language.

2. *Kajin*. Second–fourth generation *Kakyo*: Cantonese as a second or foreign language. Japanese dominant. Some Mandarin.
3. *Shin-kakyo*. Postwar newcomers: Taiwanese Mandarin, Taiwanese dialects.
4. *Hikiage* (*Chugoku-kikokusha*). These include (a) *Zanryu koji* or war orphans and (b) *Zanryu fujin* (wives of war orphans abandoned in China): mainland Mandarin dialects of Chinese, Japanese as a foreign or second language.
5. *Gaikoku-Jin Rodosha*. Foreign Chinese workers: dialects of Chinese, Japanese as a foreign language.
6. Ryugakusei. Chinese students. Chinese mainland Mandarin.

The precise (total) number of ethnic Chinese in Japan is not clear because, as indicated earlier, over 4,000 Chinese have naturalised every year in the past two decades (80,000 ethnic Chinese are therefore uncounted in the statistics for resident Chinese). Also, Chinese who are not duly registered as legal migrants (the figure 40,000 is commonly cited) are not counted. It is likely that the total number in Japan is upwards of 700,000 Chinese. Yamashita et al's (2008) analysis of transnational migration documents the tendency for many Chinese to come as college students (89,374) or pre-college students (15,915), about 69 percent of the total. There is also a high ratio (74.9 percent) of Chinese working in Japan as trainees (*kenshusei*). The population of Chinese living in Japan jumped from 606,000 in 2007 to 656,000 in 2008. During the same period, the population of, say, Americans living in Japan has hovered around 52,000 for a decade. Following the explosion of technology and job availability in the software field starting at the millennium, Chinese have made bilingalism the rule, as noted by Wang (2005) who points out that development in Sino-Japanese software is hampered by the language barrier. So in general, direct exchanges of personnel are more necessary than between India and the United States. The presence of bilingual engineers has turned out to be the key to success or failure in the joint development of software.

The number of Chinese residents in Japan is calculated using the Government of Japan's 2014 statistics on foreign residents in Japan. According to these figures from the Judicial System and Research Department, Minister's Secretariat, Immigration Bureau, as of 2013, the Chinese are numerically the largest community with China having 648,980 and China (Taiwan) having 33,322 (22,773 in 2012). The number of residents from China has jumped significantly from approximately 15,339 in 1990 (see Maher's 1995 analysis) to 335,575 in 2000. Foreign residents (i.e. those permanently residing in Japan) constitute 1.22% of the Japanese population—American military personnel are not included in these statistics. Whilst Chinese residents comprise approximately 32% of the total foreign resident population, foreign nationals from Korea comprise 26% (519,737), Brazil 10% (181,268), Philippines 10% (209,137), U.S.A. 2.5% (49,979), and Peru 2% (48,580). Foreign national residents from

Europe comprise 59,241; South America (in total) 243,174; North America (in total) 62,745; Asia (in total) 1,676,140; Africa (in total) 11,545 and Oceania (in total) 12,692.

Most of the working population seems to gather in the work intensive urban areas where employment is possible in the service industries, but also in rural areas where are jobs in the factory sector. The population spread across the top ten prefectures are:

1. Tokyo 164,424
2. Kanagawa 55,362
3. Osaka 52,392
4. Saitama 47,816
5. Aichi 47,313
6. Hyogo 25,353
7. Fukuoka 21,551
8. Hiroshima 14,559
9. Shizuoka 13,116
10. Nagano 10,943

The distribution is predictable. Many Chinese are factory workers in the manufacturing industries of the prefectures of Gifu, Fukui and Aichi. By contrast, in Fukuoka (Kyushu), and to a lesser extent in the Hiroshima area, the booming tourist industry and proximity to the continent has created dynamic population interactions among the Chinese and Korean populations from the mainland. Some long-term reconfigurations occurred in the collective mind of the non-Japanese community at the millennium, including the Chinese population. That is, the number of permanent residents doubled in four years (1998–2002) by 12 percent (Tsuda 2006: 18).

Table 10.1 Live Births Involving Japanese Fathers and Foreign Wives in Japan (adapted from Ministry of Health, Labour and Welfare 2011 and Ministry of Justice 2011)

Country of Origin of Wives	1995	2000	2005	2006	2007	2008	2009	TOTAL
Philippines	5488	4705	4441	4998	5140	4623	3815	33210
China	2244	3040	3478	3925	4271	4203	4209	25370
Korea	3519	3345	2583	2593	2530	2439	2285	19294
Thailand	851	736	509	512	507	446	427	3988
Brazil	406	397	217	256	268	249	235	2028
U.S.A.	178	142	122	130	141	124	116	953
Peru	105	85	92	99	98	84	93	656
U.K.	55	51	47	51	53	62	45	364

As the decade proceeded, and since the year 2000, two-thirds of all Chinese permanent residents have taken this step. Liu-Farrer (2011) comments that this reflects a desire to share the benefits of transnational experience and a degree of citizenship in Japan. More Chinese women come to live and work in Japan than men, for example in 2009, 58 percent of registered Chinese residents were men. Liu-Farrer analyses thus, 'This reflects the demographic consequence of the major patterns of migration. Most Chinese entered as students, spouses to Japanese nationals, dependents, and trainees and technical interns. Whereas the student population is mostly gender-equal, the spouses to Japanese nationals and dependents are predominantly women. Among the trainees and technical interns, over one-third of them work in the textile industry' (2011: 13). The emergence of mixed background, often bilingual, families can be seen in a substantial number of children born into families of Japanese fathers and Chinese mothers. Here is a comparative table.

3 TRANSNATIONAL CONNECTIONS

3.1 Identity and the War that Will Not Go Away

Many have urged a fresh look at citizenship and integration in the age of the transnational entrepreneur as well as a fresh look at the Chinese, whose sense of place and nationality is considerably more fluid than in previous generations. Expatriates aspire to a partial return to their home country and often achieve it. Indeed, it is not uncommon for Chinese couples working in Japan or the spouses of Japanese people to plan for a partial 'homecoming to China'. 'Going home' (帰国 kikoku) is a totemic theme among the Chinese diaspora in Japan and therein resides the painful issue of wartime historical dislocations that will not, even now, go away. There is a substantial population of older, mainly northeastern speakers from the northeastern provinces (Manchuria). Their children (second generation) are mostly Chinese dominant but conversationally fluent in Japanese. Among the third generation children, now attending Japanese schools, substantial language shift has occurred towards Japanese. This group can be termed Japan's 'invisible Chinese minority', dislocated from their Chinese background and with sometimes uncomfortable relations with the long-established Chinese community in Japan.

3.2 The War Orphans (残留邦人): Abandoned Bilinguals

The life trajectories of the monolingual Chinese-speaking Japanese minority abandoned in Manchuria and now 'abandoned' to their own devices in Japan is tragic. It is a paradoxical tale of a mostly Manchurian-located, Chinese-speaking minority of Japanese ethnic association, who were, in common parlance, 'tossed by the waves of history' (歴史に翻弄された), and who now find themselves a minority in Japan. How did this situation arise? How did a culturally and linguistically Chinese but ethnically Japanese minority end up in Japan?

Emulating Nazi policy, the Japanese military-industrial machine during World War II routinely tried to replace inhabitants of colonised countries with Japanese settlers (sic. 'ethnic cleansing'). Upwards of 5,000 orphans of the Japanese villages of the former Manchuko (開拓団) were abandoned, then adopted and raised by Chinese peasant families. On their return to Japan in the 1980s, they became a Chinese-speaking minority in Japan. Zanryu-hojin were Japanese civilians, mostly women and children (specifically referred to as 残留孤児 zanryu-koji), abandoned in Manchuria in 1945 when Japan's puppet state in Manchuria collapsed, and when most Japanese hikiagesha (引揚者) or repatriates (帰国者) had returned to Japan. Since 1972, the zanryu-hojin have been slowly repatriated to Japan. Orphans' repatriation has often been accompanied with several generations of their extended Chinese families. Language shift is evident in the returnee community. The third generation were educated in Japanese primary and secondary schools. In her study of the returnee community in Sakai, Osaka prefecture, Tomozawa (2001: 159) writes, 'The possibility of their becoming Japanese monolinguals is high considering that domains for using Chinese are restricted to the family and/or returnee friends, and there is a scarcity of opportunities for them to learn Chinese (especially reading and writing). Many of the respondents expressed a desire to maintain their own Chinese proficiency and that of their descendants, but seemed skeptical . . . and had no effective measures to ensure that they retained their Chinese language'.

Language provision is available for returnees in Japanese main cities, but because most returnees have daytime work, they are unable to attend. Withdrawal classes are common for Chinese returnee children; mostly these are taught by non-Chinese speaking instructors. Many returnees of the second and third generation (e.g., children of returnees) try to bring up their children bilingually—Japanese being the dominant language of their environment.

3.3   Language and Citizenship

Annually, the number of Chinese taking Japanese nationality is approximately 4000 persons. According to statistics released by the Ministry of Justice, from 1952 to 2012 (Shen Wen 2013), the number of Chinese in Japan who have taken Japanese nationality has shown a steady increase: 127,199 in total. Japanese citizenship procedures do not include an obligatory written or spoken 'citizenship test' on language and culture. The current rejection rate overall is less than 2 percent. Chinese permanent residents in Japan number 203,292 people, spouses 46,317, permanent resident spouses 8896 people.

The population structure of Chinese in Japan demonstrates stable and stereotypical characteristics. Chinese residents:

- work into the mainstream: business, the professions, trade
- include a large population of students
- live substantially in Chinatown environs but also elsewhere
- are fluent in Japanese
- are frequently trilingual (Chinese, Japanese, English)
- acquire Japanese nationality
- aquire permanent residence

Citizenship for new Chinese immigrants is a crucial issue. The Chinese community, revitalised by the influx of immigrants, demands a redefinition of the notion of civic allegiance and national citizenship. Many new citizens are not fluent speakers of Japanese. To this, Gottlieb issues the reminder that 'at the level of practice, Japanese citizenship can no longer be taken to indicate either Japanese ethnicity or that the citizen is a first language speaker of the Japanese language' (Gottlieb 2012: 2). Kibe (2006) dismantles the logic of the trope 'Japan is a country with a highly homogeneous population', suggesting the concept of a 'differentiated citizenship'. This encompasses a plurality of (ethnocultural) groups in Japan with distinct claims to differentiated citizenship but also institutions and practices accommodating them. For Kibe, the differentiated concept of citizenship differs from the conventional, unitary one in (1) disconnecting citizenship from nationality, (2) aiming at cultural pluriformity instead of uniformity, and (3) affirming positively some grey area between national and non-national categories. He goes further, 'Public policies that attempt to preserve a cultural homogeneity that does not exist and such political aims as "enhancing social unity" are morally and prudentially undesirable' (2006: 413).

4   LINGUISTIC CHANGE

4.1   Bilingual Education and Language Diversity

The language policy of Chinese schools in Japan is robustly oriented to bilingualism (at least Chinese and Japanese). Unusually for primary schools anywhere in Japan, English is introduced in the first grade. Yokohama Overseas Chinese School (YOCS) is located in Yokohama Chinatown and is the oldest of all Chinese schools in Japan. There are three full-time Chinese educational institutions in the Tokyo-Yokohama region which incorporate grades from kindergarten to senior high school (Tokyo Chinese School, Yamate Chinese School and YOCS). Most pupils of these schools are Japan-born, learning Mandarin Chinese as a second language. Japanese is mostly the home language of all pupils, and Japanese pupils in the YOCS comprise almost one-third of the school population. Parents send their children to these schools to enhance the advantages and awareness of being bilingual in both Japanese and Chinese. In Chen Pi-Chu's (2005) study of the ethnic composition and language use of the class of fifteen first grade primary school pupils, their birthplaces and language(s) spoken are as follows:

> 4 Japanese (Japanese only)
> 6 Ethnic Chinese (1 Chinese speaker, five Japanese)
> 2 Japan-born Taiwanese (Japanese)
> 2 Taiwan-born Taiwanese (Chinese and Japanese, Chinese and Taiwanese)
> 1 Mainland Chinese (Chinese only)
> This compares with the language use of the 32 schoolteachers in the institution:
> 2 Japan-born Chinese (Japanese dominant, some Chinese)
> 12 Taiwan-born Chinese (Chinese, Taiwanese, Japanese)
> 4 Mainland China-born Chinese (Chinese and Japanese)
> 13 Japan-born Japanese (Japanese only)
> 1 English (English with some Japanese)

In the majority of schools, Chinese is a privileged medium of instruction, and for most children Mandarin Chinese is learned as a second language (role-play, Chinese literature, repetition, drama). Romanisation ('Pinyin') is learned at the end of primary school and the Chinese phonological system is introduced immediately.

Chinese speaking territory born pupils to Japan-born and Japanese-speaking intake is educationally significant. A survey conducted by Qui Xiaolan (2012) in Kobe Chinese School shows the shift towards 'localisation' of education. In 1974, 100 percent of pupils (808) were of Chinese nationality, with 1.6 percent Japanese nationality. Twenty years later in 1994, the ratio was 71.2 percent Chinese: 24.6 percent Japanese; in 2004, 33.1 percent Chinese: 63.7 percent Japanese; and in 2011, of a total population of 676 pupils, 33.7 percent (203) Chinese: 63.9 percent (388) Japanese, Other 2.4 percent (16). As Qui Xiaolan (2012: 158–159) explains, the reasons are threefold. Firstly, an increase in the number of (Japanese) naturalised citizens of ethnic background, secondly, an increase in 'international marriages' between Japanese and Chinese and thirdly, an increase in non-ethnic Chinese entrants (i.e., Japanese children) to Chinese schools.

It is estimated that approximately one million Japanese are learning Mandarin or other varieties of Chinese. The 'shock to the system', in educational circles, is that Chinese has replaced the prestigious French and German that have long served as flagship foreign languages, after the most learned foreign language, English. This is not new. Pilot programmes to teach Mandarin in Japan's senior high schools began in 1987. In 2003, there were 530 schools offering Mandarin classes and there are currently 947. The Center for Testing Chinese Proficiency is one of Japan's accreditation bodies. Various tests include Chinese Proficiency Test (HSK), and the Test of Communicative Chinese (TECC).

4.2   Language Reproduction and Social Networks

4.2.1   Religion

Buddhist temples, some with international networks, are active in language maintenance with Chinese (specifically, Taiwanese, Mandarin Chinese and Japanese) services and sponsoring Chinese language classes. The languages of services are primarily Taiwanese, Japanese and some Mandarin. Whilst Yokohama churches employ Cantonese and Japanese, other congregations, like the Ikebukuro Chinese Church, employ Taiwanese and runs a 'Taiwanese dialect' class for Japan-born Taiwanese or Japanese spouses and others wanting to learn Taiwanese. In total, there are twenty-four Chinese Christian churches in Japan.

4.2.2   Chinese Language Media

Chinese language media in the Chinese community is massive and the newspaper industry—including web newspapers—is vigorous. Large circulation newspapers include the oldest, Jiyu Shimbun (Freedom News, from 1954), as well as Zhongwendaobao (Chinese newspaper), Xinjiaoliu Shibao (New Communication Newspaper), Waiguoxuesheng Xinwen (Overseas Chinese Student Newspaper) and Liuxusheng Xinwen (Overseas Student News). The extraordinary growth of Chinese language media owes its foundation to revolutionary politics in the Chinese community at the turn of the century. In 2013, there were approximately 120 magazines, newspapers, journals and periodicals published for the Chinese community in Japan. Most of the publications are in both Chinese and Japanese—the former directed to many newcomers, in particular the highly literate Chinese students who came in numbers to Japan from the 1980s, the latter for the younger generation of Japan-born ethnic Chinese who do not have a full grasp of the Chinese language. Literacy is crucial for Chinese residents: about twenty Chinese-managed bookstores cater to Chinese-language readers in the Tokyo-Yokohama region.

There are no Chinese-language TV or radio stations, but several radio networks incorporate multilingual broadcasting (Tsuda and Lafaye 2009, Kanayama 2007, Kim 2012), including Chinese-language news and other broadcasting. Recent technology platforms, such as the IPhone, Facebook and Skype, provide new linguistic opportunities for what Li Wei has felicitously termed 'translanguaging space' (Li Wei 2011a), whereby multimodalities (Li Wei 2011b) of communication serve new cultural identities and creativities (such as code-switching, see Li Wei and Wu Chao Jung 2009). Consider the following example. A 19-year-old female first year co-ed (Japanese father/Chinese mother) who goes to Japanese school at a university in Tokyo notes the possibilities now afforded for a bilingual lifestyle: 'I don't watch TV much. Quiz shows and garbage. I do stuff on the internet a lot in Japanese because it's cool and really open and that's my most comfortable language. My mom wants me to look at programmes in Chinese but they're clunky and kinda boring. Since I got a new machine . . . I skype a lot with my cousins in Taiwan. We speak Mandarin . . . they're teaching me some Tainan dialect as well . . . some Tainan slang . . . really cool. I think Skype's changed a lot for me . . . made me speak Chinese. . . . I'm kinda starting to like Chinese as well as Japanese' (Vivian Yamashita, Interview in Japanese and English, with author, 2013). This trilingual speaker quintessentially occupies the shifting and ambiguous territory described by Li Wei (2011b) as 'creativity' (challenging, testing and playing with linguistic boundaries).

5   IDEOLOGY

5.1   Intercultural Communication: Toponyms, Stereotyping and Breakdowns

As the Chinese population continues to feature as the largest foreign resident population in Japan, ideological issues revolving around politics and intercultural and interpersonal communication arise between Japanese and Chinese. The Japanese Government conducts a 'war' to protect the country's place names, such as *Kyoto* and *Hiroshima*, from being registered as trademarks in China. Currently, 261 wards and cities in Tokyo are registered as product trademarks in China.

In the bigger political arena, there are damaging disputes between China and Japan over the control of the islands. Senkaku 尖閣諸島 or Diaoyu 钓鱼岛及其附属岛屿. The toponymic but territorial dispute rumbles on related to military primacy in the Asia-Pacific. The dispute centres on eight uninhabited islands and rocks in the East China Sea south-west of Japan's southern-most prefecture, Okinawa. The islands are close to strategically significant shipping lanes and rich fishing grounds. There is also the prospect of potential oil and gas reserves. (The Sino-Japanese dispute over 'dead islands' can be compared to the 'live' linguistic implications of US-Japan issues as in the Ogasawara Islands, see Long 2011.)

At the interpersonal level, issues of ideology surface in intercultural communication. The study of stereotyping and prejudice is an aspect of intergroup relationship that analyses behaviours as mediated by perceptions, beliefs and attitudes. Stereotypes influence the force of social transmission in intergroup relations. In a study of 'bias' in intergroup perceptions, Shi Jie and Wang Jijin (2013) analysed three cohorts of young people from Japan, China and South Korea living in Tokyo. Employing a sociolinguistic survey and game-style experiment, the authors concluded that significantly negative cultural images existed among the Japanese towards China and Chinese.

The purpose of Shi and Wang's study was to ascertain the features and underpinning mechanisms of respondents' bias and, later to test the effectiveness for awareness-raising training. The results showed that 'informants held negative images of biases towards [China and] other countries.

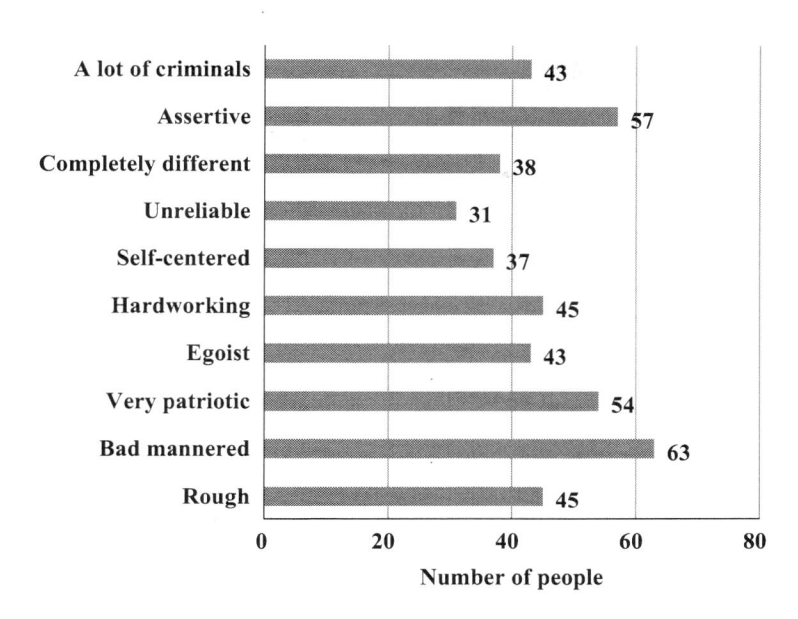

Figure 10.1   Cultural Images among Japanese towards China and Chinese.
Adapted from Shi and Wang (2013)

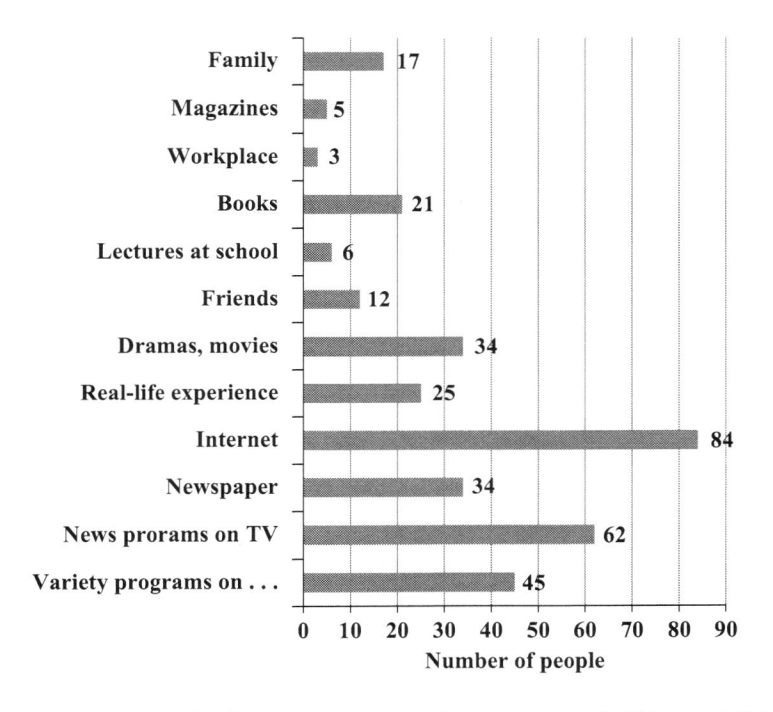

Figure 10.2   Sources of Cultural Images among Japanese towards China and Chinese.
Adapted from Shi and Wang (2013)

However, they still showed strong curiosity about and interest in each other's countries' (242). From what sources do Japanese derive images of Chinese people?

6   CONCLUSION

The Chinese community in Japan is layered and multilingual. It exists within a new stage of globalisation in Japan together with a weakening of conventional myths about language and identity. Language in Japan teems with regional and social varieties. It comprises layers of change and multi-lingual contact due to factors like migration and travel and intermarriage. Language is also extra-territorial. You are a native speaker of English or Chinese but a Japanese citizen. You are a native speaker of Japanese but a UK or French citizen. This is cosmopolitan common sense. Languages notice cultural boundaries but rarely conform to them: like birds crossing borders. Language is an archaeology of 'language contact'—the connecting of languages and language varieties. Language as a social convention encourages different styles of life and social expression. Look at language and see contact.

In Japan, the increase in bilingual populations, migrant labour, the explosion in inter-marriages, particularly Chinese-Japanese and the revitalisation of Chinatowns are well documented. I have described, elsewhere (Maher 1995, 2010), the impact of this phenomenon on language use in Japan. In addition to standard Japanese and several distinctive dialects, there are an additional several languages in active use in Japan, including varieties of oldcomer and newcomer Chinese.

Observation of the Chinese community in Japan helps us connect multilingualism with an understanding of how language and identity is changing in Japan. In a theory which I have termed 'metroethnicity' (Maher 2005), I suggest that new hybrid ethnicities and language identities are moving beyond traditional loyalties towards a performative and dynamic mode. In postmodern society, speaking fluent Korean or Chinese is no longer a badge of 'being' Korean or Chinese. Indeed, the demands of ethnic loyalty and conformity to an orthodoxy of 'being something', in postmodern Japan, are now being disengaged from language identity. An explanatory concept of metroethnic and metrolinguistic style might be a starting point (Maher 2010). 'Metro' is a multiple-signifier, pointing to phenomena that travel 'below' (métro) the radar of bordered perceptions of ethnicity and language. More underground than overground, it employs 'difference' for cultural and 'aesthetic' effect, a 'sfumato', an ethnic blurring, EA (ethnic ambiguity), rather than conformity to one ethnic orthodoxy, the celebration of momentary actions rather than ontological solidity. It is through this metrolinguistic world that return to the paradox of the mock Chinese procession of the Ryukyuans 'doing

Edo *nobori*' becomes possible. Is it, in fact, through the performance of 'doing' Chinese in Japan (revamped Chinatowns, schools attracting more Japanese pupils, Chinese Japonaise, the boom in language learning) that a new kind of Chinese will emerge? Were the Ryukyuans and Japanese—with a nod and a wink—onto something? Did the Ryukyuan performance of a cultural and linguistic *imago* of Chinese in a hegemonic Japan point to a newer postmodern reality: that identity and language will hitherto be driven by aesthetics rather than by conventional ontologies of identity?

REFERENCES

Barton, D. and Hamilton, M. 2012. *Local Literacies: Reading and Writing in One Community*. Linguistics Classics ed. London: Routledge.

Beasley, William G. 1955. *Select Documents on Japanese Foreign Policy, 1853–1868*. London: Curzon Press.

Chen, Pi-Chu. 2005. *The Overseas Chinese in the Tokyo-Yokohama Region: Language Situation and Community*. Ph.D. Dissertation. Tokyo: International Christian University.

Ferguson, Charles. 1959. Diglossia. *Word* 15: 325–340.

Fishman, Joshua. 1967. Bilingualism with and without diglossia; diglossia with and without bilingualism. *Journal of Social Issues* 23 (2): 29–38.

Gottlieb, Nanette. 1995. *Kanji Politics. Language Policy and Japanese Script*. London: Kegan Paul International.

Gottlieb, Nanette (Ed.). 2012. *Language and Citizenship in Japan*. London: Routledge.

Heinrich, Patrick. 2012. *The Making of Monolingual Japan Language Ideology and Japanese Modernity*. Bristol: Multilingual Matters.

Kanayama, Tomoko. 2007. *Community Media* (in Japanese). Tokyo: Keio Gijyuku University.

Kawakami, Ikuo. 2012. Children Crossing Borders and Their Citizenship in Japan. In *Language and Citizenship in Japan*. Nancy Gottlieb (Ed.). London: Routledge, pp.79–97.

Kibe, Takashi. 2006. Differentiated citizenship and ethnocultural groups: A Japanese case. *Citizenship Studies* 10 (4), September 2006: 413–430(18).

Kim, Chiaki. 2012. Hanshin Awaji Daishinsai kara Higashi Nihon Daishinsai e: Tabunka Kyosei no Keiken o Tsunagu (From the Great Hanshin Awaji Earthquake to the Great East Japan Earthquake: Connecting the experience of Multicultural Symbiosis). *GEMC Journal*, 2012 (7): 3.

Leung, Mathew. 2012. *Oriental Orientalism In Japan—The Case of Yokohama Chinatown*. Ph.D. Dissertation. London: University College London.

Liu-Farrer, Gracia. 2011. *Labour Migration from China to Japan*. Abingdon: Nissan Institute/Routledge.

Long, Daniel. 2011. *English on the Bonin (Ogasawara) Islands*. Publication of the American Dialect Society (PADS), Durham: Duke University Press.

Loveday, Leo. 1996. *Language Contact in Japan*. Oxford: Oxford University Press.

Maher, John C. 1995. "The Kakyo: Chinese in Japan". In *Special Issue on Japan. Journal of Multilingual and Multicultural Development* 16 (5): 125–138.

Maher, John C. 2005. Metroethnicity, Language, and the Principle of Cool. *International Journal of Sociology of Language* 175/176: 83–102.

Maher, John C. 2010. Metroethnicities and Metrolanguages. In *The Handbook of Language and Globalizaton*. Nikolas Coupland (Ed.). Wiley-blackwell, pp. 575–591.

Ministry of Health, Labour and Welfare. 2011. *Health and Social Statistics Division, Statistics and Information Department*. Government of Japan.

Ministry of Justice. 2011. *Statistics on Foreign Residents*. Government of Japan.

Qui, Xiaolan. 2012. *Tabunka Shakai Kakyo: Kajin Kyoiku* (The Overseas Chinese in Multilingual Society: Education). Tokyo: Aoyama Life Publishers.

Shao, Chunfen. 2014. Chinese Migration to Japan, 1979–2010: Patterns and Policies. In Jijao Zhang and Howard Duncan (Eds.) *Migration in China and Asia: Experience and Policy* (pp. 175–187). Dordrecht: Springer.

Shi, Jie and Wang Jijin. 2013. '"Bias" in Intercultural Communication: A Case Study of Japanese, Chinese and Korean University Students.' *Educational Studies* 55: 229–240.

Tomozawa, Akie. 2001. Japan's Hidden Bilinguals: The Language of "War Orphans" and Their Families after Repatriation from China. In Mary G. Noguchi and Sandra Fotos (Eds.) *Studies in Japanese Bilingualism* (pp. 133–163). Bristol, UK: Multilingual Matters.

Tsuda, Sanae and Beverley Elsom Lafaye. 2009. Japan's experience of language contact: A case study of RADIO-i, a multilingual radio station in Nagoya. *Language and Intercultural Communication* 5 (3–4): 248–263.

Tsuda, Takeyuki. 2006. Localities and the Struggle for Immigrant Rights: The Significance of Local Citizenship in Recent Countries of Immigration. In Takeyuki Tsuda and Chikako Usui (Eds.) Local Citizenship in Recent Countries of Immigration: Japan in Comparative Perspective. Lanham, MD: Lexington Books.

Wang, Jin. 2005. Chinese engineers and information technology in Japan. *China Perspectives* [Online] 6: 2–10.

Wei, Li. 2011a. Moment analysis and translanguaging space: Discursive construction of identities by multilingual Chinese youth in Britain. *Journal of Pragmatics* 43: 1222–1235.

Wei, Li. 2011b. Multilinguality, multimodality and multicompetence: Code- and mode- switching by minority ethnic children in complementary schools. *Modern Language Journal* 95: 3.

Wei, Li and Wu, Chao-Jung. 2009. Polite Chinese children revisited: Creativity and the use of codeswitching in the Chinese complementary school classroom. *International Journal of Bilingual Education and Bilingualism* 12 (2): 193–212.

Wen, Shen. 2013. Chinese in Japan from Several Expansion into a Qualitative Improvement. *Chinese Herald*, 207.

Yamashita, Shinji, et al. 2008. Transnational Migration in East Asia: Japan in a Comparative Focus. *Senri Ethnological Reports* 77: 3–13.

11 From Monolingualism to Multilingualism
The Linguistic Landscape in Kuala Lumpur's Chinatown[1]

Wang Xiaomei, Koh Yi Chern, Patricia Nora Riget, and Supramani Shoniah

1 INTRODUCTION

Fishman's three-generation model of language shift (1972) predicts that the development of immigrants' language will undergo three stages: (1) first generation monolingual in heritage language, (2) second generation bilingual in heritage language and host country language, (3) third generation monolingual in host country language. Accordingly, Chinese Malaysians should be experiencing the local language (Malay) monolingualism stage, as most of them represent the fourth or fifth generation of Chinese migrants to Malaysia. Despite Fishman's prediction, using the three generation model of language shift, there seems to be a contradiction. Today, most Chinese Malaysians still retain their heritage language to a large extent, in addition to being proficient in both Malay (the native language) and English (the global language) (Wang 2010). It seems that Chinese Malaysians represent a different type of stable immigrants. The development of multilingualism in Malaysia takes a different route from other immigrant communities. This chapter attempts to review the historical development of Chinese linguistic practices in Malaysia by taking a linguistic landscape approach. The main research questions are: (1) what are the different stages of Chinese multilingualism in Malaysia? (2) how are the different stages reflected in the linguistic landscape in the Kuala Lumpur Chinatown area?

This historical approach to the linguistic landscape is of theoretical and methodological significance. Theoretically, this study uses both real-time and apparent-time perspectives (Holmes 2001: 205–207), where both old signs and new signs will be investigated as the history of multilingualism manifests itself on sign-boards. Originally, real-time and apparent-time methods are used in language change studies, which investigate language change across time (real-time) or across age groups at one time (apparent-time). The historical approach broadens the scope of linguistic landscape studies, which are mainly discussed in relation to language policy (Lanza & Woldemariam 2009, Backhaus 2009), language vitality (Macalister 2010), and language identity (Curtin 2009, Taylor-Leech 2012). The real-time data are photos specially selected from two books depicting different periods of

Chinatown. These two books are *Moving Mountains* (2012), a collection of old photos of Kuala Lumpur and Selangor, and *Our Petaling Street* (2012), a collection of stories on the shops in the Kuala Lumpur Chinatown area. Some of the old signs can still be found in the present day Kuala Lumpur Chinatown area, where the present study was carried out. They are either preserved on the pillars in front of the shops or hanging inside the shops. Unfortunately, most of them have disappeared due to the renovation and development of Chinatown. The apparent-time data are photos taken by the research team in August, 2012. In total, 388 photos had been processed using FileMaker 10.0. By comparing real-time and apparent-time data, the history of language use on signs was traced, and this is closely associated with the sociolinguistic situation during different historical periods.

This chapter starts with the three historical periods of linguistic practices by Chinese diasporas in Malaysia, especially in Chinatown, Kuala Lumpur. The main section is the analysis of old photos from these three stages, which are Chinese monolingualism, Chinese-English bilingualism, and Malay-Chinese-English trilingualism. In the discussion section, the association between language development and the evolution of Chinatown in terms of language shift will be addressed. This chapter concludes by highlighting the theoretical significance of historical linguistic landscape studies and characteristics of linguistic practices by Chinese diasporas in Malaysia, focusing on Kuala Lumpur's Chinatown.

2   HISTORICAL STAGES OF LINGUISTIC PRACTICES BY CHINESE DIASPORAS IN MALAYSIA

Chinese immigrants started their settlement in Malaysia in the 15th century (Yen 2000) and underwent several stages of development in terms of linguistic practices. As these immigrants originated from different provinces in China, they spoke different varieties of Chinese dialects, such as Hokkien, Cantonese, and Hakka, and these dialects are not mutually intelligible. As such, these immigrants needed to acquire a better way to communicate with each other because they had similar cultural and religious backgrounds. As time passed, the interaction between Chinese and local Malays became more and more frequent, and they started to acquire Malay in a colloquial form or pidgin form (Wang 2012). With the start of British colonial governance in 1824, the Chinese community started acquiring English through education (Asmah 1996). English, therefore, was added to the Chinese elites' linguistic repertoire. In the 1920s, with the influence from China, Chinese schools in Malaya started to use Mandarin as the medium of instruction, which brought about a new variety of Chinese language (Mak 1985). After Malaysia gained independence in 1957, the sociolinguistic profile changed again. Many Chinese schools were transformed into national schools under the then new education policy and Malay was used as the medium of instruction. English lost its official status and Malay attained the status as the national language in 1967 (Asmah 1982). All English schools started to be transformed into national schools from 1971. As a result, Malay began to be used as the lingua franca across the different ethnic groups. Since the 1980s, the government started enforcing the use of Malay in official domains. Presently, the linguistic repertoire of the majority of the Malaysian Chinese community comprises of Chinese (Mandarin and Chinese dialects), Malay, and English. In the following section, three historical stages of the linguistic practices by the Chinese diasporas are introduced with references to the social, political, and educational domains.

2.1 Colonial Period (1824–1956)

During the British colonization of Malaya, the education system did not specify a clear national language policy. There existed basically four types of schools: English-medium, Malay-medium, Chinese-medium, and Tamil-medium schools. Each type of school had its own syllabus. The English-medium schools were run by missionaries and the British government. English, being the language of governance and education, had a higher prestige role and status. Mastering it was crucial for social and economic mobility. Hence, the learning and use of English was greatly pursued by members of the local multiracial population composed of Malays and Chinese and Indian immigrants. However, in the case of the Malays, for example, the British provided the largely rural Malay population with Malay-medium schools that did not extend beyond primary level. In fact, by developing Malay-medium schools, the British adhered to the policy of educating the rural Malay children to become farmers and fishermen, whereas the urban Malay elites sent their children to English-medium schools in order to prepare them to hold administrative positions in the colonial government (Hafriza 2006). As for the Chinese community, being immigrants living in the Malay heartland, they were given the autonomy and responsibility to set up their own schools. This included designing their own curriculum, employing teachers, and using textbooks from China. Until 1911, these schools were frequently visited and monitored by education officers from China, as the education system was based on the education system in China. The funding needed for building these schools was obtained from local Chinese businessmen and community leaders. These schools used different Chinese dialects as mediums of instruction and were funded or run by different clans. Kua K. S. (1999) notes that the struggle "to preserve and promote the language, education and culture of the Chinese in Malaya involved the active mobilization of the whole Chinese community through guilds and associations". Such high level of dedication bestowed by the Chinese to the education of their next generation greatly impressed the British colonial authorities, so much so that they left the Malayan Chinese virtually on their own to manage their affairs.

The indifference of the colonial administration and its *laissez-faire* attitude toward the non-Malay communities ended in 1920 when it introduced the "Registration of School Ordinance" in the Federated Malay

States. Firstly, the Schools Registration Enactment was passed in 1919 to restrict political activities in the schools. Then, in 1924, a new syllabus, one that centered on the local context, as well as the introduction of English and Malay, was implemented in all Chinese schools. The War years (1941–1945) marked the darkest years for the Chinese community in general. During this time, Chinese schools were suspended and a reign of terror was imposed on Chinese teachers and students by the Japanese occupation of Malaya. Prior to the independence of Malaya in 1957, a committee headed by L. J. Barnes was set up in 1950 for the purpose of "making an in-depth study of the Malay education in Malaya" (Yang 2001: 19). The Barnes Report, which was published in 1951, highlighted the following recommendations: all Malay and English schools would be preserved and should be given priority; vernacular Chinese and Tamil schools, on the other hand, would be closed down and replaced by national schools. All schools would use the same syllabus and English would be the medium of instruction at the secondary level. The Chinese and Indians in occupied Malaya were disgruntled with such recommendations and declared that their existing education systems should in fact be maintained. Thereafter, the Fenn-Wu Committee was established in 1951 and its main task was to look into the Chinese education system in Malaya. This committee recommended that English, Malay, Chinese, and Tamil should each be the medium of instruction in their respective types of school system and schoolbooks should be in those languages.

2.2 Nationalization Period (1957–1990)

On the verge of independence and in the midst of the resurgence of Malay nationalism, the leaders of the multi-ethnic groups arrived at a consensus that the Malay language, as the indigenous language of the country and the language of the majority, should be chosen as the national language. Nevertheless, Mandarin and Tamil should be allowed to be used for teaching and learning purposes. As a result, the status of *Bahasa Melayu* as the national language was enshrined in the constitution of Malaysia as stated below:

1. The national language shall be the Malay language and shall be in such script as Parliament may by law provide: Provided that-
   (a) no person shall be prohibited or prevented from using (otherwise than for official purposes), or from teaching or learning, any other language; and
   (b) nothing in this Clause shall prejudice the right of the Federal Government or of any State Government to preserve and sustain the use and study of the language of any other community in the Federation. (Constitution of Malaysia, Article 152 [1])

The national educational policy recommended by the Razak Report (1956) was incorporated into the Education Ordinance 1957 and became the foundation of the Malaysian Education system and language policy until today. It came into force on 15 June 1957. The education policy of the Federation was to establish a national system of education that was wholly acceptable to the people of the Federation. This national education system would be expected to satisfy the needs of the people to promote their cultural, social, economic, and political development as a nation, with the intention of making the Malay language the national language of the country while preserving and sustaining the growth of the languages and cultures of non-Malays living in it.

The Education Act 1961 is drawn on the basis of the Rahman Talib report (1960). It clearly emphasized the monolingual (monocultural) type of education, as some parts of the Razak Report (1956) were deliberately deleted. As a result, the Chinese community's efforts and struggle to sustain their Chinese school system were greatly impeded (Yang 2002). From 1 January 1962 onwards, 55 out of the 71 non-government Chinese secondary schools were compelled to be converted to government national-type (Chinese) secondary schools, leaving only 16 independent secondary schools to survive without any financial assistance from the government (Yang 2001).

Chinese (Mandarin) maintained its position as the medium of instruction in Chinese independent secondary schools, but the government national-type (Chinese) secondary schools were compelled to change the medium of instruction to Malay. Chinese and Chinese Literature are taught as subjects. Section 21(2) of the Education Act 1961 gave immense power to the Education Minister to convert, at any suitable time, all Chinese and Tamil primary schools to Malay primary schools (Yang 2002).

Nevertheless, in spite of all the restrictions and obstacles, with the generous monetary contributions and other forms of supports from the Chinese community, the independent schools managed to maintain their status quo until today.

2.3 Globalization Period (1991 until today)

In 1991, while tabling the Sixth Malaysian Plan, the then Prime Minister, Dato' Seri Dr Mahathir Mohammad (now Tun) introduced Vision 2020 (Wawasan 2020). The main goal of this vision is to have the nation attain the status of a self-sufficient industrialized nation by the year 2020, and it strongly emphasizes development in the fields of science and technology. Hence, for the first time since the conversion of English schools into Malay-medium schools in the 1980s, the learning of English is strongly encouraged. English is believed to be able to help in the realization of this vision.

Later, the Education Act 1996 replaced the 1961 Act and Section 17(1) of the Act states:

> The National Language shall be the main medium of instruction in all educational institutions and in the National Education system—except a national-type school established under section 28 or any other educational institutions exempted by the Minister from this subsection. (Yang 2002: 53)

Consequently, upon the implementation of the Education Act 1996, all national-type (Chinese) secondary schools were eliminated on 31 December 1997, as they were deliberately excluded from the 1996 Act. There existed only three types of school: i) national schools (Malay primary schools), ii) national-type schools (Chinese and Tamil primary schools), and iii) national (Malay) secondary schools. The part in Section 21(2) of the Education Act 1961 which gave immense power to the Education Minister to convert at any suitable time all Chinese and Tamil primary schools to Malay primary schools was dropped.

On 10 May 2002, Dato' Seri Dr Mahathir Mohammad announced the government's decision to use English to teach Mathematics and Science from 2003 onwards in all primary schools and gradually in secondary schools too. The Chinese community accepted this decision with the condition that both Chinese and English are to be used in teaching both these subjects. After implementing this policy for seven years, this decision was subsequently rescinded in 2010 due to strong opposition and dissatisfaction from the Malay loyalists.

In September 2012, the Malaysian Education Blueprint 2013–2025 was launched. Its emphasis is on providing world-class education, which includes eleven shifts in the present education system. It promises the continuation of mother-tongue education but insists on the standardization of the Bahasa Malaysia curriculum and assessment across national and national-type primary schools from 2014, starting with the Year 4 cohort. It aims to improve the proficiency level of students and elevate the status of Malay as the national language while at the same time raising the proficiency level of English across all school types. The reformation that would be brought about is yet to be seen with its implementation in the coming twelve years. The United Chinese School Committees' Association of Malaysia (Dong Zong) protested against this blueprint, saying that increasing teaching time for Bahasa Malaysia from 270 minutes to 300 minutes per week for lower primary and 180 minutes to 270 minutes per week for upper primary pupils was a move by the government to eradicate mother tongue education (The Star, September 11, 2013). Negotiations between Dong Zong and the Government are still ongoing; there is a need to find a balance between maintaining mother tongue education, strengthening the national language, and upgrading English to prepare for opportunities during the globalization era.

3   EVOLUTION OF MULTILINGUALISM IN KUALA LUMPUR'S CHINATOWN

3.1   Kuala Lumpur's Chinatown

This study uses Kuala Lumpur's Chinatown as the main site for data collection. It has a history of more than 150 years because it was founded by a group of Chinese in 1859 while searching for a new tin mining site. At first, it was under the governance of Captain Yap Ah Loy, a Hakka Chinese, before the British took over in 1880. The present Chinatown area consists of Jalan Petaling, Jalan Sultan, and the surrounding areas. But Petaling Street is the center of Kuala Lumpur's present-day Chinatown. Among the Chinese community, Petaling Street is called *Ci Chang Jie* in Mandarin or *Chee Cheong Kai* in Cantonese. *Chee Cheong Kai* is literally translated to mean "tapioca factory street". This name came about during the governing period of Captain Yap Ah Loy, as at that time there was a tapioca mill operating in Petaling Street and the flour produced by the mill was mainly used to make noodles (Sin Chew Daily 2012).

Regarded as a cultural heritage site (Bristow & Lee 1994), Petaling Street underwent a major RM11.3 million face lift in 2003 (*The Star*, 9 Aug 2007). Two large Chinese arches were placed on either end of the street to welcome visitors. The green roof constructed to cover the whole street is now dubbed the "Green Dragon". The street has now been totally transformed into a pedestrian shopping mall. It is not only famous for its all-day parade of stalls that sell a vast variety of goods, especially imitation goods; it also offers a large selection of local Chinese cuisine. It is also known for its jewelry shops with their fascinating variety of fine jewelry items. There are also many bookshops, pawnshops, and traditional pharmacies that sell traditional remedies. Besides being in a business area, Chinatown has now transformed into one of Kuala Lumpur's famous tourist hotspots. Besides tourists, locals, especially the Chinese, still throng Petaling Street to shop for their Chinese New Year essentials and other necessities for the various Chinese festivals.

3.2   Method

A historical approach to linguistic landscape studies is adopted in this study. This method compares data from different historical periods and thus reflects the change of the linguistic landscape over time in a certain place. Old photos taken in Kuala Lumpur's Chinatown from *Moving Mountains* (2012) and *Our Petaling Street* (2012) are analyzed in terms of language choice, script choice, size of various scripts, and word choice. The photos taken in present-day Chinatown are processed using FileMaker Pro 10.0. Several parameters are set in this database, such as the number of languages, dominant language, script of Chinese language, and size of Chinese scripts.

The definition of a "sign" is adopted from Backhaus (2007: 66), which is "any piece of written text within a spatially definable frame". With this broad definition, signs in this study include any visible signage from advertisements or flyers pasted on pillars and walls to huge posters or banners on perimeter fences or buildings. In total, 388 photos were taken along Petaling Street, which is the main street in the Chinatown area. In the following analysis, reference is made to some old signs on other streets in the vicinity of Kuala Lumpur's Chinatown.

3.3   Findings

In this section, Chinese monolingualism in traditional Chinese scripts and Chinese-English bilingualism during the colonial period, Malay-Chinese-English trilingualism during the nationalization period, and frequent usage of English during the globalization period are to be reviewed with the linguistic landscape data from Kuala Lumpur's Chinatown.

3.3.1   *Chinese Monolingualism*

The ancestors of Chinese Malaysians came from southern China. When they migrated to Malaysia, they spoke various Chinese dialects, such as Hokkien, Cantonese, and Hakka. When they settled down in Kuala Lumpur (hereafter KL) in late 19th century, the settlements were basically organized according to dialect groups. Hakka was the predominant group in Kuala Lumpur. At that time, the Chinese community was regarded as an immigrant community. Most of them had plans to return to China after they had saved enough money. Before the British took over the governance of KL in 1880, Chinese language was the only language on public signs. Figure 11.1 is a photo taken in 1890, which shows clearly Chinese monolingual signs on a street in KL. These Chinese signs are read from right to left following the written order of traditional Chinese texts. For instance, on the left end, the shop sign on the sun shade is 日泉 (Ri Quan). There are no other languages visible in the landscape. Figure 11.2 is a street landscape of KL's Chinatown taken in 1920. In this photo, all the signs and banners were written in Chinese characters. The banner on the left side illustrates how Chinese was used at that time: (1) traditional character was the single writing system; (2) the banner was read from right to left and from top to bottom; (3) when China was referred to, the word *Zu Guo* (祖國), "homeland", was used; (4) when Southeast Asia was referred to, the word *Nanyang* (南洋) was used. This reveals the sense of identity of these Chinese diasporas during this period. They had a strong attachment to their homeland, China. In contrast, *Nanyang* was regarded as a temporary place to stay in order to earn a living. Although there is little record on the spoken language used during that period, the medium of instruction in Chinese schools provides some clues. According to Hou (1919), both Chinese dialects and Mandarin were used as mediums of instruction when he visited Nanyang (Singapore and Malaya) in 1919.

Figure 11.1   Chinese Monolingual Signs in 1890 (*Moving Mountains* 2012: 55)

Figure 11.2   Chinese Monolingual Signs in 1920 (*Moving Mountains* 2012: 109)

3.3.2 *Chinese-English Bilingualism*

Colonial governance in KL began in 1880. During the colonial period, KL's Chinatown was developed into a Chinese settlement where various facilities flourished, such as markets, shops, temples, schools, and associations. Later, due to the civil war in China, many migrants decided to settle down in Malaya, which led to their gradual localization. As English was the official language during the British colonial period, it started to appear on public signs, and Chinese monolingual signs metamorphosed into Chinese-English bilingual signs. Dialectal pinyin written in Latin letters were added to the traditionally inscribed board. Figure 11.3 shows a photo of a Chinese traditional medicine shop in the 1950s. The main sign of the shop was bilingual, in both Chinese and English. The Chinese section was written in traditional characters and read from right to left. The English section was read from left to right and composed of two parts, the store name *Kien Fatt*, which was in Hakka, and *Medical Store* in English. The two languages were equivalent in terms of semantic coverage. A certain pattern was found among the signs in this period as illustrated in Figure 11.4. There are three signs in Figure 11.4, the main sign-board on top of the facade, the Chinese inscribed board hanging at the top grille of the main entrance, and the Chinese sign on the shop's left pillar. The main

Figure 11.3   A Chinese-English Bilingual Sign in the 1950s (*Moving Mountains* 2012:136)

sign-board is in Chinese-English bilingual with Chinese as the dominant language at the top of the sign. The English name of the hotel follows its Chinese name, which is written in dialectal (Hokkien) pinyin. The Chinese inscribed board is written in both characters and dialectal pinyin. The size of the characters is much bigger than the Latin scripts. Once again, the order of writing in these two scripts is different. The Chinese characters on the pillar are read from top to bottom and are written in traditional characters. It is noticeable that the dialectal pinyin indicates the dialect group of

Figure 11.4   Signs in the Colonial Period (*Moving Mountains 2012*: 142)

the shop owners, such as *Kien Fatt* in Hakka, *Lok Ann* in Hokkien, *Kwong Fook Wing* in Cantonese. In fact, certain dialect groups were associated with certain occupations during that particular period of time (Tan 2000). For instance, Chinese traditional medicine businesses were dominated by the Hakkas. To a certain extent, shop signs in dialectal pinyin were one of the clues to determine the relationship between occupations and dialect groups. In our current database, among the signs bearing dialectal pinyin (N=87), 40.2% of them are in Cantonese, 39.1% are in Hokkien, and 8.1% are in Hakka. This shows the dominance of Cantonese and Hokkien in the business domain during those times.

3.3.3   Malay-Chinese-English Trilingualism

Upon Malaya's independence in 1957, a majority of Chinese migrants obtained their citizenship and that hastened the process of their localization in Malaya. During this nationalization period, Malay language became a subject in Chinese primary and secondary schools. In 1967, in order to establish the national image, a Language Act was passed in parliament whereby Malay was announced as the national and sole official language. Consequently, English lost its official status in Malaysia. The government made great efforts to promote Malay in the education domain by converting English schools and Chinese secondary schools into Malay-medium schools in the 1960s and 1970s. In KL, language legislation was implemented in 1977 which made it compulsory to use Malay on sign-boards, with the stipulation that the size of its scripts must not be smaller than the other languages if more than one language is used (Asmah 1982: 58). Since then, Malay has become the dominant language used on business sign-boards in KL. Simultaneously, KL's Chinatown had metamorphosed itself into a business area that mainly served Chinese customers. This gave rise to a transformation of the linguistic landscape into a multilingual setting whereby Malay, Chinese, and English became the three main languages. Figure 11.5 illustrates the use of multiple languages on signage. Here, Malay is added onto the signage of the medical store in Figure 11.3 to highlight its dominance. In fact, the Malay section and the Chinese-English bilingual sign at the bottom should be regarded as two separate signs, as they are in two different frames. Figure 11.6 is a trilingual sign in Malay, English, and Chinese. However, the three languages convey different information. The Chinese part gives the most detailed information, that is, the name of the shop and its specialization in the western style of tailoring. The English part is also made up of two types of information, *Kwong Fook Wing*, the shop's name, and its designation as a tailor shop. However, the specialization in the western style was not indicated. The Malay part is very general, *Kedai Jahitan*, tailor shop.

Hence, it can be deduced that Malay, to some extent, is symbolic in the linguistic landscape in KL's Chinatown. Nevertheless, Malay began to take its place as an integral part of Chinese Malaysians' repertoire during the nationalization period. It became the lingua franca bringing about

Figure 11.5   Signs of a Medical store (Wang ©)

Figure 11.6   A Chinese-English-Malay Trilingual Sign (Wang ©)

communication between different ethnic groups. Its status as the national language drew respect from all ethnic groups in Malaysia.

Among the 388 entries in our database, Malay appears in 45.1% of them (N=175), and 23.5% of them put Malay in a dominant position (N=91).

In addition, Malay is used in all trilingual signs (N=71). As for the choice of Chinese characters on signage, more traditional characters are found in our database (64.4%) despite simplified script being adopted by Chinese primary schools since 1982. The frequent use of red color for the Chinese signs (N=39.6%) revealed the root of Chinese culture in the linguistic landscape. This reflects the tradition of Chinese Malaysians and their efforts to maintain their Chinese culture.

3.3.4   English in the Globalization Period

Since 1990, Malaysia has entered a new era with the implementation of Vision 2020, which aims to upgrade Malaysia into a developed country. In line with Vision 2020, English has been emphasized as a means to access the fields of science and technology. As a result, the learning of English was again encouraged, just shortly after all English schools had completed their conversion to Malay-medium schools in the 1980s. The subjects of Math and Science in primary and secondary schools have been taught in English from 2003 onwards (Gill 2005). The globalization era pushed English as a useful tool, as it was thought to help the nation gain achievements in the fields of science and technology. In the meantime, to respond to the global economy, KL's Chinatown was transformed into a tourist hotspot that has attracted tourists from all over the world. In 2003, Chinatown underwent a face-lift. More elements of Chinese culture, such as the two arches on both ends of Petaling Street and the Green Dragon cover were emphasized. The linguistic landscape has also changed due to the internationalization of Chinatown with the influx of foreign tourists. More and more English began to be used in signage. Figures 11.7 and 11.8 are two examples in our database. In Figure 11.7, Chinese is the dominant language whereas English is written in a smaller size. It is noticeable that the writing order of Chinese has changed. Signs in Chinese are now read from left to right although traditional characters are still in use. In Figure 11.8, English is the dominant language, as it provides more information than does Malay. Among the 388 entries in our database, 57.5% of them use English (N=223) and 32.7% of them use English as the dominant language (N=127). The frequency of English is higher than that of Malay. The highest frequency of English (N=100) occurs in bilingual signs.

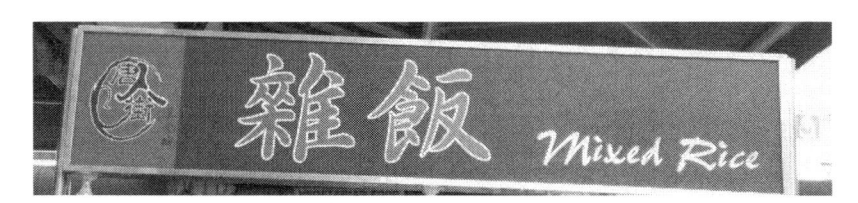

Figure 11.7   A Chinese-English Bilingual Sign (Wang ©)

Figure 11.8   A Malay-English-Chinese Trilingual Sign (Wang ©)

4   DISCUSSION: THE LINGUISTIC LANDSCAPE AND SOCIAL CHANGE

In the previous sections, different stages of the linguistic landscape in KL's Chinatown have been reviewed diachronically. In the past 150 years, it has undergone Chinese monolingualism, Chinese-English bilingualism, and Malay-Chinese-English trilingualism. The changing scenario observed in public signage is not only a direct reflection of language practices by Chinese diasporas in Malaysia but also a reflection of social and political changes within and beyond the Chinese community.

At the stage of Chinese monolingualism, Chinese diasporas consisted of immigrants from China who had a strong identification with China. They used only Chinese in public signage to present their Chinese identity. At that time, Chinatown was a closed Chinese settlement serving only Chinese immigrants. The monolingual stage was relatively short in KL due to the British invasion in 1880. During British colonial rule, Chinese-English bilingual signage became the common practice in KL's Chinatown. In these bilingual signs, Chinese was often the dominant language, appearing above English and written in a bigger font (Figures 11.3 and 11.4). This shows that the local Chinese community during the colonial period had a very strong Chinese identity. By highlighting Chinese scripts on their signs, they conveyed the message to the public that they were Chinese first. Under British rule, Chinese diasporas in Malaya still maintained their Chinese schools, although with very limited aid from the colonial government. The belief at that time was that education is the most important avenue for maintaining Chinese culture and tradition. Apart from Chinese characters, dialectal pinyin was used on signs to indicate dialectal group origins. During that period, identification with their respective dialect group was still very strong among the Chinese community (Mak 1985). Using dialectal pinyin as the English name for their shops and stores became common practice in KL's Chinatown at that time. English as the official language was the language for the elite class and English-educated people. It was neither the lingua franca across the ethnic groups nor part of the linguistic repertoire of ordinary people. To some extent, the English in signage had more of a symbolic value. The bilingual signage also reflects the composition of the local Chinese community, which was divided along the line of education (Tan 2000). The Chinese-educated and English-educated Chinese tended to have different views towards many social issues at that time. From a reader's or potential customer's view, Chinese signs served the Chinese-educated people, whereas English signs served the English-educated ones. The bilingual signs targeted both groups of readers.

Since the independence of Malaya, many social, political, and educational changes have taken place in this land. When the national ideology was proposed, the status of Malay was elevated to the national and official language in order to achieve national unity. As a result, Malay started to be used in official domains. English lost its official status and was no longer the medium of instruction in schools after the complete conversion of English schools in 1982. Chinese language never acquired official status in Malaysia, although movements have been organized by the Chinese community to fight for its official status since the 1960s (Tay 2003). The Chinese believe that language is essential for the maintenance of their Chinese culture and identity. After Malaysia's independence, the Chinese community gradually built up their national identity as Malaysians but continued to embrace Chinese ethnic identity. They had transformed themselves from immigrants to residents and later from residents to citizens. All these social changes were reflected in the linguistic landscape. A Malay-Chinese-English trilingual pattern came into being in KL's Chinatown. Malay, the national language, is attached to the national identity; English, the international language, is used for commercial purposes; and Chinese, the ethnic language, is associated with ethnic identity (Wang et al. forthcoming).

From the 1990s, the Malaysian government strived to develop the national economy and technology. Vision 2020 was introduced to propel Malaysia towards becoming a developed country by the year 2020. During this period, English regained some status, as it was regarded as a useful tool to achieve economic growth. Subsequently, the policy to teach Mathematics and Science in English has been implemented in all primary and secondary schools since 2003 in order to increase the English proficiency level in the country (Gill 2005). Proficiency in English is believed to be an effective path towards success in view of globalization and internationalization. KL's

Table 11.1   Distribution of Different Patterns of Signs in KL's Chinatown

Languages on signs	Amount	Percentage (%)
Monolingual Chinese	91	23.45
Bilingual Chinese-English	67	17.27
Trilingual Malay-Chinese-English	69	17.78
Others	161	41.5
Total	388	100.0

Chinatown responded to this new development in the country by transforming itself into a tourist hotspot. Thousands of tourists from different corners of the world visit KL's Chinatown every year. To adapt to this change, the peddlers in Petaling Street are able to speak various languages to accommodate customers. The linguistic landscape in KL's Chinatown has also undergone slight changes by using more English but not at the expense of Chinese. Table 11.1 shows the current distribution of different patterns of signs in KL's Chinatown. Out of 388 signs, 23.45% of them are Chinese monolingual signs; 17.78% of them are Malay-Chinese-English trilingual signs; and 17.27% of them are Chinese-English bilingual signs. These three patterns are most frequent in KL's Chinatown. The total occurrence of English on signs is 223, which accounts for 57.5% of total signs. Among these signs, English is used as the dominant language in 127 (32.7%) signs. These figures, to some extent, reflect the popularity of English in KL's Chinatown.

To sum up, the changing scenario of the linguistic landscape in KL's Chinatown reflects the social and political changes in Malaysia. In this process, Chinatown itself has evolved from a Chinese immigrant settlement to a tourism hotspot. The interaction between social processes and language use is exemplified by the evolution of the linguistic landscape in KL's Chinatown.

5   CONCLUSION

In this chapter, a review of the three historical stages of language practices by Chinese diasporas in Malaysia was carried out. Against this background, the evolution of the linguistic landscape in KL's Chinatown is described using a historical linguistic landscape approach. This historical approach also allows us to associate the development of multilingualism in the Chinese community with the broad social processes across time in Malaysia. This, in turn, will enhance our understanding of the interaction between language and society over time.

The evolution from monolingualism to bilingualism and multilingualism in the KL Chinatown area indicates that Chinese diasporas in Malaysia are dynamic and the local Chinese community is open to adapting to the various social, political, and global changes. Nevertheless, despite the ability to adapt easily, Chinese Malaysians are not willing to abandon their mother tongue. They exhibit strong loyalty towards their mother tongue. The common ideology within the community is that language is the symbol of Chinese identity and represents the core of Chinese culture. This explains why some fourth or fifth generation Chinese Malaysians still speak the Chinese language and do not shift to the national language or English as Fishman (1972) predicted. While maintaining the Chinese language, Chinese Malaysians also acquire Malay as their second language and English as their third language with varying proficiency levels. It can be predicted that the current multilingualism in the Chinese community will be retained as long as there are no drastic changes in national language policy.

NOTE

1. This article is funded by the research grant of the University of Malaya (UMRG369–12HNE) and the HIR Grant (UM.C/625/1/HIR-MOHE/ASH/04).

REFERENCES

Asmah O. 1982. *Language and society in Malaysia*. Kuala Lumpur: Dewan Bahasa dan Pustaka.
Asmah O. 1996. Post-imperial English in Malaysia. In Fishman J., Conrad A. and Rubal-Lopez (eds.) *Post-imperial English: Status change in former British and American colonies, 1940–1990*. Berlin and New York: Mouton de Gruyter, 513–533.
Backhaus P. 2007. *Linguistic landscapes: A comparative study of urban multilingualism in Tokyo*. Clevedon: Multilingual Matters.
Backhaus P. 2009. Rules and regulations in linguistic landscaping: A comparative perspective. In Shohamy E. & Gorter D. (eds.) *Linguistic landscape: Expanding the scenery*. New York and London: Routledge, 157–172.
Bristwo S. and Lee E. 1994. *Chinatown Kuala Lumpur*. Kuala Lumpur: Tropical Press Sdn. Bhd.
Curtin M. 2009. Languages on display: Indexical signs, identities and the linguistic landscape of Taipei. In Shohamy E. & Gorter D. (eds.) *Linguistic landscape: Expanding the scenery*. New York and London: Routledge, 221–237.
Federal Constitution of Malaysia. 2010. Retrieved on 25 July 2013. http://confinder.richmond.edu/admin/does/malaysia.pdf
Fishman, J. A. 1972. *The Sociology of Language*. Rowley: Newbury House.
Gill K. 2005. Language policy in Malaysia: Reversing direction. *Language Policy*, Vol.4, No. 3: 241–260.
Hafriza B. 2006. *Language and social behavior: Voices from the Malay World*. Bangi: Penerbit UKM.
Holmes J. 2001. *An introduction to sociolinguistics* (second edition). Harlow: Pearson Education Limited.
Hou H. J. 1919. *Nanyang lvxing ji* [Travel in Nanyang]. Wu Xi: Xi Cheng Company.
Kua K. S. 1999. *The Chinese schools in Malaysia: A protean saga*. Kajang: Dong Jiao Zong Higher Learning Center.

Lanza E. and Woldemariam H. 2009. Language ideology and linguistic landscape: Language policy and globalization in a regional capital of Ethiopia. In Shohamy E. & Gorter D. (eds.) *Linguistic landscape: Expanding the scenery*. New York and London: Routledge, 189–205.

Macalister J. 2010. Emerging voices or linguistic silence?: Examining a New Zealand linguistic landscape. *Multilingua* Vol. 29: 55–75.

Mak L. F. 1985. *Fanyanqun rentong: Zaoqi Xinma huaren de fenleifa* [Identification of dialect group: Early categorization of Singapore and Malaysian Chinese]. Taipei: The Academia Sinica.

Malaysian Education Blueprint 2013–2025. 2012. Retrieved on 30 May 2013. http://www.moe.gov.my/userfiles/file/PPP/Preliminary-Blueprint-Eng.pdf

Ministry of Education, Malaysia. 1956. *Report of the Razak Education Committee*. Kuala Lumpur: Government Printers.

Ser W. H., Teoh C. K. and Tang A. C. 2012. *Moving mountains: A pictorial history of the Chinese in Selangor and Kuala Lumpur*. Kuala Lumpur: Centre for Malaysian Chinese Studies.

Sin Chew Daily. 2012. *Women de Cichangjie* [Our Petaling Street]. Kuala Lumpur: Novum Organum Publishing House.

Tan C. B. 2000. Socio-cultural diversities and identities. In Lee K. H. & Tan C. B (eds.) *The Chinese in Malaysia*. Shah Alam: Oxford University Press, 37–70.

Tay L. S. 2003. *Malaixiya huawen jiaoyu fazhan shi* [The history of Chinese education in Malaysia]. Vol 4. Kuala Lumpur: The United Chinese School Teachers' Association of Malaysia.

Taylor-Leech K. J. 2012. Language choice as an index of identity: linguistic landscape in Dili, Timor-Leste. *International Journal of Multilingualism*, Vol. 9, No. 1. 15–34.

The Star. 9th August 2007. *Why early Chinese settlers chose the site*. http://thestar.com.my/metro/story.asp?file=/2007/8/9/central/18527005&sec= central.

The Star. 11th September 2013. *70% of English teachers not fit to teach*. http://www.thestar.com.my/News/Nation/2013/09/11/Idris-Many-teachers-not-fit-to-teach-70-of-English-instructors-found-to-be-incapable-says-Education.aspx.

Wang X. M. 2010. The sociolinguistic realignment in the Chinese community of Malaysia: Past, present and future. *International Journal of Multilingual and Multicultural Development*, Vol. 31, No. 5: 479–489.

Wang X. M. 2012. Emergent grammatical structures of Bahasa Pasar: based on Hakka-Malay and Cantonese-Malay Glossaries. *GEMA Online Journal of Language Studies*, Vol. 12, No. 3: 865–884.

Wang X. M., Patricia R., Supramani S. and Koh Y. C. forthcoming. Constructing identities through linguistic landscape: A comparison between Chinatown and Little India in Kuala Lumpur. In Asmah H. O. and Norazuma N. (eds.), *Linguistic Minorities: Their Existence in Larger Communities*. Kuching: UNIMAS Press, 120–142.

Yang P. K. 2001. The National Education Policy and the Mother Tongue Education. In Kua K. S. (ed.), *Chinese School and the Right to mother Tongue Education*. Kuala Lumpur: Dong Jiao Zong, 30–80.

Yang P. K. 2002. National education after 44 Years. *The Journal of Malaysian Bar*, Vol. XXXI, No. 1: 42.

Yen C. H. 2000. Historical background. In Lee K. H. & Tan C. B. (eds.) *The Chinese in Malaysia*. Shah Alam: Oxford University Press, 1–36.

12 Grandmother's Tongue
Decline of Teochew Language in Singapore

Lee Cher Leng

INTRODUCTION

The early Chinese immigrants in Singapore in the 19th century were dialect speakers from the southern part of China. The Teochew community forms the second largest Chinese dialect group after the Hokkiens. Singapore is a globalized city nation whose working language is English. This chapter studies the Chinese diaspora of the Teochew community in Singapore in terms of the sociocultural changes that have taken place in this community, focusing on language usage, language ideology, and identity of these Teochew speakers in a fast-changing society. The methodology is ethnographic interviews carried out with respondents from ages 13 to 86, with both male and female speakers from all walks of life to give a more comprehensive coverage.

Language maintenance and language shift (LMLS) are especially important today due to widespread globalization causing many ethnic languages to rapidly reduce in usage (Fishman 1991). Such is the case with the Teochew language in Singapore. Li et al. (1997) study the language shift in the Singapore Teochew community within the family domain. They conclude that the Teochew Chinese community has moved away from its own ethnic language to the officially recognized national languages due to institutional, status, sub-cultural, and sociocultural factors. Phua and Ho (2011) showed that there is language decline in the Teochew language in Singapore. There have been studies on Chinese diaspora, such as Li and Zhu (2010), that examined the changing hierarchies of varieties of Chinese in the postmodern era, focusing on language attitude and linguistic practices. This study continues in this vein of ethnographic study to have a better understanding of the usage of the Teochew language in Singapore among Teochew speakers from all walks of life. The following sections discuss (1) the sociolinguistics of Singapore, (2) a general overview of Teochews in Singapore, (3) factors leading to language shifts in Singapore, (4) research methodology, (5) key patterns of language use, (6) language ideology and identity of Teochew speakers, and (7) conclusion.

SOCIOLINGUISTICS OF SINGAPORE

Singapore today is a globalized multicultural, multilingual island nation of 5.3 million people. The ethnic composition is: Chinese 76.2%, Malays 15.0%, Indians 7.4%, and others 1.4% (Singapore Statistics: Population 2013). The four official languages are English, Malay, Chinese, and Tamil, with English being the main working language for economic reasons and Malay the national language for political reasons. Malay, Chinese (Mandarin), and Tamil are officially considered as 'mother tongues' for the respective ethnic groups—Malay, Chinese, and Indian—although only Malay is the home language for the Malays, Mandarin may not be the first language for the majority of ethnic Chinese, neither Tamil for the Indians.

Singapore became a British colony in 1819. Soon after Singapore was established as a British trading post in the early 19th century, the open-door immigration policy (Yeoh 2007) brought about a rapid influx of immigrants from southern China, Malaya, the Indonesian archipelago, and South Asia. By 1921, the Chinese community reached its current proportion of three-quarters of the population. Most of these Chinese immigrants were blue collar workers from the southern coast of China speaking dialects such as Hokkien (37.6%), Teochew (19.5%), Cantonese (19.2%), Hainanese (7.1%), and Hakka (6.1%), with 10.5% Straits-born (Marriot 1921, 362). During this period, Hokkien was the lingua franca among different Chinese dialect groups, whereas Bazaar Malay was the interethnic lingua franca for Singapore and the broader archipelago region. Because Singapore was a British colony, English enjoyed prestige as the language of administration, law, and business.

When Singapore gained self-government from Britain in 1959, the government decided to make it an officially multilingual state with four official languages: English, Mandarin, Malay, and Tamil. At that time, schooling was offered in four language streams: One of the official languages, English/Malay/Mandarin/Tamil, would be the MOI, with some subjects taught in another language. This was a model that stressed equality for all the official languages.

Singapore merged into the Federation of Malaysia in 1963–1965 and only became a sovereign nation in 1965. Lee Kuan Yew (Prime Minister from 1959 to 1990), the main architect of Singapore's language policy, stressed the great importance of English in order for Singapore to survive as a nation economically. He said of Singapore, 'trade and industry were her only hope'; in order to attract investors to set up their manufacturing plants, Singaporeans had to speak a language foreigners could understand. Geopolitically, Singapore is located in Southeast Asia and hence Malay is the national language. Internally, the government needed to choose a language policy that achieves racial harmony, hence the decision for bilingualism with Mandarin, Malay, and Tamil as 'mother tongues' for Chinese, Malays, and

Indians respectively. Therefore, English became the working language to give all races in Singapore a common language to communicate and work in as well as to provide equal opportunities for people to study their respective mother tongues.

After five decades, Singapore has progressed from a third world country to one whose per capita income ranks among the highest in the world. Many local and international scholars (Goh 2004; Kaplan and Baldauf 2003; Xu and Li 2002) have attributed this economic miracle to the choice of English being the main language for education.

TEOCHEWS IN SINGAPORE

The Teochew people originated from the Chaozhou region of Guangdong Province, speaking the Teochew or Chaozhou dialect. It is the second largest Chinese dialect group in Singapore (21% of the Chinese population, about half a million people). The early Teochew migrants arrived in the early 19th century in search of work to escape poverty in their hometowns.

The Teochew people are known to be hardworking and thrifty. They worked hard to secure their dominance in the local economy by trading seafood products, sundry goods, rice, textiles, charcoal, and porcelain. Many also worked as brokers and traders of goods between the many warehouses located on the shore of the Singapore River, and as financiers to fund the business transactions and ventures.

Some prominent business personalities include Seah Eu Chin, founder of the Ngee Ann Kongsi in 1845; Lim Nee Soon, Singapore's Rubber and Pineapple King and a founder of the Teochew Poit Ip Huay Kuan (The Association of the Eight Regions in Teochew) in 1929; Lee Wee Nam, Founder and President of the Malayan Confederation of the Teochew Huay Kuan in 1933; and Lien Ying Chow, Founder of the Overseas Union Bank, President of the Singapore Kwantung Huay Kuan, Chairman of the Preservation of Monuments Board, Singapore Ambassador to Japan, and President of the Ngee Ann Kongsi. These successful businessmen also contributed generously to education. The first school built by the Teochews was the Tuan Mong School built in 1906. In 1940, Lee Wee Nam built Ngee Ann Girls' School. In 1963, Ngee Ann Kongsi started the Ngee Ann College with undergraduate programs. In 1968, Ngee Ann College was converted to Ngee Ann Polytechnic.

Besides successful businessmen, many past and present cabinet ministers are also Teochew. In the year 2006, six out of 17 cabinet ministers were Teochew. They included Lim Boon Heng (Minister, Prime Minister's Office), George Yong-Boon Yeo (Minister for Foreign Affairs), Lee Boon Yang (Minister for Information, Communication and the Arts), Yeo Chao Tong (Minister for Transport), Teo Chee Hean (Minister for Defence), and

Lim Hng Kiang (Minister for Trade and Industry). Opposition politician Low Thia Kiang, the leader of the Workers' Party, is also Teochew.

The Teochew dialect spoken in Singapore includes a large amount of borrowed lexicon from Indian, Malay, and English (see Lee 2003). For example, Sikhs are referred to as *mangkali* (from 'Bengali' in English), nurses are *misi* (from 'Miss' in English), accidents are known as *lang-ga* (from *langgar* in Malay), a brand is known as *mak-tau* (from 'mark' in English and *tau* meaning 'head'), glass is known as *geh-lak* (from 'glass' in English), and 'percentage' is known as *par-siang* (from 'percent' in English). There are also terms that combine two languages, for example, biscuits are called *loti-piah* from *roti* (Malay) and *piah* (biscuit in Teochew). Since the advent of the Speak Mandarin Campaign, the Teochew dialect has been on a steady decline, with many young Singaporeans neither able to understand nor speak the dialect. Teochew may lose their identity in Singapore if the current trend of speaking only English and Mandarin continues (see Lee 2006).

FACTORS LEADING TO LANGUAGE SHIFTS IN SINGAPORE

There are two major language shifts that have taken place in Singapore. The first is from Chinese dialects to Mandarin, and the second is from Mandarin to English. The factors that led to language shifts in Singapore are as follows.

- Why Replace Dialects with Mandarin?

The government saw the Chinese dialects as 'interfering with bilingual education' as well as 'dividing the Chinese community' and decided to change the larger environment outside school by banning the use of all other dialects in radio, television, and cinema (Lee K.Y. 2011, 146ff). In 1979, the Speak Mandarin Campaign was launched with the goal to replace Chinese dialects with Mandarin. This Campaign is held annually with slogans encouraging ethnic Chinese from all walks of life to speak Mandarin. This has marked the beginning of the decline of linguistic diversity of Chinese dialects in Singapore. By 1981, the government-run Singapore Broadcasting Corporation, today's MediaCorp, had done away with programs in every Chinese dialect.

The Chinese majority in Singapore used to speak Hokkien, Teochew, and Cantonese, but in the past twenty years, there has been a strong shift toward Mandarin and/or English to phase out local Chinese dialects (Wong 1999). Today, most Singaporeans speak English as the lingua franca, and most Singaporean Chinese speak Mandarin Chinese (Kaplan and Baldauf 2003).

- Parents Choose English Education for Better Job Prospects.

The government saw the importance of English for the economy of Singapore. The English-educated graduates had better jobs. As a result, parents stopped enrolling children in non-English medium schools. This led to the closing of the Chinese-medium tertiary institution Nanyang University (a different institution from the present-day Nanyang Technological University) in 1980. In 1987, English became the medium of instruction and L1 in all schools. All second languages or designated 'mother tongues' began to be taught as stand-alone lessons. Therefore, Singapore's policy of bilingualism does not translate into what is normally accepted in academic discussions under the label 'bilingual education', which is traditionally defined as education in two languages, with instruction given in both and rough parity between the two.

• English Became the Language of Home and Media.

Because English language helps in finding better jobs, more families speak English at home. Also, American television programs have become popular. As a result, data from the Singapore Census of Population (2011) on the resident Chinese population aged 5 years and over regarding the language most frequently spoken at home show a sharp drop in dialect usage (11.5%), with a slight increase in Mandarin (2.6%), and a much higher increase in English as the home language (8.7%) between 2000 and 2010 (see Table 12.1). Research shows that 87% of children from ages 3–4 watch an average of three to nine hours of English cartoons, whereas only 27% of children of the same age watch the same number of hours of Chinese cartoons (Chen 2013). Singaporean Chinese children are fast losing their grip on the Mandarin language, not to mention their own dialects.

• English for all Subjects in School.

Students have very limited exposure time to Mandarin lessons. During the six years of primary school, 'mother tongue' takes up an average of five hours per week; over the four years of secondary school, it constitutes an average of only three hours per week. For the two years of junior college GCE 'A'

Table 12.1   Language Most Frequently Spoken at Home Among Chinese Resident Population Aged 5 and Over (Singapore Census of Population 2011)

Home language	1990 (%)	2000 (%)	2010 (%)
Total	100.0	100.0	100.0
English	32.6	19.3	23.9
Mandarin	30.1	45.1	47.7
Chinese Dialects	50.3	30.7	**19.2**
Others	0.4	0.4	0.3

level curriculum, it also represents three hours per week, and this is only for the relative minority of students who have to do the Chinese Language B syllabus and those who have elected to study it beyond 'O' levels. Most students who opted for Higher Chinese in secondary schools are allowed to 'drop' mother tongue entirely at junior college. Even students in SAP schools communicate more in English than Mandarin (Fang et al. 2010).

The language shifts from Chinese dialects to Mandarin and further from Mandarin to English have transformed Singapore students into 'English-dominant bilinguals' (Lee 2012). Today, most young Chinese Singaporeans speak a colloquial Singapore variety of English (Singlish) (Gupta 1989) as their mother tongue with some conversational competence in Mandarin. Most of these students do not understand their family dialects any more. The literacy standard of Mandarin has been on a steady decline, resulting in constant adjustments in the teaching of Chinese language in schools to make it more manageable. Due to the limited usage of Mandarin, many students express difficulties in learning the language. They find Chinese in school 'very difficult' (Goh 1997, National Day Rally Speech).

METHODOLOGY

This study uses ethnographic interviews to collect data from Teochew speakers. There are 53 informants ranging from 13–86 years of age. At each ten-year interval, there are at least two males and two females. In terms of educational levels, the informants range from those with no education at all to those with PhD degrees. In terms of profession, there are working professionals, retired individuals, homemakers, and students. These considerations ensure a wide range of different populations, giving the data a more comprehensive representation.

The author personally interviewed each informant. Each interview lasted about half an hour, with a few that lasted well beyond half an hour. The interviews are recorded both on audio-tape as well as in writing. The questions asked are as follows:

(1) To whom do they speak Teochew?
(2) What do they think of the usage of Teochew in current day Singapore?
(3) Do they think that Teochew has any value?
(4) Is it sufficient for Teochews to speak Mandarin or do they also need to speak Teochew?
(5) Is there a danger of losing the language in Singapore?
(6) Do they think there is a need to preserve the language, and if so, how?

These interviews were carried out in Teochew if the informants were able to answer in Teochew, otherwise, they were allowed to reply in Mandarin or English.

KEY PATTERNS OF LANGUAGE USE

From the data collected, there is a clear demarcation of two large age groups: ages 13–49 (younger generation), and ages 50–86 (older generation). There are 25 people in the older age group, and 28 in the younger age group.

(a) Languages spoken:

From the first row in table 12.2, there is a clear language shift from Teochew among the Teochew speakers to English and Mandarin. There is a decline of speaking other dialects, with the younger generation speaking other international languages such as Japanese, Korean, and French, etc.

(b) Languages used at the work place:

There is also a language shift from using Teochew to using mainly English and Mandarin for the Teochew speakers.

(c) Languages spoken between their parents:

Nearly all of the parents of the older generation have parents speaking Teochew to each other. For the younger generation, only 40% of their parents speak to each other in Teochew.

Table 12.2 Key Patterns of Language Usage among Teochew Speakers of Older and Younger Generations

Languages	Ages 50–86	Ages 13–49
(a) spoken	- 100% Teochew (TC) - 52% English (Eng) - 84% Mandarin (Man) - 50% TC + Man + Dialects + Eng.	- 64% Teochew - 100% English - 96% Mandarin - 1% French+Japanese
(b) workplace	- 50% TC only	Eng + Man = 50%
(c) between parents	Nearly 90% TC	- 40% TC - TC, Eng + Man
(d) with parents	- More than 80% TC only	- 20% TC only - Man./ Eng + TC, Eng + Man
(e) among siblings	70% TC only - TC + Man, TC + Can, Man + Eng	- 7% TC only - 30% Eng only
(f) with spouses	Above age 60: 50% TC only Below age 60: 30% Man + Eng	
(g) with children	Above age 60: 60% TC only Below age 60: 0% TC only, Man 22%, Man + Eng 22%	

(d)   Languages spoken with parents:

For the older generation, 80% speak Teochew with their parents, compared to only 20% among the younger generation. The younger generation use more Mandarin and English with their parents.

(e)   Languages spoken with siblings:

70% of the older generation speak only Teochew with their siblings, whereas only 7% of the younger generation do so. Most of the younger generation use English with siblings.

(f)   Languages spoken with spouses:

For the older generation above 60 years of age, 50% speak only Teochew with their spouses. For those below 60, 30% speak English and Mandarin with their spouses, others speak a mixture of Man + Eng + Teochew/Cantonese.

(g)   Languages spoken with children:

For the above 60 age group, 60% use only Teochew with their children. For the below 60 age group, there is an equal number of 22% using Mandarin or Mandarin and English with their children; the rest include some who use Mandarin and Teochew, English and Teochew, and English, Mandarin, and Teochew.

From the key patterns of language use among Singapore Teochew speakers, there is a clear language shift from Teochew more commonly used by the older generation to English and Mandarin among the younger generation.

Spoken Teochew in Singapore is going through rapid changes. During the interviews, those above 60 years of age are able to converse entirely in Teochew. Those between 40–60 years of age code-switch with Mandarin and English in their conversation. Most of the interviewees below age 40 either use Mandarin or English; few are able to use some Teochew to reply the questions. The following are three samples—the first excerpt is from an 80-year-old man, the second is from a lady in her 40s, the third is from a teenager.

A.   Mr. Tan (age 80)

When Mr. Tan (age 80) was asked if he felt that Teochew has any value in today's Singapore, he explained that the government has ordained that people speak Mandarin in the home as well, and as a result, children do not get to learn dialects any more. The entire conversation was in Teochew with no code-mixing at all.

(1)   因为伊新加坡政府是呾，是呾，汝夺爱呾英文甲华语吗。因为 伊，往的政府是呾，伊在地块呾是呾汝在厝内是爱呾华语啊，这个乜啊，就会变到哈往的仔孙啊伊就学不到啦，就学不到啦。啊是咀往这些人古早老辈的吼，往的仔孙还学得到啦。因为伊咀汝在内夺爱咀华语、英文啊，就变作这个乜汝的方言就传不到了吗，传不到汝的仔孙吗。这个乜就实践了点步错误啦。应该唔对。所以我的我的我的仔哈，还是会晓咀潮州。

[The Singapore government wants people to learn English and Mandarin. They want people to speak Mandarin in their homes. Therefore children will not get to learn dialects any more. Actually with us elderly people around them at home, they can still learn the dialect. But since they are asked to speak English and Mandarin at home, we will not have a chance to pass the dialect to our children and grandchildren any more. There are some mistakes here. So for me, my children can still speak Teochew.]

B. EK (age 47)

When EK was asked how she thinks the Teochew language can continue in Singapore society, she answered that parents have to take deliberate measures to speak to their children in Teochew. Although she speaks Teochew daily, her answer was still partly in English and not entirely in Teochew.

(2)
Q: *了汝觉得咀做呢乜则能传下来的呢？有什么方法？*
[Q: How do you think Teochew language can be continued? Any methods?]
A.: *方法啊，着着，*
it must be a very deliberate attempt on the parts of the parents to do this. That means *若是父母无甲伊的仔咀吼，伊的仔就勿咀了吗。啊是叫我逐日甲伊咀红毛话，我的仔就无晓咀。*
[A.: Methods, have to, have to, *it must be a very deliberate attempt on the parts of the parents to do this. That means* if parents don't speak (the language) with their children, then their children can't speak it. If I speak to them in English every day, my children won't know how to speak it.]

LANGUAGE IDEOLOGY AND IDENTITY OF THE TEOCHEW LANGUAGE

Interviews were conducted for all 53 interviewees. This section discusses the language attitude of Teochew speakers and their identity. Most Teochews in their twenties are not able to speak in Teochew except for a few exceptional ones. David, a 24-year-old male, is one of the few who is still able to converse in Teochew at his age. The secret of his ability to do so lies in his close relationship with his grandmother, who brought him up.

According to Silverstein (1979: 193), language ideologies are 'any sets of beliefs about language articulated by the users as a rationalization or justification of perceived language structure and use'. They are also understood as ideological appraisals of language and forms of usages based upon notions such as 'quality', value, status, norms, functions, and ownership. These ideological constructs are invested in relations of power and authority, often involving the stratification and regimentation of language usage (Blommaert 2006). As such, language ideology can be seen as 'a bridge between linguistic and social theory', relating the 'microculture of communicative action to political economic considerations of power and social inequality, confronting macrosocial constraints on language behaviour' (Woolard & Schieffelin 1994: 72). This section examines the language ideologies of the Teochew speakers in Singapore given the political economic backdrop of the nation.

- Speak Mandarin, not Teochew.

Fishman (1973: 31–32; 1989: 305) highlighted the importance between language policies and ideologies, as it is common that a state legitimizes particular policies guided by the nation's broader ideological frameworks. This was the case for Singapore when the Speak Mandarin Campaign was launched in 1979. The aims of the campaign were to unite ethnic Chinese of various dialects to bring about harmony among them, and also to 'reduce' the linguistic burden of children having to learn Mandarin and English alongside the various dialects. This was a concern of Lee Kuan Yew's that 'dialects were hindering students' ability to learn' (Lee 2011: 142). The Speak Mandarin Campaign was launched to replace dialects with Mandarin. All radio and TV dialect programs were removed with immediate effect. In a speech launching the 1988 Speak Mandarin Campaign, Prime Minister Lee Hsien Loong said, 'The Speak Mandarin Campaign is . . . meant to make dialect-speaking Chinese replace dialect with Mandarin'. As a result, parents began to converse with children in Mandarin rather than dialects. Some grandparents who could only speak dialect could no longer converse with their grandchildren (Lee 2007: 88).

All Teochew speakers interviewed say that Teochew is hardly used in Singapore society except for speaking to their grandparents at home or with venders in the markets who sell vegetables, fish, and chicken, etc. The use of Teochew fell rapidly, as did other Chinese dialects in Singapore, when the government promoted the Speak Mandarin Campaign in 1979.

In excerpt (3), David was asked about what he thinks of the usage of Teochew language in Singapore. All interviewees say that they rarely get to hear Teochew language being used in Singapore. David answered that most young people cannot speak the language as they are not living with their grandparents any more. This goes to show that Teochew can only continue to be used when the younger generation converses with their grandparents.

In other words, when their grandparents pass on, the use of Teochew language will also be reduced.

(3)
Q: 汝觉得新加坡的潮州话这阵的情况做呢乜?
[Q: What do you think of the current situation of Teochew in Singapore?]
A: 这阵新加坡的潮州话应该是无人会晓什么咀了啦，因为少年的人啊是无甲伊　人的阿妈啊是爷爷作步企，伊人甲伊人阿爸阿妈咀红毛话啊是华语. So　逐日啊　是无人甲伊人咀潮州话，伊人就勿晓咀吗。
[A: Most people can't speak the language because young people do not live with their grandparents, their parents mostly speak English or Mandarin with them. So as time goes by, fewer people will know the language.]

• Teochew: No Economic but Cultural Value.

Bourdieu's (1986, 1991) notions of *capital* and *field* are useful to discuss how public policy discourse on official languages in Singapore attempts to assign different types of capital to English, Mandarin, and dialects. It is obvious that those who know English in Singapore can find better jobs than those who only know Teochew, and those who know Mandarin can find better jobs than those who only know Teochew. For Bourdieu, *economic capital* is readily convertible into material wealth, whereas *cultural capital* is integral to the individual's *habitus* or predispositions.

When the interviewees were asked if they think that Teochew has any value in Singapore, all interviewees said that it has no economic value, most said that it has cultural value. In excerpt (4), David says that it is important for family ties and fostering closeness with his grandparents and parents. It is also important when he wants to exclude others from their conversation.

(4)
Q: 所以汝觉得咀潮州话在新加坡有价值不?
[Q: Do you think Teochew language has value in Singapore?]
A: 我想是潮州话会使付我甲我的阿公阿妈，我的爸爸妈妈嗯，feels closer LOR, like cultivate family closeness, family values, and 我我我的　daddy啊是出去吼，勿要付人知，往就会咀潮州话咯。So mm, yeah, 我觉得潮州话是 important 啦。
[A: The Teochew language makes me feel closer to my grandparents and parents. It cultivates family closeness, family values. I can use it with my family when I don't want others to know what I am saying.]

David's answer represents many of the interviewees who still feel that Teochew carries the value of a family's language and heritage. Teochew is hardly used in business transactions, one does not need Teochew for any economic activity unless one is doing business directly with the Teochew community in China. The value of Teochew therefore, is quite obviously limited to one's family heritage.

- Why Learn Teochew?

There has been an increased discussion of language as a commodity. Bourdieu (1977, 1982) pointed out that language forms part of the symbolic capital that can be interchangeable with forms of material capital. Heller (2010: 102), in her discussion on commodification of language, said that language 'is not a reflection of the social order but is part of what makes it happen'. Song (2009) states the fact that Korean mothers view English education as a commodity in the global market. De Costa (2010) illustrates the learning of English by a Chinese national in Singapore schools as an investment. Singapore has been characterized by a pervasive culture of consumerism (Baudrillard 1988; Bauman 1998), where 'people define themselves through the messages they transmit to others through the goods and practices that they possess and display' (Warde 1994: 878).

In Singapore's language policy, English is seen both as an inter-ethnic lingua franca and for global economic competitiveness. Mandarin is a language that is becoming more valued because of the economic development of mainland China. Because Singapore's education policy wants students to be fluent in English and their official mother tongue, with English being the medium of instruction and Mandarin as a subject, most parents would use English and Mandarin without dialect to better advantage their children. It would take a conscious effort to speak the dialect at home. This usually only happens when the children need to speak to grandparents who are living with them.

When the interviewees were asked if they feel that Teochews should learn how to speak the language, their answers were usually affirmative. Of course, this is because these interviewees themselves speak the language. Teochew, being a dialect, does not seem to have any economic capital. However, most interviewees said that Teochews should at least be able to use the language in everyday life. In excerpt (5), David's answer affirms that this is a matter of their own heritage, helping the Teochew people to understand their roots, their way of living, their characteristics and tastes. This answer shows that the Teochew dialect is something of a heritage language in Singapore.

(5)
Q: 按呢汝觉得咽潮州人是唔是一定要会咽潮州话?
[Q: Do you think Teochews should learn the language?]
A: 对(yes). 因为(Because) heritage吗(pt). Yeah, and it kind of really brings you back to your roots and understand like the Teochew

way of living. Because each and every one of us, our characteristic, our taste, it all goes back to our roots for being a 潮州人(Teochew).

It is particularly interesting that the two cousins interviewed have differing views on this topic. They are both 13 years of age. Alice lives with her grandmother because her parents work abroad. Jane lives with her parents. Alice speaks fluent Teochew whereas Jane cannot. When this question was asked, Alice's answer was affirmative whereas Jane's was negative. Alice's reaction to her cousin was 'I'm so ashamed of you'. Because Alice was brought up by her grandmother, she had a strong emotional attachment to Teochew, whereas Jane, living with her parents, does not feel much for the Teochew language.

- Why Mandarin can/not Replace Teochew.

Singapore's language policy emphasizes that English language proficiency is necessary for economic development—to attract foreign investment and gain access to scientific and technological know-how. However, the government wants to institute a mother tongue policy to provide Ethnic Chinese with links to their traditional cultures and values so as to prevent the effects of 'Western decadence'. Singapore's first senior minister, Lee Kuan Yew (*The Straits Times*, 11 November 1972), states in the following that bilingualism is not just a matter of learning languages, but rather different languages serve different purposes: English is for gaining 'access to science and technology' whereas the mother tongues are intended to help Singaporeans 'understand themselves', 'what they are', and 'where they came from'.

(1)　When I speak of bilingualism, I do not mean just the facility of speaking two languages. It is more basic than that, first, we understand ourselves, what we are, where we are, where we came from, what life is or should be about, and what we want to do. Then the facility of the English language gives us access to the science and technology of the West.

Lee elaborates that the different languages are associated with their own unique values:

(2)　With the language goes the fables and proverbs. It is the learning of a whole value system, a whole philosophy of life, that can maintain the fabric of our society intact, in spite of exposure to all the current madness around the world.

(3)　Only when we first know our traditional values, can we be quite clear the Western world is a different system, a different voltage, structured for purposes different from ours.

In a 1984 speech to the Chinese community, Lee stated in no uncertain terms that English is simply not acceptable as a mother tongue; English may have economic value but only Asian languages can give Singaporeans their identity and values.

(4) We have to persist in bilingualism . . . English will not be emotionally acceptable as our mother tongue. . . .

To have no emotionally acceptable language as our mother tongue is to be emotionally crippled. We shall doubt ourselves. We shall be less self-confident. Mandarin is emotionally acceptable as our mother tongue. It also unites the different dialect groups. . . .

Parents want their children to be successful. They also want their children to retain traditional Chinese values in filial piety, loyalty, benevolence, and love. Through Mandarin their children can emotionally identify themselves as part of an ancient civilization whose continuity was because it was founded on a tried and tested value system.

The question here is whether these Teochew speakers feel that Mandarin can replace Teochew, whether it is sufficient for Teochew people to speak Mandarin without speaking Teochew anymore. Quite a number of interviewees, including the oldest lady at age 86, think that it is perfectly fine to learn Mandarin without Teochew. David thinks otherwise, he feels that whereas Mandarin, like English, can meet the economic needs when China opens up its market, Teochew is still the root that brings closeness within the family. It is therefore important to preserve this heritage language. If this is the case, then unlike what the authorities assume, Mandarin cannot quite replace dialects when it comes to an identity in its core. Although the authorities wish that Mandarin can play the role of passing on Confucian ethics mentioned above, more often than not, family and cultural values are transmitted through particular sayings in the dialect. Mandarin is rather like a 'step-mother tongue' that cannot fulfill this deep desire of rootedness and cultural identity for some Teochew speakers.

(6)

Q: 汝觉得咀潮州话在新加坡应唔应该流传下去？啊是华人咀华语就够了？汝知这个 *Speak Mandarin Campaign to replace dialect* 吗, 汝觉得咀是唔是平样？

[Q: Do you think Teochew language should be preserved in Singapore or is Mandarin good enough? The Speak Mandarin Campaign replaces dialects with Mandarin, are they the same?]

A: 不平样呢。因为咀华语 is like 古早往新加坡 Lee Kuan Yew 咀逐人着读红毛，因为往后次作business拢总红毛拢总吗。等下伊就咀读华语，因为China open up 了. 伊人, 我想啦, 伊的 focus point唔是在喜个 heritage, 是在 economics, what you will use next time, what's important for your education. But for Teochew is your root lor, 汝的 family closeness, then 我甲我的 daddy mummy 咀潮州话, personally I feel close to them, because it's a language between us, and not worldwide, yeah.

[A: Not the same. Lee Kuan Yew wants us to learn English for business, now that China has opened up, we need to learn Mandarin. Their focus is not on heritage but economics. . . . But Teochew is your root, your family closeness, I feel closer to my parents when I speak to them in Teochew.]

Another interviewee, Alan (age 48), replied that his mother speaks Teochew, so his mother tongue is Teochew, not Mandarin:

'To me, it's mother tongue in school. I don't believe mother tongue is Mandarin. Because Chinese (Mandarin) is second language, mother tongue is our Teochew, Hokkien. 无理由 (no reason) mother tongue 是这个(is this) Mandarin'.

- Does it Matter if Teochew Disappears? How to Preserve the Language?

All interviewees are pessimistic about the future of Teochew language in Singapore. David said without doubt that he will be the last generation to use the dialect.

(7)
Q. 汝觉得新加坡人会继续用潮州话吗？
[Q. Do you think Teochew will continue to be used in Singapore?]
A: 我feel 我 generation 是 last 了啦.
[A: I feel that I am the last generation (who can speak Teochew in Singapore).]

When a 13-year-old Teochew girl was asked how to pass on the dialect, she said that grandparents should speak to the younger generations in dialects.

(8)
Q：汝觉得做呢乜则会传下去呢？
[Q: How do you think Teochew can continue in the society?]
A: 我觉得伊人的外公外婆应该甲伊人咀潮州话，因为这阵的外公外婆恬甲伊人的孙咀红毛话甲唐人话，了伊人大了就勿晓咀。
[A: Their grandparents should speak to them in Teochew. Because if they speak to them in Mandarin, they will not be able to speak the dialect when they grow up.]

It is indeed rare that those below age 25 are able to speak Teochew. These Teochew speakers usually grow up with their grandparents and they have a strong sense of belonging to the dialect group. However, they are all aware that the dialect is fast disappearing in globalized Singapore.

- Identity in Speaking Teochew

The state has decided that English is the medium of instruction and the designated 'mother tongues' are assigned according the father's ethnicity—Mandarin for Chinese, Malay for the Malays, and Tamil for the Tamils. Of these designated 'mother tongues', only Malay is the natural mother tongue spoken in the homes of the Malays. For the Chinese, the home language originally is likely to be Hokkien, Teochew, Cantonese, and other Chinese dialects. For the Indians, they could be speaking Malayalee, Hindi, Punjabi, Gurajati, etc.

'Mother tongue' is indeed a complex issue when it comes to Chinese families, as many spoke the southern Chinese dialects at home until the Speak Mandarin Campaign was launched. Therefore, the true mother tongue—the home language—is actually a southern Chinese dialect like Hokkien or Teochew. However, the Ministry of Education has designated Mandarin as the 'mother tongue' for all ethnic Chinese students.

During the 1988 Speak Mandarin Campaign, Prime Minister Lee Kuan Yew stated clearly that

> The Speak Mandarin Campaign is not meant to make Singapore a more Chinese society, at the expense of the Malays and Indians. It is meant to make dialect-speaking Chinese replace dialect with Mandarin.

When the Teochew speakers were asked whether the inability to speak Teochew will make them lose their identity as Singaporeans, the majority of interviewees did not feel that by not speaking Teochew, they will lose the identity of a Singaporean. However, Jonathan feels that Singapore is made up of an immigrant society. Once Singapore Chinese lose their ability to speak dialects, they will not remember their roots as coming from southern China with the distinct dialect culture. They will eventually lose their distinctiveness and follow after the Americans or British, speaking mainly English or Singlish and losing their distinct dialect identity. In other words, globalization will sacrifice the local identity of Singaporeans who used to be able to relate to their roots in dialects.

(9)
Q: 汝觉得咱若是新加坡人勿晓咱*dialects* 吼, *do you think they will lose identity as Singaporeans*?
[Q: Do you feel that if Singaporeans don't know dialects, they will lose identity as Singaporeans?]
A: I think they will. I think if let's say if you know your identity is 潮州人(Teochew), but you don't know the characteristics, you're not brought up the Teochew way, I don't know how to speak Teochew, subsequently when you go towards the later generations and all, they will start to question like you know Singapore, when you study history you know Singapore they are actually all immigrants. Then, eh? Where am I from? What if they forget their

roots? You know? And will the kids in the future, be like America. Like inculcate their traits and their characteristics because of what they learn from the internet. Is this the direction that Singapore wants to go? Or does Singapore wants to erm, you know like Singlish, what's the Singaporean way, the Teochew way? So you will start to lose all these accents and start to copy what the Americans have, what the UK says. That's what Singaporeans are going towards LAH, because we focus too much on like economics or the US. We want to be like them, we want to be like this one, when we forget that we are actually who we are.

(10)
Q: *OK, so it's like in the course of globalization, you forget your local identity?*
A: Yes, correct.
Q: *So it's sort of like you sacrifice your local identity, give way to globalization?*
A: Yes, correct.

What is interesting here is Jonathan's answer that by losing the Teochew dialect, he feels that a Chinese Singaporean has lost one's Asian identity and will not differ from a westerner. According to him, it is the family heritage language that anchors one's emotional core identity, that Mandarin as a superimposed designated language may have certain functions, but it will not be able to replace the emotional identity that the government thinks Mandarin can.

To summarize, Teochew language is very much reduced to a dialect of the grandparents' generation. It is a language that keeps the root of where the family comes from with their distinctive identity and folk culture. However, there seems to be no environment except with grandparents and in local wet markets. Grandparents who do not speak Mandarin or English will not be able to communicate with grandchildren who are not conversant in Teochew language. As a result, the older generation, who are unable to speak Mandarin or English, are totally alienated and isolated (Lee 2007). Teochew is very much like a heritage language (He and Xiao 2008).

CONCLUSION

This study is relevant as it deals with the danger of losing a heritage language in a globalized urban society. In the case of Singapore, the state has clearly implemented language policies based on the ideology of unifying diversity of dialects (Fishman 1973, 1989), causing a drastic language shift from heritage languages to English and Mandarin. The importance of this study is also in its documenting this transition from the sharp decline of the Teochew dialect to its possible disappearance in the next decade.

English is the most common language used between siblings of the younger generation. For the younger generation, Mandarin and English have taken over the language of communication between spouses and between parents and children. The language shift is so severe that many do not see any chance of reversing it. Very few children of Teochew families are able to speak the language. A few may feel that it is a language of their family roots and heritage culture, but they express helplessness to preserve it, given that the use of Teochew is reduced to only speaking to grandparents. Older generation Teochews who do not speak Mandarin or English are no longer able to communicate with their grandchildren, who hardly get to hear the language. As Singapore moves toward globalization, there is a trend of losing more local Chinese dialects, replaced mainly by Mandarin and English.

The interviewees expressed that cultural values are best retained through the heritage language of Teochew and not Mandarin. Given that most families do not speak their own dialect but Mandarin and English, one will expect that the cultural values of Mandarin (the step-mother tongue) and English will take over those of the Teochew language. The societal structure is largely driven by pragmatism, with English having the highest status, followed by Mandarin. The Teochew language is only used when speaking with grandparents or the older generation (for example, in clinics). As the Teochew language does not have any economic value, there is little incentive to preserve the language. Interviewees in their twenties predict that they will be the last generation to use the language in Singapore.

ACKNOWLEDGEMENTS

- NUS Academic research fund (ARF), Tier 1 (WBS: R-102–000–079–112)
- All 53 participants and friends who helped me in collecting all the data
- This paper is dedicated to Ms. Tay Sim Heng, who has helped me with collecting the data from Singapore Newton Life Church in March 2013 and who passed on in September 2013.

REFERENCES

Baudrillard, J. 1988. *Selected writings*. Cambridge: Polity Press.

Bauman, Z. 1998. *Work, consumerism and the new poor*. Buckingham: Open University Press.

Blommaert, J. 2006. Language policy and national identity. In T. Ricento (Ed.), *An introduction to language policy: Theory and method* (pp. 238–254). Oxford: Blackwell.

Bourdieu, P. 1977. *Outline of a Theory of Practice*. Cambridge: Cambridge University Press.

Bourdieu, P. 1986. The forms of capital. In J. G. Richardson (ed.), *Handbook of theory and research for the sociology of education* (pp. 241–258). New York: Greenwood Press.

Bourdieu, P. 1991. *Language & symbolic power*(Ed. J. Thompson and Trans. G. Raymond & M. Adamson). Cambridge, MA: Harvard University Press.

Chen, Q. 2013. Bendi diaocha xianshi huazu ertong shiyong huayu pinlv xiajiang 本地调查显示华族儿童使用华语频率下降 [Local research shows a drop of Chinese usage among Chinese children]. *Lianhe Zaobao*, September, 13, 2013, 1. Accessed on November 5, 2013 http://www.chinanews.com/hr/2013/09–13/5280788.shtml.

De Costa, P.I. 2010. Language ideologies and standard English language policy in Singapore: responses of a 'designer immigrant' student. *Language Policy* 9: 217–239.

Fang, Q.H., Zhi, S.M., Wang, X.Y., and Huang, Y.Z. (方琪惠，植思敏，王欣仪，黄宇臻). 2010. Xuesheng ketangwai de huawen shiyong (学生课堂外的华文使用) [Students' Use of Mandarin outside classroom]. In *Xinjiapo texuan zhongxue xueshu youmiao jihua lunwenji diliuji*《新加坡特选中学幼苗计划论文集，第六集[SAP Schools Mentorship Programme Volume 6] (pp. 34–50). Singapore: Lingzi Media Pte Ltd.

Fishman, J.A. 1973. Language modernization and planning in comparison with other types of national modernization and planning. *Language in Society* 2: 23–43.

Fishman, J.A. 1989. *Language and ethnicity in minority sociolinguistic perspective.* Clevedon: Multilingual Matters.

Fishman, J.A. 1991. *Reversing language shift.* Clevedon: Multilingual Matters Ltd.

Goh, C.T. 1997. *National day rally speech.* Ministry of Education. Accessed on January 31, 2012 http://www.moe.gov.sg/media/speeches/1997/240897.htm

Goh, N.W. 2004. *Huayuwen Zai Xinjiapo De Xianzhuang Yu Qianjing* 华语文在新加坡的现状与远景[The Current Practice and Prospect of Chinese Language Education in Singapore]. Singapore: Chuangyiquan Chubanshe.

Gupta, A.F. 1989. Singapore colloquial English and standard English. *Singapore Journal of Education* 10(2): 33–39.

He, A.W. and Xiao, Y. (eds.). 2008. *Chinese as a heritage language: fostering rooted world citizenry.* Honolulu: National Foreign Language Resource Centre and University of Hawaii Press.

Heller, M. 2010. The commodification of language. *Annual Review of Anthropology* 39:101–114.

Kaplan, R.B., and Baldauf, Jr., R.B. 2003. *Language and language-in-education planning in the Pacific Basin.* Dordrecht, Netherlands: Kluwer.

Lee, C.K. 2007. Ageing in place—An unattended barrier. *Prime*, p. 88.

Lee, C.L. 2003. Xinjiaporen shuo de chaozhou hua 新加坡人说的潮州话 [Teochew spoken in Singapore]. In C.H. Lee (Ed.), *haiwai chaoren de yimin jingyan*《海外潮人的移民经验》 [*The Migration Experience of the Overseas Teochew Community*] (pp. 240–260). Singapore: Global Publishing Company (In Chinese).

Lee, C.L. 2006. Teochews in Singapore. In *Singapore Encyclopedia* (pp. 569). Singapore: Didier Millet, 2006.

Lee, C.L. 2012. Saving Chinese language education in Singapore. *Current Issues in Language Planning* 13, 285–304.

Lee, K.Y. 2011. *My lifelong challenge: Singapore's bilingual journey.* Singapore: Straits Times Press.

Li, W., Saravanan, V. and Ng, J.L.H. 1997. Language shift in the Teochew community in Singapore: A family domain analysis. *Journal of Multilingual and Multicultural Development* 18(5): 364–384.

Li, W., and Zhu, H. 2010. Voices from the diaspora: Changing hierarchies and dynamics of Chinese multilingualism. *International Journal of Sociology of Language* 205: 155–171.

Silverstein, M. 1979. Language structure and linguistic ideology. In P. Clyne, R.W.F. Hanks, and C. Hofbauer (Eds.), *The elements: A parasession on linguistic units and levels* (pp. 193–247). Chicago: University of Chicago.

Singapore Statistics. 2013. *Population Census.* Accessed on November 5, 2013 http://www.singstat.gov.sg/statistics/browse_by_theme/population/statistical_tables/popinbrief2013.pdf

Marriott, H. 1921. The peoples of Singapore. In W. Makepeace, G. E. Brooke, & R. Bradell (Eds.), *One hundred years of Singapore* (pp. 341–362). London: John Murray.

Phua, C. P. and Ho, P. Q. 2011. Yuyan de xiaowang—yi xinjiapo chaozhouhua wei ge an: jianlun jiben cihui de youjie fenbu 语言的消亡—以新加坡潮州话为个案：兼论基本词汇的有阶分布 *Yuyanxue Luncong* 《语言学论丛》 42: 141–182.

Song, J. 2009. Language ideology and identity in transnational space: Globalization, migration, and bilingualism among Korean families in the USA. *International Journal of Bilingual Education and Bilingualism* 13(1): 23–42.

Warde, A. 1994. Consumption, identity-formation and uncertainty. *Sociology* 28(4): 877–898.

Wong, R. Y. L. 1999. *Medium of instruction in schools in Singapore.* Regional report submitted to SCOLAR, Hong Kong Government.

Woolard, K. A. and Schieffelin, B. B. 1994. Language ideology. *Annual Review of Anthropology* 23: 55–82.

Xu, D. M., and Li, W. 2002. Managing multilingualism in Singapore. In W. Li, J-M, Dewaele, and A. Housen (Eds.), *Opportunities and challenges of bilingualism* (pp. 275–296). Berlin, New York: Mouton de Gruyter.

Yeoh, Brenda B. S. A. 2007. *Singapore: Hungry for foreign workers at all skill levels.* Migration Information Source. Country Profiles. Washington, DC: Migration Policy Institute. Accessed on January 31, 2012 http://www.migrationinformation.org/Profiles/display.cfm?ID=570

13 Multilingual Mediators
The (Continuing) Role of the Peranakans in the Contact Dynamics of Singapore

Lisa Lim

1 PREAMBLE

In 1856, John Crawfurd, Scottish physician and Company surgeon of the East India Company, colonial administrator and diplomat, notably the second British resident of Singapore (after Raffles' departure), and author of numerous works on Asian languages and India and the East Indies, wrote:

> the [Chinese] settlers, whenever it is in their power, form connections with the native women of the country; and hence has arisen a mixed race, numerous in the older settlements, known to the Malays under name of Paranakan China [*cina* 'Chinese'], literally, 'Chinese of the womb', that is, Chinese of native mothers . . . (1856: 96, in Tan 1988a: 44).

This would appear to be the first description of such a community, viz. that of the Peranakans[1] ([pranakán], from the Malay root *anak* "child", meaning a locally born person), the descendants of Southern Chinese traders who settled in Southeast Asia who intermarried with local Malay/Indonesian women,[2] who, in Singapore, are also known as Babas or Straits (-born) Chinese.[3] Such a description identifies two characteristics of the Peranakans that are significant for our purposes: their early, settled presence in the region, and their mixed origins. This chapter highlights the significance of these factors in the ecology of Singapore and in the Peranakans' linguistic practices and the evolution of what later became Singapore English. This chapter also underlines how such a community—seemingly of the past—does in fact continue to impact on ecology and evolution in the present day.

2 ARRIVAL AND ACCULTURATION

Whereas the Chinese had been an important maritime and trade power in Southeast Asia from as early as the 12th century, it was the Ming Dynasty (1368–1644) which witnessed relatively large Chinese settlement in the Philippines, the Strait of Malacca, and the Malay archipelago. One of the most prominent figures was Zheng He, who, in command of an extensive fleet, and leading expeditions to Southeast and South Asia more than eight times in the early 15th century, apparently established small communities along the route (Pan 2000). It is believed that the earliest Chinese stable trade colonies date back to this period, although Chinese settlers in Malacca were already reported to be found during their expeditions (Tan 1988a: 28–29). A longer-lasting Chinese maritime empire developed in the 16th and 17th centuries, led particularly by Fujian-based traders (Pan 2000: 49) who are said to be among the earliest to actually settle down in Southeast Asian ports and establish local communities (Norman 1988). These comprised what Wang (1991) identifies as the huashang—Chinese trader—pattern of Chinese emigration, the other three being huagong, Chinese coolies; huaqiao, Chinese sojourners; and huayi, Chinese descendants (Wang 1991: 5–9). Merchants travelled by land or sea to distant countries to seek goods to trade with China, some of whom, over time and after several trips, settled there. In fact, by the time the Europeans, starting with the Portuguese, started trade colonies in the 16th century in the "East Indies"—the region extending either from India or from Malaysia to New Guinea—they found several Chinese-based communities already established; in Malacca, in particular, they encountered the demographically most important Peranakan colonies. Later, once Singapore was established as a British trading post in 1819 (to later become a Crown Colony of Britain in 1867, forming together with Malacca and Penang the Straits Settlements), many Malacca Babas moved there in the early 19th century, attracted by the trading opportunities which arose there (Pakir 1986).

With the fall of the Ming to the non-Chinese Manchurian Qing Dynasty in 1644 came a larger wave of emigration to Southeast Asia (as well as Taiwan). During most of that period, migration from China was illegal, with migrants disallowed from returning to China after they left. Female emigration was also strongly discouraged by the Manchu regime (Tan 1988a: 34). The Chinese traders thus typically were male, with females staying behind to take care of their households and to observe filial piety and ancestor worship (Lim 1967: 63–65). The women that did get brought over to the Straits Settlements were there for the purpose of prostitution, and by the 19th century they comprised a significant proportion of the Chinese women there (Tan 1988a: 35). Nonetheless, in Malaya, Chinese women were still greatly outnumbered by Chinese men—by 4 to 1 in 1881 in Malaya, and by 15 to 1 in 1864 in Singapore (Liu 1999: 85)—an imbalance which led to frequent inter-ethnic marriages involving local women. Marriages to non-Muslim women, often slaves of Balinese, Bugis, or Javanese origin, required no religious conversion (Tan 1988a: 40–41; Pan 2000), whereas those marriages which involved Muslim Malay women entailed conversion of the males to Islam in only a subset, and in general, such conversion was clearly nominal: this can be seen in the fact that the Chinese generally continued observance of Chinese folk religion and brought up their children as Chinese (Skinner

1960: 96–97; Tan 1988a: 38f). Gradually, especially once the community attained a critical mass, marriages between the Baba men or the Nyonya women with the locals were discouraged, and an endogamous practice was established (Lim 1917: 876–877, in Tan 1988a: 37, 47).

The new hybrid culture that emerged in this context shows unique traits that set the Peranakans apart from other Chinese, the more indigenous local populations, and other ethnically mixed groups (Tan 1988b; Rudolph 1998). Non-linguistic examples include a mixed nyonya cuisine largely influenced by Malay traditions, and the wearing of Malay/Indonesian sarong and kebaya, instead of the Chinese dress, by the women. These contrast with the retention of Chinese rituals, such as religious practices mentioned above and traditional wedding customs involving imperial era wedding costumes (Tan 1988b: 299). According to some observers, the Peranakans had "lost touch with China in every respect, except that they continued to uphold Chinese customs, and to practice, in variously modified forms, the social and religious practices of the forefathers" (Lim 1917, in Kwok 2000: 202; Tan 1988a: 47).

Linguistically, Baba Malay (BM), a restructured, contact variety of Malay, developed as the mother tongue of the community, distinct from other Malay varieties due partly to the large amount of Chinese influence on it, particularly from Hokkien, Teochew, and Cantonese.[4] By around the 19th century, the Peranakans had shifted to BM as their vernacular: Song (1923/1967: 3) refers to this period in his observation that "in Malacca, however, where the Chinese had formed a continuous colony for about six centuries, the women-folk had entirely dropped the use of Chinese, while the Malacca-born Chinese males only acquired the Hokkien dialect colloquially for the purpose of trade".

BM is the vernacular for which the community is most well known, and garners particular attention in creole studies and in the world of endangered languages; collected corpora are for the most part entirely BM (e.g., Pakir 1986; Lim 1988; Ansaldo and Matthews 1999, Ansaldo, Lim and Mufwene 2007; Wee 2000; Tan 2014). We return to the issue of the Peranakans' linguistic repertoire in section 4.

3   PERMANENCE, POWER, PRESTIGE

In contrast with the majority of the (non-Peranakan) Chinese in 19th-century Singapore who continued harbouring plans to return to China—statistics from 1881 up to the 1960s show not only a continuous stream of Chinese immigration but also return emigration (Kwok 2000: 200)—the Peranakans considered Malacca and Singapore their home. The early Peranakan Chinese males did return regularly to China to ship more goods (Lim 1917: 876), as did the sons of the wealthier ones (a minority) to receive education—the presence of "many boys of partly Malay blood" is documented in the emigrant villages in Southern China, especially in schools supported by the emigrants in Southeast Asia (Chen 1939: 143). However, they always returned to the Straits. Until as late as the 1950s, only the Peranakan Chinese could be considered "permanent", "native", or indigenised Chinese communities in the region (Song 1923/1967).

Due in no small part to the fact that they had been in the region longer, more continuously, and more permanently than the other Chinese immigrants, the Peranakans formed the larger proportion of the influential class of Chinese capitalists in the Straits Settlements, having established themselves in the mining of gold and tin, the large-scale commercial agriculture business (in gambier, pepper, tapioca, and especially rubber), import-export business, and other economic enterprises that had been drawing Chinese to Malacca for years (Tan 1988a: 48). By the time of the European exploitation and colonisation of the region in the 19th century, most Babas of Malacca had accumulated much wealth and become prestigious subgroups in the region, forming separate communities of their own. In particular, they distinguished themselves from later Chinese immigrants, referring to them derogatorily as *sinkeh* "new guests", i.e., "new arrivals", whom they considered poor and with low social status (Tan 1988a: 45). In Singapore as well, the Babas were a class apart from the other ethnic groups. Although small in number ("Malacca men" comprised only 2.5% of the Chinese population in 1848, growing to just 9.5% in 1881), their social and economic influence was disproportionately strong in comparison, and they formed an important sector of the local elite (Kwok 2000: 202–204). By the 1920s, Singapore-born Peranakans controlled the pineapple industry, and most of the rubber which was cultivated, at one time more than 8000 hectares in Singapore as well as in Malaya—which together with tin drove Singapore's prosperity in the late 19th to 20th centuries (Liu 1999: 98). In Malacca, the well-off Baba were able to take over the houses of the great Dutch merchants in Heeren Street, which then became "the fashionable and aristocratic resort of the Chinese" (Braddell 1853: 74). In Penang, it was also noted that the Chinese "who have long been settled in the place, and who have wedded native wives, dwell in large and elegant houses environed with fruit and flower-gardens" (Thomson 1875: 13). In Singapore, the Peranakans were wealthy enough to afford weekend retreats or second homes in the form of seaside bungalows—some with swimming enclosures—in the East Coast of the island, an increasingly attractive residential area from the end of the 19th century (Liu 1999: 148).

They additionally distinguished themselves from the continuously increasing population of China-oriented immigrants by their local (Malayan) orientation and their pro-British sentiments (Tan 1988a: 54f.). Not an uncommon observation then was for Peranakans "on being asked if they were Chinamen [to] bristle up and say in an offended tone 'I am not a Chinaman, I am a British subject'" (Vaughan 1879). In their social clubs "to which they will admit no native of China . . . they play billiards, bowls, and other European games, and drink brandy and soda ad libitum" (ibid.). Identifying politically with the British (Kwok 2000: 205), they formed the Straits Chinese British Association (SCBA) in August 1900,[5] with an admitted aim to promote trade with, and foster loyalty to, the British Empire (Song 1923/1967: 319).

The Peranakans' early economic, social, and political establishment in the region, as outlined above, had important implications for their language and education. English had become, since the early 19th century, an increasingly important language in Southeast Asia, and the Peranakans were amongst the privileged few who acquired and benefited from it. They held a high regard for English-medium education, sent their children to English-medium schools, and were amongst the early advocates of education for girls (Liu 1999: 162). The establishment by members of the community of four early educational institutions—the Anglo-Chinese College of Malacca (1818), Penang Free School (1816), Singapore Institution (1823; later, renamed the Raffles Institution, 1868), and Malacca Free School (1826, Malacca High School since 1878)—was especially important to the development of the community (Tan 1988a: 52). The establishment of the Queen's Scholarship in 1885 for British subjects in the Straits Settlements further enabled a few Peranakans to be educated in higher institutions in Britain, producing scholars and leaders (Tan 1988a: 65, 82). Notably, the language in the SCBA was exclusively English, and the association's *The Straits Chinese Magazine*, first appearing in 1897, was published in English. The Peranakans were amongst the earliest groups in the region, certainly in Singapore, to adopt the English language. Whereas in earlier days they were noted to have spoken English "tolerably well" (Earl 1837, in Tan 1988a: 50), by the mid-19th century, their ability to converse in this colonial language was clear.

4 MULTILINGUAL REPERTOIRE, MULTILINGUAL MEDIATORS

The account so far may lead the reader to form the impression that it is merely Baba Malay followed by a shift to English that collectively characterise the Peranakans' linguistic practices, and indeed these codes are usually the only ones reflected in studies and corpora of the community. What I highlight in this paper is their multilingual reality, which can be understood in two respects: a multilingual repertoire, i.e., the various linguistic varieties that they had in their repertoire at their disposal, and their mixed code, both of which were critical to their positioning in the ecology in which they existed.

We first consider the myth of the Peranakans' inability to speak Chinese, which has been countered by scholars noting that, throughout the 19th century, many Babas could indeed speak Hokkien or other Chinese varieties, had their sons taught by Chinese tutors at home or sent to Chinese-medium schools, or at least learned or brushed up their Chinese for interaction with China-born Chinese immigrants (Tan 1979: 72; Rudolph 1998: 312–314).

Four examples of prominent Peranakans of the 19th century are provided in Rudolph (1998: 314), including Song Ong Siang's father, Song Hoot Kiam (1830–1900), a Melaka-born Baba, who learned Cantonese while in Hong Kong as a 13-year-old; Tan Jiak Kim (1859–1917), educated privately in Chinese and English, and who supported Chinese vernacular education; and Melaka-born Tan Boon Chin (1857–1933), who preached in Malay and who had spent four years at a Chinese school before attending Raffles Institution.

In the next generation too, that is, those of the early 20th century, a shift from BM to English would be taking place, in an ecology which was itself transforming to become English-dominant. Nonetheless, a picture is painted of a rich tapestry of languages wielded, illustrated in the following ethnographic accounts.[6]

(1) Cheong Keong Tuan (CKT, 1921–2011) traces her family's settlement in the region along her paternal line five generations to her great-great-grandfather, Cheong Joo Keng, who sailed from China to Malacca in the early 1800s. Her father, Cheong Koon Seng (b. 1880), educated, like many other Babas then, at the Anglo-Chinese School where the teachers were American missionaries, was a renowned comprador, auctioneer, philanthropist (making donations particularly to schools, such as his alma mater), and founder and President of the Chinese Swimming Club. Her mother, Chia Siew Tin (b. 1896), went to the Singapore Chinese Girls' School, where the teachers were English missionaries, studying there up until Standard 5 when she turned about 12. She could read and write, and sign her name, and is remembered for having won a prize for reading *Little Lord Fauntleroy*. CKT's grandfather on the maternal side, Chia Hood Theam, a third-generation Peranakan, was a comprador of the Mercantile Bank in Singapore. CKT grew up speaking BM and English with her parents and husband, but primarily English with her siblings, together with some BM. She spoke Cantonese with the live-in Cantonese maid, and Hokkien at the market. She and her three sisters attended the Methodist Girls' School, where the majority of the teachers were American missionaries, and where the language medium was English, with Latin taught as a subject. She studied there until she was 16 years old, completing her Senior Cambridge examinations, then went to the Teachers' Training College and became a secondary school teacher.[7]

(2) Koh Kong Hai (b. 1910), CKT's husband, spoke Baba Malay to his parents. His father, Koh Sek Lim, originally from Malacca, owned a large stretch of coastal land at the eastern end of Singapore, on which estate the family grew up fishing, sailing, and hunting. With his siblings, whereas BM was predominant, English was also used. He attended St Andrew's School until Secondary 3

when he was about 15 years of age; there the teachers were English missionaries. Because he was proficient in English, he became a foreman in a government office, which raised his social status in relation to Asians, as he worked directly under the British, in charge of distributing the weekly salary to the Singaporean civil servants.

The command that the Peranakans had of the English language certainly afforded them closer contact with British administrators and merchants, and positions of higher status, whether as government foremen or teachers, or as prominent agriculture capitalists or compradors. Their prominent socioeconomic position in relation to the British was so strengthened by the position of English in their repertoire that they were often referred to as the "King's Chinese" (Tan 1988a: 53), in reference to the King of England. What should not be overlooked is the fact that it was also their knowledge of Malay, various Chinese languages, and the local ways which afforded them a significant role as intermediaries between Europeans, locals, and Asian newcomers (Lim 1887; Tan 1988a; Kwok 2000), with many working for the Dutch and British East India Companies (Tan 1988a: 51f.). It is perhaps not surprising that the Peranakans were seen to be the "more enlightened, and better merchants" (Earl 1837: 363), and the best educated, the wealthiest, and the most intelligent section of the Chinese community (Nathan 1922: 77).

The Peranakans' multilingualism is also worthy of note in the form of the mixed codes which formed their linguistic practice. Baba Malay is well documented as a restructured Malay variety, with clear Sinitic elements, such as the southern Min pronominal system and lexis from Hokkien and other Chinese varieties in the domains of kinship and religion. The English of the community also shows itself to be a restructured variety, as seen in recent work on Peranakan English (PerE, Lim 2010a, 2014). Example 3 illustrates speech representative of the generation of Singapore Peranakans born in the early 20th century (CKT of example 1), here, in a typical conversation in a three-generation family gathered on Sunday for family lunch, in the early 2000s (English, *Baba Malay*).

(3)

1 When you think of having babies, don[t] drink! . . . For one year! . . . Abstinence. Really clean . . . your system. You never know what you get.

2 Like drugs you know when you're under drugs. . . . The babies come out crying crying *Apa dia mo? mo?* Drugs. *Nanti* alcohol the same. They get into their system.

3 *Kita semua tak drin[k].* . . . Keep yourself clean and healthy. Don[t] drin[k] don[t] drin[k]. Don[t] say oh it's only beer never min[d]. Beer also has alcohol!

4 Before you get the child, you mus[t] already tell yourself, if you're going to have children, you very well keep your blood clean.

5 And don[t] don[t] have furry animals also. You never know, you breathe the thing, it's carried in your blood system. . . . Go and get stuck somewhere in the chil[d] . . . also . . .

6 Animals! Animals also can affect. . . . Very fine fur. Don't keep animals. And *chium-chium* them. Ee uh. Enough!

7 You want to have babies, you don't *a24*. One year you give yourself cleansing. . . . No alcohol.

As noted in Lim (2010a), variation between more acrolectal features approximating Standard British English and more vernacular BM features is found in a single conversation, at times within a single turn or utterance. Features of BM phonology include unaspirated voiceless plosives and consonant cluster simplification, as well as phrase-final prominence with pitch peak located on the final word of phrases. Features of BM syntax are also evident, such as absence of copular and topic-comment structure. Also noteworthy is the presence of BM,[8] as single words, phrases, or utterances: the switch to BM in Turn 6 for the lexical item *chium* "to kiss", reduplicated as *chium-chium* for attenuation or continuation to mean "to kiss a little, continuously"; the very common *nanti* "in future = wait and see" used in Turn 2 in a largely English utterance *Nanti alcohol the same*; Turn 3's *Kita semua tak drin(k)* "All of us didn't drink" in BM with English verb; and entire BM utterances: speaking of babies, born of drug-addict mothers, who cry constantly, the question "What do they want?" is presented in Turn 2 in BM *Apa dia mo?*. Significant for the premise in this chapter is the point, also made in Lim (2010a), that the linguistic practice observed, viz. the alternate use of English and BM (where BM in turn would involve Hokkien[9] loanwords for address practices, food, certain cultural and religious practices, and terms of emotive import and value judgment) should really be viewed as a single English-BM mixed code in its own right. In other words, it is mixed codes—such as BM and Peranakan "English"—that characterise the Peranakans' multilingual repertoire.

5 SIGNIFICANCE FOR THE EVOLUTION OF SINGAPORE ENGLISH

The Peranakans and their vernaculars are not just of interest unto themselves. Recognising their presence in the ecology of Singapore in fact makes a significant contribution to our understanding of the evolution of New Englishes such as Singapore English (SgE).

In analyses of the restructuring of SgE from a contact perspective, the usual suspects identified are the (southern) Sinitic languages: SgE is analysed as relexification of Chinese grammar (Bao 2005); a vast majority of (more recent) SgE particles come from Cantonese, with the few older ones from Hokkien/Bazaar Malay (BZM) (Lim 2007); and typological congruence and reinforcement is seen amongst southern Sinitic varieties and BZM (Ansaldo 2004, 2009). Prosody, however, presents a more complex picture. Sinitic languages certainly also have had a dominant role in the evolution of SgE prosody: SgE is analysed as having tone in addition to and being predictable from stress (Wee 2008; Ng 2011), and is considered a tone language of a particular kind (Lim 2009a, 2011). Sinitic-type tone is clearly found in the Cantonese set of particles in SgE (Lim 2007: 451). Tone is also noted at the level of the word and phrase (4, 5),[10] with the phrase-level contour comprising sequences of sustained level tones which step up or down to each other, rather than glide more gradually from one pitch level to another (Lim 2004: 42ff.).

(4) `manage, `teacher 33–55 / MH   (Wee 2008)

    in`tend, a`round   11–55 / LH
    `origin, bi`lingual   11–33–55 / LM
    o`riginal, se`curity   11–33–33–55 / LMMH
    o`riginally   11–33–33–33–55 / LMMMH

(5) I think happier   LHLLM   (Lim 2004)

Suprasegmental features, including tone, are widely recognised as susceptible to being acquired in contact situations (Curnow 2001), and tone is often acquired in a non-tonal language by borrowing or imitation due to the presence of tone in the broader linguistic environment (Gussenhoven 2004: 42f.). In contact language formation scenarios involving European accent languages and substrate tone languages, tone evolves in the contact language. Fine examples include Saramaccan, an English-based Atlantic maroon creole of Surinam, with African languages Gbe and Kikongo as substrates (Good 2004), Portuguese-lexifier Papiamentu (Kouwenberg 2004; Rivera-Castillo and Pickering 2004); and the Austronesian language Ma'ya, in contact with tonal Papuan languages (Remijsen 2001: 43).

In Singapore, the Chinese form the vast majority of the population, and Sinitic languages dominate the ecology: Hokkien was the intra-ethnic lingua franca amongst the Chinese and a widely understood and spoken language by ethnic groups in colonial and early independence eras, Mandarin was made one of the four official languages soon after independence and eventually became the new intra-ethnic lingua franca, Cantonese was one of the prominent Chinese languages of the early immigrants, as well as a popular language in the golden years of Cantonese cinema and Cantopop in the late 1980s to 1990s, boosted by significant immigration from Hong Kong (see details in Lim 2010b). Clearly tone languages have been in the majority and are dominant in the ecology, and tone has thus been a salient aspect of the feature pool. An initial assumption would almost automatically be that the tone observed in SgE originates in the Sinitic substrates, as opposed to the other substrates, which are not tone languages. With the particles, this is clear: the tones in SgE particles are the exact same tone as in the Cantonese particles. A slightly more complex and intriguing situation emerges, however, with the tone patterns at word and phrase level.

In other contact varieties of English in which tone has evolved, the general pattern locates high (H) tones on what would be stressed or accented syllables at word- or phrase-level, e.g., in Nigerian English (6) and Hong Kong English (7, 8). In contrast, as seen earlier, SgE locates H tones on the final syllable of the word, and tends to prefer prominence on the phrase-final syllable such that the pitch is perceived as relatively high. What might account for this distinctive patterning?

(6) ˋsomething   HH   (NigE, Gut 2005)

conˋtinued   LHH

(7) inˋtend   11–55 / LH   (HKE, Wee 2008)

ˋorigin, ˋphotograph   55–11–11 / HLL

oˋriginal   11–55–11–11 / LHLL

(8) I saw the manager this morning   LHHHHHHHL!   (Luke 2008)

An obvious candidate amongst the languages that are or have been in widespread use in the ecology would be a Malay variety, with Malay the vernacular of the ethnic Malays, and colloquial Bazaar Malay (BZM) the main inter-ethnic lingua franca in Singapore from the earliest era until as recently as the 1970s, and the trade language used in the region for millennia. Most Malay/Indonesian varieties prefer prominence on the penultimate and/or final syllable at word level (with some variation; see Gil in press), and prominence at phrase level tends to be located phrase-finally (with acceptability increasing closer to the right edge of phrase-final word) (e.g., Goedemans and van Zanten in press). BZM as spoken in the earlier era of Singapore's ecology has not had its intonation described, but recent work by Ng (2012) suggests frequent word-final rises or H tone, as well as the use of level tones. Baba Malay too shows phrase-final prominence, in the form of an utterance-final rise-fall, often manifested as step-up progressions across the final syllables of the utterance (Wee 2000). The structural features do support the hypothesis that some Malay variety/ies may well be the source for SgE's word-/phrase-final prominence.

If we consider social factors of the ecology, we make some headway in distinguishing between the potential influences that the different Malay varieties and their communities may have had on early SgE. The ethnic Malays have comprised a minority of the population (no more than 15%) since the second decade of the populating of Singapore under British colonial rule, which started in the early 1800s; thus, numerically, and consequently socially, they have not been as dominant (as the Chinese) in Singapore's ecology. This is, of course, not to downplay the significant presence of the early Malay royalty as well as numerous influential and wealthy Malays and Arabs, such as the late-19th-century community leaders. However, although the Malay language is still the most frequently spoken home language in 91.5% of Malay homes (2000), BZM is currently no longer widely spoken by Singaporeans outside of the Malay community, its role as a main inter-ethnic lingua franca only lasting until the 1970s, and its position then replaced by English, in particular in the new generations of native English speakers. In other words, when Malay varieties were widely spoken in Singapore's ecology, English was not—it would have been in the repertoire of a very small minority of the population, and would have been acquired in education, again by a minority, those in English-medium schools. The time that English started becoming more widespread in the ecology was about the time when BZM lost currency. The timing, as it were, for contact and transfer would have been a bit off. Finally, even if we assume that Malay did influence SgE through the first and second points, that is, in the earlier era when BZM was a dominant language in the ecology, why would it be that features of this earlier Malay influence appear to be maintained in spite of more recent Sinitic dominance?

Quite a compelling answer can be found if we consider the Founder Principle in the ecology paradigm (Mufwene 2001, 2008), which suggests that the founder population in an ecology exerts a strong influence on features, an influence which persists in the emergent variety, and if we consider the Peranakans as a founder population in Singapore's ecology, one with significant economic and social prominence in the ecology. In their Baba Malay vernacular lies the word-/phrase-final prominence that also developed in PerE as a result of contact in their multilingual repertoire. The Peranakans, although a small minority, were clearly dominant in the external ecology due to their political, economic, and social status, and their position as intermediaries, and later as teachers. As early English adopters, crucially during the British colonial period, theirs would have been the early features influencing the emerging variety of SgE—this would have been a time when the majority of the population, in contrast, even if BZM users would hardly have been using English in any sustained, systematic way. In short, if we consider both structural features and sociohistorical factors, in the Peranakans we find this a plausible explanation for the prosodic patterns observed in SgE.

6   THE CONTINUING EVOLUTION—OF THE PERANAKANS, AND OF SGE

Is the Peranakans' role as multilingual mediators in Singapore's ecology relevant only in the past? A century and a half on from the very first acknowledgement of the Peranakans in the region, the community is still around, and in fact proclaimed in 2010 by Singapore's Arts and Information Minister Lui Tuck Yew as "multiracial emblems of [Singapore's] social mix". As suggested in Lim (2014), the Peranakans have been seeing a renewed relevance in late modernity, and, in their current positioning in their 21st-century cultural revival in the changed sociolinguistic context of Singapore, may even play a role in the continuing evolution of SgE.

As noted in Lim (2010a), the Peranakans, along with other communities such as the Eurasians and Anglo Indians, were groups which saw their formation and evolution in a particular sociohistorical context. Bloom (1986: 360) recognises this very fact, pinpointing "the amalgam of Asian cultural traits and the English language in groups such as the Straits Chinese, Anglo Indian groups and Portuguese Eurasians, in particular in the Straits Chinese, [was] unique to the Straits Settlements, which made them an indigenous culture in a palpable sense". The ecology in which they were formed has however certainly changed, and, for a period, the Peranakan community seemed not to have been evolving along with the times: as noted by Peter Lee, a core figure in the community, the community had chosen what has been seen in retrospect as a self-imposed exclusivity during the 1960s–70s, and who had remained in "ultra-conservative mode, lost touch with the reality of the world then and painted itself into a corner" (Yap 2008). Some even predicted "the dying out of the Peranakans" (Kwan-Terry 2000: 96).

In the past decade or so, however, their ethnolinguistic vitality has been injected with new life. The Peranakan Association has always been extremely active and dedicated, organising well-attended activities throughout the year including food festivals, talks, annual conventions, and their annual dinner and dance, and their membership has been stable and has even continued to grow annually. In the late 2000s, however, the community started receiving increased formal institutional recognition or support, for example in the form of a restored traditional Baba House and a dedicated Peranakan museum, both opening in 2008. Above all, they started being recognised as an important cultural group in the country.

What of their linguistic vitality? A reasonable prognosis is put forward in Lim (2010a) along these lines. On the one hand, given Singapore's rapidly changing linguistic ecology, driven to a large extent by language policies (Lim 2009b), the positioning of English has led to the evolution and establishment of SgE as the mother tongue of most young Singaporeans. Young Peranakans, classified as "Chinese", have studied Mandarin as a second language in school, and have little or no exposure to Baba Malay, due to the move from extended to nuclear family units and the demise of the BM-speaking older generation, as well as the general shift already in place from BM to English in the community at large. Such a decrease in (speakers of) BM means a reduction in their presence in the ecology, and consequently a reduction in their influence on English in Singapore, even if we only consider the community of Peranakans. All these circumstances suggest that the conditions which were vital for the formation of PerE are no longer applicable, and thus a natural disappearance of PerE may be expected, in particular in the face of the extremely vital SgE. On the other hand, the high vitality of the community that is undeniably in existence may well go some distance in the maintenance of PerE. For one thing, even if BM is gradually disappearing as a widely-used vernacular, there are clearly conscious efforts being made in its maintenance and revitalisation: publications such as a BM dictionary and a collection of BM idioms (Gwee 1993, 2006) have appeared recently, plays are written and performed regularly in BM, and churches in traditional Peranakan districts have services in BM. For a while, at least, the presence of BM in the ecology of the Peranakans may still be assured, even if only passively in the younger generation. The socio-psychological dimension also seems promising, because with the revival of interest in all things Peranakan comes the recognition, especially amongst the younger generation, that the culture is not obsolete but relevant. The Peranakan Association's youth group has regular gatherings, which involve not only engaging in Peranakan cultural activities but also revitalising BM and using it in popular culture; and there is even a Peranakan presence in the virtual world of Second Life. Such identification with and reinforcement of the culture may well lead to a focusing (in Le Page and Tabouret-Keller's 1986 sense) and maintenance of features at least in the Peranakan community.

Since these predictions in Lim (2010a) at the end of the last decade, there have been new developments: most recently, the reinvention and rebranding of what it means to be Peranakan is notable along several lines. The Peranakan culture has now been taken beyond Singapore and undergone global branding: in 2010, the musée du quai Branly in Paris hosted an exhibition on Peranakan jewelry entitled *BabaBling*. The Peranakan community continues to actively engage in ways to retain their relevance via reinvention: for instance, BM has been used in rap and hiphop by the Main Wayang Company who set out to modernise Peranakan entertainment as a way to keep the heritage alive through innovation and reach out to as many people as possible. There appears to be a rebranding—even a commodification—of Peranakan culture in the context of Singapore: being "multiracial emblems of [Singapore's] social mix", Peranakan performances are featured at international events representing Singapore, such as at the 2009 Asia-Pacific Economic Committee forum. There are increasing possibilities to "do" PerE: in drama series and sitcoms centering around Peranakan families, such as the 2008 local English comedy series *Sayang Sayang*, as well as Peranakan events such as the museum's Sarong Kebaya Exhibition storytelling in 2011.

In the 21st century, it appears that the Peranakans still have relevance in Singapore's multiracial ecology, their position as mediators as a consequence of their multilingual resources still maintained in a slightly different form, viz. as representatives of the multicultural ecology and ethos that Singapore styles for itself. And this may well have implications for linguistic practices. It is still early days yet, but this chapter (following Lim 2014) ventures the following prediction for the evolution of SgE in response to the recent unease towards population groups and language in Singapore's ecology. Just as factors of immigration and language policy were instrumental in shaping Singapore's linguistic ecology in colonial times (see Lim 2010b), its population make-up, in particular, continues to impact on SgE's evolution. The last decade has seen a surge of mainland Chinese immigration, part of the government-engineered push to counteract Singapore's low birthrate. About a million mainland Chinese have arrived in the past decade—where the total population in Singapore is about 5.07 million, this means they comprise a fifth—drawn by financial incentives and a liberal visa policy, but who are felt by Singaporeans not to have assimilated well or at all to Singapore's culture, values, and languages. The impact on Singapore's linguistic ecology is significant, as Mandarin—more specifically, mainland Chinese Mandarin—is increasingly dominant in the ecology, as already predicted in Lim (2010b). This is due not only to sheer numbers but also to the Singapore government's pandering to the mainland Chinese. A pointed illustration of this is Singapore's Mass Rapid Transport initiating a three-month "trial" in October 2012 to announce station names in Mandarin but not in Malay or Tamil, the two other official languages in Singapore. This attracted widespread criticism amongst Singaporeans with regard to the unequal treatment of Singapore's "Mother Tongues", with many speculating that this was to cater to the growing number of arrivals from mainland China; the trial was subsequently suspended. With the Peranakans increasingly identified as all that is emblematic of Singapore's history and multiracial social mix, and with PerE displaying more saliently than mainstream SgE particular features that index languages and identities other than "Chinese", the evolution of SgE may well move in the direction of selecting more features from PerE which distinguish it from a more Sinitic variety and identity to set it apart from a more (mainland) Chinese identity—a change not dissimilar to what was observed decades ago on another small island seeing influx from the mainland (Labov 1972).

In the Peranakans we see how the earliest Chinese diaspora to the Southeast Asian region put down their roots—early and deep. This not only had implications for their place in the cities in which they located themselves, and their position in society, but also in the languages that were in currency and were evolving in the region then. That the Peranakans commanded a multilingual repertoire, which crucially also included the lingua franca of the region and the language of the colonisers, meant that they could fill the significant position of intermediary. With all these factors coming together, it is not surprising to identify the persistent influence of linguistic features of the Peranakans—as a founder population in an ecology—in the evolving contact variety. In a sense then, they put down their roots in language as well. And in the Peranakans we also see how an early, older diaspora, if they maintain a high ethnolinguistic vitality even while the ecology evolves, may well maintain their position as mediators of the territory's multicultural self in late modernity.

NOTES

1. I am grateful to Umberto Ansaldo and Salikoko Mufwene for our earlier collaboration on the Peranakan community and its languages, and for their views of the Peranakans being the founder population in the evolution of Singapore English, which have shaped my work on the community. I also thank Katherine Chen, Ana Deumert, Randy LaPolla, and Li Wei for their comments on two recent presentations. Above all, my heartfelt appreciation goes to my consultants, who have, all these years, gladly put up with being scrutinised, recorded, and interrogated, even during the most intimate of family gatherings.

2. The label Peranakan is also used to refer to other mixed communities in Malaysia and Indonesia. For example, the Jawi Peranakan in Penang and Singapore are offspring of mixed unions between South Indian Muslims and Malay women (Tan 1988a: 26); the Chitty Melaka (*chitty* Tamil "merchant") or Peranakan Indians of Malacca and later Singapore are the result of contact between early South Indian settlers and indigenous Malay, Javanese, or nyonya women (Dhoraisingam 2006: xi).

3. These terms are not entirely synonymous and have been used variably by different authors. The term "Peranakan" can be—and is often—used to refer to most individuals of Chinese origin living in the Malay/Indonesian region; Song's (1923/1967: 69) distinction, for instance, is between the "Dutch Peranakans", i.e., those of Indonesia, and the "Straits-born Chinese", i.e., those born in the Straits Settlements (namely Malacca, Penang, and Singapore), who would be associated with English. Whereas the term "Straits-born" refers to all people of Chinese ancestry born in the Straits Settlements, a distinction has been made between "a first-generation Straits-born Chinese who lived and acted much like his immigrant Chinese parents" and "a third, fourth or fifth generation Baba whose customs, language and behaviour were Straits Chinese" (Png 1969: 98). For instance, only the latter group has Malay as their only vernacular, while the former also spoke (some) Chinese (Png 1969: 99). The more inclusive usage serves a political ideology (Tan 1988a: 10; see also The Peranakan Association 2006). The term "Baba", originally used as an honorific term in the early 19th century, came to be used to refer to locally born Chinese in the Straits Settlements by around the mid 1800s (Tan 1988a: 44–45), or more specifically the locally born descendants of a mixed Malay-Hokkien culture original to Malacca and later Singapore. "Baba" also refers to male Peranakans, in opposition to the "Nyonya", the females. In this chapter I use the label "Peranakans" to refer to the Peranakan Chinese of Malacca and Singapore.

4. Whereas Ansaldo and Matthews (1999) note several grammatical similarities between Hokkien and BM which can be attributed to Hokkien substrate influence or the congruence of the latter and nonstandard Malay varieties, they also acknowledge the presence and potential influence of other southern Chinese groups and languages, such as Teochew and Hakka.

5. The Malacca branch of SCBA was formed in October of the same year (1900), and the Penang branch was founded later in 1920. The Associations are all still extremely active to date, the Singapore one renamed The Peranakan Association.

6. These are based on interviews conducted in September 2002.

7. Note that only those who obtained the highest level of Grade 1 in English could go on to train to become teachers, and the only ones who could do this at that time were the Eurasians and the Peranakans, those who typically were proficient and fluent in English.

8. The data in Lim (2010a) are more English-dominant, because PerE is the focus; in interactions between Peranakans in whom BM is more active, usually in the older generations, a greater proportion of BM is documented.
9. But tone as in Hokkien is not transferred to BM, nor is it realised in PerE (cf. Sinitic tone being acquired in SgE, Lim 2009a).
10. Tones are represented as pitch level numbers 1 to 5 where, in the Asianist tradition, the larger the number the higher the pitch; thus *55* represents a high level tone, *24* represents a rising tone, etc., and in the phonological tradition where L = Low tone, M = Mid tone, and H = High tone, the latter as in the original sources.

REFERENCES

Ansaldo, Umberto. 2004. The evolution of Singapore English: Finding the matrix. In *Singapore English: A Grammatical Description*, Lisa Lim (ed.), 127–149. Amsterdam/ Philadelphia: John Benjamins.

Ansaldo, Umberto. 2009. The Asian typology of English: Theoretical and methodological considerations. In *The Typology of Asian Englishes*, Lisa Lim and Nikolas Gisborne (eds.), *English World-Wide* 30(2): 133–148.

Ansaldo, Umberto, Lisa Lim and Salikoko S. Mufwene. 2007. The sociolinguistic history of the Peranakans: What it tells us about 'creolization'. In *Deconstructing Creole*, Umberto Ansaldo, Stephen Matthews and Lisa Lim (eds.), 203–226. Amsterdam/ Philadelphia: John Benjamins.

Ansaldo, Umberto and Stephen J. Matthews. 1999. The Minnan substrate and creolization in Baba Malay. *Journal of Chinese Linguistics* 27(1): 38–68.

Bao, Zhiming. 2005. The aspectual system of Singapore English and the systemic substratist explanation. *Journal of Linguistics* 41(2): 237–267.

Bloom, David. 1986. The English language in Singapore: A critical survey. In *Singapore Studies*, Basant K. Kapur (ed.), 337–458. Singapore: Singapore University Press.

Braddell, T. 1853. Notes of a trip to the interior from Malacca. *Journal of the Indian Archipelago and Eastern Asia* 7: 73–104.

Chen, Ta. 1939. *Emigrant Communities in South China: A Study of Overseas Migration and Its Influence on Standards of Living and Social Change*. Shanghai: Kelly & Walsh Ltd.

Crawfurd, J. 1856. *A Descriptive Dictionary of the Indian Island and Adjacent Countries*. London: Bradbury & Evans.

Curnow, Timothy Jowan. 2001. What language features can be 'borrowed'? In *Areal Diffusion and Genetic Inheritance: Problems in Comparative Linguistics*, Alexandra Y. Aikhenvald and Robert M.W. Dixon (eds.), 412–436. Oxford: Oxford University Press.

Dhoraisingam, Samuel S. 2006. *Peranakan Indians of Singapore and Melaka: Indian Babas and Nonyas—Chitty Melaka*. Singapore: Institute of Southeast Asian Studies.

Earl, George Windsor. 1837. *The Eastern Seas or Voyages and Adventures in the Indian Archipelago in 1832–33–34*. London: Allen & Co.

Gil, David (ed.). in press. *Malay/Indonesian Linguistics*. London: Routledge Curzon.

Goedemans, Rob and Ellen van Zanten. in press. Stress and accent in Indonesian. In *Malay/Indonesian Linguistics*, David Gil (ed.), 35–62. London: Routledge Curzon.

Good, Jeff. 2004. Tone and accent in Saramaccan: Charting a deep split in the phonology of a language. *Lingua* 114: 575–619.

Gussenhoven, Carlos. 2004. *The Phonology of Tone and Intonation*. Cambridge: Cambridge University Press.

232   *Lisa Lim*

Gut, Ulrike. 2005. Nigerian English prosody. *English World-Wide* 26: 153–177.
Gwee, Thian Hock William. 1993. *Mas Sepuloh: Baba Conversational Gems*. Singapore: Armour Publishing Pte Ltd.
Gwee, Thian Hock William. 2006. *A Baba Malay Dictionary*. Singapore: The Peranakan Association; Tuttle Publishing.
Kouwenberg, Silvia. 2004. The grammatical function of Papiamentu tone. *Journal of Portuguese Linguistics* 3: 55–69.
Kwan-Terry, Anna. 2000. Language shift, mother tongue, and identity in Singapore. *International Journal of the Sociology of Language* 143: 85–106.
Kwok, Kian Woon. 2000. Singapore. In *The Encyclopedia of the Chinese Overseas*, Lynn Pan (ed.), 200–217. Singapore: Chinese Heritage Centre; Cambridge, Mass.: Harvard University Press.
Labov, William. 1972. *Sociolinguistic Patterns*. Philadelphia: University of Pennsylvania Press.
Le Page, Robert and Andrée Tabouret-Keller. 1986. *Acts of Identity*. Cambridge: Cambridge University Press.
Lim, Boon Keng. 1917. The Chinese in Malaya. In *Present Days' Impressions of the Far East and Prominent and Progressive Chinese at Home and Abroad: The History, People, Commerce, Industries and Resources of China, Hong Kong, Indo-China, Malaya and Netherlands India*, W. Feldwisk (ed.), 875–882. London: Globe Encyclopedia Co.
Lim, Hiong Seng. 1887. *A Manual of the Malay Colloquial such as Is Spoken by All Nationalities in the Colonies of the Straits Settlements, and Designed for Domestic and Business Purposes*. Singapore: Koh Yeu Hean Press.
Lim, Joo Hock. 1967. Chinese female immigration into the Straits Settlements 1860–1901. *Journal of the South Seas Society* 22: 58–110.
Lim, Lisa. 2004. Sounding Singaporean. In *Singapore English: A Grammatical Description*, Lisa Lim (ed.), 19–56. Amsterdam/ Philadelphia: John Benjamins.
Lim, Lisa. 2007. Mergers and acquisitions: On the ages and origins of Singapore English particles. *World Englishes* 27(4): 446–473.
Lim, Lisa. 2009a. Beyond fear and loathing in SG: The real mother tongues and language policies in multilingual Singapore. In *Multilingual, Globalizing Asia: Implications for Policy and Education*, Lisa Lim and Ee-Ling Low (eds.), *AILA Review* 22: 52–71.
Lim, Lisa. 2009b. Revisiting English prosody: (Some) New Englishes as tone languages? In *The Typology of Asian Englishes*, Lisa Lim and Nikolas Gisborne (eds.), *English World-Wide* 30(2): 219–240.
Lim, Lisa. 2010a. Peranakan English in Singapore. In *The Lesser-Known Varieties of English*, Daniel Schreier, Peter Trudgill, Edgar W. Schneider and Jeffrey P. Williams (eds.), 327–347. Cambridge: Cambridge University Press.
Lim, Lisa. 2010b. Migrants and 'mother tongues': Extralinguistic forces in the ecology of English in Singapore. In *English in Singapore: Modernity and Management*, Lisa Lim, Anne Pakir and Lionel Wee (eds.), 19–54. Hong Kong: Hong Kong University Press.
Lim, Lisa. 2011. Tone in Singlish: Substrate features from Sinitic and Malay. In *Creoles, Their Substrates and Language Typology*, Claire Lefebvre (ed.), 271–287. Amsterdam/ Philadelphia: John Benjamins.
Lim, Lisa. 2014. Yesterday's founder population, today's Englishes: The role of the Peranakans in the (continuing) evolution of Singapore English. In *The Evolution of Englishes*, Sarah Buschfeld, Thomas Hoffmann, Magnus Huber and Alexander Kautzsch (eds.), 401–419. Amsterdam/ Philadelphia: John Benjamins.
Lim, Sonny. 1988. Baba Malay: The language of the 'Straits-born' Chinese. In *Papers in Western Austronesian Linguistics* No. 3, Hein Steinhauer (ed.). Department of Linguistics, Research School of Pacific Studies, The Australian National University.

Liu, Gretchen. 1999. *Singapore: A Pictorial History 1819–2000*. Singapore: National Heritage Board and Editions Didier Miller.

Luke, Kang-kwong. 2008. Stress and intonation in Hong Kong English, 14th Conference of the International Association for World Englishes (IAWE), Hong Kong.

Mufwene, Salikoko S. 2001. *The Ecology of Language Evolution*. Cambridge: Cambridge University Press.

Mufwene, Salikoko S. 2008. *Language Evolution: Contact, Competition and Change*. New York: Continuum.

Nathan, J. 1922. *The Census of British Malaysia, 1921*. London: Waterloo & Sons.

Ng, E-Ching. 2011. Reconciling stress and tone in Singaporean English. In *Asian Englishes: Changing Perspectives in a Globalised World*, Lawrence J. Zhang, Rani Rubdy and Lubna Alsagoff (eds.), 48–59. Singapore: Pearson Longman.

Ng, E-Ching. 2012. Chinese meets Malay meets English: Origins of Singaporean English word-final high tone. Special issue, *International Journal of Bilingualism* 16(1): 83–100.

Norman, J. 1988. *Chinese*. Cambridge: Cambridge University Press.

Pakir, Anne. 1986. *A linguistic investigation of Baba Malay*. PhD dissertation, University of Hawai'i.

Pan, Lynn (ed.). 2000. *The Encyclopedia of the Chinese Overseas*. Singapore: Chinese Heritage Centre; Cambridge, Mass.: Harvard University Press.

Peranakan Association Singapore. 2006. Peranakan History. *The Peranakan Association*. Singapore. Accessed on 11 March 2007 http://peranakan.org.sg/index.php?option=com_content&task=view&id=26&Itemid=56

Png, Poh Seng. 1969. The Straits Chinese in Singapore: A case of local identity and socio-cultural accommodation. *Journal of Southeast Asia History* 10(1): 95–114.

Remijsen, Bert. 2001. *Word Prosodic Systems of Raja Ampat Languages*. Utrecht: LOT.

Rivera-Castillo, Yolanda and Lucy Pickering. 2004. Phonetic correlates of stress and tone in a mixed system. *Journal of Pidgin and Creole Languages* 19: 261–284.

Rudolph, Jurgen. 1998. *Reconstructing Identities. A Social History of the Babas in Singapore*. Aldershot, Vermont: Ashgate Publishing Co.

Song, Ong Siang. 1923. *One Hundred Years' History of the Chinese in Singapore*. London: John Murray. Reprinted 1967, Singapore: University of Malaya Press.

Tan Chee Beng. 1979. Baba and Nyonya: A study of the ethnic identity of the Chinese Peranakan in Malacca. PhD dissertation, Cornell University.

Tan, Chee Beng. 1988a. *The Baba of Malacca. Culture and Identity of a Peranakan Community in Malaysia*. Petaling Jaya, Selangor: Pelanduk Publications.

Tan, Chee Beng. 1988b. Structure and change: Cultural identity of the Baba of Melaka. *Bijdragen tot de Taal, Land- en Volkenkunde* 144: 297–314.

Thomson, J.T. 1875. *The Straits of Malacca, Indo-China and China, or Ten Years' Travels, Adventures and Residence Abroad*. London: Sampson Low; Marston: Low & Searle.

Vaughan, J.D. 1879. *Manners and Customs of the Chinese in the Straits Settlements*. Singapore: The Mission Press. (Reprinted by Oxford University Press 1971, 1992).

Wang, Gungwu. 1991. *China and the Chinese Overseas*. Singapore: Times Academic Press.

Wee, Kim Soon Gabriel. 2000. *Intonation of the Babas: An auditory and instrumental approach*. BA Honours thesis, National University of Singapore.

Wee, Lian Hee. 2008. Phonological patterns in the Englishes of Singapore and Hong Kong. *World Englishes* 27(3/4): 480–501.

Yap Koon Hong. 2008. Here's re-looking at you, Bibik. *The Straits Times*. 2 February 2008.

Part IV

Transnational Families, Transcultural Living

14 The Transnational Journey of an Indonesian Chinese Couple in Hong Kong

The Story of One Family, Three Places, and Multiple Languages

Katherine Hoi Ying Chen

1 INTRODUCTION

A proliferation of research on transnationality has emerged over the past few decades in the fields of cultural anthropology, population studies, social and cultural geography, and economics, to name but a few of the pertinent social sciences. Research in linguistics, and more specifically sociolinguistics, has produced relatively little work on the ethnography and linguistic practices of transnationals.

Ong (1999) exposes the need for observing the environs concerning transnationals, arguing that if "we pay attention to the transnational practices and imaginings of the nomadic subject and the social conditions that enable his flexibility, we obtain a different picture of how nation-states articulate with capitalism in late modernity. . . . His very flexibility in geographical and social positioning is itself an effect of novel articulations between the regimes of the family, the state, and capital, the kinds of practical-technical adjustments that have implications for our understanding of the late modern subject" (p. 3). An investigative inclination of ways in which versatility of individuals appropriates larger regimes of social organization grounds the current research.

Research concerning contemporary Chinese diaspora and transnationalism (in particular, work by Ien Ang (2001), Aihwa Ong (2003), Johanna Waters (2005, 2007, and 2008)) has informed an understanding of trends in transnational configurations and spectra. A sociolinguistic approach to transnational studies can contribute highly while providing unique insights and perspectives into the micro-social relations of these people in transition. Furthermore, this sociolinguistic approach differs from, while complementing, other disciplines in the social sciences and humanities in current scholarly discourses on transnationalism and globalization.

Hong Kong provides an optimum locale for this transnational research, as Hong Kong has always represented a transient region for many, and a gateway between China and the rest of the world. People of Hong Kong have traversed numerous political and social changes, and a significant number that have become mobile and flexible in their citizenship, as such, represent perfect consultants for transnational and bilingualism research.

This paper takes Indonesian Chinese in Hong Kong as a starting point for investigating the personal experience of these transnationals, their multilingual linguistic repertoire, and generational language shifts. This research focuses on micro-level and individual ethnography, which is distinctive from and complementary to the more common quantitative and macro-research on globalization, people's movement, and transnationalism. This paper is organized into the following sections. Section 2 describes the historical development of Indonesian Chinese from early days to the time when the massive "return" to China occurred in the 1950s and 1960s. Section 3 includes the personal narratives of an Indonesian Chinese couple, Lee and Tan, who made their journey from Indonesia to China, and then to Hong Kong. Section 4 focuses on the couple's respective multilingual repertoire and the development of their own and their family's generational linguistic shifts. Section 5 gives a preliminary sketch of two relatively new varieties of Chinese spoken by Indonesian Chinese: Huaqiao Mandarin and Siantar Mandarin. Section 6 connects the transnational journey of Indonesian Chinese in the last few decades to the understanding of Indonesian Chinese identity in Hong Kong.

2   HISTORICAL DEVELOPMENT OF INDONESIAN CHINESE

2.1   Indonesian Chinese in Indonesia until the Massive "Return" to China in the 1950s and 1960s

Early traces of Chinese trade and settlements in Indonesia dated back to the Sung dynasty (around 900 AD). Tang (2006) mentions that there were Chinese villages found in Belitung off the coast of Sumatra as early as 1293. But major migration of Chinese to Indonesia did not start until the beginning of the Dutch colonization in the 1600s, when workers for various plantations and mines were highly sought after. Since then there had been a steady increase of Chinese migration to Indonesia despite fluctuating government policies, and even brutal killing of "excess Chinese" in the 1740 massacre in Jakarta. In 1853, the Dutch colonial government announced a ban on Chinese migration, yet in 1858 abolished the ban (Li and Huang, 1987).

The number of Chinese population in Indonesia reported by various sources showed that by the 1930s, there were 1,190,014 Chinese in Indonesia, in contrast with only 221,438 in 1860 (government census reported by Li and Huang, 1987). The number was relatively steady with an increase to 1,430,528 in 1930 (*Al-Hayat*, 14 August 1950). Chen (1938) reports a 1930 survey of 900 Chinese families in Indonesia who stated their reasons to come to Indonesia; the majority, 70% of them, listed economic hardship in China as their reason for coming to Indonesia, 20% stated relatives and connections with South East Asia promoted their migration, and 10% listed natural disasters, family problems, outcasts, etc. as their reasons for migration.

Most of the Chinese who came to Indonesia were from South China. Wen and Hong (1985) reported a 1930 government census of the place of origin of the 1,190,014 Indonesian Chinese (see Table 14.1), which provides a good indication of the language background of these migrants. From the second column of the table, those whose place of origin was Fukien (Hokkien) constituted 47% of the Indonesian Chinese population, followed by Hakka (17%), Canton (11%), and Teochew (7%); all of these four areas are in Southern China, and the place of origin of the remaining 18% is unknown.

2.2 Anti-Sinicism in Indonesia Since the 1950s and the Massive "Return" to China, 1950s to 1970s

In 1957, Sukarno, the first president of Indonesia, issued Presidential Regulation 10 (PR-10), a law prohibiting foreign nationals to run businesses in rural areas, which forced Chinese to pay an expensive amount to become Indonesian nationals. By 1958, all Chinese schools were shut down, and any Chinese religious and cultural practices were forbidden, which started a prevailing period of anti-Sinicism in Indonesia. It is the same period as the massive migration of Indonesian Chinese to China.

Wang (2003) estimates that nearly half a million Indonesian Chinese "returned" to China in the 1950s and 1960s, motivated by new Chinese nationalism and the establishment of the People's Republic of China in 1949, and by Indonesian policies aimed at marginalizing ethnic Chinese. In particular, waves of anti-Chinese measures and riots happened at the time to drive Chinese refugees out of Indonesia. Between 1952 and 1965, China

Table 14.1   Place of Origin of Indonesian Chinese in 1930 Census

籍貫別 Place of Origin	人口總數 Total	在荷印出生者 Born in Indonesia	百分比 (%)
Fukien 福建	(47%) 554,981	427,962	77.1
Hakka 客家	(17%) 200,736	121,734	60.6
Teochew 潮州	(7%) 87,812	32,822	37.4
Cantonese 廣府	(11%) 136,130	45,636	33.5
Others 其他	(18%) 210,355	128,018	60.9
合計	1,190,014	756,172	63.5

資料來源：《1930 年人口調查》卷七，294 頁。

Table data from Wen & Hong, 1985, p191

sent ships, sometimes hiring cargo ships from the USSR to go around SE Asia to pick up Chinese who wanted to return to China.

Wang describes the " 'Return' as re-embracing Chinese ethnicity, culture, and a political decision to join the new Chinese nation. . . . However, their journey to China turned out to be painful and traumatic. This was not so much because of ill adjustments to the Chinese society on their part, but was mainly due to the Chinese state's refusal to recognise them as 'one of us'. They were turned into an isolated group excluded from 'the People' (renmin)".

Thousands of returnee families, upon arriving in China, were sent to farms for overseas returned Chinese (Huaqiao Nongchang 華僑農場) in remote and underdeveloped parts of the country, a destination and life in stark contrast with the utopia they were promised before returning to China. As of 2015, the Overseas Chinese Affairs Office of the State Council reports a total of 85 such farms in China, mainly spanning from Fujian to Guangxi and Hainan, but an account of the actual number of farms set up in the 1950s and 1960s is yet to be found. Life on those farms was harsh and resources were extremely limited.

2.3 From Disappointment to New Life as New Immigrants in Hong Kong Since the 1970s

Godley and Coppel (1990) report that because of the disappointment in their experience in China, more than 250,000 returned Indonesian Chinese left for Hong Kong and Macao along with their families in the late 1970s once China loosened its control. From my knowledge, many of those who made it to Hong Kong had attended higher education in China, yet their qualifications were not legally recognized in Hong Kong in the 1970s. Many ended up working in factories and various low-end jobs to survive. Godley and Coppel describe them as "a minority community in transition", as they were yet again marginalized as new immigrants in Hong Kong.

Indonesian Chinese in China and Hong Kong retain distinctive language and cultural practices. They are typically multilingual in Huaqiao Guoyu (華僑國語), a variety of Mandarin with a marked non-mainland Chinese accent, a local variety such as Siantar Mandarin, varieties of Indonesian languages such as Bahasa Indonesian and Javanese depending on where in Indonesia they came from, and varieties of Chinese dialects such as Teochew, Hokkien, and Hakka depending on their original Chinese heritage. They listen to and dance to Indonesian folk songs, particularly songs popular in the 1930s to 1940s before their departure from Indonesia, and cook Indonesian and Peranakan (fusion Indonesian and Chinese) food. Many of them had close kinship ties with Indonesia and maintain frequent communication as well as visits to Indonesia. Many of them who lived in Hong Kong for more than thirty years still feel that they are rootless and marginalized. However, the next generation, those who were born after the 1970s and grew up in Hong Kong, identify themselves as Hong Kongers.

3 THE PERSONAL NARRATIVES OF AN INDONESIAN CHINESE COUPLE IN HONG KONG: LEE AND TAN

3.1 Lee in Indonesia

Lee was a third generation Chinese born and raised in Pemangkat (邦戛), a small town near a river delta in North West Kalimantan, Indonesia. Lee's grandparents came from South China to Pemangkat in the 1930s and settled there. Similar to those reported in the 1930 survey, Lee's grandparents came to Indonesia because of civil wars and economic hardship in China.

The town of Pemangkat had a little less than 10,000 residents in the 1950s. Lee remembers that 80% of the town's people were ethnic Chinese, and most were Hakka speaking. Lee's parents were from Shantou, a Teochew speaking area of Guangdong Province, South China, came to Pemangkat in the 1930s, and ran a small grocery store in town. Like all other Chinese children in Pemangkat, Lee studied in a Mandarin-medium school run by the pro-PRC Pemangkat Chinese Association (邦戛中華公會). The textbooks and school material were published in PRC and contained propaganda material about the newly established China.

Lee studied for five years until the Indonesian authority shut all of the Chinese schools down in 1958, while PR-10 in 1957 practically stopped Lee's family business, and the 1960 big fire that wiped out the entire town sent the family into poverty. The Chinese that Lee knew of lived a segregated and threatened life on foreign land. Going to China, "a safe place that belongs to us", became an appeal as the livelihood in Indonesia turned from bad to worse.

After the big fire, the Chinese Association called for help from the PRC government, who responded by sending multiple cargo ships, beginning in March 1960, to Pemangkat to transport the refugees to China. Lee's father secured two seats from the fifth ship leaving on July 12, 1960. He asked two of the eldest children to go first so that they would be on time for the start of the new school year in September. Lee was barely 17 when she took her 15-year-old sister with her on board the cargo ship. The two sisters were assured that the rest of the family would join them shortly when the next ship came. Little did they know that was the very last time they saw their father, and it would take almost thirty years for them to see the rest of their family again. The rest of the Lee family was not able to board the sixth ship, which never came.

When these refugees left Indonesia, they all had to sign a document stating that they gave up their rights to return to Indonesia once they left. When they arrived in China, all of the identification documents they had were taken by the Chinese government, they were each given a new document for their new lives in China, a document that does not allow them to leave China unless with governmental permission. It was a road with no return.

3.2 Lee's Arrival in China

After about ten days in the ocean, on July 18, 1960, they landed in Shantou on the Eastern Coast of Guangdong Province in China. Those who came to China as a family were all sent to various overseas Chinese farms where the living conditions were poor. About twenty of the teenagers, including Lee and her sister, were sent to a remedial school for the overseas Chinese in Shantou city.

When Lee considered what subject to study at the university, it was the first time she realized her background as an overseas returning Chinese was stigmatized in the pre-cultural revolution China. She was interested in studying foreign trade, hoping that it would give her opportunities to see the world, but her schoolteachers warned her that only those locals with good "elements", i.e., those whose parents were farmers, workers, or government officials, would be selected—she would have no chance. She could only choose from a couple of universities designated for overseas returning Chinese, she was told, again, that the best universities in the country would only admit students with good "elements". In the end, she selected Chinese language and literature, a safe subject for her overseas Chinese background, hoping for a future teaching job upon graduation. In 1965, five years after returning to China, she was admitted to a university in Guangzhou dedicated mainly for overseas returning Chinese. This was where she met her husband, Tan, also a fellow Chinese returning from Indonesia.

3.3 Tan in Indonesia

Tan was also a third generation Chinese born and raised in Sumatra, Indonesia. His grandfather came to Penang, Malaysia at the turn of the 20th century because of economic hardship in his hometown in Jieyang, a Teochew speaking area in Guangdong, South China. Tan's father grew up in Penang and studied in an English school, and found a job as an accounting clerk in the Goodyear Rubber Plantations Company in Northern Sumatra. Tan grew up in the multilingual and multi-ethnic plantation estates in which the Chinese were the minority. As a child, he and his siblings played with children of the Javanese plantation workers and local Batak workers and learned various Indonesian languages. Details of his multilingual experiences are discussed in Section 4.

As a teenager, Tan moved out of the plantation and into the nearest city, a Chinese-populated Pematang Siantar (shortened to Siantar), to further his study in a boarding secondary school. The secondary school was run by the pro-PRC Chinese Merchants' Association (先達中華總會) in Siantar and taught pro-communist and pro-PRC material to the students. Going to China was a popular trend then, and for the Tan brothers, it was the only way to further their study because China provided free education, whereas if they stayed in Indonesia, their family wouldn't be able to afford to send them to Indonesian universities. "We were told wonderful things about China and were motivated to go to China. They told us they need young Chinese people from overseas to help them build the new country", said Tan, who went to China when he was 22.

3.4 Tan's arrival in China

Tan arrived in Shantou, China in 1961. He noticed that those who returned to China with the whole family were sent to overseas Chinese farms. Tan was sent to a school to further his study. When he applied for university entrance, the teachers told him that he could only apply to three universities that were designated for overseas Chinese. He was told that the best universities in China, such as Beijing University and Tsinghua University would never admit students like Tan who had an "overseas connection". Tan wanted to study journalism; but he was told those with overseas connections were not allowed in professions like that. The Chinese government did not trust them and suspected they could be spies. Tan chose to study Chinese language and literature and was admitted to one of the designated university for overseas returning Chinese, Jinan University in Guangzhou, where he met his future wife, Lee.

One year after Lee and Tan started university, in 1966, the Cultural Revolution swept across China and their education stopped. The students at Jinan were sent to participate in various mass rallies in Beijing and Guangzhou, and were later sent to work in rural farms. Their experience during the Cultural Revolution, witnessing the insanity of what horrid acts human beings can do to each other, shocked them deeply.

In 1969, Lee and Tan, who requested to be relocated together as they were planning to get married, were sent to Hainan Island as teachers. Their futures were not ones they chose, but were assigned by the government. Hainan Island was a remote and underdeveloped area in China then; food, clothing, and other basic resource were extremely scarce. But the worst part in their experience was the local officials' discrimination against Lee and Tan because of their overseas Chinese background. Tan was denied a few important promotions or transfer opportunities and was told as overseas Chinese he and his wife would not be considered for better jobs. When their daughter was born, they worried about her future too. Their experience of being discriminated against, of disappointment with the government, and seeing no hope for their own or their daughter's future drove them eventually to leave China.

3.5 A New Start as New Immigrants in Hong Kong

Life as new immigrants in Hong Kong was not easy. Mainland Chinese qualifications were not recognized in Hong Kong in the 1970s, so Indonesian Chinese who had some university education were considered the same as the illiterate. They did not speak Cantonese, the dominant language in Hong Kong, which made it difficult for them to find jobs that required Cantonese interaction. Lee and Tan were only able to find manual labor work in the factories and got paid barely enough for food. They lived in the squatter area/slum on a hillside with no fresh water and limited electricity, and under risk of fire and typhoons. It took ten years for them to successfully apply for government-subsidized rental housing to leave the dilapidated squatter area and eventually as their children grew up their living conditions improved.

Lee and Tan's social network in Hong Kong was mainly made up of other Indonesian Chinese. Gatherings with friends and families were filled with Indonesian food, Indonesian folk music and dance, and reminiscences of their old days in Indonesia and their hardships in China and Hong Kong. They speak a Huaqiao Mandarin mix with some lexical items of Indonesian, especially food terms. Unlike the strict control in mainland China, they enjoy freedom to go outside of Hong Kong as long as they can afford it, so many Indonesian Chinese reconnect with their families in Indonesia. Once their finances allowed, Lee visited Indonesia in 1989 and reunited with her mother and siblings 29 years after she left home; whereas Tan waited until 1993, 32 years after he left, to be able to visit his family in Indonesia.

4   LEE AND TAN'S MULTILINGUAL REPERTOIRE AND THE THREE GENERATIONAL LINGUISTIC SHIFTS

Most Indonesian Chinese are multilingual given the language contact situation they encounter when they migrate from one continent to another. They exhibit diverse patterns of linguistic repertoire and interesting generational shifts. Below we show the linguistic repertoire of Lee and Tan respectively as compared to their parents and their children.

Lee's native language and her home language as she grew up is Teochew, as her parents and grandparents are native Teochew speakers from South China. In Pemangkat, where Lee grew up, the Chinese, who constituted 80% of the town's population, are mostly Hakka speakers, and therefore Hakka became the lingua franca among the Chinese. Lee's family all learned or acquired fluent Hakka. Lee's parents' grocery store business required them to be multilingual. Their customers included ethnic Chinese speakers of various dialects, but Hakka was the lingua franca used for business transactions among the Chinese. Lee's parents bought goods from Indonesians for sale in the store, and their transactions were conducted in the limited Indonesian they knew. Lee's parents did not want their children, especially girls, to interact with Indonesians, so Lee and her sisters know limited Indonesian only from the two years of basic Indonesian learned at primary school. As an adult, Lee said she forgot most of the Indonesian she learned at school, except food terms and local common lexicon she often uses.

Table 14.2   Lee's Multilingual Repertoire as Compared to her Parents, her Husband, and her Children

Languages/ Family members	Overseas Chinese Mandarin/ Huaqiao Mandarin 華僑國語	Cantonese	Hokkien	Teochew	Hakka	Bahasa Indonesian	English
Lee's mother			✔ for business transactions	✔✔✔ native and home language	✔✔✔ lingua franca among Chinese in Kalimantan	✔ for business transactions	
Lee's father			✔ for business transactions	✔✔✔ native and home language	✔✔✔ lingua franca among Chinese in Kalimantan	✔ for business transactions	
Lee Age: 72 Hong Kong	✔✔✔ home language with children	✔✔✔	✔ only passive knowledge	✔✔✔ native and home language with parents	✔✔✔ lingua franca among Chinese in Kalimantan	✔ very weak (studied 2 years P4–5)	
Tan (Lee's husband) Age: 77 Hong Kong	✔✔✔ also native in Siantar Mandarin 先達國語	✔	✔✔✔ naitive and home language with parents			✔✔✔	✔
Son Hong Kong	✔✔ home language	✔✔✔ native					✔✔
Daughter Hong Kong	✔✔ home language	✔✔✔ native					✔✔✔

Keys:

✔	Limited Knowledge
✔✔	Fair
✔✔✔	Very good or native fluency

Lee's generation was a new generation of Chinese in Indonesia in the 1940s and 1950s who were educated in Mandarin Chinese schools, whereas her parents' generation did not speak Mandarin at all. The Mandarin variety Lee learned at school is Huaqiao Guoyu (Overseas Chinese Mandarin), with significant differences from Putonghua, the standardized variety promoted in China since 1949. The label "Huaqiao Guoyu" (華僑國語) was not an official linguistic term but a local term referring to the common accent of the Indonesian Chinese. At schools in Indonesia, the language subject and the language of medium was referred to as simply "Guoyu" (國語) or Chinese (中文). After Lee went to China and stayed there for over 12 years, she mostly interacted with other Indonesian Chinese who used Huaqiao Mandarin, so in her own account, her accent of Mandarin didn't change to the standardized Putonghua. As Huaqiao Mandarin is the lingua franca among Indonesian Chinese of her generation, Lee and her husband choose to use it as their home language with their children. Lee retains knowledge of her native language Teochew, and the Pemangkat Chinese lingua franca, Hakka, but she never teaches them to her children. Lee cooks both Indonesian and Chinese food, and she taught her children various Indonesian food terms.

After Lee came to Hong Kong, she started learning Cantonese and practiced with her co-workers in a textile factory often. In the 1980s, more than ten years after she came to Hong Kong, Lee's Cantonese was fluent enough that she was able to find a job as a cashier in a children's gaming gallery which requires Cantonese interaction with customers. Lee's children grew up in Hong Kong and went to local Hong Kong schools where they learned Cantonese among their peers and English in the classroom. Lee and her husband insist on using Huaqiao Mandarin at home, even though, similar to the classical language shift situation, when they speak to the children in Huaqiao Mandarin, the children often reply to them in Cantonese.

Tan's linguistic experience in Indonesia was quite different from Lee's. Tan's mother was born in Penang, Malaysia, and spoke Penang Hokkien as her native and home language. Tan's father was born in Sumatra, Indonesia, but was sent by his father to Penang at the age of six to study in English-medium schools. Neither of Tan's parents could speak or write Chinese. Tan's father's English ability helped him get an accounting job in the American plantation, but he didn't teach his children English. Tan's parents learned a colloquial form of Indonesian when they lived in the rubber plantation, as they often interacted with local Indonesians. They both learned to write Indonesian, and when there were times when Tan's father was sent to another Goodyear plantation hundreds of miles away for a few months, they communicated with each other by writing letters in colloquial Indonesian.

Tan's family lived among the Javanese and Batak Indonesian in the Rubber Plantations Company Estates. The small amount of local Indonesians working in the Sumatra plantation were of the Batak ethnic group, they occupied supervisor positions in the plantation, and the Javanese were

Table 14.3 Tan's Multilingual Repertoire as Compared to his Parents, his Wife, and his Children

Languages/ Family members	Overseas Chinese Mandarin/ Huaqiao Mandarin 華僑國語	Cantonese	Hokkien (Penang variety)	Teochew	Hakka	Bahasa Indonesian	English
Tan's mother Indonesia	passive knowlege		✔✔✔ native and home language			✔✔✔	
Tan's father Indonesia			✔✔✔ native and home language (studied in Penang, Hokkien speaking)	✔ some konwledge		✔✔✔	✔✔✔
Tan Age: 77 Hong Kong	✔✔✔ home language with children also fluent in Siantar Mandarin 先達國語	✔	✔✔✔ native and home language with parents			✔✔✔ also has some knowledge of Javanese and Batak language	✔ some knowledge, learned in school and in the American Goodyear Plantation
Lee (Tan's wife) Age: 72 Hong Kong	✔✔✔ home language with Children	✔✔✔ (HK)	✔ passive knowledge	✔✔✔ native and home language	✔✔✔ lingua franca among Chinese in Kalimantan	✔ very weak (studied 2 years P4–5)	
Son Hong Kong	✔✔ home language	✔✔✔ native					✔✔
Daughter Hong Kong	✔✔ home language	✔✔✔ native					✔✔✔

Keys:
✔   Limited Knowledge
✔✔   Fair
✔✔✔   Very good or native fluency

recruited from Java to be the rubber collection workers under the Batak Indonesians' supervision. Tan's father and other ethnic Chinese in the plantation occupied mid- to high-ranking office positions mainly as administrators and accountants. The senior management of the plantation were English-speaking white European Americans sent from the headquarters in America. As a child, Tan played with the Javanese and Batak Indonesians and spoke some Javanese, some Batak language, and fluent Bahasa Indonesian, as it was the lingua franca among the children in the plantation. As Tan's father was a high-ranking staff, Tan had the opportunity to go to the senior staff club for the white American and Chinese families. One of the American staff, a retired professional baseball player in America, established a baseball team by recruiting the teenaged children of the senior plantation staff. Tan joined the baseball team when he was a young teenager and learned some English from the team.

Tan's home language as a child was mainly Penang Hokkien, mixed with a small amount of colloquial Indonesian. Later, when Tan and his siblings went to Chinese language school and learned Huaqiao Mandarin and Siantar Mandarin, the siblings alternated between Hokkien, Indonesian, and the two varieties of Mandarin in their speech. Tan's family moved a few times among different plantation estates in Northern Sumatra, so he studied in various Chinese-medium primary schools near the plantations and started learning to speak Huaqiao Mandarin and write Chinese as a young child. The family stopped moving when Tan was about eight, when they were stationed only in the Goodyear Rubber Plantations Wingfoot Company Estates.

The nearest city from the Wingfoot Estates is Siantar, short for Pematang Siantar, and it was where Tan went to senior primary school and secondary school. Tan studied both Chinese and Bahasa Indonesian in primary school, and English was added to the curriculum in secondary school. Tan said that English was available as a subject only in the secondary schools in large cities because not many Chinese schools could find teachers of English. Tan recalled one of his English teachers was an ethnic Chinese person who had studied in an Indian-run English school in Siantar. Local Indonesian teachers taught Bahasa Indonesian. The Chinese teachers were mixed, some were graduates from Chinese secondary schools in other large cities in Indonesia, such as Medan and Jakarta, and some were recruited directly from China, such as Zhejiang and Fujian. From what Tan described, there could be a language-leveling phenomenon as the schoolteachers were from different geographical backgrounds, and yet the students considered themselves to be learning one formal variety of Chinese called Guoyu, later referred to as Huaqiao Guoyu/Mandarin. Tan said the term Huaqiao Mandarin became popular after he went to China. It was a term the overseas returned Chinese used to refer to their own Chinese variety as different from the mainland varieties.

Tan's experience in China was similar to Lee's, in which they mainly interacted with other Indonesian Chinese and retained Huaqiao Mandarin.

The three years they spent in Hainan Island gave them some exposure to the local Hainanese language, but they never learned to speak it. Tan learned to understand Cantonese when he came to Hong Kong but he did not speak it fluently, as his various jobs, from working in a factory when he first came to Hong Kong to being a commercial oil painter, did not require much interaction with other Cantonese speakers.

5 A PRELIMINARY SKETCH OF NEW FORMS OF CHINESE: HUAQIAO MANDARIN AND SIANTAR MANDARIN

Further linguistic analysis will be needed to get a full picture of the difference between Putonghua and Huaqiao Mandarin. But here is a preliminary sketch of the characteristics of Huaqiao Mandarin:

- Non-rhotic: Putonghua Retroflex affricates [ʈʂ, ʈʂʰ, ʂ] are realized as alveolar affricates [ʈʂ,, ʈʂ,, s] in Huaqiao Mandarin.
- Inclusion of Indonesian words, especially food items and place names (i.e., mostly noun/NP).
- Terms that distinguish between "us" and "them", e.g., "Sagaai", meaning those from the countryside, backward and uncivilized, as a slur referring to mainland Chinese.
- In-group identification among the Indonesian Chinese, especially when they were in China, and later in Hong Kong.

The more formally learned Mandarin, or Huaqiao Guoyu, was the variety used in the classroom. But outside of the classroom, students in Siantar speak a colloquial Mandarin variety they call Siantar Mandarin. From what Tan knows, Siantar Mandarin came into being from around the 1920s, when Chinese primary and secondary schools in Siantar were established. As the previous generations, such as Tan's parents, spoke only regional Chinese varieties such as Hokkien, Teochew, and Hakka, not Guoyu/Mandarin, the Chinese schools had to recruit teachers directly from China. For unknown reasons, some of the teachers were recruited from the Guilin area in Guangxi, China, who brought with them a variety of Chinese that was a regional standard Mandarin. Tan and Siantar Chinese refer to that variety as Guilin speech. This variety of Mandarin developed in Siantar and mixed with local varieties of Chinese and Indonesian to become Siantar Mandarin. By the time Tan went to school in Siantar in the 1950s, this new variety had developed into a colloquial lingua franca among the younger generation of Chinese in the city, which contrasted with the older generation's lingua franca, Hokkien. The Chinese teachers in the schools in Siantar were no longer those from Guilin or Sichuan, and the variety of Chinese taught in school was the more leveled Huaqiao Mandarin, while Siantar Mandarin continued to flourish as a colloquial variety. Tan said new teachers coming from outside of Siantar at first would have difficulty understanding Siantar Mandarin because the accent, grammar, and lexicon were quite distinct from Huaqiao Mandarin.

Siantar Mandarin is spoken in Siantar, as well as among Siantar Chinese in China and Hong Kong. Tan uses Huaqiao Mandarin with his Indonesian Chinese friends and relatives, but when he meets his Siantar friends, they naturally switch to use Siantar Mandarin. Tan's description of Siantar Mandarin, as influenced by Guilin Chinese and mixed with Hokkien and Indonesian, was echoed by others who wrote on the Internet about their experience with Siantar Mandarin. A Hong Kong author, likely a returned overseas Chinese him/herself, described the use of Mandarin in Siantar's classrooms, but Siantar Mandarin outside the classroom, and that it was a common language among those from the same hometown of Siantar in Hong Kong (Ta Kung Pao 2007). Another self-identified Siantar Chinese, Liang, recalled that when he and his other Siantar Chinese friends visited Guilin years ago, a local Guilin person told them they were speaking an official Guilin speech, which was almost obsolete in Guilin now (Liang, 2012). A mainland Chinese newspaper journalist, Jiang, from Guangxi, wrote of her experience of visiting Siantar and was amazed that her hometown Guilin language was intelligible with Siantar Mandarin (Jiang, 2013).

Below are a few examples comparing the three varieties of Mandarin: Standard Mandarin (i.e., Putonghua), Huaqiao Mandarin, and Siantar Mandarin. The latter two varieties are transcribed based on Tan's pronunciation.

Example 1.

In example 1, Siantar Mandarin retains the alveolar affricates of Huaqiao Mandarin in /sən/, but /giɑŋ/ is a unique Siantar pronunciation influenced by Guilin speech.

講　什　麼?	<<What to say?>>	
Standard Mandarin Pinyin:	jiǎng shén me	
Standard Mandarin IPA:	/tɕiɑŋ ʂən mɤ/	
Huaqiao Mandarin IPA:	/tɕiɑŋ sən mɤ/	
Siantar Mandarin IPA:	/giɑŋ sən mɤ/	

Example 2.

Tan speaks of frequent code-mixing between Mandarin, Hokkien, and Indonesian in Siantar Mandarin. In Example 2, the term "wanton" /wən tʰən/ is a Hokkien pronunciation that does not occur in either Standard or Huaqiao Mandarin.

先達人做的雲吞麵很好吃！

<<Siantarese made tasty *wanton* noodles.>> ("Wanton" in Hokkien pronunciation)

Standard Mandarin Pinyin: xiān dá rén zuò de yún tūn miàn hěn hǎo chī

Standard Mandarin IPA: /tɕiɑŋ ʂən mɤ/

Huaqiao Mandarin IPA: /ɕjɛn ta jən tswɔ tɤ yn tʰyn mjɛn xən xɑʊ tsʰẓ/

Siantar Mandarin IPA: /ɕjɛn ta jən tsɔ tɤ wən tʰən mjɛn xən xɑʊ tsʰẓ̪

Example 3.

Example 3 shows a mix between Mandarin and colloquial Indonesian as a feature of Siantar Mandarin. The word "Kalo", meaning "if", is an Indonesian word commonly used in Siantar Mandarin.

如果不是這樣 <<If it is not that way.>>

kalo不是這樣 <<If it is not that way.>> ("if"in Indonesian)

Standard Mandarin Pinyin: rú guǒ bù shì zhè yàng

Standard Mandarin IPA: /ʐu kwɔ pu ʂʈʂɤ jaŋ/

Huaqiao Mandarin IPA: /ju kwɔ pu sʐʈʂɤ jaŋ/

Siantar Mandarin IPA: /ga lòk̚ pu sʐʈʂɤ jaŋ/

Gan and Shan (2013) conducted research on the current situation of Siantar Mandarin in Indonesia and estimate that it has only 2000 speakers left in Siantar, mainly among the older generation aged above 60. The middle-age Siantar Chinese below 50 know little written Chinese and have limited spoken Mandarin ability because of the long period of anti-Chinese legislation in Indonesia. The young generation, who grew up after Chinese was allowed to be taught in schools in Indonesia, learns the more standard Putonghua variety and do not speak Siantar Mandarin either. Gan and Shan (2013) provide a list of elements found in Siantar Mandarin, which can trace their origins from Min dialect (Hokkien), Cantonese, hybrid words between Southwestern Mandarin (Xinan Guanhua 西南官話) and Indonesian, and hybrid words between Southwestern Mandarin and Hokkien. They detailed characteristic features in grammar and lexicon of Siantar Mandarin, and conclude that Siantar Mandarin is disappearing because only the older generation uses it in Indonesia. Simliar to Gan and Shan's prediction, Tan and other Siantar Chinese in Hong Kong, who are now in their 60s and 70s, continue to use Siantar Mandarin, but the variety has not been passed down to the next generation, and will likely disappear in the next few decades.

6 INDONESIAN CHINESE IN HONG KONG: FROM TRANSITIONAL EXISTENCE TO EXTRATERRITORIAL IDENTITY

In the above sections, we get a good picture of the history of the Indonesian Chinese who moved from Indonesia to China and then to Hong Kong. We look at the general historical development in literature, the personal narratives of a couple who went through the journey, as well as their multilingual repertoire and generational linguistic shifts. Hong Kong was the end stop for most of these Indonesian Chinese's cross-continental journey. Although Hong Kong was not a planned destination, its status as a British Colony provided an alternative to these transnationals whose hopes were crushed by their experience in China.

Tan described in his private memoir his sense of frustration and disappointment as he left China, a place he used to consider his "mother country", to go to the British-ruled Hong Kong in 1973:

> 從深圳跨過那羅湖鐵路橋走去香港時，那心情無法用語言文字來形容。上世紀五六十年代，當大批僑生回國時，看到飄揚的五星紅旗和聽到高音喇叭傳出《歌唱祖國》的旋律時，很多僑生都興奮的流下眼淚；如今，我們卻帶著失望和無奈的心情，不得不反方向跨出去，追尋當年祖輩「賣豬仔」出洋的不歸路「流浪」去了。
>
> <<When I went across the Shenzhen Lo Wu Bridge walking towards Hong Kong, my feelings were not describable by words. In the 1950s and 1960s, when massive amount of overseas Chinese (like me) return to China, going into China, seeing the China flag hoisted, hearing the song "Sing for our mother land" through the public speakers, many of us teared with excitement. Today, we carry with us a deep sense of disappointment and helplessness as we go the opposite way (to leave China), and follow the footsteps of our great grandparents who left China to drift overseas.>>

After living in Hong Kong for 40 years, Tan and Lee both think of Hong Kong as more than a transitional place, but a safe home. They no longer carry the patriotic feelings towards China they had when they were teenagers in Indonesia. Tan sighed, "I love my country, but my country does not love me". His ambivalence about where he belongs is not settled yet. Tan mentions when he dies, he wants his ashes to be spread towards the Southern Sea, the direction of Indonesia, "so that I can go *home*". Tan's home is a nostalgic state in the past, unconnected to the current Indonesia in reality.

Tan's and Lee's networks and connections are mainly with other Indonesian Chinese in Hong Kong, with whom they share similar history, sentiments, and experiences. They feel most strongly about their Indonesian Chinese identity (more so than being Chinese, being Hong Konger, and being Indonesian), but such identity is not bounded by nationality or citizenship. They still think of Indonesia as someone else's country, but the Indonesian culture and their childhood experiences are still a quintessential part of their lives. Wang (2003) describes such seemingly puzzling sentiments regarding their identity as "extraterritorial":

> [The Indonesian Chinese in Hong Kong] could not be able to identify with the local majority or any sub-ethnic groups in Hong Kong, be they Cantonese, Fujianese, Hakkas, Chaozhounese or Mandarin, but to embrace a new identity of their own, which I shall term an "extraterritorial identity". This identity, . . . highlights their internal ethnic and cultural commonalities while disregard differentiations in national belongings and economic status. With this identity, the [Indonesian] Chinese "no longer count on the 'country', a human and territorial entity, instead, one must place one's faith in the group, a social entity (Wang 2003: 266).

Such extraterritorial identity resembles the flexible citizenship Ong (1999) describes. The concepts of nation state and of citizenship are no longer clearly defined, at least from the perspective of the transnationals who made their decision to move from one place to another. In the 1950s and 1960s when these young Indonesian Chinese thought of China, the ideology of nation state, of "our own country" was strong, so the economic hardship and anti-Chinese movements drove families to return to China. Their move from China to Hong Kong was one driven by the loss of acceptance as legitimate members in the nation state as they were outcast and rejected. In early 1990s, as the hand-over of Hong Kong from Britain to China was looming, Lee and Tan seriously considered migrating to Singapore, the closet place with a similar "safe" environment as Hong Kong, and with their familiar South East Asian culture. This migration plan did not get carried out, but it shows their fear as the rootless ones and their difficulty finding a place to truly call home. The next generation, those who grew up in Hong Kong but are accustomed to their parents' Indonesian Chinese culture, seem to be the more lucky generation: at least they consider Hong Kong their real home, despite its status as a city rather than a nation state.

ACKNOWLEDGEMENTS

This research was supported by HKU Seed Funding and RGC GRF 17615215.

REFERENCES

Ang, Ien (2001). *On Not Speaking Chinese: Living between Asia and the West.* London: Routledge.
Chen, Da (1938). *Nán yáng huá qiáo yǔ mǐn yuè shè huì.* China: Commercial Press. 南洋华侨与闽粤社会 / 陈达 長沙：商務印書館

Da Gong Ping Lun (unknown date)大公評論，普通話在港還未普及<<Putonghua is not yet popular in Hong Kong>> http://www.hkpecs.org/epaperDetail.asp?ep_id=146

Gan, Yu En and Shan, Shan (2013). On the Lexical and Grammatical Features of Siantar Mandarin in Indonesia. *TCSOL Studies* 4, 94–99. 甘于恩;单珊 2013 印尼"先达国语"词汇语法特点概说,华文教学与研究 4, 94–99.

Godley, M.R. & Coppel, C.A. (1990). The Pied Piper and the Prodigal children: A report on the Indonesian-Chinese students who went to Mao's China. *Archipel* 39, 1pp. 179–198.

Jiang, Lin Yun (2013) 美麗神奇的多巴湖 <<Beautiful Toba Lake>>. 廣西日報 <<Guangxi Daily>> http://big5.xinhuanet.com/gate/big5/www.asean-china-scenter.org/2013–03/27/c_132264527.htm

Li, X. and Huang, K. (1987). *Yinni hua qiao shi*. Canton: Guangdong gao deng jiao yu chu ban she.

Liang Quan (2012) 良全,家鄉先達遊 <<Visiting hometown Siantar>> http://www.siantarpeople.org/portal.php?mod=view&aid=1206

Ong, Aihwa (1999). *Flexible Citizenship: The Cultural Logics of Transnationality*. USA: Duke University Press.

Ong, Aihwa (2003). Cyberpublics and diaspora politics among transnational Chinese. *Interventions* 5, 82–100.

Tang, Hui (2006). *Yindunixiya li jie zheng fu Hua qiao Hua ren zheng ce de xing cheng yu yan bian*. Beijing Shi: Shi jie zhi shi chu ban she. 印度尼西亚历届政府华侨华人政策的形成与演变 / 唐慧/北京市：世界知识出版社

Wang, C. (2003). *Re-establishing networks: Capital, power and identity in the making of an Indonesian Chinese community in Hong Kong* (Hong Kong University Theses Online.)

Waters, Johanna L. (2005). Transnational family strategies and education in the contemporary Chinese diaspora. *Global Networks* 5, 4, pp. 359–377.

Waters, Johanna L. (2007). 'Roundabout routes and sanctuary schools': The role of situated educational practices and habitus in the creation of transnational professionals. *Global Networks* 7, 4, pp. 477–497.

Waters, Johanna L. (2008). *Education, Migration, and Cultural Capital in the Chinese Diaspora: Transnational Students Between Hong Kong and Canada*. USA: Cambria Press.

Wen, Guangyi and Hong Si Si. (1985). 溫廣益, 洪絲絲. *Yindunixiya Hua qiao shi* <<*The history of Indonesian Chinese*>>印度尼西亞華僑史. China, Beijing: Hai yang chu ban she. 北京：海洋出版社.

15 Family Language Policy in the Chinese Community in Singapore
A Question of Balance?

Xiao Lan Curdt-Christiansen

Hong: Actually both of us [husband and Hong] were brought up in a Chinese-speaking environment, when we were young.

R: Oh, any dialect?

H: Dialect, of course, is Hokkien. So when we were young, mainly is Chinese and Hokkien.

R: So for your generation, you and your husband, when you were small, so at home, parents will speak Mandarin? Or most of the time, they will speak Hokkien or other . . .

H: Hokkien, I think most of the time they will speak Hokkien. But we will speak Mandarin most of the time with our friends.

R: Oh, why?

H: That was the environment, because most of the kids at that time don't come from English-speaking family.

R: Oh, but they don't speak Hokkien?

H: They don't speak Hokkien, they speak Mandarin most of the time.

R: Oh, they understand dialects, but they will answer in Mandarin?

H: Actually in our generation [1970s], you can see, a lot of them don't speak Hokkien, don't speak dialects as much already, a lot of them don't have a good understanding of dialect.

R: Oh, like the situation today, right? You speak Chinese to your kids, they answer in English. And your generation, parents speak Hokkien to you, and you answer in Mandarin?

H: In our time, I think we converse in dialect with our family members. But when we go out and meet with friends, and in school, we speak Mandarin. There are some campaign going on, just like now, the school, the Speak Mandarin Campaign, right, it is an opposite scenario last time

R: Oh . . .?

H: *But of course, there are days we were forced to speak English by our teacher.*

[R= researcher; H=Hong, a participant]

With its account of the language practices of the generation growing up in the 1970s and 80s, Hong's story captures the characteristics of multilingualism and the complexity of the language shift situation in Singapore. A city-state, Singapore is inhabited by a population of 5.08 million (Statistics Singapore, 2010) divided into four major ethnic groups—Chinese (76%), Malays (13%), Indians (8%) and others (3%). In order to maintain racial harmony, Singapore's government applies strong interventionist measures in all its management, including language policies, such as the globally known bilingual policy and the Speak Mandarin Policy. Although these policies have enabled new generations to speak Mandarin, the 'standard' variety of the Chinese language, and have created a new 'English-knowing' bilingual generation (Pakir, 2008) that is able to use English and the designated mother tongues in both social and official situations, serious language shifts and loss have accompanied these top-down interventions.

This chapter focuses on the language shift phenomenon in Singapore as a consequence of the top-town policies. By looking at bilingual family language policies, it examines the characteristics of Singapore's multilingual nature and cultural diversity. Specifically, it looks at what languages are practiced and how family language policies are enacted in Singaporean English-Chinese bilingual families, and to what extent macro-language policies, i.e., national and educational language policies, influence and interact with family language policies. In doing so, it describes the actual language practices in Chinese and English speaking families against the background of the Speak Mandarin Campaign and the current bilingual policy implemented in the 1970s. It discusses the reality of such language management measures in contrast with the government's 'separate bilingualism' (Creese & Blackledge, 2011) expectations with regard to 'striking a balance' between Asian and Western culture (Curdt-Christiansen & Silver, 2013; Shepherd, 2005) and between English and mother tongue languages (Curdt-Christiansen, 2014a). Demonstrating how parents and children negotiate their family language policy through translanguaging or heteroglossia practices (Canagarajah, 2013; Garcia & Li Wei, 2014; Li Wei, 2011), this chapter argues that 'striking a balance' as a political ideology places emphasis on discrete and separate notions of cultural and linguistic categorization and thus downplays the significant influences from historical, political and sociolinguistic contexts in which people find themselves. This simplistic view of culture and linguistic code will inevitably constrain individuals' language expression, as it regards code-switching and translanguaging as a delimited and incompetent language behavior.

FAMILY LANGUAGE POLICY, BALANCED BILINGUALISM, TRANSLANGUAGING

Family language policy (FLP) has received increased attention over the last decades as researchers seek to understand how intergenerational transmission takes place (Canagrajah, 2011; Fishman, 2004; Gafaranga, 2010; Li Wei, 1994, 2005, 2011), what mechanisms and linguistic conditions parents provide for bilingual development and language acquisition (de Houwer, 2009; Lanza, 2007), and how parental attitudes to languages are influenced and shaped by broader sociolinguistic forces and political discourse (Curdt-Christiansen, 2009; 2013a; 2014a). As an interdisciplinary field of inquiry, the study of FLP draws on theoretical frames of language policy, language socialization, home literacy studies and child language acquisition. It seeks to gain insights into how macro-political policy decisions and sociolinguistic contexts (external factors) influence and interact with micro-level parental language-discourse strategies.

Studies of transnational families have found that parents tend to surrender to external forces, resulting in intergenerational language shift within three generations. The process of language loss and shift is often related to political structures, migration pressures, economic considerations and public education demand. Lane (2010), for example, showed how a minority group of Kven speakers in Norway were 'coerced' to change their FLP and cease to speak Kven to the younger generation as a result of the official Norwegianization policy. Studying Sri Lankan Tamils in diasporic communities, Canagarajah (2011) found that Tamil migrants often have to consider issues of heritage language maintenance in relation to other needs and priorities, such as economic pressure and legal survival. Li Wei (1995) studied Chinese immigrant families in Britain and found that language shift underwent different stages of linguistic practice. As such, language choices and code-switching patterns were dependent on community norms of language use and individual conversational strategy. These studies shed light not only on parental beliefs about their heritage language but also on the xenophilia and xenophobia of politically powerful languages.

Recently, research into FLP has begun to pay attention to how parents and children negotiate their policies in everyday, face-to-face interactions; how parents translate their FLP through socialization routines; and how children comply with, reject or change parents' language choice. In tracing the language shift process of Rwandans in Belgium, Gafaranga (2010) showed that Kinyarwanda-French bilingual children constantly use 'medium request', thus indirectly demanding medium-switch from Kinyarwanda to French. Curdt-Christiansen (2013b), based on conversation discourse analysis, demonstrated that a range of FLPs are established and enacted in Singaporean Chinese bilingual families through parental discourse strategies, from highly organized and overt policies to unreflective and *laissez-faire* attitudes to managed language practices. Inconsistent language choices are also found in families in other contexts. Zhu Hua (2008) showed that intergenerational conflict talk existed among different generations in the UK when family members try to use different languages to assert their cultural values.

These studies have revealed that translanguaging is a distinctive feature of the everyday interactions in these bi/multilingual homes despite parents' cautious control over which language to use for what purposes. Generally, parents require children to separate linguistic codes and to practice what Creese and Blackledge (2011) call 'separate' bilingualism with expectations of achieving 'balanced bilingualism'. Such belief about 'parallel monolingualism' (Heller, 1999) is deeply rooted in a monolingual view of bilingualism and code-switching as a less acceptable language behavior for political, social or cultural reasons. The negative attitude toward code-switching, otherwise a sense-making act of individuals to maximize their communicative potential, is derived largely from a deficit view of translanguaging as lacking mastery of both languages (Garcia & Li, 2014).

The ideology of one language, one culture, one nation and one identity is another factor that affects people's attitudes on translanguaging. Language practice, however, is a social phenomenon, therefore not always fixed and straightforward. It is linked to social practices, language policy, political discourse and sociolinguistic forces in speech communities. Within linguistic contact zones, and in this global-transnational era, treating bi/multilingual practices as separate and discrete codes of practice is to deny the realities of historical trajectory, political development and sociocultural evolution. As such, the study of FLP can offer a new lens to 'make visible the relationships of private domains and public spheres' (Curdt-Christiansen, 2013a, p. 1) and advance our understanding of the essential interplay between macro-, messo- and micro-level of linguistic practices and policy decisions.

In order to capture how macro-level language policies interact with micro-family language policies and how family members' language repertoires are constructed, built and developed, the study addresses the following questions:

- What languages are practiced by family members in Singapore's Chinese community?
- What is the relationship between parental language repertoire and the mother's educational level?
- To what extent do parental language input patterns relate to their children's language output practices?
- How do family members negotiate FLP through different languaging and translanguaging strategies?

CONTEXTUALIZING THE STUDY

Top-down Policies in Singapore

Governing a multi-ethnic nation, Singapore's government has from its inception been concerned with language policy. With racial harmony as its priority, the government adopted a bilingual policy in 1965, which recognizes four official languages: English, Mandarin, Malay and Tamil. Although the largest population group has always been Chinese and Singapore is located in the Malay Peninsula, English has been promoted as the language of government, business and education. The prestige positioning of English has resulted in a visible language shift from mother tongues to English language among all ethnic groups (Curdt-Christiansen, 2014b; Lim, 2009; Zhao & Liu, 2008).

The bilingual policy has in particular affected the language repertoire of Singaporean Chinese, as Mandarin was designated as the mother tongue although the Chinese community comprised different 'dialect' speakers who spoke a multitude of Chinese varieties, including Hokkien, Teochew, Cantonese, Hainanese, etc. (Teo, 2005). As a result, this deliberate political intervention has inflicted a double shift—Mandarin to English and 'dialect' to Mandarin (Curdt-Christiansen, 2014a; Li, Saravanan, & Ng, 1997). The latter was perceptibly influenced by the annual Speak Mandarin Campaign (SMC), launched in 1979. Targeting various audiences, such as hawkers, taxi drivers and white-collar workers, the Campaign has had different focuses over the years: to unite the Chinese community and promote social cohesion; to demote 'dialects' as underdeveloped varieties of the Chinese language; and to establish the economic power associated with Mandarin.

As a result of these political interventions, the linguistic behavior of Singaporeans has visibly changed from generation to generation as indicated by the dialogue in the beginning of the chapter. Although researchers have studied different aspects and effects of these policies, few studies have reported on the gradual language shift taking place in the homes, on what family language polices have been implemented to support/undermine the government's political decisions and on what linguistic practices have been negotiated among family members in everyday conversation.

The Study

This study is part of a larger research project, investigating the biliteracy development of primary school children of grade 3 from four government schools involving 545 students. Of these are 273 girls and 272 boys 8–9 years old. These children are mostly the third generation of school children being educated under Singapore's bilingual policy.

In order to understand how the bilingual policy has changed the linguistic landscape in Singapore, we took a holistic stance by using multiple factors to locate the children's biliteracy practices. We included parents and grandparents as participants to trace the trajectory of the policy history. The grandparent generation (1960–70s) typically had little education in English and spoke generally dialects among themselves. The parent generation (1970–80s) went through both bilingual policy and the SMC, and subsequently used dialects at home, Mandarin with friends and English at school. The participating children (2000s) are the third generation educated under the bilingual policy and typically use English at school and with friends whereas some use Mandarin at home.

By means of a survey, we were able to obtain basic demographic information about parental educational level and their SES, as these factors provide information on how educational language policy influenced the job market and shaped the linguistic repertoires of households. Table 15.1 presents the parents' and grandparents' educational profiles and SES backgrounds. Indirect financial information, such as type of housing, was used to determine the family's SES, as the HDB (Singapore's Housing Development Board) exercises a policy of property allocation based on household income level.[1]

Data Sources

In this chapter, data sources include two parts: 1) a prescribed linguistic practices survey; and 2) participant observation of actual negotiation of FLP in face-to-face social interaction in bilingual English-Chinese families.

The linguistic practices survey serves to illuminate the process of language shift from one generation to the next. Encompassing various conversation partners, it breaks the types of language used into more refined units from 0–25%; 26–50%, 51–75% and 76–100% (see Table 15.2). It captures the patterns of *de facto* linguistic practices of FLP in relation to 'a wide range of socio-historical, political, cultural and linguistic variables' (Curdt-Christiansen, 2013a, p. 1), especially the language policies imposed by the Singaporean government.

The face-to-face interactions were part of our ethnographic endeavors to provide detailed information to supplement the larger quantitative survey data. These everyday interactions not only capture the details of how FLP is established, negotiated and constructed in the families but also encapsulate the communicative strategies of using translanguaging when parents and children translate their language beliefs into linguistic practices. Two families are chosen for the purpose of this chapter. Regular home visits were carried out once a week/two weeks for a period of one school semester, depending on the family's availability. Recordings were made by the families

Table 15.1 Demographic Characteristics of Participating Families (in percentages)

Percentage of mother's educational attainment		Percentage of housing types	
N= 545		N= 545	
PSLE Cert	9	3 room	12
O-Level	23	4 room	26
A-Level	15	5 room	28
Poly	31	Private Housing	33
University +	17	Not answered	1
Not answered	4		

Table 15.2 Languages Used among Family Members 家庭成员间语言使用情况

Language	Up to ¼ of the time 0–25% 的时间	From ¼ to ½ of the time 26 % –50 % 的时间	From ½ to ¾ of the time 51% – 75% 的时间	More than ¾ of the time 76% –100% 的时间
English				
Mandarin				
English & Mandarin				
Mandarin & Dialect				
Dialect				

What languages are used *between parents (between mother and child etc.)* and how often are they used? Please tick where applicable. You may tick more when more languages are used. 父母之间使用什么语言，使用频率如何？请在合适的地方打'√'。如果使用多种语言，您可以多种语言都选。

at will without researchers present, usually every week. Each recording lasted 25–40 minutes.

In what follows, I present the quantitative findings of the *de facto* FLPs of Singaporean Chinese families. I then illustrate how families use different discourse moves to establish the 'rules' of language use and negotiate FLPs through analysis of their everyday interactions.

PATTERNS OF LANGUAGE PRACTICE

With regard to language practice information, we include all family members and possible language interlocutors, including language used between parents, between parents and children, grandparents, and domestic helper, and among siblings.

Table 15.3 shows the general language practice patterns between family members. We are aware that the self-reported information may not accurately present the actual practices at homes of the participating families. As in any type of survey, these data provide an estimated language behavior of Singaporeans today.

For parents who use dominantly either English or Mandarin between themselves for more than 75% of the time, the percentage is comparable with 28% for English and 29% Mandarin. When it comes to using English and Mandarin as a mixed mode, the frequency is almost 10% higher at 37%. This statistic indicates that language meshing is a rather common mode of communication (Canagarajah, 2013), and linguistic separation in

Table 15.3 Language Practice Information between Family Members

Language Language use	English	Mandarin	English & Mandarin	Mandarin & Dialect
Between parents	28	29	37	4
Parents/children	40	24	36	0
Between siblings	47	15	37	1
Grandparents/ Grandchildren	10	26	12	4
Domestic helper/children	34	1	2	0

language contact zones is insufficient for effective communication. Only 4% of parents reported using mixed Mandarin and dialect in the homes.

Language use between parents and children clearly indicates that English is a much preferred language choice, with a high percentage of 40%. No parents reported using dialect with their children.

With regard to languages used between siblings, English is used in almost half of the participating families (47%), whereas 37% of the families used mixed English and Mandarin for communication. Only 15% of the families used Mandarin and 1% used mixed Mandarin and dialect between the siblings.

MOTHERS' EDUCATIONAL LEVEL AND LANGUAGE PRACTICE PATTERNS

Decades of research have strongly suggested that mothers' education level plays an important role in both children's language and cognitive development. Taking the research evidence into consideration, we used maternal education level as an indicator to establish whether there is a strong relationship of language practice patterns between parents and children.

Maternal Education Level and Language Practice Between Parents

Figure 15.1 indicates that the higher the mother's educational level, the more English language is used between the couple. The opposite can be said for the Mandarin language use between parents.

Maternal Education Level and Language Input Pattern

Whereas mother's education can shape child language outcomes, our goal in the current study was to examine how maternal language use had changed

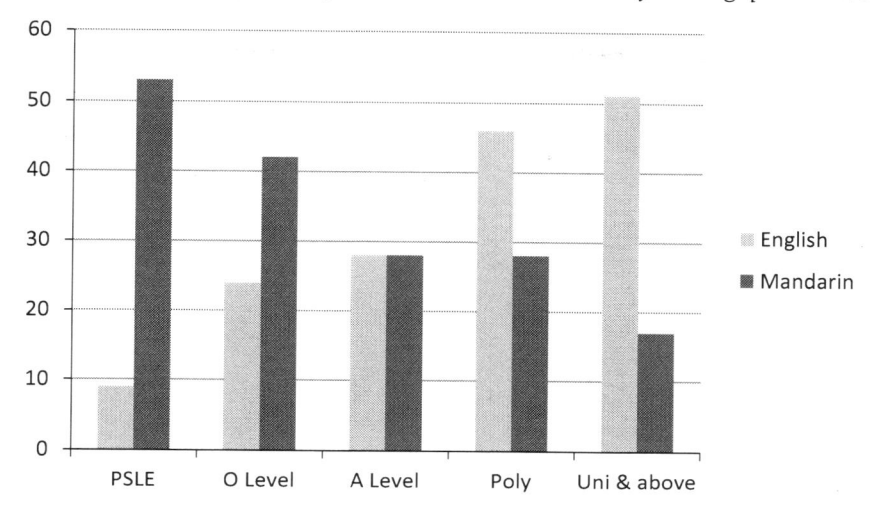

Figure 15.1 Mothers' Educational Level and Patterns of Parental Language Practice

along with their educational attainment as well as how that indirectly influenced children's language outcomes.

The yellow arrows in this table indicate the increasing percentage of language choice, and the black arrows indicate where the increase and changes of pattern are possibly from. In general, based on the language pool to which they have access, mothers tend to use different languages with their language partners with a tendency to use the language of higher status established in the sociolinguistic context of Singapore. The flow shows that PSLE mothers' language repertoire normally includes Mandarin and dialect, with some English proficiency indicated in the previous figure. When speaking to their children, they tend not to choose dialects but Mandarin with limited attempts at using English. Mandarin use in this group decreases from 53% between parents to 47% from mother to children, which suggests that mothers mix more English into the Mandarin pattern, leading to the mixed practice of English and Mandarin increasing from 21% (between parents) to 40% between mother and children. Regarding mothers with O-level education, a similar pattern is seen. This group of mothers, however, has better command of English. More mothers choose to use English with their children as dominant English language practices increase from 24% between parents to 42% between mother and children. The possible cause is likely to be that mothers who use mixed language with their husbands now switch to English. Mandarin users now switch to mixed language, where we can see a decrease of Mandarin practice from 42% between parents to 32% between mother and children. When it comes to mothers with university education, mothers using English to communicate with their children increase to 56%. For this group of families, the language use is more or less

Table 15.4   Maternal Education Level and Language Input Pattern

Mother's Education	Language Use Pattern	English	English & Mandarin	Mandarin	Mandarin & Dialects
6 years (PSLE)	Between parents	9	21	53	11
	From mother to student	13	40	47	0
10 years (O Level)	Between parents	24	24	42	9
	From mother to student	42	26	32	0
12 years (A Level)	Between parents	28	37	28	6
	From mother to student	45	39	15	1
12–14 years (Poly)	Between parents	46	23	28	3
	From mother to student	52	30	18	0
16 years & above (U-degree & above)	Between parents	51	25	17	7
	From mother to student	56	23	19	2

stable; the changes from the language use between parents to the children are not as drastic as in other groups. With regard to dialect use, there is a sign of revitalization even though the percentage is only 2%.

Language Input Pattern and Language Output Practice

Finally, we look at how mother's language input to children influences the language practices produced by siblings.

Clearly the table indicates that across all the groups, mothers make different choices in their language use with their husbands and children. A small number of mothers use mixed Mandarin and dialects with their husbands, but almost none of them use the mixed codes with their children.

Regarding children with mothers who have obtained PSLE and O-level education, their language practice in mixed English and Mandarin shows an increase up to 59% from 40% of mother to children input and up to 38% from 26% between mother and children. The percentage increment clearly

Table 15.5 Language Input Pattern and Output Practice

Mother's Education		English	English & Chinese	Chinese	Chinese & Chinese Dialects
6 years (PSLE)	Language used between parents	9	21	53	11
	Language used from mother to student	13	40	47	0
	Language used from student to siblings	8	59	32	0
10 years (O Level)	Language used between parents	24	24	42	9
	Language used from mother to student	42	26	32	0
	Language used from student to siblings	40	38	21	0
12 years (A Level)	Language used between parents	28	37	28	6
	Language used from mother to student	45	39	15	1
	Language used from student to siblings	55	26	12	0
12–14 years (Poly)	Language used between parents	46	23	28	3
	Language used from mother to student	52	30	18	0
	Language used from student to siblings	62	30	8	0
16 years & above (U-degree & above)	Language used between parents	51	25	17	7
	Language used from mother to student	56	23	19	2
	Language used from student to siblings	64	27	8	0

indicates a strong relationship between mother's language input and children's language output practices. For the rest of the groups, it is noticeable that more English is used among siblings. The high percentage of English output can be explained by two factors: more mothers speak English to their children, meaning more input from home, and the language practice in school as a result of English being the MoI for all subjects. It confirms Baldauf's (2005) argument that school is the most effective site for changing language behavior. What is most striking from the survey is the translanguaging practices between family members.

Whereas Tables 15.4 and 15.5 and Figure 15.1 provide quantitative descriptive statistics about family language practices in Singapore, further study of how family language policy is enacted and language practices are negotiated, and of what linguistic practices have been changed or abandoned, are needed to enhance our understanding of the subtleties and processes of language (dis)continuity in relation to policy interventions. In the next section, I present everyday interactions taking place in two families to capture the changing linguistic landscape between generations and language interaction patterns.

FROM TEOCHEW TO MANDARIN MESHING WITH ENGLISH

Singapore's Chinese community has traditionally comprised several linguistic and cultural groups, mostly from the southeastern coast of China and the provinces of Fujian, Guangdong and Hainan. The largest Chinese dialect groups are Hokkien, Teochew and Cantonese. Before the Speak Mandarin Campaign in 1979, Hokkien was the lingua franca of the entire community, although many had knowledge of Teochew. Mandarin has now become the most commonly spoken variety of Chinese in Singapore, but dialects are still used among members of the older generation, although much less frequently and for limited purposes within restricted contexts.

The following excerpt is a typical example of everyday interaction representing Singaporeans' translingual practice and demonstrating the subtle changes of language ecology shaped by language policy and educational policy.

Excerpt 1: 补习—*Doing Tuition*

(The conversation took place at a HDB housing community center hosting various local facilities, including private tuition classes, government sponsored daycare, small shops and clinics. Outside one of the tuition classes, the mother of Family Teo sat at a stone table with her younger daughter, D2, waiting for her older one, D1, to finish her class. A neighbor passed by and started a conversation in Teochew. M=mother in the mid-30s, N1= neighbor in the 70s. Translation is provided below the original text; **bolded** text indicates code switching).

N1: 今天也有补习吗？ Hah? (in Teochew)

You are also here for tuition today?

M: [讽刺]*学校教！你不知道吗？不懂什么鬼啊！汉语拼音* (in Mandarin), 小小就是学学学! (in Teochew)

[scornfully] (because) *The school teaches!* Don't you know? Don't know what 'ghost-related' matter this is! Little ones have to learn **Chinese phonics!**

N1: 由学校有教嘛! (in Teochew)

The school would teach that!

M: [讽刺]*学校教！* 哎哟！如果没有跟人补习就怎么办？ (in Teochew)

[scornfully] *The school teaches!* Oh dear! [literally: don't know] what would happen if she didn't get help from a tuition teacher?

N1: 我只是读到中二而已。(in Teochew)

I only studied till Secondary 2.

M: [用高音]自己处理。(in Teochew)

[in a high pitched voice] You have to settle the problem yourself.

N1: [小声笑] 哈哈！管你让你去补！(in Teochew)

[giggles] Ha-ha! It's up to you to let her go for tuition!

M: 想不要给她补了！(in Teochew)

(I am) thinking about stopping the tuition for her!

N1: **OK,** 那就停止吧！(in Teochew)

OK, then stop it!

M: 让我这个大人 就麻烦了！(in Teochew)

It'll be troublesome for adults like me!

One of the noticeable features in this dialogue is the use of Teochew, despite the young age of the mother. Actually, except the insertion of 汉语拼音 (hanyu pinyin) in Mandarin, the entire conversation is conducted in Teochew. Clearly the mother has undergone schooling in the 1980s when the language-in-education policy had been implemented with English as MoI and Mandarin as the required mother tongue subject. The education has enabled her to use Mandarin and English (evidenced in the next excerpt), but she chooses to converse in Teochew with the elderly neighbor who had not received education in English.

The linguistic choice she made could be attributed to her habitual language use, formed in her early years with family members who spoke only Teochew. This habitual language practice has been comparatively more common in HDB community contexts where the elder generation don't have good command of Mandarin or English because of their restricted access to education in these languages. Using Teochew in this context also indicates that the language has a limited space of practice although it is slowly fading out of the Singaporeans' multilingual repertoires in step with the forcefully implemented government policies. Li Wei, Saravanan and Ng (1997) reported that such decrease of Teochew practices was already taking place in the 1990s, when Teochew and other 'dialects' were no longer transmitted to the children as the primary language of family communication. In the next excerpt, I illustrate the shift of language use between the mother and her two young daughters.

Excerpt 2: *Mummy* 叫我 *Take!*

(The conversation took place before D1 went to her tuition class. Mrs. Teo was examining the contents of D1's school bag).

1 M: 我问你：做什么你死人书包这样重？ 你是补习还是做什么鬼你告诉我？

Let me ask you: Why is your bag damn heavy? Tell me: Are you preparing for tuition or up to some kind of mischief?

D1:   我在补习 . . .

I am preparing for tuition . . .

M: 还有这本东西做完了没有？

Have you finished this book?

D1:   还没有。

Not yet.

5 M: 我很讨厌你*leh*！你每次去学校借这种书来做什么？呵？这两本多么重，你跟我讲？

I really dislike you! Why do you go to school and borrow such books? These two books are really heavy. Why did you borrow them?

D1:   这个是补习的!

This is for tuition!

M: 这本 leh？

How about this book?

D1:   **Chinese** 写字 (Teochew: Writing).

Chinese Writing (Teochew: Writing).

M: 你这本要拿去还，对吗？

You're going to return this book, aren't you?

10 D1:   (whining) Hmmmmm!
M: 你书本就没有看到 . . . 也不会读story . . .

You didn't read this book . . . you don't know how to read the **story** . . .

D1:   *Han lah* (Teochew: Yes), 我刚才读过了一本.

Yes, I have already read one book.

M: 受不了你哦！ 这整个书包这么重你知道吗？

I can't stand you! Don't you know this entire bag is so heavy?

D1:   这是阿妹的. (pointing to a pile of cards).

This is my younger sister's (pointing to a pile of cards).

15 D2: 我的牌！

They are my cards!

D1: 这你的...

This is your own . . .

M: 妈妈才教你们做 . . . 不要**take**!

Only Mother will teach you how to do . . . don't take it!

D1: (whining) Hmmmmm!
D2: **Mummy** 叫我 **take**!

Mummy asked me to **take** it!

20 M: 这个校长也 是 **xiao** (Teochew: crazy) 的! **That day**, 你的那 个 . . .

This principal is **crazy**! **That day**, your . . .

In this conversation between Mrs. Teo and her two daughters, three languages are at play, Mandarin, Teochew and English. Mandarin is the main code of communication, whereas Teochew and English are only inserted as single words to signal the tones and changes of the topic of conversation. For example, in lines 5, 7 and 13, *leh* and *lah*, affirmative particles (Singlish expressions), are used at the end of sentences to stress special pragmatic functions. *Leh* in line 5 is used by Mrs. Teo to soften the brusqueness of her nagging and complaining. *Leh* in line 7 conveys Mrs. Teo's disapproval of her daughter's heavy bag contents. *Lah* in line 13 shows D1's frustration and impatience with her mother's accusation about her inability to read the book. Other Teochew words such as 写字 and *xiao* in the conversation are probably employed habitually in the family and can therefore facilitate the meaning making process and make expressions more to the point. As to the insertion of English words such as *take* in line 17, it functions as an emphasis or a warning sign to the children 'not to **take** the cards'.

The meshing of the three languages in this everyday conversational interaction is not atypical in contact situations. Li Wei, for example, documented such translanguaging practices in Chinese families (2005) as well as in the translanguaging space of multilingual Chinese youth (2011) in the UK; Canagarajah described the way communication works in South Asia as translingual dispositions (2013). Such linguistic practices illustrate that mixing of languages or linguistic pluralism arises in response to situated practices in order to achieve communicative success. Linguistic practices in private domains in Singapore are no exception, as members in any given family are required to negotiate meaning through the use of multiple codes to accomplish their communicative goals in relation to their purposes and interests.

Despite the fact that translanguaging practices are visible and inevitable in almost all domains, the government advocates separate bilingualism, viewing the use of mixed codes such as Singlish[2] as equivalent to poor command of English. Through mass media and official language campaigns, the government strongly discourages the use of Singlish in favor of Standard English and Mandarin. The use of mixed code is interpreted as uneducated, indicative of less intelligence and less competence (Bokhorst-Heng et al., 2010). Consequently, parents' attitudes toward and beliefs about languages are influenced and shaped by this political discourse. In the next excerpt, I present such ideological convictions in an everyday, mundane interaction taking place during a homework session in a typical Singaporean family.

怎么办?怎么办?—WHAT SHOULD WE DO?: FACING TRANSLANGUAGING REALITIES

Excerpt 3: 怎么办?怎么办?—*What Should We Do?*

(Family Chew has just finished dinner; the mother, Mrs. Chew, is urging her two daughters, D1 (age 11) and D2 (age 6), to do their homework. D2 is making a lantern for school and D1 is doing her math work. M = the mother; D1 = daughter 1; D2 = daughter 2; English code in bold font.)

1 D2:   我用，我**paste** 那个花，到 . . .

   I use, I [want to] **paste** that flower, on . . .

M: //你**paste**哪个花?//

   //You want to **paste** which flower?//

D2:   //灯笼，我**paste** 那个花，黄色的。也有粉红色的花。//

   //[On] the Lantern, I [want to] **paste** that flower, yellow color. And pink flowers too. //

M: 诶 (sigh), 为什么你, 为什么你一句话里面全部讲了,有时英语有时华语, 这样讲的啊?

   Ai (sigh), why you, why [is it] in one sentence, you use all [both] languages? Sometimes in English, and sometimes in Mandarin, why do you speak that way?

5 D2:   因为, 我**some** 我不懂华语跟英语，**some** (incoherent)

   Because, I, **some**, I don't understand English and Mandarin, **some** (incoherent)

M: 啊?

   What?

D2:   有时我不懂, 我不懂

Sometimes I don't understand, I don't understand.

M: 我在用华语跟你讲的时候， 你就要用华语回答我。如果别人用英语跟你讲的时候， 你就用英语回答他。要全部用华语，或者全部用英语。你一句话里面啊，一半华语，一半英语，那句话我都听不懂你在讲什么。因为我不懂英语，怎么办？

When I talk to you in Mandarin, you should answer me in Mandarin. If other people talk to you in English, you need to answer them in English. Should use Mandarin only, or English only. In your sentence, half is Mandarin, half is English. I don't even understand what you are saying. If I don't understand English, what should we do?

D1: (joking) 啊！ 怎么办?怎么办? 不懂英语怎么办? 我的天啊。(D2 Laughing)

(joking) ah, what should we do? What should we do? What are we going to do without understanding English? Oh, My God! (D2 laughing).

In this exchange, D2 requests Mrs. Chew's help to find flowers of the right color for decorating a lantern. She inserts the content word 'paste' in English. To accommodate her daughter's language practice, Mrs. Chew did not correct D2 or provide her with the Chinese input for 'paste'; instead, she makes a clarification '你paste哪个花?' (you [want to] paste which flower?) by repeating the verb 'paste' in English. This medium repair move (Gafaranga, 2010) indicates her compromise with D2's choice of linguistic practice. Noticeably, such a move may facilitate a smooth communicative exchange; it may, nonetheless, also give concession to the mixing of communication modes, thus leading to language shift. The subsequent moves show that Mrs. Chew is upset with D2 for mixing the languages in her utterances. She asks, 'Why you, why [is it that] in one sentence, you use all [both] languages? Sometimes in English, and sometimes in Mandarin, why do you speak that way?' Mrs. Chew's question indicates a conscious observation of the language mixing practice that is unremittingly used and negotiated in this family. D2 is unable to explain her language behavior, answering her mother that '因为,我some 我不懂华语跟英语, some' (*Because, I, some, I don't understand English and Mandarin, some.*). Not believing what she heard, Mrs Chew then makes a rather long speech, stating the family language policy (turn 8):

When I talk to you in Mandarin, you should answer me in Mandarin. If other people talk to you in English, you need to answer them in English. Should use Mandarin only, or English only. In your sentence, half is Mandarin, half is English. I don't even understand what you are saying. If I don't understand English, what should we do?

However, this policy announcement does not seem to have any effect on the children because D1 starts mocking her mother by imitating her: 'Ah, what should we do? What should we do? What are we going to do if we don't understand English? Oh, My God!' The mocking seems to suggest that it is impossible for the announced policy to replace the already existing and long established language practice in the family, as all the family members seem to be comfortable with and fully accepting of this practice.

Mrs Chew's beliefs in separating linguistic codes seem to be rooted in the concept of bilingualism as double monolingualism. Her FLP, which requires her children to practice English or Mandarin separately, is based on the view that competent bilinguals should have a balance or two fully developed languages. In Garcia's words (2013, p. 142), such monoglossic vision of bilingualism suggests that balanced bilingual practices are 'language practices of a monolingual individual, simply by multiplying them by two'. From a language maintenance perspective, Mrs. Chew's FLP may be crucial for developing her daughter's Mandarin, but striking a balance between the two languages in this communicative act seems impossible for D2, as she claims, '有时我不懂, 我不懂'. Her response seems to suggest that using only one language for communication is insufficient to maximize her potential and will not allow her to achieve her communicative purpose. D2's remark reflects not only complex ways of language communication, but also the realities that bilinguals/multilinguals face in their everyday communicative routines when language contact in the community is intense and lively.

CONCLUSION

In this chapter, I have described the language shift phenomenon that has occurred in Singapore in recent years. With examples from the general patterns of linguistic practice of 545 bi/multilingual families, I illustrate how Singaporeans' language repertoires have gradually undergone changes from one generation to the next as the result of top-down language policies. To facilitate our understanding of the process of language change, I have documented everyday language interactions in two families, demonstrating how family language policies are associated with sociocultural and political forces.

As in any contact situation, translanguaging is a distinctive feature of the family discursive practices. This multilingual feature, however, has not been welcomed and embraced by either the government or many parents, despite the vibrant use of different forms of hybridity in public and private domains. The unacceptance of and discouragement of using hybrid forms of languages are associated with powerful and persuasive linguistic, academic and political discourse that views languages and cultures as self-contained systems. Any mixing and meshing of different languages and diverse cultures would disrupt the notion of 'purity' in linguistic and social systems. When situated in a multilingual society where multiple languages are used and different cultures are practiced by different ethnic groups, according to the government, the best way to keep the languages and cultures 'pure' is to separate them and develop monolingual competencies of the languages, as indicated in one of the policy statements by the Singaporean government:

> Our bilingual policy aims to equip our students with the language competencies to access Asian cultures and develop a global outlook. This will give our students a competitive edge, enable them to appreciate their culture and heritage and connect with people from different backgrounds, so that they can thrive in a globalised world. (MOE, 2012, p. 1)

This statement represents a balanced view of bilingualism and biculturalism when language competencies are concerned. It seems to suggest that Asian cultures are only accessible when full command of an Asian language is developed. The ideological conviction is tied to the notion of language and culture in simplified ways which lead to a political decision on 'striking a balance' between the Western cultures and the Asian cultures, associated with English and the designated Asian mother tongues. The political intervention has complicated the linguistic practices that were already multilingual and hybrid. The argument for developing separate bilingualism or double monolinguals in English and the mother tongue has been an appealing political move, but it has failed to recognize the complexity of translanguaging practices brought to the forefront by the various linguistic contacts. Hybrid language use is strongly discouraged by parents, school teachers and government officials, believing that such language practices (as for example the use of Singlish) can hinder children's bilingual development and even damage their intellectual growth.

I would argue that developing linguistic competencies should take into consideration the children's language environment and Singapore's language ecology. 'Balancing' the language development needs to give recognition to Singapore's linguistic nature, which is interactional, dialectic and interdiscursive. Instead of condemning children's translanguaging behavior, parents as well as teachers should consider how to take advantage of such linguistic practices so as to maximize the children's opportunities, enhance their language competencies and celebrate 'their culture' in more creative ways and through more resourceful means.

ACKNOWLEDGEMENTS

This research was partially supported by funding from the Education Research Funding Programme, National Institute of Education (NIE), Nanyang Technological University, Singapore (Grant#: OER35/09XLC). The views expressed in this paper are the author's and do not necessarily represent the views of NIE.

NOTES

1. Because household income is a sensitive issue, we used housing type as an indicator of household income level, as the Housing Development Board is responsible for public housing in Singapore and exercises a policy of property allocation based on income level. For example, to acquire a 4-room flat, the lessee's gross monthly household income must not exceed S\$8,000. If a household monthly income exceeds S\$12,000, the family/individual has to purchase a private condo or house).
2. Singlish, also known as **Colloquial Singaporean English**, is an English-based creole language. Its vocabulary and grammar/syntax are heavily influenced by Malay, Hokkien, Teochew, Cantonese and Tamil.

REFERENCES

Baldauf, R. B. Jr. (2005). Language planning and policy research: an overview. In E. Hinkel (Ed.), *Handbook of research in second language teaching and learning* (pp. 957–970). New Jersey and London: Lawrence Erlbaum.

Bokhorst-Heng, W., Rubdy, R., McKay, S. L. & Alsagoff, L. (2010). Whose English? Language ownership in Singapore's English language debates. In L. Lim, A. Pakir and L. Wee (Eds.), *English in Singapore: Modernity and management* (pp. 133–157). Hong Kong: Hong Kong University Press.

Canagarajah, A. S. (2011). Diaspora communities, language maintenance, and policy dilemma. In T. L. McCarty (Ed.), *Ethnography and Language Policy* (pp. 77–97). London and New York: Routledge.

Canagarajah, A. S. (2013).*Translanguaging practice: Global Englishes and cosmopolitan relations*. London and New York: Routledge.

Creese, A. & Blackledge, A. (2011). Separate and flexible bilingualism in complementary schools: Multiple language practices in interrelationship. *Journal of Pragmatics, 43*, 1196–1208.

Curdt-Christiansen, X. L. (2009). Visible and invisible language planning: Ideological factor in the family language policy of Chinese immigrant families in Quebec. *Language Policy, 8*(4), 351–375.

Curdt-Christiansen, X. L. (2013a). Editorial: Family language policy: Realities and continuities. *Language Policy, 13*(1), 1–7.

Curdt-Christiansen, X. L. (2013b). Negotiating family language policy: Doing homework. In M. Schwartz & A. Verschik (Eds.), *Successful family language policy: Parents, children and educators in interaction* (pp. 277–295). *Series Multilingual Education 7*. Dordrecht, Netherlands: Springer. doi: 10.1007/978–94–007-7753-8_10

Curdt-Christiansen, X. L. (2014a). Family language policy: Is learning Chinese at odds with leaning English in Singapore. In X. L. Curdt-Christiansen and A. Hancock (Eds.), *Learning Chinese in diasporic communities: Many pathways to being Chinese* (pp. 35–58). Amsterdam: John Benjamins.

Curdt-Christiansen, X. L. (2014b). Planning for development or decline? Education policy for Chinese language in Singapore. *Critical Inquiry in Language Studies, 11*(1), 1–26.

Curdt-Christiansen, X. L. & Silver, R. E. (2013). New wine into old skins: The enactment of literacy policy in Singapore. *Language and Education, 27*(3), 246–260. doi:10.1080/09500782.2012.704046

De Houwer, A. (2009). *Bilingual first language acquisition*. Clevedon, UK: Multilingual Matters.

Fishman, J. A. (2004). Language maintenance, language shift, and reversing. In T. K. Bhatia and W. Ritchie (Eds.), *The handbook of bilingualism* (pp. 406–436). Oxford, UK: Blackwell.

Gafaranga, J. (2010). Medium request: Talking language shift into being. *Language in Society, 39*(2), 241–270.

Garcia, O. & Li, Wei. (2014). *Translanguaging: Language, bilingualism and education.* Basingstoke, UK: Palgrave MacMillan.

Heller, M. (1999). *Linguistic minorities and modernity: A sociolinguistic ethnography.* London and New York: Longman.

Lane, P. (2010). We did what we thought was best for our children: A nexus analysis of language shift ina Kvan community. *International Journal of Social Language, 202,* 63–78.

Lanza, E. (2007). Multilingualism in the family. In P. Auer and Li Wei (Eds.), *Handbook of multilingualism and multilingual communication* (pp. 45–67). Berlin: Mouton de Gruyter.

Li, Wei. (1994). *Three generations two language one family: Language choice and language shift in a Chinese community in Britain.* Clevedon: Multilingual Matters.

Li, Wei. (1995). *Three Generations Two Language One Family: Language choice and language shift in a Chinese community in Britain.* Clevedon: Multilingual Matters

Li, Wei. (2005). "How can you tell?": Towards a common sense explanation of conversational code-switching. *Journal of Pragmatics, 37,* 375–389.

Li, Wei. (2011). Moment analysis and translanguaging space: Discursive construction of identities by multilingual Chinese youth in Britain. *Journal of Pragmatics, 43,* 1222–1235.

Li, W., Saravanan, V. & Ng, J. (1997). Language shift in the Teochew community in Singapore: A family domain analysis. *Journal of Multilingual and Multicultural Development, 18*(5), 364–384.

Lim, L. (2009). Beyond fear and loathing in SG: The real mother tongues and language policies in multilingual Singapore. *AILA Review, 22,* 52–71.

MOE (Ministry of Education). (2012). *Education in Singapore.* Retrieved 6 June 2013, from http://www.moe.gov.sg/about/files/moe-corporate-brochure.pdf

Pakir, A. (2008). Bilingual education in Singapore. In J. Cummins and N. Hornberger (Eds.), *Encyclopedia of Language and Education: Bilingual Education* (pp. 191–204). Amsterdam: Springer.

Shepherd, J. (2005). *Striking a balance: The management of language in Singapore.* Berlin: Peter Lang Publishing.

Singapore Statistic. (2010). *Census of population 2010.* Retrieved 17 March 2010, from http://www.singstat.gov.sg/pubn/popn/c2010asr/10A1.pdf

Teo, P. (2005). Mandarinising Singapore: A critical analysis of slogans in Singapore's "Speak Mandarin" campaign. *Critical Discourse Studies, 2*(2), 121–142.

Zhao, S. & Liu, Y. (2008). Home language shift and its implications for language planning in Singapore: From the perspective of prestige planning. *The Asia Pacific-Education Researcher, 16*(2), 111–126.

Zhu, Hua. (2008). Duelling languages, duelling values: Codeswitching in bilingual intergenerational conflict talk in diasporic families. *Journal of Pragmatics, 40,* 1799–1816.

16 Language Maintenance in the Chinese Diaspora in Australia

Linda Tsung

INTRODUCTION

The family home is an important domain for children's multilingual acquisition and maintenance. Abundant literature can be found on family language policies and parents' language attitudes in relation to their children's multilingual development (Pauwels, 2005; King and Fogle, 2008; Baker, 2006; Sakuragi, 2008). This chapter explores the role of family language policies in the context of family language maintenance, multilingualism and language shift among Chinese diaspora in Australia. Chinese, mainly from Southern coastal China, were among the earliest migrant groups to arrive in Australia. Before looking at the topic in depth, the beginning of this chapter gives a brief background of Chinese settlement in Australia. Their story, particularly up to the 1960s, has been one of hardship and discrimination from both government policies and racial attitudes of other immigrant groups. Notwithstanding this historical background, or perhaps because of it, many of them have managed to maintain their language and cultural heritage due to strong family language policies and community support to younger generations. Against this background, the theoretic framework of the family language policy will be discussed, followed by a detailed analysis of two Chinese families and their members' personal experience in the local Chinese diaspora.

THE CHINESE DIASPORA IN AUSTRALIA

The history of Chinese immigration to Australia dates back to the earliest days of the British Colony, when Australia was established in 1788. The earliest recorded Chinese immigrant in Australia was Mak Sai Ying in 1818. But early seventeenth century Chinese immigration was sporadic and limited to arrivals on trading ships which had passed through Asia on their way to Sydney Cove. In the 1840s, when Australia faced the curtailing of the supply of convict labour, the Colonial authorities experimented with the importation of coolie labour, mainly from the coast of Amoy (Xiamen) in the Fujian region. Between 1848 and 1853, over 3000 Chinese workers were brought to Australia, mainly to be engaged in agricultural labouring.

In the 1850s, attracted by the discovery of gold in New South Wales and Victoria, Chinese immigrants, along with a much larger number of mainly European immigrants, arrived. Tensions and conflicts developed within the gold fields between the Chinese and European miners; for example, in 1861, riots broke in Lambing Flat (in NSW) as 3000 European miners attacked 1000 Chinese.

More tensions developed among the European and Chinese migrants during the period between 1888 and 1973, reflecting the general population's fear that the influx of large numbers of Chinese would put their jobs and economic well-being at risk. The government adopted a policy in favour of European migrants and supported the anti-Chinese movement. For example, in 1888 a shipload of Chinese, many of whom were residents or born in Australia, was turned back from Melbourne and refused permission to disembark in Sydney. Crowds marched on the NSW State Parliament house and demanded the Premier "stop the invasion". Under such pressure the NSW Government enacted Anti-Chinese Legislation, which was subsequently adopted as the "Immigration Restriction Act" by the Federal Government and became known as "The White Australia Policy". This act stood in place until its final elimination by the Whitlam Government in 1973 (Fitzgerald, 2008).

The discriminatory policies against Chinese are reflected in the decreasing numbers of Chinese recorded by the Australian Bureau of Census between 1881 and 1921. Many Chinese migrants returned home (see Figure 16.1 below).

Nevertheless, over this period "China-towns" appear in all major Australian cities, and the Chinese became dominant in the growing and distribution of fruit and vegetables in the Colony. These people and their subsequent

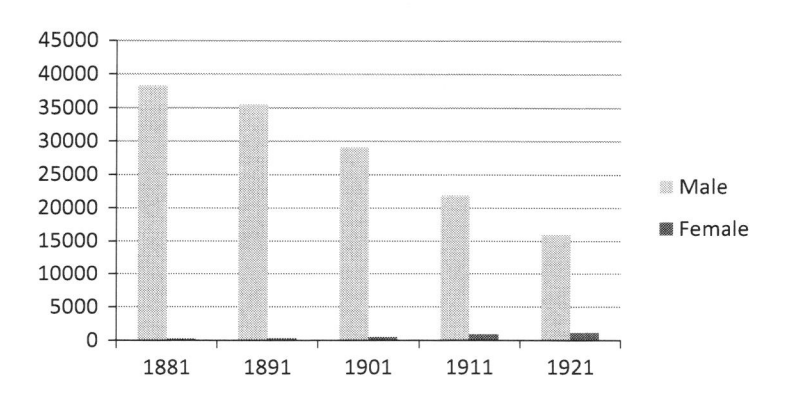

Figure 16.1   Chinese Migration between 1881–1921

offspring, mainly Cantonese speakers, formed the Chinese community until the end of the White Australia Policy in 1993.

The period from 1973 saw a new wave of Chinese migrants, initially ethnic Chinese arriving as wartime refugees from Cambodia and Vietnam during the 1970s, followed by economic migrants from Hong Kong before 1997. Following the 1989 Tiananmen movement, all mainland Chinese students in Australia at the time were allowed permanent residence, and since then the numbers of migrants from the mainland have grown steadily.

Since 2000, as China has become the fastest growing economy in the world, many economic and skilled Chinese migrants have arrived in Australia. In 2012–13, mainland immigrants formed the largest migrant intake into Australia, supplanting the numbers from the UK for the first time.

The Chinese diaspora population, including newly arrived migrants and those Australian-born claiming Chinese heritage, comprises well over 5.39% of the population in Sydney today (Australian Bureau of Statistics 2007). In 1996, there were 99,600 Chinese-born living in Sydney. This had risen to 146,000 by 2006. When those with a Chinese parent were added in, the number rose to 292,400, and these figures do not include any of the descendants of the story told here. Areas of most dramatic population growth have been the City of Sydney and Hurstville, with growing numbers in Auburn, Parramatta, Ryde, Hornsby and Willoughby.

In spite of cultural transition difficulties, language barriers and having to cope with racial discrimination, Chinese Australians have evolved dramatically from working as indentured labourers to being one of the most well-established immigrant ethnic groups in Australia. They record high levels of educational attainment that match and occasionally surpass the national average. With a high degree of upward academic and socioeconomic advancement and achievement, Chinese Australians are among the most well-educated groups in Australia and comprise a large percentage of Australia's educated class, and hold higher educational records of achievement among most demographic groups in the country. Although many earlier Chinese diaspora have shifted their own language to English under pressure of the assimilationist policy in Australia, some Chinese families have maintained their own language and have expanded their linguistic repertoires.

FAMILY LANGUAGE POLICY

Kenner (2004: 107) states that "home, school and community together make up pieces in the jigsaw of children's lives". In the field of language policy studies, family is another important domain involved in language policy processes from "bottom-up". The language or languages used in the family help shape and maintain a society's language use and practice. As an important domain within sociolinguistic ecology, it constitutes a specific type of language policy, which exerts great influence on other domains, and which in turn is also influenced by other domains. Thus it is of critical importance to study the role of family in the maintenance of intergenerational language transmission or in the language shifting that "marks changes of social and demographic environment typified by migration, urbanization or conquest" (Spolsky, 2012: 6).

Family language policy can be defined as involving explicit and overt planning in relation to language use within the home among family members (King et al., 2008). It is a deliberate attempt at practising a particular language use pattern and particular literacy practices within home domains (Curdt-Christiansen, 2009). Whereas language policies at a macro level tend to be established and implemented in order to change or influence social structures and processes, FLP tends to be based on the individual family's perception of social structures and social changes (Curdt-Christiansen, 2009). It is usually shaped by family beliefs about what will strengthen their family's social standing and best serve and support the family members' goals in life.

Like language policy at large, family language policy consists of decisions and actions in three areas: status planning (when parents make decisions concerning when and whether to use a language with their children), corpus planning (when parents decide which variety of a language to use for what types of literacy activities) and acquisition planning (when decisions are made regarding how and when to formally or informally instruct a language). Connected in significant ways with children's formal school success, FLPs and their implementation together shape children's cognitive development and determine the maintenance of that particular language (King et al., 2008). In some cases, siblings (Kyratzis, 2004) may play a crucial role, whereas in other situations grandparents (Kenner et al., 2007) or even peers (Zadunaisky Ehrlich and Blum-Kulka, 2010) may exert a great influence.

- **Parental Language Ideologies and Family Language Practice**

Language ideology has been defined as the subconscious beliefs and assumptions about the social utility of a particular language in a given society that reflect values and patterns rooted in a society's linguistic culture (Schiffman, 2006). It has often been taken as the driving force of language policy, because it is based on the perceived value, power and utility of various languages.

As a major component of FLP, the underlying language ideology always reflects the sociopolitical and economic interests of the parents. In addition, it is also related to linguistic factors as well as parental educational experiences and expectations. All these factors are interrelated and exert influence on an individual person's belief systems.

It is believed that parents' language ideologies play a crucial role in determining their child's language development. De Houwer (1999) draws a model to illustrate the relationship between beliefs, practices and outcomes in childhood bilingualism (see Figure 16.2).

Based on this model, De Houwer (1999) further identifies three types of parental ideologies or attitudes impacting on linguistic practices in bilingual families. First, parents have a clear idea about which languages should be used for what purposes with their children. This can be best illustrated by the example of Quechua parents in the Peruvian Andes. Despite government efforts to provide Quechua-Spanish bilingual education in public schools, parents perceived the school as a Spanish-only domain for formal learning and thus resisted Quechua-medium schooling. Second, parents' attitudes towards particular types of interactions impact their own child-directed speech. For example, code-switching may be taken as a means to establish their ethnic identity. This has been documented by Zentella (1997). Last, parents' attitudes concerning language learning and bilingualism also come into play in influencing their interactional strategies. An example was given by King (2001), who explains how indigenous Ecuadorian parents' belief that early second language exposure confuses children leads them to promote Spanish only in the home and shift away from their indigenous language.

However, it is evident that although children's language behaviour is largely shaped by parental language, it, in turn, can also impact on parents' beliefs and strategies (King et al., 2008). Tuominen's study (1999: 73) on the bilingual child in the USA found that parents' policies were often affected

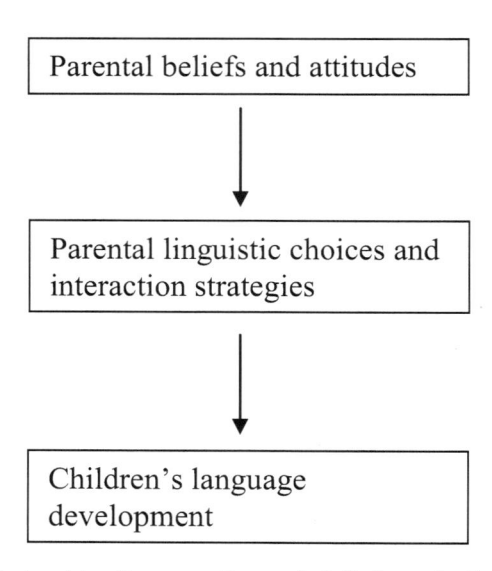

Figure 16.2 Relationship Between Parental Beliefs and Children's Language Development

by school-age children's attitudes and practice: "Children in multilingual families are socializing their parents. . . . They are teaching their parents to 'speak the same language' as the rest" of the dominant society.

Therefore the relationship between parental beliefs and children's language development is an interactive and bidirectional process. Language ideologies of parents are both formed and enacted through parent-child interactions.

FLP AS A COPING OR DEFENCE MECHANISM

There are many reasons behind immigration families' choice of languages for the family domain. Languages are linked closely to their livelihoods in the adopted country. The major dilemma concerns the varying levels of commitment to acquiring the new dominant language on the one hand and to maintaining the heritage aspect on the other (Spolsky, 2012). Family language policy is different from broad national and social policies, as it is usually affected by a range of implicit and unconscious dynamics, accompanied by strong emotional involvement (Tannenbaum, 2012). As various factors are involved in family life, such as past and present experiences, hopes and worries about the future, close interactions, etc., the emotional aspect of FLP decisions has emerged as the centre of FLP studies (Barkhuizen, 2006; Guardado, 2008; Pavlenko, 2004; Smolicz, Secombe, and Hudson, 2001). Tannenbaum (2012) takes a psychoanalytic approach to the emotional explanation of family language policy, which she argues reflects the way a family perceives its external reality and its internal status. In her study (2012), FLP is seen as either a "coping or defence" mechanism. It is, on the one hand, coping with competing demands of its heritage and of its new environment, and on the other hand, providing a defence against external pressures. A typical example of FLP as a coping mechanism is the decision to promote bilingualism in an immigrant family. Immigrant parents often attribute their decision or efforts to encourage majority language acquisition for themselves as well as for their children to the potential economic benefits of bilingualism (Curdt-Christiansen, 2009; King and Fogle, 2006). They usually emphasise the advantages of being absorbed into the wider society and the necessity of mastering the majority language for the sake of better work prospects in the future (Tannenbaum, 2012). Their insistence on their children's language maintenance can also be seen as a coping mechanism if it involves explicit, conscious ideas about language and family dynamics to increase adaptiveness. However, it can also be seen as a defensive mechanism. By promoting language maintenance, they may employ a range of defensive strategies to protect the integrity of the family system unconsciously. These strategies include "maintaining strong emotional contact with the past, with childhood memories, parents and grandparents via language maintenance" (Tannenbaum, 2012: 62).

In order to understand the multilingual attainments of Chinese diaspora in Australia, I have adopted the theoretical framework of family language policy discussed above. The paper will explore issues between parents' language ideology and family language practice, in particular how parents shape their children's language development, why and how they determine a particular home language will be maintained or not maintained in the family domain.

METHODOLOGY

The study adopts a narrative approach to examine the micro aspect of family language policy and the rationale behind it. Small-scale in-depth interviews were conducted with the key participants to reconstruct a family language history. This method is important for exploring explicit and overt planning in relation to language use among family members and the language attitude and choices of the participants towards multilingual achievement or under-achievement. The study mainly focuses on family members' personal experience in the local Chinese communities in Australia. These interviews aimed to disclose the influence of the family language policy and ideologies on shaping family language practice and people's language attitude on the carrying out of the linguistic practice. Language attitudes may be positive or negative, and may be motivated by instrumental or integrated attitudes (Gardner and Lambert, 1972), based on a range of extra-linguistic factors, either socioeconomic, cultural or political.

Three extended families in Sydney were selected for this project. In-depth face-to-face interviews or telephone conversations were conducted with the third generation of the Chinese diaspora family members. The interviews with each participant lasted about two to three hours and were recorded. Content analysis was the method used for data analysis. Only two of the families are presented in this paper, as the third family case was very similar to the Chan family.

1   Multilingual Attainments: The Chan Family

There have been four generations of the Chan family in Sydney. I was able to interview most family members of the third generation, from whom I recorded the family history. The first generation, John Chan, was born in Doumen in Guangdong, China. He arrived in Australia in the last years of the nineteenth century and, after working in the North Queensland goldfield for several years, became a market gardener, then moved to Melbourne. During this time, John returned to Doumen and married, bringing his wife to Melbourne. Their family languages were Doumen and limited English. His son David was born around 1905 in Australia and was sent back to Doumen at age of 7 for Chinese primary schooling. David returned to Australia when he was 18 and worked with his father in the Melbourne vegetable markets. When David was 23, he returned to Doumen and married a Doumen girl. His first son, Stephen, was born there. Over the next eight years David lived in Melbourne while his family lived in Doumen. He sent money to the family and occasionally joined them in Doumen. His daughter Jane was born in Doumen during that time.

When the Japanese war started, his wife and family joined David in Melbourne. At that time Stephen was 12, and Jane was 10. The family moved to the countryside in NSW where they operated a general store and market gardens. In the following years, three more children were born: Mary, Sam and Helen. At the time the family was united in Australia David was bilingual, whereas his wife and their children Stephen and Jane spoke only Doumen.

Chan's second generation was more bilingual than their first generation; David had good Chinese literacy and spoken home dialect as well as good command of spoken English, and his wife spoke their home dialect and limited English. The third generation, however, developed multilingual skills, whereas most of the fourth generation became monolingual in English. Stephen had had a few years of Chinese education in his hometown and then, at the age of 14 went to school in rural Australia. From this he learned English and later went on to learn Cantonese and Mandarin. He explained:

> I am the first son of the family. My father had a lot of expectations from me, I suppose this is our Chinese culture, I cannot escape. My father was always strict on me and insisted I make a good model for my siblings, I started working with him in the market when I was very young, I had to look after the family. As for language at home, I always had to remind my siblings to speak Doumen otherwise Dad would be upset. So we only speak Doumen when we talked to each other. My dad always boasted about his Chinese literacy skills and how good he could write Chinese characters. He bought some Chinese calligraphy and paintings from China every time he visited home. He bought Chinese books for us to read, but it was very difficult for us, there was no Chinese schools in rural NSW.

Stephen mastered bilingual skills when he was a child through his primary schooling in China and his later schooling in Australia. He also expanded his language skills when he was an adult. He stated:

> I had a Chinese education in Doumen until 10 years old, so my Chinese literacy was at primary school level. I went to school in rural Australia. From this I learnt English and later on picked up Cantonese as I have many Cantonese friends. I need to use Cantonese to do business with local Chinese.
>
> I learned Mandarin out of the necessity to communicate with people from the Chinese Consulate in Sydney when I was the president of

the Chinese Association. I hired a private tutor to teach me Mandarin. Since 1993, I have received many official visitors from China.

In a traditional Chinese family, the eldest son takes more responsibilities in the family life. This was particularly true for Stephen.

> Dad was very strict with me. I had to speak Doumen at home. He said I needed to set a good example for my siblings. Mum could only speak limited English, I often helped her manage the family store after school. At home we always spoke Doumen. Until now when my sisters and brothers meet once a month we still speak it.

As a father, Stephen also insisted his children learn more languages. He and his wife provided Cantonese as a home language and also sent their children to weekend Chinese community schools. He was proud of his FLP and he explained that his children have benefitted by being bilingual. He said:

> My children speak English and Cantonese. My wife and I only speak Cantonese to them. I sent them to the community school to learn Cantonese, and Chinese characters, as there were no schools teaching Doumen. Cantonese was an important language in Sydney. They needed it for communicating with local Chinese. My elder son is a doctor and he has a clinic in China Town and a lot of patients only speak Cantonese.

Stephen speaks good Cantonese and explained Doumen is very close to Cantonese; as he had many Cantonese friends, he soon picked up Cantonese. He learned Mandarin out of the necessity to communicate with people from mainland China in Sydney. "I hired a private tutor to pick up my Mandarin", he explained. Stephen often returned to his hometown with his father and still retains strong links there.

Mary was the first child born in Australia. She is the one with the best education with a multilingual repertoire. She speaks English, Doumen, Cantonese and Mandarin. She studied Mandarin Chinese at a university and became an academic at a university. In the interview she explained:

> My father was very strict with our language at home. He said if we did not speak our hometown language we could not eat any food at home. We only spoke Doumen at home when I was young. Even now we speak Doumen when we have family gathering. My dad also encouraged me to learn Mandarin Chinese at the university. He was very proud of me when I got a university degree in Chinese studies. He always reminded us of our Chinese culture and the value of our language.

May obtained Mandarin through her academic studies and activities and the necessity of being able to communicate with students from the mainland with whom she came into contact. May's husband was from Taishan, a different Cantonese dialect, so she learned to speak it too. May's only child speaks Mandarin, German and English, which she learned from a private secondary school. Her daughter understands Taishan but does not speak it. May explained:

> I was not very strict with my daughter. My daughter understands Taishanhua. When we spoke to her Taishan, she often replied in English. We sent her to a community school to learn Mandarin. I think Mandarin is more important for her career. I am teaching Chinese and I often invite a lot Chinese scholars to my home, my daughter picked up Mandarin from them. The problem was the teaching method in the weekend school was very poor. Her day school only offered German and French. However she studied Chinese as her major at the university and went to China as an exchange student for one year.

Sam was the second son of the Chan family; he speaks English, Doumen and Cantonese, but he cannot read and write Chinese. His wife is from Hong Kong. They have two children who both speak Cantonese and English. Sam explained:

> I did not go to weekend schools to learn Chinese formally, I am basically illiterate in the Chinese written language. We sent our children to Chinese community language school when they were young, they were reluctant to go. I simply forced them to go like my father did to us. My son went to China as an exchange student, he is now fluent in Mandarin.

The youngest daughter in the family, Helen, speaks Doumen, Mandarin and English. She was not impressed by her father's language policy at home and said:

> I did not speak English when I went to school. It was very embarrassing. I did not do this to my children. I think it was cruel. I was upset with my parents. I left school early, because I was discriminated against by my teachers and peers as I am a Chinese.

Because of her bad experience in school, she wants her children to be bilingual. However, her choice of language is Mandarin, not Doumen. She explained the reason for her choice:

> My husband is from Qingdao, I picked up Mandarin. I think Mandarin is more important than Doumen, because Mandarin is spoken in mainland China, Singapore and Taiwan. It is more useful for my children's future careers. My husband and I speak Mandarin at home. We often

took my children to China. My children realized they need to learn Mandarin as they need to talk to their cousins in China. Now they can talk to their clients in China too.

The data show the Chan family is multilingual, through marriage (Helen and Sam), by formal study (May) or by transnational schooling with the home country (David, Stephen and Jane), by weekend schools or university exchanges (Sam's children). The most important factor for the third generation being multilingual is the family language policy and practice enforced by their father, David, who insisted on speaking the home tongue language. This policy was against the trend for Australian assimilationist language policy and anti-Chinese migration legislation during the time that the third generation was growing up. The period also saw the turmoil period in China of the Cultural Revolution 1966–1977, which completely removed the ability for any Chinese families to have interactions with their hometown.

There are certainly many gains and pains for the third generation, as Helen indicated above. The ideology of the family language policy has been expanded to the fourth generation children, as China has opened doors and provided many opportunities for the fourth generation, who are multilingual if their parents have insisted on speaking the home language.

The first and second generations of this Chan family are bilingual or multilingual. They have had strong emotional connections with their hometown. The retention of bilingualism in the face of a largely monolingual environment is due to the efforts of the individual families. The third generation's ability to expand their bilingualism demonstrates marriage, economic activities and education playing important roles.

2　Language Shift: The Lee Family

William Lee arrived in Australia as human cargo in a shipload of Chinese from Xiamen who were brought to Australia by an enterprising Chinese

The first generation: monolingual	Speaking Doumen (one of the Chinese dialects) [John and his wife]
The second generation: bilingual	Speaking English and Doumen [David and his wife]
The third generation: multilingual	Speaking English, Doumen, Cantonese and Mandarin [Jane, Mary, Sam and Helen]
The fourth generation: multilingual	Speaking English, German and/or Mandarin [Geoff, etc.]

Figure 16.3　Chan Family's Language Tree

national who ran a supply business in Bathurst NSW. This business supplied miners on the Bathurst Goldfields with vegetables and equipment in 1884. William spoke Hokkien and was indentured for 18 months as a miner on the goldfields. During this period, William became very aware of the danger posed to a Chinese from aggressive, racist behaviour of the white miners. When he completed his apprenticeship, he went to Sydney and joined a group of former miners from Xiamen in establishing market gardens near Mascot in Sydney.

William prospered during the 1880s in a sustained period of economic development in Australia. He became registered as a resident of the Colony of NSW. In 1886, he returned to Xiamen and got married. He returned to Sydney in 1888 and was surprised to find that it took some time before he and his wife were allowed off the boat. He subsequently learned that an earlier ship from China had been turned back by angry mobs who were against the "invasion" of Chinese. Remembering his experiences on the goldfields, Lee resolved to stay as far away from confrontation as he could.

William had two sons, Bob and Andrew, and one daughter, Anne, and they were born in Sydney. The family prospered and lived quietly in the south of Sydney on their small market garden. He supplied Chinese stall-holders at the markets and dealt occasionally with Chinese restaurants.

All the children in the second generation spoke English and Hokkien, because his wife spoke Hokkien (the language from her hometown in Amoy) to their children when they were little. They grew up bilingual.

Bob married a Chinese girl in Australia and had two sons: Harry and Richard. The third generation, however, are monolingual. As Harry explained:

> We only speak English at home. My mum can speak some Cantonese as her family was from Guangdong. Dad wanted us to learn better English, and try to demonstrate that we were Australian. He did not give us any Chinese names. Because of his experiences he did not want his children to suffer discrimination. We have a lot of Australian friends and he often invited Australian friends over for a BBQ.

Richard mentioned that his wife is Australian, so they only speak English at home. He has very little knowledge about his family history and has never been to China. He said:

> I only speak Hokkien with Mum and Dad. My wife and I spoke English at home. We hardly know our hometown. Neither my father or Grandfather ever mentioned our hometown. I only knew we came from Amoy.

Bob's brother, Andrew, has two daughters: Jenny and Barbara. Jenny married an Australian doctor and Barbara remained single. Jenny is concerned

The first generation: monolingual	Speaking Hokkien (one of the Chinese dialects) [William and his wife]
The second generation: bilingual	Speaking English and Hokkien [Bob, Andrew and Anne]
The third generation: monolingual	Speaking English [Harry, Richard, Jenny and Barbara]
The fourth generation: monolingual	Speaking English [Kathy, etc.]

Figure 16.4   Lee Family's Language Tree

her children don't know her family history and sent them to a Chinese Saturday school. She explained:

> I felt it was a great shame for me not to have learned Hokkien and I sent my children to Chinese school every Saturday to learn Mandarin as there were no Hokkien lessons. But they refused to go after a few weeks. It was very hard as their friends only speak English.

The Lee family only maintained their home language until the second generation. The third and fourth generations only speak English. Their family language tree is very different from the Chan family's.

The Lee family took an approach to be integrated with the dominant English-speaking people. Integration was their purpose. The revival of bilingualism in the family needed outside support, such as that available from the education system.

Discussion and Conclusion

The Chan family case shows a transnational multilingual acquisition involved in the second and third generations. David had Chinese education until 18, his son Stephen had Chinese education until 10. It is clear the family took a defensive strategy as their FLP, with mother tongue maintenance at home and English learning at school, and the third generation also expanded their linguistic repertoires. Like any other language planning, three-stage family language planning was undertaken by the Chan family.

- Corpus planning:
  Parents decided on Doumen as a home language with connection to hometown in China.
- Status planning:
  Parents made decisions to choose the home language, not the dominant language. They regarded the hometown language as the most important language for the home.

- Acquisition planning:
  Schooling in the hometown; marriage in the home country; hometown language only at home; weekend community schooling.

The Lee family made their decision to give up Hokkien in favour of English. The family took the coping strategy as their FLP; the third generation children became monolingual. They also had three stage planning:

- Corpus planning
  Parents decided on English for its connection with new home, Australia.
- Status planning:
  Parents made decisions on FLP.
- Acquisition planning:

Schooling in English; speaking only English at home.

The cases of the Chan and Lee families show that family ideology has an important role to play in their children's multilingual attainment. Their choices and decisions are driven by ideological, pragmatic and emotional factors (Stavans, 2012).

It is clear the Chan family maintained bilingualism or multilingualism for four generations, whereas the Lee family had a language shift in the third generation. Analysing FLP through the perspective of coping and defence mechanisms helps us get a better understanding of the emotional aspects involved in language decisions in multilingual families and explains their unconscious, defensive and adaptive roles. Due to the dynamic nature of defences, FLP also exhibits a dynamic aspect. FLPs might change in response to external or internal changes, although this may not be conscious. Families' linguistic "behaviours can change, preferences modify and ideological stances transform, just like in other contexts of language policy or indeed of any policy" (Tannenbaum, 2012: 64).

This study has shown the influence of family language policy and ideologies in shaping family language practice and people's language attitudes on the carrying out of the linguistic practice. Language attitudes may be positive, for example, to maintain the home language, like the Chan family who were motivated by keeping the home heritage, or negative, for example, like the Lee family who were motivated by instrumental and integrated attitudes (Gardner and Lambert, 1972). Such attitudes are based on a range of extra-linguistic factors, either socioeconomic, cultural or political.

The results of this research have provided crucial insights into the parents' and family members' decision-making process. The study shows that age and gender are the least influential factors, although the person's position in the Chinese family structure plays an important role, such as Stephen who, as the eldest child of the Chan family, had a family duty to implement his father's language policy. Education in the home language is another significant factor that has influenced multilingual achievement and career success among the Chinese diaspora in Australia, as indicated by the examples of the Chan family. Li and Zhu (2011) indicate that there is changing linguistic hierarchy among the varieties of the Chinese language in Britain. This paper confirms the same situation in Australia. Despite the fact that the third generation of the Chan family mainly speaks Doumen and Cantonese, Mandarin has become the language of the fourth generation, as parents want their children to learn Mandarin in order to gain economic benefit from the fast growing economic development in China.

Whereas some Chinese diaspora families in Australia have shifted to English, the dominant language, which holds political and economic capital, such as for employment and education opportunities, some Chinese families have maintained multilingualism and strong cultural identities. Given the strong political and economic power China has gained in recent years, multilingualism may return as a major trend of the Chinese diasporas in Australia against language shift and monolingual assimilation.

REFERENCES

Australian Archives (NSW), Security Service Investigation Branch files, 1940–44, C320C9.

Australian Bureau of Statistics (25 October 2007). Sydney (Statistical Division). *2006 Census QuickStats*. Retrieved 4 January 2010.

Baker, C. (2006). *Foundations of Bilingual Education and Bilingualism*. Clevedon: Multilingual Matters.

Barkhuizen, G. (2006). Immigrant parents' perceptions of their children's language practices: Afrikaans speakers living in New Zealand. *Language Awareness*, 15(2):63–79.

Caldas, S.J. (2006). *Raising bilingual-biliterate children in monolingual cultures*. Clevedon, UK: Multilingual Matters Press.

Curdt-Christiansen, X.L. (2009). Invisible and visible language planning: Ideological factors in family language policy of Chinese immigrant families in Quebec. *Lang policy*, 8: 351–375.

De Houwer, A. (1999). Environmental factors in early bilingual development: The role of parental beliefs and attitudes. *Bilingualism and migration*, (eds) Guus Extra and Ludo Verhoeven, 75–96. New York, NY: Mouton de Gruyter.

Doyle, W. (1998). John Shying, 1815–1992, Research Papers, State Library of NSW, Mitchell Library manuscript 5857.

Fitzgerald, F. (2008). *Red Tape Gold Scissors: The Story of Sydney's Chinese*, second edition, Sydney: Halstead Press.

Fogle, L.W. (2008). Home-school connections for international adoptees: Producing academic language in parent-child interactions. *Child's play? Second language acquisition and the younger learner*, (eds) Jenefer Philp, Rhonda Oliver and Alison Mackey, 279–301. Amsterdan, The Netherlangs: John Benjamins.

Gardner, R.C. & Lambert, W.E. (1972). *Attitudes and motivation in second-language learning*. Rowley, Mass: Newbury House.

Gregory, E. (2001). Sisters and brothers as language and literacy teachers: Synergy between siblings playing and working together. *Journal of Early Childhood Literacy*, 1(3): 301–322.

Guardado, M. (2008). Language, identity, and cultural awareness in Spanish-speaking families. *Canadian Ethnic Studies*, 40(3), 171-181.

Jones, P. (2007). *New Pathways or Old Trajectories? The Chinese Diaspora in Australia, 1985 to 2005*. Papers presented at workshop on Chinese in the Pacific: Where to Now? Canberra: The Australian National University.

Kenner, C. (2004). *Becoming Biliterate: young children learning different writing systems*. Stoke-on-Trent: Trentham Books.

Kenner, C., Ruby, M., Jessel, J., Gregory, E., & Arju, T. (2007). Intergenerational learning between children and grandparents. *Journal of Early Childhood Research*, 5(3): 219–243.

King, K. A. (2000). Language ideologies and heritage language education. *International Journal of Bilingual Education and Bilingualism*, 3(3): 167–184.

King, K.A. (2001). *Language revitalization processes and prospects: Quichua in the Ecuadorian Andes*. Clevedon, UK: Multilingual Matters.

King, K. A., & Fogle, L. (2006). Bilingual parenting as good parenting: parents' perspectives on family language policy for additive bilingualism. *International Journal of Bilingual Education and Bilingualism*, 96: 695–712.

King, K.A., Fogle, L. and Logan-Terry, A. (2008). Family language policy. *Language and Linguistics Compass* 2(5): 907–922.

Kyratzis, A. (2004). Talk and interaction among children and the co-construction of peer groups and peer cultures. *The Annual Review of Anthropology*, 33: 625–649.

Lanza, E. (1997). *Language mixing in infant bilingualism*. Oxford, UK: Clarendon Press.

Li, Wei & Zhu, Hua. (2011). Changing hierarchies in Chinese language education for the British Chines learners. *Teaching and learning Chinese in global contexts*, (eds) L. Tsung & K. Cruickshank, 11–27. London: Cuntinuum.

Okita, T. (2001). *Invisible work: Bilingualism, language choice and childrearing in inter-married families*. Amsterdam, The Netherlands: John Benjamins.

Pauwels, A. (2005). Maintaining the community language in Australia: challenges and roles for families. *The International Journal of Bilingual Education and Bilingualism*, 8(2–3), 124–131.

Pavlenko, A. (2004). 'Stop doing that, ia komu skazala!' Language choice and emotions in parent–child communication. *Journal of Multilingual and Multicultural Development*, 25(2/3): 179–203.

Piller, I. (2002). *Bilingual couples talk: The discursive construction of hybridity*. Amsterdam: John Benjamins.

Sakuragi, T. (2008). Attitudes toward language study and cross-cultural attitudes in Japan. *International Journal of Intercultural Relations*, 32: 81–90.

Schiffman, H. (2006). Language policy and linguistic culture. In *An introduction to language policy: Theory and method*, (ed) T. Ricento, 95–110.Oxford: Oxford University Press.

Smolicz, J., Secombe, M.,& Hudson,D. (2001). Family collectivism and minority languages as core values of culture among ethnic groups in Australia. *Journal of Multilingual and Multicultural Development*, 22(2), 152–172.

Spolsky, B. (2006). Language policy failures-Why won't they listen? In *'Along the routes to power': Explorations of empowerment through language*, (eds) M. Putz, J.A. Fishman, and J.N.v. Aertselaer, 87–106. Berlin: Mouton de Gruyter.

Spolsky, B. (2008). Family language management: Some preliminaries. In *Studies in language and language education: Essays in honor of Elite Ohlstain*, (eds) A. Stavans and I. Kupferberg, 429–450. Jerusalem: The Hebrew University Magnes Press.

Spolsky, B. (2012). Family language policy-the critical domain, *Journal of Multilingual and Multicultural Development*, 33(1), 3–11.

Stavans, A. (2012). Language policy and literacy practices in the family: The case of Ethiopian parental narrative input. *Journal of Multilingual and Multicultural Development*, 33(1): 13–33.

Takeuchi, M. (2006). *Raising children bilingually through the 'one parent-one language' approach: A case study of Japanese mothers in the Australian context.* Bern, Switzerland: Peter Lang.

Tannenbaum, M. (2012). Family Language Policy as a Form of Coping or Defence Mechanism. *Journal of Multilingual and Multicultural Development*, 33(1): 57–66.

Tuominen., A. K. (1999). Who decides the home language? A look at multilingual families. *International Journal of the Sociology of Language*, 140: 59–76.

Wood, J. (1994). *Chinese Residency in the Haymarket and Surry Hills 1880 to 1902*, BA Hons thesis, University of Sydney.

Zadunaisky Ehrlich, S., and Blum-Kulka, S. (2010). Peer talk as a 'double opportunity space': The case of argumentative discourse. *Discourse & Society* 21: 211–233.

Zentella, A. C. (1997). *Growing up bilingual: Puerto Rican children in New York.* Malden, MA: Blackwell Publisher.

17 Across Generations and Geographies
Communication in Chinese Heritage Language Speaking Households

Agnes Weiyun He

1 HERITAGE LANGUAGE

Whereas current scholarship has problematized the notion of "heritage language" both on the basis of "heritage" learners' own orientations toward such a notion (Blackledge & Creese, 2008) and in terms of lifespan development of the "heritage" speaker (He, 2013), the term "heritage language" (hereafter HL) has conventionally referred to an immigrant, indigenous, or ancestral language that a speaker has a personal relevance and desire to (re) connect with (Fishman, 1991; Valdés, 2001; Wiley, 2001). In the United States, Canada, and the UK, the term "heritage language" has often been used synonymously with "community language," "home language," "native language," and "mother tongue" to refer to a language other than English used by immigrants and their children. Accordingly, a heritage speaker is someone who is raised in a home where a non-mainstream language is spoken and who is to some degree bilingual in the home language and in the mainstream language (Valdés, 2001: 38), but whose home language does not typically reach native-like attainment in adulthood (Benmamoun et al., 2010). HL speakers have most likely been exposed to the HL since birth and may have used the HL during the initial years in their life and on and off subsequently, but have never developed the full range of phonological, morphological, syntactic, pragmatic, and discourse patterns which will enable them to use the HL in the scope and sophistication characteristic of and comparable to the native speaker. HL speaking households thus refer to families where there are at least two generations who have different linguistic and cultural upbringings and who speak the HL to varying degrees and at varying proficiency levels.

This chapter examines features of communication in American households where Chinese is used as a heritage language against this backdrop of global migration. It focuses on everyday interactions that take place in CHL speaking households. It aims to address the following two broad questions: How is discourse in heritage language speaking households impacted by immigration, cultural and linguistic contact/conflict/convergence, and global information networks? And what is the role of child HL speakers in shaping their family discourse?

2   DATA AND METHODS

Data are drawn from a dozen households with child or teen speakers of Chinese as a heritage language. Participants in this study include five child CHL speakers and eight teen CHL speakers and their family members. Naturally occurring interactions during dinner time, playtime, homework time, and telephone/video call time were recorded and transcribed. Informal interviews were conducted in the participants' households over the course of one year.

Elsewhere (He, 2013, 2014), I argued for a lifespan approach to address the complex relationships that obtain between heritage language practices, identities, and cultures. My proposal is that scholarship in heritage language use should consider more comprehensive settings beyond schools, broader time spans beyond childhood, participant structures that go beyond the individual to include relevant generations and social networks, and a wider range of communicative resources beyond speech. Only then may we appreciate the fact that language competencies, choices, and ideologies change over the speaker's lifespan, along with changing motivations, social networks, and opportunities.

To understand this complex trajectory of growth and change, I portray a prototype speaker of Chinese as a heritage language named "Jason" and reconstruct his language development process from a collage of different Chinese HL speakers of various ages I have encountered in my research over the last ten years (He, 2006, 2011, 2014). In other words, my goal is to present a linguistic and cultural biography of "Jason" that is a synthesis of the observational, interview, reported, and audio/video recorded data that have been collected from a range of subjects in settings and situations that "Jason" would have experienced at various stages of his life from early childhood to early adulthood. This composite "Jason" represents a model script of the life experiences of Chinese HL speakers with respect to their language development. In some sense, this approach parallels a number of recent efforts in applied linguistics and linguistic anthropology, including studies of interactional and sociocultural aspects of language learner discourse (Kanagy, 1999; Lerner, 1995; Ohta, 1999), the research on identity investment and language learning over time and space (Norton, 2000; Rampton, 1995), the examination of socialization across speech events (Wortham, 2005), and the tracking of a language learner's behavioral change across interactions (Markee, 2008). Conceptualized and implemented in this way, the composite lifespan approach is thus able to reveal that, in the complex process of HL socialization, Jason's family's linguistic landscape evolves as Jason undergoes various stages and phases of his life.

In what follows, I present a re-storied chronological account of Jason's family discursive practices, on the basis of a dozen households with child or teen speakers of Chinese as a heritage language, as described previously. I focus on the following two aspects: (1) the ways in which child HL speakers (re-)shape their parents' language forms (lexical choice, pronunciation, syntactic structure, interactional strategy); and (2) the ways in which children and parents complement each other's language and cultural skills as they navigate and negotiate with other members of their extended families as well as with the local and global communities. In all data extracts, J stands for Jason; M stands for Mother.

Data analysis will be guided by Goffman's (1981) concept of "footing," which refers to the "alignment we take up to ourselves and the others present as expressed in the way we manage the production and reception of an utterance" (1981: 128). In his model of communication, Goffman outlines varying forms and degrees of participation in social interaction and breaks down the roles of speaking and hearing into specific "footings." With regard to the production of utterances, speakers may take up various footings in relation to their own remarks. By employing different "production formats" (1981: 145), they may convey distinctions between the (a) animator, (b) author, and (c) principal of what is said. The "animator" is the person who produces the utterance. The "author" is the person who originates the beliefs and sentiments and composes the utterances through which they are expressed. And the "principal" is the person whose viewpoint or position is being expressed in and through the utterance.

With regard to the reception of utterances, the recipient of an utterance may also assume (or be assigned by another speaker) various "participation statuses" (1981: 137). The recipient may have an official status of a "ratified participant" in interaction, in which case she may either be "addressed" (as in two-party conversation) or "unaddressed" (as in multiparty conversation wherein each given moment only the participant may receive the speaker's visual attention while the others are included in interaction but not directly addressed). The recipient may also not be an official, ratified participant in the interaction but have access to the interaction as a "bystander" in two different ways. She may be an "eavesdropper," purposely and maybe secretively listening in on conversations, or an "overhearer," unintentionally and inadvertently hearing the conversation. A speaker may purposely design her talk in order to be heard by someone who is not officially participating in interaction, in which case the otherwise "unintended overhearer" becomes an "intended overhearer."

3   CHILD HL SPEAKERS' IMPACT ON THEIR PARENTS' LANGUAGE

It is worth pointing out at the outset that bilingual communication begins at the very early stage, even before the child becomes proficient in English.

Jason's mother, who immigrated to the US in her early 30s, gave the following account of the beginning of bilingual practice at her home.

Extract (1) Mother's account

We knew from the very beginning that English will be very important for our children. They are going to need it for school and later for life. Our English is not good. So we cannot teach them good English. When Jason was young, he didn't have much exposure to English, except for watching TV programs such as Sesame Street, Barney and Blue's Clues. I had wanted to send him to preschool so that he can learn properly, but it was too expensive. In the beginning we took him to work at our store, where we kept a separate space for him to play, sleep, and watch TV. Sometimes our customers would play with him or give him some little toy. Somehow he could figure out that they didn't speak Chinese and he would always say to them the only two English expressions we taught him: "Thank you" and "Bye bye." After Jasmine was born, my mother came to help us and to live with us. So we would leave Jason at home with Grandma and baby sister when we attended the store. We worked long hours those years. When we finally got home for dinner, Jason was usually almost ready for bed. I would bathe him and read him some stories when I was not too tired. The stories were mostly in Chinese, like 孙悟空 Sun Wukong (the Monkey King), 葫芦娃 Hulu Wa, 盘古开天地 Pangu kai tiandi, 女娲补天 Nuwa Bu Tian, etc. We had some children's books in English too, from some of our kind customers. But I always felt funny reading them. I never actually read them to Jason. It was unnatural to me and I felt somewhat embarrassed too, I guess.

Jason was a pretty smart little kid. He learned from Grandma how to count in Chinese and he was even able to do some rudimentary math such as two plus three and later on two digit additions and subtractions. He was very observant and very talkative. He was reading a little bit in Chinese too. I don't really remember exactly how he learned English. It must be the TV. Or maybe it was from the other kids that he met in the play area in the neighborhood. I still feel bad that I didn't do anything about his English in those years. With his sister Jasmine it was better. I knew better. I took her to our local library for the "Mommy and Me" program and other activities for toddlers. For Jason, I did nothing. I only remember one day he started calling me "mom" instead of "mama." I was surprised. But I was happy too. I knew an excellent command of English is the key to a bright future. Maybe our own life goals cannot be fully reached because of language deficiencies, but our children should have no reason not to fulfill their dreams. Jason started Kindergarten when he was almost 6. The first day of school, I walked him to the bus stop. When the bus pulled up, I said to him, "Have a nice day!"—something I heard our store customers say often. As he boarded the bus, I added, "I love you!" I would never say such things in Chinese. It's strange. I never felt comfortable with English, but those words simply slipped out of my mouth and expressed precisely how I felt. As I watched the bus leave, tears rolled down my cheeks.

As we can see from this account, the process from "necessary" to "natural" bilingualism in fact begins at a rather early time, even before Jason started schooling. Parents orient to the child's needs (needs as perceived by parents themselves) and adjust their language choice accordingly. Concurrently, as the parents' own socialization into the US society and the English language unfolds, the social meaning and personal significance of language choice evolves as well. In Jason's mother's case, English transformed from a useful but alien, unnatural, uncomfortable language to an occasionally more spontaneous, more expressive form of communication. The young Jason, simply by virtue of his presence (rather than his competence in English), already has a silent but salient influence on his mother's gradual shift toward mixed language use.

Below, I will delineate a number of ways in which child HL speakers shape their parents' language forms. I highlight the discourse strategies of *reformulation* and *repair* that are used by the participants during language mediation both among themselves and with the outside world. *Reformulation* refers to the presentation of the same communicative goal with an alternative linguistic structure, affective stance, or conversational style. *Repair* refers to the deployment of conversational-structural resources to address problems in speaking and understanding.

3.1 Reformulation

In second language acquisition literature, a *recast* is a discourse strategy used by expert speakers (such as language teachers) to correct the novice speakers' (e.g., language learners') errors in such a way that communication is not obstructed (Ellis & Sheen, 2006). To *recast* the novice speaker's speech, the expert speaker will re-present the novice speaker's speech back to the novice in a modified, corrected form. Recasts are often used both by teachers in formal educational settings and by interlocutors in naturalistic language acquisition settings. "Reformulation" differs from "recast" in that there may or may not be any speech "errors" involved. Reformulation is the hearer's alternative rendering of the speaker's utterance in part or in whole with the purpose of clarifying and promoting the speaker's communicative purpose and goal.

Reformulation: Children's Tacit Scaffolding
In the following segment, Jason is playing with another boy who also comes from a CHL family background. The boys were fussing and fighting over

some toy. To distract them from the squabble, Jason's mother asked if either of the boys would like to play with a different toy—a caboose.

Extract (2) "Caboose"

((1st grade, during a play date))
     001 M: 来来你跟他玩（.）来呀跟-
     Come come you and he play together ok?
     002 ((pause))
     003 M: Ni::ce 不抢啊：：
     Don't' fight ok.
     004 I give you I give you-
     005 J: You take this I ta[ke this
     006 Playdate: [I don wannit=
     007 M: =who want the kooboose?
     008 J: Caboose (.2) mine=
     009 Playdate: =I want the caboose
     010 M: 这个 caboose- caboose 大家 share, OK?
     This everybody

As can be seen from the extract, when Mother says the word "caboose" incorrectly (line 007), young Jason did not actually explicitly correct her. Instead, he reformulates the pronunciation of the word in his exhibited orientation toward the ownership of the toy (line 008). From Jason's re-production of the word "caboose" in the immediate next turn, we can tell that he (a) comprehends his mother's erroneous speech, (b) is in command of the correct form, and (c) does not explicitly correct his mother's error, as evidenced by the fact that the "fighting sequence" between Jason and his playmate continues smoothly without any insertion or side sequence specifically dedicated to fixing Mother's mistake. Whereas Jason appears to target his playmate as his primary addressee with the production of "caboose" (008), Mother, as a bystander, overhears and notices Jason's and his playmate's correct rendering of the word "caboose" and corrects herself in the next turn (010). This is perhaps an example of what Evelyn Hatch (1978) called "discourse scaffolding" in the context of SLA, although in this case the scaffolding may not be intentional.

Reformulation: Children Coaching Parents

Sometimes children's reformulation does concern parents' apparent mistakes, but is geared toward reaching a more expedient or desirable interactional outcome, as is the case in (3).

Extract (3) "I don't speak English"

((9th grade, phone ringing; some market survey))
     001 M: Hello

002 (.4)
003 M: Who?
004 (.5)
005 M: No:: he not home=
006 J: =°I don't speak English°
007 M: I don't have time. Don't speak English. Bye.
008 ((off the phone))
009 M: 我还以为是你二姑呢!
I thought it was your second aunt!

Unlike (2), where Mother pronounced "caboose" wrongly, in this case, nothing is "wrong." As Mother is engaged in the phone conversation (lines 001–005) and explaining to the caller (a telemarketer) that her husband is not home (005), Jason, a bystander, overhears the conversation and thinks of a more efficient way to close the conversation. Exploiting the obvious non-native-ness of his mother's English, Jason suggests that his mother tell the caller that she does not speak English (006). He does so not by issuing a directive to his mother (for example, "Say . . ."), but by ventriloquizing his mother in a soft and quiet voice (006). His suggestion is designed as a replacement for, or at least an addition to, Mother's original response ("he not home," 005). The upshot is that Mother indeed appropriates Jason's suggestion, presenting it as an additional reason (besides "I don't have time") for hanging up the phone immediately (007). As can be seen from Mother's remark off the phone (009), she indeed had no interest in speaking to the caller (whom she had assumed to be a relative when she picked up the phone). Thus in this case, Jason's reformulation contributed to Mother's expedient closure of an unintended phone conversation. In Goffmanian terms, Mother becomes the animator, Jason becomes the author, and both Mother and Jason become principals as they both share the same viewpoint. Jason and Mother collaboratively perform the role of the addressee in this phone conversation.

Reformulation: Children Refocusing Adults' Utterances
Although cases like (3) do happen, they are relatively rare. More commonly, children proffer reformulations of their parents' utterances as they assert/ insert themselves in the actual interaction which they find is taking place in a less than desirable fashion due to their parents' inadequate proficiency in English or lack of familiarity with the discourse norms in English speaking contexts. In the next episode, Jason's mother is explaining to a professional plumber the problems with her kitchen.

Extract (4) "Drain open no use"

((10th grade, interaction with a professional plumber))
001 Serviceman: You have a problem?

002 M: Yes water always stop. Many time don't go down.
003 We try the liquid. Didn't work!
004 (.4)
005 J: It's totally clogged. We tried the drain opener. It didn't work=
006 M: =Right. Drain [open no use.
007 Serviceman: [Ok where's the ((inaudible))

In (4), even though Mother's utterances (lines 002–003) are comprehensible, they are not getting an immediate reaction and response from the plumber (pause in line 004). At this point, Jason interjects by summarizing and sharpening Mother's utterances. Mother's "always" and "many time" (002) become Jason's "totally" (005). Mother's "stop" and "don't go down" (002) evolve into Jason's "clogged" (005). Mother's generic noun "liquid" gets clarified in Jason's "drain opener" (005). Although Jason does not contribute any new information, his reformulation gives Mother's utterances more focus and greater clarity, which successfully leads to the plumber's immediate response and action (007, "Ok" overlapping with Mom's turn echoing Jason and "where's the . . ." suggesting the physical action he is about to take). In terms of participation structure, it is in fact very difficult to tease apart the speech roles that Mother and Jason play in strictly Goffmanian terms. As they mirror and modify each other's wordings and utterances, they share the roles of the animator, the author, and the principal. In a quite literal sense, Jason and Mother become one speaker and one voice.

3.2   Repair

It has been documented elsewhere (e.g., He, 2003, 2011) that CHL children play an active role in both semiformal interactional settings with CHL teachers and informal settings with parents. The conversation structural mechanism of *repair* affords us an empirically accountable anchor position to carry out investigations into the interactional opportunities, rights, and obligations in the give-and-take between children and adults in CHL contexts.

When trouble in conversation occurs, it is noticed and then corrected, either by the party whose turn contains the source of trouble or by some other party. This sequence of trouble + initiation-of-correction + correction is known as a *repair trajectory*. Repair occurs when one party corrects his or her own talk or that of another party and can be accomplished in a number of ways (Sacks et al., 1974; Schegloff et al., 1977). Of particular relevance to our data are the following:

- *Self-initiated same turn repair* refers to the situation when the current speaker initiates and completes the repair within her current turn of talk and before coming to a possible completion of a complete grammatical, lexical, intonational, and pragmatic unit, also known as the turn-constructional-unit (TCU) (Ford and Thompson, 1996). It is the earliest position in which repair can be undertaken, as well as the most frequent and the most preferred type of repair (Schegloff et al., 1977).

- *Other-initiated self-completed next turn repair* is when repair is initiated by a participant other than the speaker of the trouble-source. When this happens, the repair initiation usually comes in the turn immediately subsequent to the trouble-source turn (known as next-turn-repair-initiation, or NTRI).
- *Other-initiated other-completed repair* occurs when a participant other than the speaker of the trouble-source both initiates and completes the repair.

Of the types of repair outlined above, the most preferred is self-initiated and self-completed in the same turn as the trouble-source. Other initiation and other completion of repair can index a stance of disaffiliation with the interlocutor; and the farther the distance between the trouble source and the completion of the repair, the greater and the longer the miscommunication.

Repair the Repair: Children Supplying and Substituting Lexis

In the following case, Mother is having trouble describing to her friend about the setting where she sees someone that both she and her friend know. The trouble begins in line 002 when she is searching for a word (questions addressed to herself twice ["what"], pauses, elongated filler "u:::n"), continues in line 003 when she switches to Chinese in a think-aloud monologue, and culminates in line 004 where her speech becomes full of perturbations as evidenced by fillers ("u::n", "y'know"), audible breathing, and self cut-offs ("Grey-Greyhound") until she is able to recall the word "Greyhound" and the occasion which she knows as "Greyhound Day."

Extract (5) "Groundhog party"

((7th grade, at an informal gathering with friends))
    001 M: yes yes that day the party in the party-
    002 called what (.2) u:::n called what (.2)
    003 叫什么 u::n (.2)
    what is it called
    004 last week u::n y'know (.hhh) Grey-Greyhound Day=
    005 J: =Groundhog=
    006 M: =Groundhog Groundhog party
    007 yes I see him and her (.2) her daughter I see him

Thus Mother first self-initiates and self-implements repair within her own speaking turn as she finally produces "Greyhound Day" as a smooth string of utterance, except that her recall and lexical repair is wrong—she has confused "groundhog" with "greyhound" (004). At this juncture, Jason overhears Mother's trouble and latches onto Mother's turn by proffering a next-turn, other-initiated, other-implemented, repair of Mother's self-repair. He supplies an explicit corrective substitution, "Groundhog" (005). As outlined above, of all the repair structural mechanisms, this is the type that most saliently indexes disaffiliation with the speaker and is a least preferred form of repair. Furthermore, Jason, in this case, is not the primary addressee of Mother's talk. His eavesdropper status makes his repair all the more glaring. However, Mother exhibits no reservation whatsoever about Jason's move. Just as the repair is made with no hesitations or mitigations (latching of 005 to 004), the reception of repair is equally smooth and instantaneous, as seen in the latching of 006 to 005 as well as Mother's immediate appropriation and repetition of Jason's repair, "Groundhog" (006). This example corroborates the longitudinal ethnographic observation that CHL children across all age groups play an active role in assisting and refining their parents' communication by "butting in," even when they themselves are not the intended addressees in interaction and even when they are not recruited or requested by parents.

Quasi-Repair: Children Paraphrasing Parents

In some cases, children's repair of parents' talk is rather subtle and sophisticated. It is less easily identifiable through tracking lexical choice or structural features of turn-taking. In Extract (6), Jason's mother meets Jason's teacher on the school field day. After exchanging "hellos" with Teacher, Mother asks Teacher how Jason has been doing at school.

Extract (6) "not follow"

((3rd grade, school field day))
    001 Teacher: He is such a bright kid, a real pleasure to have=
    002 M: =Really? He's not good at home (.2) not follow hhehehe
    003 ((to J)) right? Not follow?
    004 ((Teacher looks somewhat puzzled))
    005 J: ((to M)) I always listen to your words
    006 Teacher: ((to J)) Ah following the ru:les
    007 yes you do a good job following the rules.

Out of Chinese modesty, upon hearing Teacher's praise of Jason, Mother expresses surprise ("really?," line 002) and counters the teacher's compliment by characterizing Jason as "not good at home" and "not follow[ing rules at home]" (line 002) and seeking Jason's confirmation of her account (line 003). Apparently the teacher does not follow Mother's line of thought (visible puzzlement, line 004). At this point, Jason strategically answers Mother's question "Not follow?" (003) in a way that interprets "not follow" (002 and 003) as "not following Mother's words" (005). It is a very subtle form of correction of Mother's expression "not follow" (both 002 and 003), as instead of a direct repair of Mother's question, Jason embeds his repair in his response to Mother's question. His effort consequently leads to Teacher's much improved comprehension of Mother's speaking turns, as indicated by a revelation-marker "ah" (006) and an affirmation of Mother's lexical choice "follow" (006 and 007).

4 PARENT-CHILD LANGUAGE MEDIATION

Language brokering has received much scholarly attention in recent years. It refers to the practice of children of immigrant families who translate and interpret a variety of talk and texts for their parents and grandparents who have limited access to the mainstream language and culture and limited proficiency in contemporary technology. Such practice may begin in childhood or preadolescence and may continue throughout the lifespan. Tse (1996) points out that language brokers are intermediaries between linguistically and culturally different parties. Rather than rendering literal translations (as is the case with professional translators and interpreters), language brokers influence the contents and the nature of the messages they convey, and ultimately affect the perceptions and decisions of agents for whom they act. In other words, language brokers play not merely a transmission role, but a transformational role, in shaping the messages they relay. Along similar lines of thought, other scholars have used the term "culture brokering" (Trickett, Sorani, & Birman, 2010), or "para-phrasers" (Orellana, 2009; Orellana et al., 2003) to describe children of immigrants who interpret and translate.

Missing from the existing literature are, however, two important pieces of information. The first one concerns the lexical-syntactic-interactional details of language brokering. We know language brokering takes place, but we don't know the sequential, interactional, and grammatical context of such occurrences. We do not know, for example, whether language brokers volunteer brokering or are asked to broker, how their brokering is reacted and responded to, or what linguistic and interactional resources are used to accomplish the brokering. The other missing piece is the reciprocal, bidirectional nature of language and cultural brokering in which both parents and children participate. Parents, as well as children, function as brokers as they engage in multiparty, multidirectional, intergenerational, intercultural, and cross-linguistic interactions.

4.1 Interactional Context of Language Brokering

Volunteered Brokering: Literal Translation: Speaking:
Young Child for Grandmother

Language brokering starts very early, before children are even conscious of it. Jason's Grandmother speaks no English at all. Here is her account about an incident that occurred before Jason started schooling:

Extract (7) Grandma's account

*Whenever the weather was good, I'd push Jasmine [Jason's baby sister]
in a stroller for a walk and Jason would walk with me. Our favorite
destination was the playground about five minutes' walk from home.
There was a sandbox, a seesaw, and a couple of swing sets. We would
spend as much time there as possible until I needed to cook meals. Other
families in the neighborhood took their children there too. Because we
went often, we saw each other all the time. I don't know where those
families come from. Definitely not from China. Many of them are not
whites either. You always hear that America is a country of many different races; that is not false at all. . . . One day a kind-faced lady handed
me a baby bottle and said something. I didn't know what she wanted
and didn't know what to do. At this point, Jason said to that lady,
"No." I reprimanded him right away. I said how can you be so rude
and disrespectful? Jason explained to me that the lady was asking if the
bottle was ours. You see, was my grandson capable or not?!*

From this account, we can see that young Jason, even when he is merely a
bystander in the described interaction, volunteers to bridge the communication gap between Grandma and the outside world. Without Jason, Grandma
would not have been able to understand the "kind-faced lady" and would
have wronged her own grandson. Grandma is delighted by and proud of the
role Jason plays.

Solicited Brokering: Literal Translation: Reading: Teenager for Mother
As children get older, they are more frequently called to provide assistance,
as in the case below. A letter arrived from Jason's high school informing
parents of an upcoming talk for parents on college admissions. Mother read
the beginning of the letter, glanced at the rest of the letter, gave up reading,
and turned to Jason for help.

Extract (8) "What does this say?"

((10th grade))
001 M: 这说什么? 要家长都去听啊?
what does this say? Want all parents to listen?
002 哪天呢? 也没说呀
which day? It doesn't say
003 J: Thursday at 7pm. It says right here.
004 (.2)
005 J: Ok, you don't have to go. It's for juniors and seniors.

It is noteworthy that Mother does have the ability to read the letter.
She has functional reading literacy in English and if she applies herself she

should have no problem getting all the necessary information from the letter. In fact, she has had plenty of successful experience reading letters like this one when Jason was in lower grades. Judging from her question in line 001, it is clear that she understands what the letter is about. The language in the remainder of the letter is not any more difficult than what she has already read and understood in the beginning of the letter. Nonetheless, Mother stops trying to read, because of the greater ease afforded by Jason's presence. Existing literature has focused on children acting as linguistic intermediaries in contexts where adults are not functional in English; the example here suggests that this type of mediation may indeed continue even when parents become more proficient in English as their immigration experiences unfold.

Solicited Brokering: Literal Translation: Writing: Teenager for Mother

The same applies to Extract (9), where Mother is capable of writing a note to Jason's sister's teacher but nonetheless asks Jason to write it on her behalf. Hence in writing, Jason becomes Mother's animator and author.

Extract (9) "Write a note to your sister's teacher"

((10th grade))
    001 Jasmine: Mr. G said that we need a note from parents to say
    002 it's okay to stay for the club after school
    003 M: Ask 哥哥. Jason-啊,
    Ask your older brother. Jason-a:
    004 你给妹妹的老师写个条,
    you write a note to your sister's teacher
    005 就说我们同意, 啊?
    just say we agree, ok?
    006 J: o[kay
    007 M: [thank you

It is possible that the kind of distribution of discursive rights and obligation in CHL households documented in Extracts (8) and (9) coincides with the overall tendency of parents gradually relinquishing authority and expecting their children to shoulder greater responsibility as their children get older. The exact relationship between the shift of household discursive responsibility and that of responsibility in other domains of life is yet to be investigated empirically.

Cultural Brokering

A cultural broker commonly refers to a person who facilitates the border crossing of another person or group of people from one culture to another culture by bridging, linking, or mediating between groups or persons of differing cultural backgrounds. The role covers more than being an inter-preter, although this is an important attribute in cross-cultural situations where language is part of the role. CHL children, especially older children, often function as cultural brokers for their parents, as can be seen in Extract (10), where someone at the door is asking for Mother's signature and address in order to put a political candidate on the ballot.

Extract (10) "She doesn't vote"

((10th grade))
    001 M: You want me- my name? No, no, I don't want to buy=
    002 Visitor: =no ma'am I'm not selling any[thing
    003 J: [ma-
    004 M: 跟他说我们不要,
    Tell him we don't want.
    005 刚才就来过一个人
    Someone else came just a moment ago
    006 J: U:m my mom says she doesn't vote.

In this case, Mother's request is for Jason to interpret for her ("Tell him we don't want," 004). However, Jason realizes that Mother has misunderstood the visitor's intent. Hence instead of interpreting for Mother as she requested, Jason improvises a response that is relevant to the question and that effectively puts an end to the interaction between the visitor and Mom ("my mom says she doesn't vote," 006). Furthermore, Jason frames (and fakes) the response as a translation of Mother's words ("my mom says," 006). In so doing, Jason is able to accomplish multiple communicative goals. He protects Mother from the embarrassment of not comprehending the visitor, presents Mother as a competent interlocutor, meets the interactional need of the visitor, and prevents potential conflicts and breakdown in communication between Mother and the visitor. With confidence, Jason makes the visitor believe that Mother is the author and he (Jason) is merely the animator, while in effect Jason appropriates all three roles of the animator, the author, and the principal, with neither the visitor's nor Mother's knowledge.

4.2   Bi-directional Brokering

As stated previously, the literature on language and cultural brokering in immigrant families has considered the role of the children in communication in the new country but has not paid attention to that of the parents in immigrant households where communication is becoming increasingly intergenerational, cross-cultural, and global, given the advancement and availability of technology. In the following extract, (11), Jason is trying to finish an email that his mother has asked him to write to Grandpa to wish him happy birthday.

Bidirectional Brokering: Mother Co-Authoring Email to Grandpa

Extract (11) "How do you end this?"

((7th grade, writing an email in Chinese wishing Grandpa happy birthday))
001 M: Hurry up. Finish. We must go.
002 J: 'kay:: how do you end this?
003 M: Just say 祝你健康，长寿，快乐
Wish you health, longevity, joy
004 J: But I already said 健康，快乐 'n all that stuff in the beginning.
health, joy
005 Ss-so stupid!
006 M: Not stupid! That's nice. Nice thing to say.
007 Let me see . . . ((pause; reading J's computer screen))
008 Yeah yeah yeah you just- you just say
009 再次祝您健康快乐！
Once again wish you health and joy
010 ((Jason inputs Chinese using *pinyin*))
011 M: No no no not this one.
012 Not number one. Number two, next one.
013 ((differentiating two characters with the same pronunciation 在 vs. 再))

In this case it is Jason's turn to ask Mother for assistance, as he does not know how to end the email (002). After Mother gives her suggestion (003), however, Jason resists it (004) and criticizes it (005). Only after Mother's persuasion (006), careful scrutiny (007), and second attempt (009) does Jason accept her suggestion (010). As Jason inputs Chinese using the Latin alphabet-based phonetic annotation system (*pinyin*), he enters the wrong character (在 *zai* meaning *at*, which is a homophone with the correct character (再 *zai*, meaning *again*) and is thus represented by the same alphabetic letters). At this point Mother corrects Jason's mistake (011 and 012). Hence Mother plays a crucial role in authoring this email. She asks Jason to write the email. She provides wording when Jason is at a loss. And she edits Jason's writing to ensure readability. The communicative roles of the animator, the author, and the principal become blurred and blended between Mother and Jason. Comparing Jason's reaction to Mother's help in (11) with Mother's response to Jason's help in (10), we see that children are more likely to be critical of their parents' input than vice versa.

Parents' indispensable role as cultural and communicative intermediaries between CHL children and grandparents can perhaps be best illustrated by the next data extract, which captures a moment in a triadic interaction among Jason and Mother in the US and Grandma in China, via webcam.

Bidirectional Brokering: Conversation via Webcam

Extract (12) "This kid has no manners"

((11th grade))
001 M: 妈, 生日快乐啦
ma, happy birthday
002 G: 啊呀, 快乐快乐,
oh, happy happy
003 你们吃饭了吗?
Have you had dinner?
004 M: 我们挺好的, 吃了.
We are pretty good, had dinner.
005 Jason 快来, 跟姥姥说生日快乐
Jason, come quick, say happy birthday to Grandma
006 ((G and M talk about a neighbor who just visited G))
007 M: Jason, can you please come?
008 J: O::K::
009 M: ((to G)) 他特忙,
He's extremely busy,
010 学校事儿特别多
Lots of things to attend to from school
011 J: ((to G)) HI, 姥姥好, 生日快乐
Hi Grandma, happy birthday
012 G: ((to J)) 啊呀, 怎么也带了眼镜?
Oh, how come you wear glasses too?
013 学习太用功了吧?
Studying too hard?
014 J: ((to M)) Can I go now?
015 M: ((to J)) Ok, thank you.
016 ((to G)) 这孩子没礼貌,
This kid has no manners.
017 这么大了还不懂事
[He is] so big but still doesn't know how to behave

Here, after initial greetings between Mother and Grandma, Mother makes her first attempt to recruit Jason to participate in the interaction, using an imperative in Chinese (line 005). When Jason fails to respond to the summons, Mother makes another attempt, this time posing a question in English (007). As Jason reluctantly joins the conversation ("O::K::," 008), Mother justifies Jason's behavior to Grandma by citing Jason's school workload (009–010). Jason subsequently engages in minimal exchange with

Grandma, wishing her happy birthday perfunctorily (011), not replying to Grandma's queries (012, 013), and swiftly asking for Mother's permission to exit the conversation (014). Mother gives Jason permission and thanks him in English (015) on the one hand, and reprimands him in front of Grandma in Chinese (016, 017) on the other.

Mother in this case functions as an intermediary on both linguistic and cultural levels. She uses exclusively Chinese with Grandma and primarily English with Jason. She both makes excuses for Jason when he fails to show up (009 and 010) and criticizes Jason when he takes an early leave (016 and 017) to appease Grandma, but also shows appreciation for Jason's however limited participation (015). Mother is thus able to maintain rapport between Grandma and Jason, between Grandma and herself, and between Jason and herself. Through her language and cultural mediation, Mother effectively translates, transposes, and transforms linguistic information and cultural values while transcending generational and geographical divides.

5   CONCLUSIONS AND DISCUSSION

CHL children play a wide range of speech roles in family discourse and an important role in shaping their parents' discourse. Through reformulation and repair, they intentionally or unintentionally scaffold their parents' language use (Extract (2)), coach their parents (Ex. (3)), refocus their utterances (Ex. (4)), supply lexis (Ex. (5)), and strategically paraphrase their parents (Ex. (6)). They also function as language and cultural brokers for their parents as they are engaged in various everyday activities of socializing with neighbors (Ex. (7)), reading (Ex. (8)), writing (Ex. (9)), and negotiating with strangers (Ex. (10)). Parents, too, are an integral part of their children's discourse, particularly in contexts where grandparents are involved. They initiate and facilitate interaction between their children and grandparents (Exs. (11) and (12)).

In all cases above, children and parents appropriate each other's vocabularies and voices, mimic and modify each other's utterances, and collaboratively (de-)construct the speech roles of the animator, the author, and the principals, rendering them virtually indistinguishable. The highly inter-textual nature of CHL family discourse provides compelling evidence for what Goodwin terms "interactive footing" (Goodwin, 2006). It highlights the very dialogic and dynamic nature of language use in general as well as of speakership in particular. It shows that speaker agency is not an a priori given feature of a participant but is the outcome of interactions between the heterogeneous participants. Speaker agency is not located in an individual participant, but is distributed among diverse participants that jointly form a collective speaker.

This study also has implications for heritage language maintenance. We can see from this study that HL use and change is a familial and communal, rather than individual, process. Language shift within HL households entails evolving participation frameworks and evolving discursive opportunities and obligations. The multiplicity of speech roles and distributed agencies analyzed in this study may well function as resources for multidirectional, bilingual, and translingual socialization of not only the heritage but also the mainstream language and culture.

REFERENCES

Benmamoun, E., Montrul, S. & Polinsky, M. (2010). *White paper: Prolegomena to heritage linguistics.* National Heritage Language Resource Center, http://nhlrc. ucla.edu/pdf/HL-whitepaper.pdf

Blackledge, A. and Creese, A. (2008). Contesting 'Language' as 'heritage': Negotiation of identities in late modernity. *Applied Linguistics* 29 (4): 533–554.

Ellis, R. & Sheen, Y. (2006). Reexamining the role of recasts in second language acquisition. *Studies in Second Language Acquisition* 28 (4): 575–600. doi:10.1017/S027226310606027X

Fishman, J. A. (1991). *Reversing language shift.* Clevedon, UK: Multilingual Matters.

Goffman, E. (1981). Footing. In E. Goffman (ed.), *Forms of talk* (pp. 124–159). Oxford: Blackwell.

Goodwin, C. (2006). Interactive footing. In E. Holt and R. Clift (eds.), *Reporting Talk: Reported Speech in Interaction* (pp. 16–46). New York: Cambridge University Press.

Hatch, E. (1978). *Second language acquisition.* New York: Newbury House Publishers.

He, A. W. (2003). Novices and their speech roles in Chinese heritage language classes. In R. Bayley & S. Schecter (eds.), *Language Socialization in Bilingual and Multilingualsocieties,* 128–146. Clevedon, UK: Multilingual Matters.

He, A. W. (2006). Toward an identity-based model for the development of Chinese as a heritage language. *The Heritage Language Journal* 4 (1): 1–28.

He, A. W. (2013). *Language of the Heart and Heritage: A Tangled Tale.* Plenary address delivered at the Annual Meeting of the American Association for Applied Linguistics (AAAL). March 16–19, Dallas, Texas.

He, A. W. (2014). Identity construction throughout the life cycle. In T. Wiley, J. K. Peyton, D. Christian, S. Moore & N. Liu (eds.), *Handbook of Heritage and Community Languages in the United States: Research, Educational Practice, and Policy* (pp. 324–332). New York: Routledge.

Kanagy, R. (1999). Interactional routines as a mechanism for L2 acquisition and socialization in an immersion context. *Journal of Pragmatics* 31: 1467–1492.

Lerner, G. H. (1995). Turn design and the organization of participation in instructional activities. *Discourse Processes* 19: 111–131.

Markee, N. (2008). Toward a learning behavior tracking methodology for CA-for-SLA. *Applied Linguistics* 29(3): 404–427.

Norton, B. (2000). *Identity and language learning: Gender, ethnicity, and educational change.* Essex, England: Longman.

Ohta, A. S. (1999). Interactional routines and the socialization of interactional style in adult learners of Japanese. *Journal of Pragmatics* 31: 1493–1512.

Orellana, M. F. (2009). *Translating childhoods: Immigrant youth, language, and culture.* New Brunswick: Rutgers University Press.

Orellana, M. F., Reynolds, J., Dorner, L. & Meza, M. (2003). In other words: Translating or "para-phrasing" as a family literacy practice in immigrant households. *Reading Research Quarterly* 38: 12–34.

Rampton, B. (1995). *Crossing language and ethnicity among adolescents*. New York: Longman.

Sacks, H., Schegloff, E. A. & Jefferson, G. (1974). A simplest systematics for the organization of turn-taking in conversation. *Language* 50 (4): 696–735.

Schegloff, E. A., Jefferson, G. & Sacks, H. (1977). The preference for self-correction in the organization of repair in conversation. *Language* 53 (2): 361–382.

Trickett, E. J., Sorani, S. & Birman, D. (2010). Towards an ecology of the culture broker role: Past work and future directions. *mediAzioni* 10: 88–104.

Tse, L. (1996). Language brokering in linguistic minority communities: The case of Chinese and Vietnamese-American students. *The Bilingual Research Journal* 20: 485–498.

Valdés, G. 2001. Heritage language students: Profiles and possibilities. In J. K. Peyton, D. A. Ranard & S. McGinnis (eds.), *Heritage Languages in America. Preserving a National Resource*, 37–80. McHenry, IL: Center for Applied Linguistics.

Wiley, T. G. 2001. On defining heritage languages and their speakers. In J.K. Peyton, D. A. Ranard & S. McGinnis (eds.), *Heritage Languages in America: Preserving a National Resource*, 29–36. McHenry, IL: Center for Applied Linguistics.

Wortham, S. (2005). Socialization beyond the speech event. *Journal of Linguistic Anthropology* 15: 95–112.

Contributors

Katherine Hoi Ying Chen is a sociolinguist and linguistic anthropologist at the University of Hong Kong specializing in language ideologies, identities, multilingualism, ethnography, and sociolinguistic documentary film. She has published in *Multilingua, Discourse & Society*, *Journal of Language and Sexuality*, and through Films for the Humanities and Sciences.

Koh Yi Chern is a language teacher at the Faculty of Languages and Linguistics, University of Malaya. She teaches German as a Foreign Language for beginners. Her main research interests are language learning, multilingualism, language shift and maintenance, and linguistic landscape. She co-authored a book chapter entitled, "Will Tamil be Endangered in Malaysia? A Linguistic Landscape Perspective", in *Language Endangerment in South Asia*, Volume 1.

J. Clancy Clements is Professor of Linguistics and Spanish and Portuguese at Indiana University, USA. His research interests cover contact linguistics, pidgins and creoles, sociolinguistics, lexical semantics, functional syntax, and morphology and he has carried out extensive empirical work on Spanish and Portuguese in contact situations. Amongst his numerous publications are *The Linguistic Legacy of Spanish and Portuguese: Colonial Expansion and Language Change* (2009, Cambridge University Press),and *Functional Approaches to Spanish Syntax: Lexical Semantics, Discourse, Transitivity*, co-edited with Jiyoung Yoon (2006, Palgrave Macmillan).

Xiao Lan Curdt-Christiansen is Associate Professor in the Institute of Education, University of Reading, UK. Educated at McGill University, Montreal, Canada, she has previously worked at the National Institute of Education, Singapore, and been actively involved in research projects on children's literacy practices and language development in family domains, heritage language schools, and mainstream classrooms. She is the guest editor of a special issue on Family Language Policy for *Language Policy* and an associate editor of *International Journal of Learning*. She is co-editor of Learning Chinese in Diasporic Communities: Many Pathways to Being Chinese, with Andy Hancock (2014, Benjamins), and *Language, Ideologies and Education: The Politics of Textbooks in Language Education*, with Csilla Weninger (2014, Routledge). Her publications have appeared in *Language Policy; Canadian Modern Language Review; Cambridge Journal of Education; Language and Education; English Quarterly; Language, Culture and Curriculum; Sociolinguistic Studies;* and *Heritage Language Journal*, among others.

Ana Deumert is Associate Professor in Linguistics in the School of African and Gender Studies, Anthropology and Linguistics, University of Cape Town, South Africa. Her work is in the area of African sociolinguistics, with particular attention to questions of mobility and migration, as well as new media studies. Her most recent book is *Sociolinguistics and Mobile Communication* (2014, EUP).

Paul Tjon Sie Fat is an independent academic researcher. He studied Sinology at the University of Leiden and received a PhD from the University of Amsterdam (Chinese New Migrants in Suriname: The Inevitability of Ethnic Performing, 2009). His recent publications include "They Might as Well Be Speaking Chinese; The Changing Chinese Linguistic Situation in Suriname under New Migration", in Eithne Carlin, Isabelle Leglise, Bettina Migge, and Paul Tjon Sie Fat (eds), *In and Out of Suriname; Language, Mobility and Identity* (2015, Brill); "Old and New Chinese Organizations in Suriname", in Zhang Jijiao and Howard Duncan (eds), *Migration in China and Asia: Experience and Policy* (2014, Springer Netherlands); and "Old Migrants, New Immigration and Anti-Chinese Sentiments in Suriname", in Walton Look Lai and Tan Chee Beng (eds), *The Chinese in Latin America and the Caribbean* (2010, Brill).

Agnes Weiyun He is Professor of Applied Linguistics and Asian Studies and Founding Director of the Center for Multilingual and Intercultural Communication (MIC) at SUNY-Stony Brook University, USA. Her research has been devoted to the study of how language use is intricately motivated by contextual and co-textual contingencies and how everyday human interaction (re)constructs identities, communities, and cultures on a moment-by-moment basis. In the last decade, she has focused on the socialization of Chinese as a heritage language across different times and different settings. Her work has been supported by the Spencer Foundation, the National Academy of Education, the US Department of Education, and more recently, the John Simon Guggenheim Foundation. Her books include *Reconstructing Institutions: Language Use in Academic Counseling Encounters* (1998, Greenwood); *Talking and Testing: Discourse Approaches to the Assessment of Oral Language Proficiency* (edited with Richard Young, 1998, Benjamins); and *Chinese as a Heritage Language: Fostering Rooted World Citizenry* (edited with Yun Xiao, 2008, NFLRC/University of Hawaii Press).

Kasper Juffermans is a postdoc at the University of Luxembourg, where he leads a funded project on language and migration between West Africa and Europe. He is the author/co-editor of two books (*Local Languaging, Literacy and Multilingualism in a West African Society*, 2015; *Multilingual Matters and African Literacies: Ideologies, Scripts, Education*, 2014; Cambridge Scholars) and two special issues (*Analyzing Voice in Educational Discourses, Anthropology and Education Quarterly*, 2013; *Digital Language Practices in Superdiversity, Discourse, Context and Media*, 2014).

Lee Cher Leng is Associate Professor and Deputy Head of the Department of Chinese Studies at the National University of Singapore. Her research interests include pragmatics, sociolinguistics, and Chinese Language Education. She has published extensively in these areas and her recent publications include: "The Deixis of First Person Pronouns in the Analects", 《当代语言学》, *Contemporary Linguistics* 2014; "Politeness in Singapore", in *Politeness in East Asia* (2012, Cambridge University Press); and "Saving Chinese Language-Education in Singapore", *Current Issues in Language Planning* (2012).

Jinling Li is a professional translator (Chinese, English, Dutch) and Chinese language teacher with experience in both China and the Netherlands. She is presently finishing her PhD at Tilburg University.

Li Wei is Chair of Applied Linguistics and Director of the UCL Centre for Applied Linguistics at the UCL Institute of Education, University College London, UK. He has previously worked at Birkbeck College, University of London, University of Newcastle upon Tyne, and Beijing Normal University. He is Principal Editor of the *International Journal of Bilingualism*, and co-editor of *Global Chinese, Chinese Language and Discourse*, and *Applied Linguistics Review*. Amongst his numerous publications are *Translanguaging: Language, Bilingualism and Education* (with Ofelia Garcia, 2014, Palgrave Macmillan), *Applied Linguistics* (2014, Wiley), *The Routledge Applied Linguistics Reader* (2011, Routledge), *The Bilingualism Reader* (2nd edition, 2007, Routledge), and *The Blackwell Guide to Research Methods in Bilingualism and Multilingualism* (with Melissa Moyer, 2008, Blackwell). He is a Fellow of the Academy of Social Sciences (AcSS), UK.

Lisa Lim is Associate Professor at the School of English, the University of Hong Kong. Her research encompasses contact language varieties in multilingual ecologies and language shift and endangerment in minority communities. Her most recent work includes *Languages in Contact* (2016, Cambridge University Press, with Umberto Ansaldo), and the online resource *LinguisticMinorities.HK*.

Nkululeko Mabandla is a researcher at the Centre for African Studies at the University of Cape Town, South Africa. His work focuses on questions of land, class and globalization in South Africa. His most recent book is *Lahla Ngubo—The Continuities and Discontinuities of a South African Black Middle Class* (2013, Leiden).

John C. Maher is Director of the Institute for Educational Research and Professor of Linguistics in the Department of Media, Communication and Culture at International Christian University, Tokyo. He has lectured at De La Salle University, Philippines, and was Senior Academic Member at St Antony's College, Oxford. His research interests include multilingualism, language and identity, 'metroethnicity', globalization, topopnyms, and the languages of Japan. He is the author/editor of several books, including *International Medical Communication* (1992, University of Michigan Press), *Diversity in Japanese Culture and Language* (1995, Routledge), *Linguistics for Language Teaching, Multilingual Japan* (1998, Multilingual Matters), and *Introducing Chomsky* (1996, Icon Books). He is a founding member of the Japan Association of the Sociolinguistic Sciences.

Patricia Nora Riget is currently a French lecturer and Head of the Department of Asian and European Languages, Faculty of Languages and Linguistics, University of Malaya. She teaches courses in French linguistics and applied linguistics. Her main research interests cover teaching and learning of foreign languages, language education, and ethnolinguistics. Her recent publications include "Language Vitality among the Bidayuh of Sarawak (East Malaysia)" (2013, *Oceanic Linguistics*) and *Pertinence de la formation en France et adéquation aux besoins malaisiens: entre théorie et pratique* (2014, L'Harmattan).

Charlotte Setijadi is a Postdoctoral Fellow at the School of Humanities and Social Sciences, Nanyang Technological University, Singapore. Her research interests lie in the fields of oral history, overseas Chinese identity politics in Southeast Asia, and new Chinese migration in Asia-Pacific.

Supramani Shoniah is a senior lecturer and Tamil Linguistics Programme Coordinator in the Faculty of Languages and Linguistics at the University of Malaya. He teaches Tamil linguistics and applied linguistics. His research interests are language shift and maintenance, language endangerment, linguistic landscape, discourse analysis, and language teaching. He co-authored two books, titled *Discourse—Form and Function* (2009, Katarkuthirai Patippagam) and *Tamil Morphology* (2014, University of

Malaya). At present, he is the principle investigator of the research titled "Language Attitude of Tamil Community as reflected in the Linguistics Landscape".

Juldyz Smagulova is Assistant Professor at KIMEP University, Almaty, Kazakhstan. Her research interests cover multilingualism, ideologies of language, nation-building, and education with special attention on the role of language in the construction of social difference and social inequality in post-Soviet Kazakhstan. She co-authored the bilingual Kazakh-Russian *Dictionary of Sociolinguistics*, *Dictionary of Linguistics* and has published in *Journal of Sociolinguistics* and *International Journal of Bilingual Education and Bilingualism*.

Josh Stenberg is a postdoctoral researcher at the University of British Columbia, Canada. His research interests include Chinese theatre and public performance in southern China, Taiwan, and Southeast Asia. His recent publications include articles on Sino-Indonesian puppetry and on contemporary *xiqu* (Chinese opera) in Fujian.

Linda Tsung is Associate Professor in the Department of Chinese Studies, University of Sydney, Australia. Her research interests are in multilingualism, multilingual education, language policy, second language learning, and cultural identity in Australia and China. Her recent book is *Language Power and Hierarchy: Multilingual Education in China* (2014, Bloomsbury).

Jie Wang is a postgraduate from Leiden University, the Netherlands, holding a Research Master's degree in Middle Eastern Studies. Her research interests include exile politics, political and social movements in the modern Middle East and North Africa (MENA), gender issues in modern MENA, and transnational demographic movement between China and MENA. Her recent publications include an article coauthored with Josh Stenberg, "Localizing Chinese Migrants in Africa: A Study of the Chinese in Libya before the Civil War", *China Information* 28.1 (2014): 69–91.

Wang Xiaomei is a senior lecturer at the Faculty of Languages and Linguistics, University of Malaya. She teaches courses in Chinese linguistics and applied linguistics. Her main research interests cover language maintenance and shift, language spread, multilingualism, and Malaysian Mandarin. Her recent publications include "Language Planning for Malaysian Chinese Community" (2014, *Journal of Malaysian Chinese Studies*), *Mandarin Spread in Malaysia* (2012, University of Malaya Press) and "A Hierarchical Model for Language Maintenance and Language Shift: A Focus on Malaysian Chinese Community" (2011, *Journal of Multilingual and Multicultural Development*).

Index